J. A. Gilles

Hebrew and Christian Records

Vol. II: Christian Records

J. A. Gilles

Hebrew and Christian Records
Vol. II: Christian Records

ISBN/EAN: 9783743382558

Manufactured in Europe, USA, Canada, Australia, Japa

Cover: Foto ©Lupo / pixelio.de

Manufactured and distributed by brebook publishing software (www.brebook.com)

J. A. Gilles

Hebrew and Christian Records

HEBREW AND CHRISTIAN RECORDS;

AN HISTORICAL ENQUIRY CONCERNING THE

AGE AND AUTHORSHIP OF THE OLD

AND NEW TESTAMENTS;

BY THE

REV. DR GILES,

RECTOR OF SUTTON, SURREY, AND FORMERLY FELLOW OF CORPUS
CHRISTI COLLEGE, OXFORD.

NOW FIRST PUBLISHED COMPLETE.

VOL. II.—CHRISTIAN RECORDS.

LONDON:
TRÜBNER & CO., LUDGATE HILL.
1877.

CONTENTS.

CHAPTER	PAGE
I. Introduction	1
II. Canon of the New Testament—Reputed Authors, Places, and Dates of the several Books	4
III. The New Testament considered as a whole—Interpolations and Variations in the Text	11
IV. The Three Principal Manuscripts of the Greek Testament—their Various Readings	14
V. Apocryphal Gospels, Acts, Epistles, and Revelations	18
VI. The New Testament wholly written in Greek—The Greeks unknown to the Hebrews until Alexander the Great—Syria and Antioch—Egypt and Alexandria—Hebrew still spoken, not Greek—Josephus learnt Greek with difficulty—Evidence of coins	34
VII. Hebraisms few or none in the New Testament—No connection between its writers and the Jews who remained in Judæa—Its Style and Language closely copied from the Septuagint	48
VIII. Latinisms in the New Testament	53
IX. Christianity not mentioned by Josephus or Philo—Notice of the other Hebrew Writings—Targums—Mishna and Gemara—Talmud	60
X. Testimony of the early Greek and Latin Writers, Suetonius, Tacitus, Pliny the younger, Seneca, Epictetus, Marcus Aurelius, Lucian, Story of Peregrinus—Letter of Hadrian—Character of the Egyptians in the Second Century	68
XI. The Testimony of the Apostolical Fathers, Barnabas, Clement, Hermas, Ignatius, and Polycarp	88
1. Barnabas, 90—2. Clement of Rome, 93—3. Hermas, 96—4. Ignatius, 97—5. Polycarp, 103.	

VOL. II.   *b*

CHAPTER	PAGE
XII. Papias quoted by Irenæus and Eusebius	113
XIII. Justin Martyr—Irenæus—Clemens Alexandrinus	117
XIV. Minor Writers of the Second Century	138
XV. Internal Evidence concerning the Four Canonical Gospels—§ 1. Matthew—§ 2. Mark—§ 3. Luke —§ 4. John	151
XVI. Genealogies of Christ, in the Gospels according to St Matthew and St Luke	166
XVII. The Two Accounts of the Annunciation	174
XVIII. Different Views entertained by the Four Evangelists concerning the Duration of Christ's Ministry	177
XIX. Uncertainty about the Place of Christ's Birth	183
XX. Uncertainty about the Time of Christ's Birth—Anachronism of the Census—Christ born before A.D. 1	189
XXI. Flight into Egypt—Murder of the Innocents, &c.	198
XXII. Relation of John the Baptist's Ministry to that of Christ	203
1. John's preaching and doctrines, 207—2. First meeting of Jesus and the Baptist, 209—3. Imprisonment of the Baptist, 211—4. John's doubts about the Messiahship of Jesus, 212.	
XXIII. The Temptation in the Wilderness	213
XXIV. The Twelve Apostles—Variation, 1. In their Names; 2. In the Time, Place, and Manner of their being called to the Apostleship—The Seventy	218
XXV. Sermon on the Mount	228
XXVI. The Lord's Prayer	241
XXVII. Jesus always accompanied by a Multitude of Followers	245
XXVIII. Purification of the Temple	249
XXIX. Healing of the Centurion's Servant	253
XXX. Healing of Two Blind Men near Jericho—Other such cases	255
XXXI. The Miracle of the Loaves and Fishes	259
XXXII. The Demoniac among the Tombs and the Swine	266
XXXIII. Instructions and Conduct of Jesus towards the Samaritans	270
XXXIV. Christ anointed by a woman at a feast	273

CONTENTS. vii

CHAPTER		PAGE
XXXV.	Jesus raises Jaïrus's daughter—Heals the Woman who had an Issue of Blood	277
XXXVI.	Christ's last Journey and Triumphal Entry into Jerusalem	281
XXXVII.	The Barren Fig-Tree	286
XXXVIII.	The Last Supper	289
XXXIX.	Christ's Agony in the Garden of Gethsemane	296
XL.	Christ's Arrest and Examination before the High-Priest	299
XLI.	The Trial of Jesus before Pontius Pilate, the Roman Procurator	307
XLII.	The Crucifixion	316
XLIII.	The Resurrection of Christ and the Witnesses thereof	331
XLIV.	Christ's Appearances after the Resurrection	340
XLV.	The Death of Judas, and Purchase of the Potter's Field	346
XLVI.	Development of Later Ideas	348
XLVII.	Summary of the Acts of the Apostles, &c.	359

1. Paul otherwise called Saul, 364—2. The Ascension, 364—3. Simeon and Simon, 365—4. Theudas and Judas, 366—5. The conversion of St Paul, 368—6. Use of the word Christians, 373—7. Seeming anticipation of regular Christian worship, 374—8. Variation in the names of the disciples and brethren of Christ, James, Judas, &c., 375.

XLVIII.	St Paul and his Epistles	377

Thessalonians, 385—Galatians, 387—Corinthians, 390—Romans, 391—Ephesians, 392—Philippians, 393—Colossians, 393—Philemon, 393—Timothy, 394—Titus, 395.—Hebrews, 396.

XLIX.	General Epistles of St James, St Peter, St John, and St Jude—The Revelation of John the Divine	399
L.	Uncertainty in identifying various names, James, Judas, Simon, Mary, and others in our canonical books	406

I. St James, 409—II. Judas, 412—III. Barnabas and Barsabas, 412—IV. Mary, 414—[1. *Witnesses of the Crucifixion*, 415—2. *Those who visit the Tomb*, 415—3. *The sisters Martha and Mary*, 416—4. *Other Maries*, 416]—V. Simon, Peter, Cephas, and Symeon, 416.

LI.	The Canon generally—The Greek Language—Antioch—Conclusion	417
	Index	429

CHRISTIAN RECORDS.

CHAPTER I.

INTRODUCTION.

THE early records of the Christian religion, from the nature of the case, bear a strong likeness to those of Judaism: they are, indeed, regarded by all orthodox Christians as a supplement to the more early writings, founded upon the same facts, and developing a scheme of religion which had been rather shadowed out than fully revealed to the Jews in the first ages of the world. This connection between the books of the Old Testament and those of the New is distinct from any connection, real or supposed, between the two creeds of which these writings give us the history; for it is possible to conceive that two modes of faith and worship may have been entirely distinct in their origin, and were afterwards assimilated the one to the other from causes operating extensively among the first followers of those religions in a variety of ways, according to the peculiar circumstances of the case. As regards Christianity and Judaism, it is evident that, though the Jews have mostly disclaimed all connection with Christians, yet the Christians will not consent to give up their connection with the Jews. On the contrary, they maintain that their own faith is derived from Judaism, of which it is a sort of fulfilment; and they point out to the incredulous unbelievers numerous passages in the Jewish Scriptures foretelling the more enlarged system into which their narrow ritual would be developed. It is this circumstance which makes it so important to examine, carefully and critically, both Christian and Jewish writings, to ascertain their historical character, and to test their authorship, their authenticity, the age in which they were written, and every other point which may serve to throw light on the momentous questions which they involve. If we reflect that the religion of the ancient Jews is known only from the accounts which have come down to us in the Old Testament, and that almost the only witness of primitive Christianity is the picture of it which the New Testament unfolds, it is clear that all the questions which can arise upon the subject must be settled almost wholly— for tradition and contemporary history lend little or no additional help—according to the evidence which those two ancient volumes furnish. This course of inquiry may, it is evident, interfere greatly with our preconceived notions of the affinity between the Christian and the Jewish religions. For, even if we admit that their historical records bear a striking resemblance, the one to the other, leading to the inference that the religions themselves were analogous, and were from the first intended to be so, yet the conclusion to which this might lead would be greatly shaken if it could be shown that those respective records were not compiled until many ages after the beginning of the religious systems which they describe, and it might fairly be asked whether the religions themselves may not have been changed or modified in the course of so long a time. These observations point out the importance of our present work, which is to examine the books of the New Testament, with reference to the age when they were written, the sources from which they were derived, and the authority which they consequently possess, either as descriptive of Christianity in its first stages, or as a rule of conduct which it behoves us to follow in the actual condition of the world. Such an inquiry, in the case of the Old Testament, has led to the conviction that its compilation is to be ascribed to a date later than the Babylonish captivity, and consequently that it is not to be considered as a contemporary narrative of the events which happened in the times of Moses, Joshua, Samuel, David, and others, by whom it is generally supposed to have been written. In the same way, if it were shown that the several books of the New Testament were not written until a hundred years later than the events which they record, it would in like manner follow that their contemporary character would be lost. But here a caution seems necessary, lest men, with that precipitancy which unhappily attends too many of our inquiries after truth, when they find that an extreme opinion cannot be maintained, run into its opposite, like the crew of an ill-ballasted ship, who rush from side to side, as their vessel rolls, until all are overwhelmed in the storm, which with prudence they might have ridden out in safety. To calm the fears of such imprudent inquirers, it may be stated in the outset that the inquiry here to be instituted concerning the New Testament, lies within narrow limits; its authorship can in no way be referred to a date much later than one hundred and fifty years after the birth of Christ; and this circumstance exempts it from unfavourable comparison with the Scriptures of the Old Dispensation of the Jews. We read the acts of Moses, his miracles and his legislation, in a book compiled a thousand years after Moses was dead; but we read the acts and miracles of Jesus Christ in a book which some say is contemporary with its subject-matter, but which all admit to have been written very near to the time of which it treats.

There is another point of difference between the two books of which we are speaking. The Old Testament was written whilst literature was still rising even in the most polite nations of the world: little or nothing had been written among the Greeks, if we except the ancient writings of Homer, Hesiod, and other heroic poets, when the Pentateuch appeared among the Israelites; but literature had risen to its highest point, and even begun to decay, before the books of the New Testament were written. This fact, although a point of difference, is at the same time a point of likeness between the two: for whilst, on the one hand, those who have descended from an eminence are not more distant from its top than those who have not yet mounted, yet, on the other hand, the models of a literature once flourishing were still, we may believe, open to the age which saw the birth of the evangelic narratives, and could hardly fail to give a colouring to those narratives not to be found in the first and ruder, however sublime, essays of the old Hebrew writers. This difference is, indeed, plainly to be observed in the comparison of the Old and New Testaments. Though the several parts of both are in many cases ill joined together and show their separate origin, yet these breaks in their style of composition are less apparent in the New Testament than in the Old. This circumstance is of course to be ascribed to the different circumstances under which each was written. The compilers of the Old Testament, from the age of Ezra downwards, had to deal with old documents of different ages, extending over many hundred years; but those to whose diligence we owe the preservation of the Christian

Scriptures, compiled from records which ascended not more than a hundred years, or thereabouts, earlier than their own time; and, it may be remarked, all that they have left us is of a singularly uniform character, evidently the work of one age, and presenting no such varieties of thought and style as strike us so forcibly in various passages of the Old Testament, where ancient documents, however short, have plainly been inserted. But, that we may not anticipate what must hereafter be brought before our notice in a regular form, let us proceed first to enumerate the several books of which the New Testament is composed, and then, having stated the opinions which generally prevail on the subject of their authorship and various other points concerning them, to examine on what grounds, either of internal or of external contemporary evidence, such opinions may be maintained.

CHAPTER II.

Canon of the New Testament—Reputed Authors, Places, and Dates of the several Books.

The canon of the New Testament, as we are told by the Commentators, consists of twenty-seven books, which are said to have been written by eight different authors, all of whom were contemporary with our Saviour. These books were written at different times, and at places remote from each other; so that when the latest of them was published, the Gospel had been preached, and churches founded, in many parts of Asia, Europe, and Africa. Different churches at first received different books, according to their situation and circumstances; their canons were gradually enlarged, and it was not long, though the precise time is not known, before the same, or very nearly the same, books were acknowledged by the Christians of all countries. These books may be divided into four parts; namely, the Gospels, the Acts of the Apostles, the Epistles, and the Revelation.

The idea, which this account presents, concerning the assemblage of writings that passes under the name of the New Testament, is that which generally prevails among the people of Christian countries, and can be traced back to the second or third century of our era. An opinion so long prevalent should be treated with the utmost caution and respect; though it must be remarked at once, that the proposition as above stated is of a complex nature, involving several questions, each of which is really distinct, and can only for the purpose of an abstract be presented to the thoughts in one general assertion, with others that are of a wholly different nature.

1. The first question which we should have to decide is whether the several books of the New Testament, as we have them at present, are really the works of separate authors—either those commonly said to have written them, or possibly others—or whether they are the work of some compiler who put them into their present form to be read in the religious assemblies of the Christians.

2. In the next place it is a fair subject of inquiry whether the authors of the separate books, or the compiler who collected them, were contemporary with our Saviour, or lived in a later age.

3. Whether the several books or divisions of the New Testament were written at different times, and irrespective of one another, or whether they were written at the same time, with a co-operative design.

4. Whether the separate books passed current, in early times, among various classes of Christians, who knew of no other writings than those which they severally possessed.

5. Whether the canon which we have was gradually enlarged; and if so, what was the process, until it reached its final state.

6. How long was it after the occurrence of the events that the final canon of their history was formed.

It is manifest that all these questions are perfectly distinct, and consequently, that the blending of so many subjects into one proposition can only be admitted in a summary or popular view of the whole subject. It is my present purpose to bring together, from various sources, all the original authorities, which may enable the reader to answer these questions for himself. And though those who follow us into the depths of so dark an age as the two first centuries of the Christian era will have frequent cause to lament the fewness of our original documents, on the other hand they must not be surprised if our inquiry should lead us to modify, very considerably, the summary which the Christian world at large is content to receive respecting the various questions here enumerated.

The names under which the several books of the New Testament are commonly received, are these:—

1. Gospel according to St Matthew,
2. Gospel according to St Mark,
3. Gospel according to St Luke,
4. Gospel according to St John,
5. The Acts of the Apostles,
6. St Paul's Epistle to the Romans,
7. — First Epistle to the Corinthians,
8. — Second Epistle to the Corinthians,
9. — Epistle to the Galatians,
10. — ———— Ephesians,
11. — ———— Philippians,
12. — ———— Colossians,
13. — First Epistle to the Thessalonians,
14. — Second Epistle to the Thessalonians,
15. — First Epistle to Timothy,
16. — Second Epistle to Timothy,
17. — Epistle to Titus,
18. — Epistle to Philemon,
19. — Epistle to the Hebrews,
20. The General Epistle of St James,
21. The First General Epistle of St Peter,
22. The Second General Epistle of St Peter,
23. The First General Epistle of St John,
24. The Second General Epistle of St John,
25. The Third General Epistle of St John,
26. The General Epistle of St Jude,
27. The Revelation of St John the Divine.

It is generally believed that these twenty-seven books were written by eight different writers, all of whom must have been contemporary with the events which they relate. The following table will show the chronological order in which these books are popularly thought to have been written, together with the names of the places in which those eight writers are supposed to have been resident when they wrote them. I say "supposed," because there is not a particle of evidence for the space of a hundred and fifty years which bears upon the subject; and I use the words "popularly thought to have been written," because, with one only exception (II Peter, iii, 15), there is no indication in any of the books by which it is possible to infer that either of them was written at an earlier or later date than the others.

II.] CANON OF THE NEW TESTAMENT. 7

A.D.
52. St Paul supposed to have written the First Epistle to the Thessalonians, at Corinth.
52. St Paul's Second Epistle to the Thessalonians, at Corinth.
52 or 53. St Paul's Epistle to the Galatians, at Corinth.
56 or 57. — First Epistle to the Corinthians, at Ephesus.
57 or 58. St Paul's Epistle to the Romans, at Corinth.
58. St Paul's Second Epistle to the Corinthians, in Macedonia.
61. St Matthew is supposed to have written his Greek Gospel, somewhere in Judea; but it has been suggested by others that the Greek text which now remains is a translation of an earlier Hebrew work.
61. St Paul supposed to have written the Epistle to the Ephesians, at Rome.
61. St James supposed to have written his General Epistle, at Jerusalem, of which city he is said to have been the first bishop.
62 or 63. St Paul; his Epistle to the Philippians, at Rome.
— — his Epistle to the Colossians, at Rome.
— — his Epistle to Philemon, at Rome.
— (?) the Epistle to the Hebrews, in Italy.
63 or 64. St Mark; his Gospel, at Rome.
63 or 64. St Luke; his Gospel, in Greece.
— (?) the Acts of the Apostles.
64. St Paul; his First Epistle to Timothy, in Macedonia.
— his Epistle to Titus in Macedonia.
St Peter; his First General Epistle, at Rome.
64 or 65. St Jude; his General Epistle (where?).
65. St Paul; his Second Epistle to Timothy, at Rome.
— St Peter; his Second General Epistle, at Rome.
68 or 69. St John; his three General Epistles, at Ephesus.
96 or 97. — his Revelation, at Ephesus.
97 or 98. — his Gospel, at Ephesus.

In this table the names of SS. Matthew, Mark, Luke, and John are given as showing that those apostles are supposed to have written the Gospels and Acts which pass under their names, at the times and places above mentioned, just as SS. Paul, Peter, James, and John are given as the writers of the other works; but there is this difference between the two classes, that, whereas the Epistles bear the names of their writers embodied in their composition, the Gospels have only the superscription, "according to St Matthew," "according to St Mark," &c., a fact which has not been overlooked by critics, but which has not been allowed its due weight, nor has, on the other hand, been explained away by any of the commentators.

The ascription of the twenty-seven books to these writers

is supported, in the case of sixteen of them, upon a declaration which they bear upon their face, that they were written by those authors. Thus, thirteen of the Epistles bear the name of St Paul as their writer, " Paul, an apostle of Jesus Christ," one is ascribed to James, " a servant of God and of the Lord Jesus Christ," two bear the name of Peter, with a slight but not unimportant difference, which may be here noticed. The first Epistle is headed " Peter, an apostle of Jesus Christ, to the strangers scattered throughout Pontus, Galatia, Cappadocia, Asia, and Bithynia;" whereas the second begins " *Simon* Peter, a servant and an apostle of Jesus Christ, to them that have obtained like precious faith with us," &c. The General Epistle of St Jude also bears the name of its writer in the manner usually found in the epistolary correspondence of the ancients. Sixteen therefore of the Epistles profess to be the works of St Paul, St James, and St Peter, but four others, namely, the Epistle to the Hebrews, and the three ascribed to St John, are anonymous, and only bear the names of those by whom later writers and the majority of the Early Christian Church have supposed them to have been written. The Epistle to the Hebrews, usually ascribed to St Paul, and that which is called the First Epistle of St John, cannot indeed with certainty be called Epistles at all, but have more the appearance of being short tracts, perhaps sermons, addressed to Christian congregations or to be read in the closet, and treating of various points of the Christian faith. The last two Epistles ascribed to St John are addressed—the Second by " the Elder unto the Elect lady," and the Third " unto the well-beloved Gaius, whom I love in the truth." The Revelation declares expressly, in the first chapter, that its author bore the name of John, but whether the same who wrote the Gospel and the Epistles, was the subject of debate and doubt in the very earliest age of the Church. The title which it bears in the manuscripts, ascribes it to John the ' Divine ' or ' Theologian,' but these titles are admitted to have no authority to determine either the age or the authorship of the works to which they are prefixed. The Preface to the Revelation is as follows:—

The Revelation of Jesus Christ, which God gave unto him, to show unto his servants things which must shortly come to pass; and he sent it and signified it by his angel unto his servant John, &c. . . . John to the seven churches which are in Asia, &c.

It appears then that the four Gospels, as well as the Acts

of the Apostles, and four of the Epistles, are really anonymous—they give no direct intimation of their writers, and there is no other foundation for the ascription of them to their received authors than the voice of tradition handed down through several hundred years. This tradition is not strong enough to put the matter wholly out of doubt; for although it ascends far into the early ages of Christianity, it does not go far enough to support a conclusive inference. We can trace the books of the New Testament, with their attendant traditions, up to a certain point—the second century after Christ; but we cannot trace them farther; there is no evidence that either the Gospels, the Acts of the Apostles or the other writings, as we have them, existed within a hundred and twenty years after the Crucifixion, much less that they were from the first known to be the productions of the writers to whom tradition generally assigns them, and whose names they bear.

This is the true issue between the two parties who have written on this subject,—not whether we can trace a long chain of Christian evidence up to a period very near to the times of the Apostles, but whether this chain does not fail us at the very point where all depends upon its strength; for whilst, in judging of a history written many ages after the event, we should pass lightly over many exaggerations, erroneous views, and other defects, as the accumulation of a later age, or the result of defective memory about former times, yet in examining a history which professes to be contemporaneous or almost contemporaneous with the event, our requirements become necessarily more strict and searching, and if at this early stage of the matter tradition alone is found to supply the only argument of authorship, it becomes a grave question whether the contemporary character of such a history is not to be pronounced doubtful, perhaps to be rejected altogether. In saying this, I do not imply that the facts which such a book relates are to be rejected, but that the book in which these are found is no longer to be received as written by the eye-witnesses of those facts. The facts still remain for consideration, though the book is not in itself a conclusive guarantee for their truth, because the evidence which it affords is proved to be anonymous evidence: we no longer regard it as the writing of one who had witnessed with his own eyes the truth of what he has written. It cannot be denied that such a doubt about the authorship of any book that enters into the momentous question of religion, is at once a great difficulty in the way of fully testing the doctrines of that particular form of religion, and the truth of the facts on which those doctrines rest. The truth of a fact may indeed be established, even by a writing whose author is unknown; but in such a case, the fact must bear probability upon its surface, or the arguments which are brought to support it must be proportionably stronger—at all events, the world at large will examine them the more rigidly, according as they lead to substantiate facts divergent from the general experience of mankind. With those doctrines and opinions we have nothing to do at present; they have stood their ground against more forcible discussions than they are ever again likely to encounter, and the beneficial teaching of their Founder, although sadly neglected in practice, is still followed by all those who wish to maintain the standard of a pure faith amid the conflicting elements of human speculation.

If, therefore, any one of the separate books of the New Testament comes before us anonymously, we are bound to examine it with the most scrupulous accuracy, that, if possible, we may discover who wrote it, as well as when it was written, and what sources of information its writer may have had for knowing that he wrote nothing but the truth. Neither are we debarred or excused from fulfilling this duty by the silent consent of so many centuries, which would seem to infer that the question here agitated has long ago been set at rest. For this notion of its having been set at rest is erroneous. There is positive proof, in writings of the first ages of Christianity, that the same question as to the age and authorship of the books of the New Testament was even then agitated, and if it was then set at rest, this was done, not by a deliberate sentence of the judge, but by burning all the evidence on which one side of the controversy was supported. From that time, almost down to the present day, the process has been continued, and often, not only the writings which raised a doubt, but those who produced such writings, have been burned also. Such then having been the state of things, it is no wonder if a question involving such consequences has generally slumbered, or been roused to life only when that love of sifting the truth which is so natural to our species, has prompted some bolder spirit to renew a controversy that seemed never to have been fully settled. It is, happily, unnecessary in the present day to abstain from following wherever truth may lead us. On the contrary, it is thought good service to the world to illustrate and define, in every possible way, all the moral and political obligations which are thought to be incumbent on mankind: and it is hardly denied by any one that good service is done by those also who endeavour to test the history of the past as being the chief foundation upon which those duties rest.

CHAPTER III.

The New Testament considered as a Whole—Interpolations and Variations in the Text.

NOTWITHSTANDING the observation, so often repeated by biblical critics and commentators, that the books of the New Testament have a separate origin and consequently a separate authority, it must not be forgotten that this view of them is not the primary one, as regards ourselves. It may have applied to the first two centuries, before the canon was complete; but at present, we know these books, not in their individual, but in their aggregate form, and according to this view must all our arguments be conducted. It is evident that the New Testament, besides having separately had eight different writers, must also have had a compiler,—an editor or body of editors, to whom we owe the form in which the books now appear. Possibly, the editor, or editors, were content to copy the twenty-seven books into one volume, without altering in the slightest degree the text of them. But the same conditions allow us also to suppose that a further editorial process took place, extending to changes more or less extensive, in order to mould separate writings into one harmonious body. It will be replied perhaps to this, that no variation of reading, of any consequence, has been discovered in all the manuscripts of the Sacred Text that have come down to us. Such a reply has often been made, but it is not true; for many important variations are found between the various manuscripts of the New Testament; and even if it were true it would be of little weight; for it is not to be expected that important differences of reading would be found in manuscripts so modern as the greater part of those which now remain. With the exception of three or four ancient copies which will be noticed in the next chapter, no others can be traced higher than the seventh and eighth centuries after

Christ, and we know for certain that in the time of Eusebius, about A.D. 320, the canon of the New Testament was more or less complete. It is not in the fifteen centuries since Eusebius, but in the three before his time, that we must search for all our evidence as to the text and authenticity of the New Testament canon and the books that it contains. It was manifestly a very early step for the founders of our ecclesiastical system to reduce to uniformity all the copies of those books which they selected to form their canon; this necessity, together with the general tendency of the Christian community to have accurate copies of books which were held in such general estimation, are quite sufficient to account for the trivial variations of reading which are found in the greater part of the MSS of the New Testament now existing. Notwithstanding all this, however, it is well known that the text of our books has been tampered with and interpolations have been made in certain passages, which shows the necessity of our relaxing none of that vigilant criticism by which the whole truth may be ascertained on all these and other corresponding subjects of inquiry. It would add greatly to the proposed extent of this work, if we were here to enter minutely into the consideration of the various words and passages which have been proved to be interpolations, and not from the first genuine portions of the original text. The most important of them is the verse, 1 JOHN, v, 7.

There are three that bear record in heaven, the Father, the Word, and the Holy Ghost; and these three are one.

The authenticity of this passage has long been disputed in the Church, and has at last been thoroughly sifted by the learned and justly celebrated Professor Porson, who, in his able work, "Letters to Archdeacon Travis," has set the question at rest, and clearly shown this much canvassed passage to have been interpolated in the text, perhaps with no dishonest intention, by a later copyist.

To the foregoing instance may be added also the doubtful passage with which St Mark's Gospel now ends, from the ninth to the twentieth verses of the last chapter, which, Jerome tells us, in his numerous critical works *Ad Hered. Qu.* iii, 4, were wanting in every Greek copy that he had seen. Gregory, bishop of Nyssa, a contemporary of Jerome, confirms this statement, and those verses may therefore be considered to be the unauthorized addition of a later age.

Similar criticism has been applied to the last chapter of

St John's Gospel and also to that passage in St Matthew, xvii, 27, where it is related that St Peter was told by Jesus to pay the tribute with money that he should find in the belly of the first fish which, in his capacity of fisherman, he should catch.

Moreover, the allusion to the descent of an angel in St John's Gospel, v, 3, 4, and to the woman taken in adultery, in the same Gospel, vii, 53—viii, 11, have long been abandoned as unauthentic additions to the text; whilst another appearance of an angel, found only in the Gospel of St Luke, xxii, 43, 44, "whose complete vindication (according to a recent critic) ranks among the happiest fruits of modern research," is still thought by many to be among the least defensible passages in our Sacred Books.

"It may be hoped," is the observation of Gibbon on this subject, in his fifteenth chapter, "that none except the heretics gave occasion to the complaint of Celsus (Origen, ii) that the Christians were perpetually correcting and altering their Gospels;" but the term heretic has been in all ages freely given to all who have differed in the smallest degree from the opinions which at any time have had the mastery; and it is not safe to infer that all those to whom Eusebius gave that name were the only classes among the early Christians against whom the charge of corrupting the Scriptures might be brought. He is speaking principally of the heresy of Artemon, when he quotes, in the fifth book of his Ecclesiastical History (ch. xxviii,) from an anonymous writer, as follows :—

> The Sacred Scriptures have been boldly perverted by them; the rule of the Ancient Faith they have set aside, Christ they have renounced. . . . . . They fearlessly lay their hands upon the Holy Scriptures, saying that they have corrected them. And that I do not say this against them without foundation, whoever wishes may learn, for should any one collect and compare their copies one with another, he would find them greatly at variance among themselves. For the copies of Asclepiodotus will be found to differ from those of Theodotus. Copies of many you may find in abundance, altered by the eagerness of their disciples to insert each one his own corrections, as they call them, that is, their corruptions. Again, the copies of Hermophilus do not agree with these, and those of Apollonius are not consistent with themselves. For one may compare those which were prepared before by them, with those which they afterwards perverted for their own objects, and you will find them widely different.

Such points as the foregoing, though they may bear with

great weight upon doctrinal investigations, have little interest for those who pursue an historical investigation like the present. For though it should be proved that the verse where the " Three Heavenly Witnesses " are named, the last chapter of St John, and the last twelve verses of St Mark were not to be found in the New Testament in the time of Eusebius, about A.D. 320, yet if all the rest of the New Testament was then what it now is, we are not in the least degree nearer to the discovery when the book was first written; its general identity has never been disputed, though in a few places the reading has certainly been altered, not always, it may be hoped, from dishonesty, nor always in such a way as to introduce into the text a passage that has touched so closely upon doctrine, and led to such bitter discussions as the verse which contains the Three Heavenly Witnesses.

CHAPTER IV.

THE THREE PRINCIPAL MANUSCRIPTS OF THE GREEK TESTAMENT—THEIR VARIOUS READINGS.

It is well known to students of biblical literature, that as late as the beginning of the fifteenth century, copies of the Greek Testament, as well as of all other books, were produced only by the slow process of the pen. Probably more than a thousand manuscripts of the Bible, written before the year 1500, still remain in the various public libraries and monasteries of Europe and Asia. A comparatively small number contain, besides the New Testament, the Greek version of the Old Testament, commonly known by the name of the Septuagint. But all of them, with few or no exceptions, were intended by the copyists to represent either the whole of the New Testament, or the historical books collectively, or the Epistles in like manner bodily, and not any separate Gospel or Epistle by itself alone. Thus the evidence of these manuscripts confirms the view here taken, that we know the Christian Scriptures only in their collective shape, and not as a miscellaneous assemblage of separate works, each having an independent origin, and possessing independent authority on all questions that might concern the Christian community. We, as well as all Christians from the second century to the present time, know the New Testament only as one book, and we find from the evidence of manuscripts still remaining, that other works, besides those which we call canonical, were added to the collection as possessing equal authority with those which are still retained. Of the thousand manuscripts which remain, there are three which are thought to have been written not later, and possibly earlier, than the fifth century of the Christian era.

The first which became known to scholars is called the Vatican MS, because it is preserved in the Vatican Library at Rome, where it has been at least since the year A.D. 1475, as appears from a catalogue of the library made in that year. It contains both the Greek Septuagint and the New Testament: but the Epistles to Timothy, Titus, and Philemon, the Revelation, and part of the Epistle to the Hebrews, from Chapter ix, 14, to the end, are missing. A fac-simile of this volume was printed in the year 1868.

The second, called the Alexandrian MS, from Alexandria, whence it came, was presented by Cyril Lucar, Patriarch of Constantinople, in 1628, to King Charles the First, and is preserved in the British Museum. This also contains both the Greek Septuagint and the New Testament, but all the beginning of St Matthew's Gospel up to xxv, 6, is wanting; as well as John vi, 50, to viii, 52; and II Corinthians, iv, 13, to xii, 6. But, besides the Old and New Testaments, this book contains the only remaining manuscript copy of Clemens Romanus, a Treatise of Eusebius on the Psalms, and a letter of Athanasius. That part of the MS which contains the New Testament was printed in 1768 by Woide, in fac-simile as to the size of the volume, the page, and the spelling of the words, but not as to the shape of the letters. The volume has since been re-edited by B. H. Cowper, in a smaller and more convenient size.

The third MS, which we shall here notice, is the Sinaitic, so called from Mount Sinai, where it was discovered in 1844 by Professor Tischendorf, and brought by him in 1859 to Russia for the Emperor Alexander the Second. Besides the Greek Septuagint and the whole of the New Testament, it contains the Epistle of Barnabas, and part of the Shepherd of Hermas: "two books," says Tischendorf, "which down to the beginning of the fourth century, were looked upon by many as Scripture. All the considerations which tend to fix the date of manuscripts lead to the conclusion that the Sinaitic Codex belongs to the middle of the fourth century. Indeed, the evidence

is clearer in this case than in that of the Vatican Codex;
and it is not improbable (which cannot be the case with
the Vatican MS,) that it is one of the fifty copies of the
Scriptures which the Emperor Constantine, in the year
331, directed to be made for Byzantium, under the care
of Eusebius of Cæsarea. In this case it is a natural
inference that it was sent from Byzantium to the monks
of St Catharine by the Emperor Justinian, the founder
of the convent. The entire Codex was published by its
discoverer, under the orders of the Emperor of Russia, in
1862, with the most scrupulous exactness, and in a truly
magnificent shape; and the New Testament portion was
issued in a portable form in 1863 and 1865."

The evidence of these early copies has been brought
to bear with great force upon some of the doubtful and
disputed passages of Scripture which have been named
in the last chapter; and, whilst that evidence has been
almost conclusive against the authenticity of some of
the passages, yet the authority of these MSS has been
of no weight to disturb the general tenor of the Gospel
narratives. "The notion," says one of the most zealous
defenders of our Vulgate Greek text, "of a literal identity
between the present copies of the inspired text, and
the original edition which was published by the sacred
writers, is a vulgar error which finds as little foundation
in reason as justification in fact. It would require no
labour of deduction to prove that notion unreasonable
which presupposes that every person who undertakes to
copy the sacred writings should be withheld from wilful
or inadvertent error by preternatural power, were it not
demonstrably refuted by the publication of one hundred
and fifty thousand various readings, which have been
collected against the authorized text." These are the
words of Dr Nolan, in the Preface to his Inquiry into the
Integrity of the Greek Vulgate.

Notwithstanding this reasonable view of the matter, a brief
notice of the principal variations which lie between these
three manuscripts may not be out of place. Designating the
Alexandrian MS by A, the Sinaitic by S, and the Vatican
by V, we find the following differences between them:—

ST MATTHEW'S GOSPEL. In x, 2, S and V omit the words
Lebbæus, whose surname was—xii, 47, S and V omit this verse—
For *Joses*, in xiii, 55, S has *John*, and V *Joseph*—For *Magdala*,
in xv, 39, S and V have *Magadan*. In xx, 22 and 23, S and V
omit *and to be baptized with the baptism that I am baptized with*—

IV.] THE THREE PRINCIPAL MANUSCRIPTS. 17

xxiii, 35, S omits *son of Barachias*—xxvii, 46, S and V read *Eloi, Eloi, lema*. A has *lima*—xxvii, 49, after this verse, S and V insert *But another took a spear and pierced his side, and there came out blood and water*. In xxvii, 56, S omits the word *mother*, and reads *Joseph* altered in a less ancient hand to *Joses*.

ST MARK'S GOSPEL. In i, 1, S omits *the Son of God*—i, 2, S and V read *Esaias the prophet*.—v, 1, S reads *Gerasenes*, altered in a less ancient hand to *Gergesenes;* V reads Gerasenes—vi, 3, S reads *James and Joseph*—ix, 44, S omits this verse—ix, 45, S and V omit *into the fire that never shall be quenched*—ix, 49, S and V omit *and every sacrifice shall be salted with salt*—xi, 26, S and V omit this verse—xv, 28, A, S, and V omit this verse —xv, 34, A has *lima sabacthani*, S has *lema sabactani*, and V has *zabaphthani*. In xvi, S and V omit the last twelve verses, from 9 to 20.

ST LUKE'S GOSPEL. In iii, 23, S and V read *was, when he began, about thirty years of age*—iii, 23 to 38, A, S and V differ very much not only in spelling these names, but in the names themselves and in the number of the generations—viii, 26, S has *Gergesenes*, V *Gerasenes*—xiv, 5, for *an ass* A and V read *a son*—xxii, 43, 44, A, S, and V omit these two verses.

ST JOHN'S GOSPEL. In i, 28, for *Bethabara* A, S, and V read *Bethany*—iii, 8, S reads *of water and of the Spirit*—v, 2, S reads *Bethzatha*, V *Bethsaida*—v, 4, S and V omit this verse —vii, 53 to viii, 11, S and V omit all these verses—ix, 38, S omits this verse—xx, 16, S and V have *saith unto him in Hebrew* —xx, 15, 16, 17, for *Jonas* S and V read *John*—xx, 25, S omits this verse.

ACTS. In i, 19, A and S read *Acheldamach*, V *Aceldamach* —vii, 43, A has *Rephan*, S *Romphan*, V *Rompha*—xviii, 24, S has *Apelles*—xxvii, 8, A reads *Alassa*—xxvii, 14, A, S, and V read *Euraquilon*—xxviii, 19, A, S, and V omit this verse.

EPISTLE TO THE ROMANS. i, 16, V omits *first*—xi, 12, A omits this verse—xv, 31, for *service* V reads *ministration of alms* —xvi, 3, for *Priscilla* A, S, and V read *Prisca*—xvi, 5, for *Achaia* A, S, and V read *Asia*—xvi, 8, for *Amplias* A and S have *Ampliatus*—xvi, 24, A, S, and V omit this verse.

FIRST EPISTLE TO THE CORINTHIANS. In i, 1, V omits *called to be*—ix, 2, A omits this verse—xvi, 19, A omits this verse; S and V read *Prisca*.

EPISTLE TO THE GALATIANS. In ii, 9, A omits *Cephas*—ii, 11 and 14, for *Peter* A, S, and V have *Cephas*.

EPISTLE TO THE HEBREWS. In vii, 21, S and V omit *after the order of Melchisedec*.

FIRST EPISTLE OF ST JOHN. In v, 7, 8, A, S and V omit the Three Heavenly Witnesses.

REVELATION. In v, 4, A omits this verse.

CHAPTER V.

APOCRYPHAL GOSPELS, ACTS, EPISTLES, AND REVELATIONS.

OUR investigation into the time when the volume of the New Testament collectively, or its several parts, may be supposed to have been written, would be very incomplete, if it were thought that these books alone remain from the earliest ages of Christianity. So far, however, is this from being the case, that a much larger number of other Gospels, Acts, Epistles, and Revelations still exist, besides many kindred works professing to be equally ancient and to be equally authentic with those which now form part of the canon. It is true that these audacious pretensions have long been repudiated, and the books themselves would have long ago perished were it not that truth itself derives most of its brightness from the existence of error, and the world would hardly form so safe a judgment of genuine and authentic documents unless they were aided in forming a conclusion by the juxtaposition of what is spurious. It will, therefore, not be a superfluous task to take notice of many works which at one time or other competed with the books of our canon for acceptance among Christians, and this notice will lose none of its importance from the fact that some of these books have been quoted by early Christian writers as of equal authority with those which are accounted canonical and authentic.

The second century of our era has been fixed on as the period when those numerous uncanonical or Apocryphal Gospels and other writings, many of which still exist, first made their appearance and seem to have had much influence among the Christians of those days. But it is the object of this work to show that the books which are still deemed canonical owe their existence to that same period, and were compiled in part out of the same original documents which were the ground-work of the less authentic Christian histories. Nor will this imply any charge of spuriousness or want of authenticity in our canon; for the existence of what is false infers also the existence of that which is true, and although many writings on the life and teaching of our Lord, besides those which are canonical, still remain and, in fact, were received by some of the early Churches; yet their evident inferiority, both as regards their origin, their statements, and other points, caused them, within a comparatively short space of time, to be eliminated from the catalogue of Christian writings, and to owe their present existence to no other cause than to the curiosity of literary men, the general neglect of the old volumes in which they were written, or the death-like repose of the libraries on the shelves of which they have slumbered.

But a graver accusation than that of inaccuracy or deficient authority lies against the writings which have come down to us from the second century. There can be no doubt that great numbers of books were then written with no other view than to deceive the simple-minded multitude who at that time formed the great bulk of the Christian community.

"It greatly affects me (says the learned Casaubon) to see how many there were in the earliest times of the Church, who considered it a holy task to lend to heavenly truth the help of their own inventions, in order that the new Revelation might be more readily admitted by the wise among the Gentiles. These officious lies, they declared, were devised for a good end. From this source sprang up innumerable books published under the name of the Lord Jesus Christ."

The celebrated Eusebius, bishop of Cæsarea, and friend of Constantine the Great, is our chief guide for the early history of the Church; and we learn from his own confession that he was by no means scrupulous to record the whole truth concerning the early Christians in the various works which he has left behind him. The historian Gibbon, whose researches into the history of those ages are only equalled by the language in which he has recorded them, has given his judgment on this subject in the following passage*:—

The gravest of the ecclesiastical historians, Eusebius himself, indirectly confesses, that he has related whatever might redound to the glory, and that he has suppressed all that could tend to the disgrace, of religion. Such an acknowledgment will naturally excite a suspicion that a writer, who has so openly violated one of the fundamental laws of history, has not paid a very strict regard to the observance of the other; and the suspicion will derive additional credit from the character of Eusebius, which

---

* Decline and Fall of the Roman Empire, chapter xvi: Eusebius, Historia Ecclesiastica, viii, 21: and De Martyribus Palæstinæ, xii.

was less tinctured with credulity, and more practised in the arts of courts than that of almost any of his contemporaries.

But Eusebius wrote at the beginning of the fourth century, and it is evident from his Ecclesiastical History, which remains still perfect, that the task of writing the annals of the Early Church had become by no means easy. Notwithstanding all the disingenuousness of which he was capable, and which has been the safer from detection in consequence of the destruction that has befallen the chief works written by the enemies of Christianity, we nevertheless observe that he was constrained to mention, in his Ecclesiastical History, the names of numerous Gospels, Epistles, and other treatises of which some members of the Church still even then thought highly; but which have since sunk into merited oblivion. In his review of the Scriptures, both those which are genuine and those which are not, in the twenty-fifth chapter of his third book, he writes as follows:—

Among the first we must range the holy quaternion of the Gospels, which are followed by the treatise of the Acts of the Apostles. But after these we must reckon the Epistles of Paul; after which, in order, we must confirm the first which is in circulation of John, and also the Epistle of Peter. After these we must range, if it should seem fit, the Apocalypse of John, about which we shall at the proper time set forth the various opinions. And these are among the acknowledged [books]; but of those which are disputed, but yet however are known to most men, is circulated that which is called of James, and that of Jude, and the Second Epistle of Peter, and that which is named the Second and the Third of John, whether being of the Evangelist or even of another having the same name with him. Among the spurious let there be reckoned also the treatise of the Acts of Paul, and that called the Shepherd, and the Apocalypse of Peter, and in addition to these that which passes as the Epistle of Barnabas, and what we call the Doctrines of the Apostles: and further, as I said, if it seem fit, the Apocalypse of John, which some reject, as I said, and others rank among the acknowledged. But now some reckon among these also the Gospel according to the Hebrews, in which those who have received Christ take pleasure, the most of all the Hebrews. All these may be of the number of those which are disputed. But we have, however, necessarily made the list of these also, distinguishing both the writings which are true, and genuine and acknowledged, and the others besides these, not indeed canonical, but also disputed, but yet known among most of our ecclesiastical writers, so that we may be able to know both these very ones and those which are put forth by the heretics in the name of the Apostles, as containing, that is, the Gospels of Peter and Thomas and Matthias or even of some others besides these, as the Acts of Andrew and John, and of the other Apostles, which no one of the ecclesiastical writers in succession has at all thought fit to bring to our memory in any history.

I shall here subjoin a list of the various apocryphal works which have been ascribed to the Apostles, to their contemporaries or immediate followers, and even to Christ himself.

1. *Historia Josephi fabri lignarii, Arabice.* The history of Joseph the Carpenter, in Arabic. This work has come down to us from the fourth century, if we may believe Wallin, who first published it at Leipsic in the year A.D. 1722. It is the opinion of Professor Tischendorf that the Arabic text is a translation from a Coptic original, and if this supposition be true, the conjecture of Thilo, that it is much later than the fourth century, is proportionally weakened; for the Coptic language was the vehicle of Christian legends at a very early date of our era.

2. *Evangelium de Nativitate Mariæ, Latine.* Gospel of the birth of Mary, in Latin. A short tract, similar in some of its legends to the former, and towards the end closely copying the language of the canonical Gospel concerning the birth of Jesus. It is thought to have first seen the light in the sixth century, as translated from a Hebrew original by the Evangelist St Matthew. It is found among the spurious works in the editions of Jerome, to whom it was once ascribed.

3. *Epistolæ Ignatii et Beatæ Virginis Mariæ, Latine.* Epistles of Ignatius and the Blessed Virgin Mary, in Latin. Eight letters first printed in 1495 at the end of the Quadripartite life of Becket, commonly called the *Quadrilogus*.

4. *Apocalypsis Mariæ, Græce.* The Revelation of Mary. A tract written in very late Greek, and, if possible, of less than no value, although found in very many manuscripts.

5. *Johannis Liber de Dormitione Mariæ, Græce.* The Book of John concerning the falling to sleep of Mary.

6. *Transitus Mariæ, Latine*, A. The Transition of Mary, in Latin, No. 1.

7. *Transitus Mariæ, Latine*, B. The Transition of Mary, in Latin, No. 2.

These three tracts, concerning the miraculous incident said to have accompanied the decease of the Virgin Mary, are perhaps not all of equal antiquity, although they most probably owe their origin to the same traditional source. The manuscripts of them vary very much: in one of them there is prefixed to the second Latin work an epistolary preface bearing the name of Melito, a bishop of the second century, to whom have been ascribed a large number of writings published within the last thirty years, but all equally apocryphal, if not spurious.

8. *Evangelium Infantiæ Arabicum.* The Arabic Gospel of the Infancy. A tract full of the agency of Satan, devils, and necromancers; it also abounds with historical inaccuracies and anachronisms, which show it to have been written at a late date, and possibly is a compilation from various earlier tracts.

9. *Abgari Regis Edessæ Epistola ad Christum, Græce.* Letter from Abgarus, king of Edessa, to Christ.

10. *Christi Epistola Responsoria ad Abgarum, Græce.* Letter from Christ in answer to King Abgarus.

These two letters were first made known to the world by Eusebius, who tells us in his Ecclesiastical History (i, 13) that he found them in the Archives of Edessa, in the Syriac language, from which he translated them into Greek.

11. *Fragmenta Hymni quem Christus in monte Olivarum dixit, Latine.* Fragments of an Hymn which Christ spake on the Mount of Olives. This fragment was copied by St Augustine (*Epist. ad Ceretium*) out of a book belonging to the sect of the Priscillianists.

12. *Epistola Salvatoris quæ de cælo lapsa est, Latine.* Letter from our Saviour which fell from heaven. A monkish forgery to enforce the observance of the Sabbath: printed for the first time by Baluzius in Appendix ad Acta Vetera Capitularium Regum Francorum, ii, 1396.

12.* *Fragmentum Epistolæ alius Christi, Latine.* Fragment of another Epistle from Christ. It occurs in the Chronicle of Sigebertus Gemblacensis ad An. Ch. 1032. Several other similar worthless compositions occur in manuscripts and printed books which occupy the shelves of the various public libraries of Europe.

13. *Abdiæ Historia Apostolica, Latine.* Abdias's History of the Apostles. Prefixed to this work is a preface bearing the name of Julius Africanus, as the translator from the original Hebrew, of which Abdias or Obadiah is said to have been the writer. We learn from the sixth book of the work that Abdias or Obadiah was bishop of Babylon, that he had come, with the Apostles, from Judæa, and had himself seen the Lord Jesus. The facts related in the work

coincide in many instances very closely with those found in earlier writings, and this shows that these are either copied from them or are derived from the same source as those, but otherwise the work is altogether spurious, of no authority whatever, and was written, in Latin, about the end of the ninth century.

14. *Doctrinæ Apostolorum, Græce.* The Doctrines (or Teachings) of the Apostles. Eusebius, in his Ecclesiastical History, iii, 25, 4, mentions a work bearing this title, and Hilgenfeld has collected the few fragments which remain. He adds also a short notice of a similar work, entitled *Didascalia Apostolorum Ægyptiaca,* which is not quoted by any ancient author.

15. *Evangelium secundum Ægyptios.* Gospel according to the Egyptians. Mentioned by Clement of Rome, Origen, and others. If we could be certain that the Epistles of Clement were genuine, this Gospel would compete for antiquity of date with the canonical Gospels of the New Testament. Hilgenfeld has collected two pages of fragments.

16. *Evangelium Ebionæorum, Hebraice.* Gospel of the Ebionites. This Gospel is thought to have been the same as that of the Hebrews in a more advanced stage of development, in the same way as the canonical Gospel of St. John is thought to be a further development of Christianity, concerning the Divinity of our Saviour, beyond the three Synoptical Gospels. A few fragments of a Greek translation of it are given in the work of Hilgenfeld, but it is thought to have been written originally in Hebrew.

17. *Evangelium Hebræorum vel Nazaræorum.* The Gospel of the Hebrews or of the Nazarenes. There was a Gospel under this name, as Eusebius tells us, (III, xxxix, 11,) mentioned by Papias, and other later Fathers of the Church. Different opinions have been given concerning its age, authorship, and contents. If written in Hebrew, as is most probable, it may have been in use among the Jews even at an earlier date than the canonical Gospels; but all the dissertations that have been written on the subject have only shown that we know nothing whatever about it, and only a few supposed fragments of it in Greek and Latin have been as yet found and published by Professors Tischendorf and Hilgenfeld.

18. *Acta Andreæ, Græce.* The Acts of Andrew. These Acts occur in manuscripts of the eleventh century, but they certainly, either wholly or in part, are earlier than that date. Certain facts mentioned or alluded to by some of the

early Fathers of the Church are still found in this book, but how far the original text of the work has been altered or even wholly recast by intermediate copyists and editors, cannot now be ascertained.

19. *Acta Andreæ et Matthiæ in urbe Anthropophagorum, Græce.* The Acts of Andrew and Matthias in the city of the Cannibals. This tract occurs in manuscripts of the eleventh and the eighth centuries, and is thought to derive its origin from those earlier writings of Leucius, to whom so many apocryphal and heretical narratives are due. The nature of this work may be seen from the first paragraph or chapter, and will perhaps be of interest to the reader as showing the method which the authors of these forgeries endeavoured to introduce into the proceedings of the first Christian missionaries, so different from what might be expected from the disciples who, when Jesus was arrested in the garden, all forsook him and fled.

At that time all the apostles were gathered together, and divided out among themselves the countries, casting lots, how each should go to the lot which fell to him. By lot then it happened that Matthias went into the country of the cannibals. Now the men of that city neither ate bread nor drank wine, but were eating the flesh of men and drinking their blood. Every man therefore who went into their city, they seized him, gouged and dug out his eyes, and made him drink poison prepared from pharmacy and magic; and by their making him drink poison, his heart was alienated and his mind underwent a change. When therefore Matthias came into the city, the people of that city laid hold of him and forced out his eyes, and after carrying him out they gave him to drink the poison which caused the magical aberration of mind, and led him away in custody, and put before him fodder to eat, and he would not eat it.

20. *Evangelium Barnabæ, Italice.* Gospel of Barnabas. From a manuscript belonging to Prince Eugene, and said to be a translation from an Arabic original.

21. *Revelationes Bartholomæi, Sahidice.* The Revelations of Bartholomew. A fragment perhaps of a larger work, and found in the National Library of Paris, in a volume containing other fragments in the Sahidic tongue. A French translation of it was published with the original text, and is given by Professor Tischendorf in his collection of *Apocalypses Apocryphæ.*

22. *Martyrium Bartholomæi, Græce.* The Martyrdom of Bartholomew. Similar in subject to the notice of Bartholomew found in the Apostolical History of Abdias, who

either must have copied his facts from this book, or from an earlier book, which also was the ground-work of this Martyrdom.

23. *Apocalypsis Danielis, Græce.* The Revelation of Daniel. A short tract found in several Venetian and Parisian manuscripts.

24. *Apocalypsis Esdræ.* The Revelation of Esdras. This book is similar in subject to the Second Book of Esdras found in the Apocrypha of the English Version. The monks of the middle ages seem to have been fond of the various mystical traditions attached to the name of Esdras or Ezra, as is shown by the large number of manuscripts in which such subjects are contained. The names of angels, Michael, Gabriel, Uriel, &c., which occur in this book, might seem to throw it back to the ante-Christian age, but, as the names of Paul, Peter, and Christians generally occur therein, we must refer it to a later and perhaps very late age.

25. *Protevangelium Jacobi Minoris, Græce.* The Primitive Gospel of James [the Less]. This is one of the most ancient of the Apocryphal writings of the New Testament. It was first published in a Latin translation, Basil. 1552; and the Greek text in Neander's Apocrypha, twelve years afterwards. The existing work is supposed to be the same which Clement of Alexandria quotes under the name of *Book of James,* and some think that Justin Martyr (*Dial. Tryp.* 78) relates, on the authority of this book, fifty years earlier than Clement, how Joseph and Mary placed the child Jesus in a cave near Bethlehem, because there was no room for them in the village. This work is found in a large number of manuscripts, and under a different name in almost every one of them. An ancient Syriac version of it has been published by Dr W. Wright, in his "Contributions to the Apocryphal Literature of the New Testament, 8vo, London, 1865."

26. *Acta Johannis, Græce.* The Acts of John. This work is one of the best known of the Apocryphal writings, and is mentioned by Eusebius and other Fathers of the Church. Some parts of it correspond with passages in the *Liber de Passione* S.J., by Mellitus, and others have their counterpart in the Apostolical History of Abdias.

27. *Liber Sancti Johannis Apocryphus, Latine.* The Apocryphal Book of St. John. This tract was first printed in Benedict's Histoire des Albigeois, &c., tom. i, page 283. Its origin is as obscure as its contents are worthless. These

were most probably copied by the author out of various writings by Leucius Charinus, of whom mention is made by so many ecclesiastical writers, and who occurs in so many manuscripts as a heretic and author of works which either as he wrote them, or in an altered shape, still exist as exponents of the Gnostic and Manichæan doctrines.

28. *Epistolæ Sancti Johannis et Hydropici, Latine.* Epistles of Saint John and the man who had the dropsy. Fragments of five lines only.

29. *Melliti Liber de Passione Sancti Johannis, Latine* Mellitus, his book on the Passion of St John. The author says that he had before him as an authority the Acts of John, written by Leucius. A doubt seems also to exist about the real name of the writer, whether Mellitus or Miletus is the true reading. It has also been suggested whether Melito, a well-known bishop of Sardis, may not be its author, but this doubt was suggested only to be as speedily dismissed, for the contents of the work are much later than the date of Bishop Melito.

30. *Apocalypsis Johannis.* The Revelation of John. This is simply one out of many patent forgeries of the middle or even earlier ages. It has been two or three times printed, but no manuscript of it now extant is earlier than the fifteenth century.

31. *Narratio Josephi Arimathiensis, Græce.* Narrative of Joseph of Arimathæa. The History of the two thieves is contained in this short tract, of which the earliest manuscript is of the twelfth century.

32. *Evangelium Marcionis.* The Gospel of Marcion. There is no such work now in existence, and it is doubtful whether such a work ever existed. Irenæus, Origen, and others thought that the Gospel ascribed to this early heretic was only a corrupted copy of St Luke, and on this supposition Professor Thilo compiled out of our present third canonical book that which he thought might represent the Gospel of Marcion. Such a task is interesting and even useful to its author, but has very little weight to commend itself to the judgment of the public.

33. *Acta et Martyrium Matthæi, Græce.* The Acts and Martyrdom of St Matthew. This tract, closely connected with the preceding both in style and subject, if not even a portion with it of some larger original work, was unknown to the learned until it was published by Professor Tischendorf from a manuscript of the eleventh century.

34. *Pseudo-Matthæi Evangelium.* The spurious Gospel

of Matthew. This tract is probably a Latin imitation of the Pseudo-Matthæi Evangelium, which certainly was in existence about the year A.D. 200, and no doubt would become known to the Christians in Western Europe. It occurs also under the title *Historia de Nativitate Mariæ et de Infantia Salvatoris*, and twenty-four chapters of it are so printed in the first Leipsic edition of 1832, but the text differs much in various passages. Its value arises from the fact that, although perhaps not earlier than the fourth or fifth century, it contains legends of a much earlier date.

35. *Matthiæ traditiones*. The traditions of Matthias. Origen writes in his *Philosophumena*, vii, 20: "Basileides and Isidore the legitimate son and disciple of Basileides, say that Matthias told them secret sayings which he heard from our Saviour, having been taught by him privately." Clement of Alexandria also speaks of the *Traditions* of Matthias.

36. *Apocalypsis Mosis*. The Revelation of Moses. The age of this tract is unknown, but from the fact of its being quoted by the writer of the Protevangelium Jacobi, Professor Tischendorf ascribes it to a very early date. It seems also to be quoted by the author of the Descent of Christ into Hell; and the character of the legends which it contains places it not much below the Apocryphal Book of Tobit either in point of time or of historical accuracy. The general subject of the work is a legendary narrative of events in the lives of Adam, Eve, Cain, Abel, Seth, and concludes with the burial of Eve, by the Archangel Michael and three attendant angels.

37. *Evangelium Nicodemi*. The Gospel of Nicodemus. Two works had been published under this title, one in Greek and one in Latin, neither of these being a translation nor yet an exact paraphrase of the other. The number of manuscripts in which it is found is considerable, and they all vary widely in language, although they describe the same facts and mostly in the same order. The latest editor, Professor Tischendorf, has separated these two works into their component parts, having, as he believes, detected that they have been formed by blending into one several works which are mentioned by other writings under the following titles.

i. *Gesta* [or *Acta*] *Pilati Græce* A. Acts of Pilate in Greek, No. 1.

ii. *Gesta* [or *Acta*] *Pilati Græce* B. Acts of Pilate in Greek, No. 2.

iii. *Gesta* [or *Acta*] *Pilati Latine*. Acts of Pilate in Latin.

iv. *Descensus Christi ad Inferos Græce.* Descent of Christ into Hell, in Greek.

v. *Descensus Christi ad Inferos Latine,* A. Descent of Christ into Hell, in Latin, No. 1.

vi. *Descensus Christi ad Inferos Latine,* B. Descent of Christ into Hell, in Latin, No. 2.

Both Justin Martyr and Tertullian mention a work called the Acts of Pilate, and it is not improbable that it coincided generally in substance, if not in language, with some of the documents here enumerated.

38. *Pauli Epistola ad Corinthios Tertia, Latine.* Third Epistle of St Paul to the Corinthians, in Latin.

39. *Epistola Corinthiorum ad Paulum, Latine.* Epistle of the Corinthians to Paul.

These spurious epistles were written in Armenian and published in a Latin translation by Wilkins and afterwards by La Croze. The latter refers their origin to some Armenian "impostor" who wrote about the beginning of the eleventh century.

40. *Pauli Epistola ad Laodicenses, Latine.* Epistle of Paul to the Laodicensians. Philastrius is the first Father of the Church who mentions such an epistle. Jerome also refers to it, but as he says "It is exploded by all," we need not inquire whether the epistle now remaining is the same as the one of which Jerome disposes so summarily.

41. *Pauli et Senecæ Epistolæ, Latine.* Epistles of Paul and Seneca. Fourteen letters under this title were at one time supposed to be genuine. But the fact that Paul and Seneca were contemporary, so far from favouring the authenticity, is a strong reason for condemning them. If Seneca was acquainted with St Paul, we can hardly doubt that the result would have been an important historical record of it, whereas the short letters which have come down to us are worthless scraps, the first of which indicates great intimacy between the two and ends in nothing. They all show very low intellectual powers in the writers between whom they are said to have passed. There is, indeed, a notice in the works of St Augustin, St Jerome, and others, of such letters having existed in their times, but whether they are the same which we now have, must be well established before any credit whatever can be given to their authenticity.

42. *Acta Pauli et Theclæ, Græce.* The Acts of Paul and Thecla. These Acts are probably the oldest of all the uncanonical writings now remaining. They are mentioned by Tertullian and afterwards from him by Jerome, and there-

fore may be considered to owe their origin to the second century, although some modern writers have suggested a doubt whether the work which we have now is identical with that which they had in those early times. However this may be, the subject of the book does not commend itself to the approbation of reasonable judges ; the safety of the denuded virgin in the presence of the wild beasts, her defence by the lioness, and the subsequent baptism reduce the work to the class of shameless fictions, by which the second and following centuries of our era are strongly marked.

43. *Acta Barnabæ, auctore Marco, Græce.* The Acts of Barnabas, written by Mark. This work is found in one of the same early manuscripts (written about A.D. 890) in which the Acts of Peter and Paul occur. Its subject is in some respects similar to that of the Apostolic History by Abdias, but the fictitious character of its contents is evident from the very commencement, where the change of its author's name from John to Mark is mentioned.

44. *Evangelium secundum Petrum.* The Gospel according to St Peter. Mentioned by Jerome, *De Viris illustribus, cap.* i.

45. *Marcelli de Actibus Petri et Pauli Apostolorum, Latine.* Marcellus on the Acts of the Apostles Peter and Paul. This tract, similar in part of its contents to the foregoing Acts of Peter and Paul, was first printed in the *Martyrologium Hieronymianum* of Florentinius, but is a very late work, and of no more authority than the great mass of these apocryphal writings. The writer in the course of his work speaks of himself as "Marcellus, an illustrious man," and concludes with stating that he was a disciple of Peter, and wrote what himself had seen.

46. *Acta Petri et Pauli.* The Acts of Peter and Paul. Three of the manuscripts in which this tract is found appear to have been written as early as the ninth and perhaps even the eighth century of our era. At what time the work was itself composed is wholly uncertain, and it has been thought worth notice principally from the well-known but equally uncertain tradition that St Peter and St Paul were at Rome at the same time, and there established the episcopate which is the origin of the papacy.

47. *Apocalypsis Pauli.* The Revelation of Paul. In Eusebius's Ecclesiastical History (vii, 25) is a passage quoted from Dionysius respecting the Revelation of St John, the authenticity of which he says is doubtful, because no mention is made of it either in the Gospel or the Epistles of St John, whereas St Paul "in his Epistles gives some

intimation of his Revelations, although he never wrote these in a separate work." Whether it is meant that St Paul ever embodied them in a larger work, is doubtful; but it is tolerably certain from those words that the Revelation published by Professor Tischendorf was not extant in the time of Eusebius and cannot be earlier than the end of the fourth century.

48. *Acta Petri.* Acts of Peter. Named by Jerome, *De Viris illustribus*, cap. i, as forming one of the five apocryphal books ascribed to that Apostle; it was perhaps a distinct work.

49. *Epistola Petri ad Jacobum, Græce.* Epistle of Peter to James. Such an Epistle is named first by Photius, and demands no further notice.

50. *Prædicatio Petri.* The Preaching of Peter. Named by Jerome, *De Viris illustribus*, cap. i, as forming one of the five books ascribed to St Peter, but accounted apocryphal by the Church.

51. *Petri et Pauli Prædicatio.* The Preaching of Peter and Paul. How far this is connected with the preceding work, ascribed to Peter alone, cannot be known for certain. Hilgenfeld has collected a few fragments and quotations.

52. *Duæ Viæ vel Judicium Petri.* The Two Ways, or the Judgement of Peter. It is the opinion of Hilgenfeld that this is no other than a short Greek tract published by Bickel in 1843, containing some ecclesiastical canons of the holy Apostles, and he has accordingly added these to his collection under the above-named title, which connects them with St Peter.

53. *Apocalypsis Petri, Arabice.* The Revelation of Peter, in Arabic. This work is found in manuscript in the Bodleian library at Oxford, also in the Vatican at Rome, and elsewhere. It has never been published, but Professor Tischendorf has given the headings of its eighty-eight chapters, from which it would appear that no great gain to either history or religion would result from its publication.

The Apocalypsis Petri named by Jerome, *De Viris illustribus*, cap. i, was probably a different work altogether and of earlier date.

54. *Acta Philippi, A, Græce.* The Acts of Philip, No 1.
55. *Acta Philippi, B, Græce.* The Acts of Philip, No 2.

These two works have been published from manuscripts not earlier than the eleventh century. They probably have come down through divergent channels from some common original, as there is a singular community of ideas exemplified in passages which occur in the two works. In the former of these Philip is said to have "begun to curse them, calling out and crying in the Hebrew tongue, Abalo, aremoun, idouthael, tharsaleon, nachoth, aidounaph, teleteloï! In the latter work the High Priest says to Philip, "I know that thou art a magician and a disciple of Jesus, thou dost not enchant me;" and the Apostle said to Jesus, Sabarthan, sabathabt, bramanouch, come quickly!

56. *Acta Pilati.* The Acts of Pilate. See Evangelium Nicodemi.

57. *Epistola Pilati A Græce.* Letter from Pontius Pilate to the Emperor Claudius, No 1—Printed in the Acta Petri et Pauli, of which it forms the fortieth section.

Epistola Pilati B Latine. Letter from Pontius Pilate, No 2—A Latin version of the preceding, and forming chapter xiii of the Descensus Christi ad Inferos, A.

58. *Anaphora Pilati A Græce.* The Report of Pilate, No 1.

Anaphora Pilati B Græce. The Report of Pilate, No 2. Two Epistles, Reports from Pontius Pilate to the Roman emperor concerning the marvellous events which had happened at Jerusalem.

59. *Paradosis Pilati, Græce.* The delivering up of Pilate. The first paragraph of this tract states that "when the letters reached the city of Rome and were read to the emperor before a large number of persons, they were astounded at hearing that Pilate's lawless conduct had caused darkness and an earthquake over the whole world, and Cæsar in anger sent soldiers to bring Pilate bound to Rome."

60. *Mors Pilati, qui Jesum condemnavit.* The Death of Pilate, who condemned Jesus. This tract might be supposed to relate the natural result of Pilate's offence as related in the foregoing report; but the writer of this present had no knowledge of the former narrative. He ascribes the anger of Cæsar to a different cause. The emperor, he says, was afflicted with a severe disease, and being informed, on the testimony of Veronica, who bore about her the handkerchief impressed with the image of Christ's face, that there was a great prophet in Judæa who cured all kinds of disease, he ordered him to be sent for to Rome, and when he learned that Pontius Pilate had put him to death, he ordered him to be brought prisoner to Rome. The series of events which followed led to Pilate's committing suicide.

61. *Acta Thaddæi Græce.* The Acts of Thaddeus. This tract contains little more than a short account of the corre-

spondence between Christ and Abgarus. It is printed from a manuscript of the eleventh century.

62. *Evangelium Thomæ Græcum.*—No 1. First Greek Gospel of Thomas.

63. *Evangelium Thomæ Græcum.*—No 2. Second Greek Gospel of Thomas.

64. *Evangelium Thomæ Latinum.* Latin Gospel of Thomas.

These three tracts have been printed from numerous manuscripts found in various European and Eastern libraries, but it is uncertain to what period of the Christian era they may be assigned. It is true that a Gospel written by the Apostle Thomas is quoted by Irenæus, Origen, Hippolytus and Eusebius, but no proof can be given that either of the three here named is the one, which existed at so early a date, and the omission of the name Apostle from the designation of the writer seems to imply that the three works are of a later and spurious origin. The author is named Thomas the Israelite, in the first sentence of both the Greek texts.

Acta Sancti Thomæ, Latine. The Acts of St Thomas. This was the first Apocryphal Book published by Thilo, at Leipsic, 1823. Its age cannot be ascertained, but it is as early as any of the uncanonical scriptures now remaining.

66. *Consummatio Sancti Thomæ, Græce.* The end of St Thomas—A short account of his death and miracles. It was printed from a Paris manuscript of the eleventh century.

67. *Vindicta Salvatoris, Latine.* Vindication of our Saviour. Another legend in which Titus, Vespasian, Joseph of Arimathæa, and Veronica appear as actors, and the power of Christ to heal diseases again is made the subject of the story.

68. *Epistola Judæorum ad fratres transmarinos tempore Jesu crucifixi missa, Latine.* Epistle from the Jews sent to their brethren beyond the sea at the time of Christ's crucifixion. Twelve lines only, printed by Martin Crusius, and again by Fabricius, from an unknown source.

69. *Fragmenta Apostolorum, Latine.* Fragments of the Apostles, in Latin—Worthless scraps, first published by St Prætorius in 1595, copied from Abdias and other sources.

70. *Libellus a muliere hæmorrhousa Herodi oblatus.* Petition presented to Herod by the woman who had the issue of blood—John Malalas has this tract in his Chronographia; he relates that, King Herod being in Paneas a town of Judæa, Veronica, the woman in question, presented the petition to him, asking permission to erect a statue to Christ in gratitude for the cure which he had wrought in her.

Such being the list*—and that probably not complete, for many remain still unexamined in various foreign libraries —of the spurious works bearing on early Christianity, it is obvious to ask why they were ever recognized as of any authority at all, and why, after the lapse of so many hundred years, they have occupied the attention of so many learned men. A bishop† of the English Church has given, in a single sentence, an answer to this question.

"Our vital interest in Him of whom they pretend to tell us more than the canonical Scriptures have recorded, is the real, though it may be the hidden reason, why these poor figments are read with interest even whilst they are despised."—*Essay*, p. 156.

But the Bishop adds in the next page, "We know *before we read them*, that they are weak, silly, and profitless—that they are despicable monuments even of religious fiction, &c."—a dangerous principle to admit, this judgment of books before they have been read, and only to be maintained, when others have read them, whose ability to discover and honesty to declare the truth, are acknowledged to be beyond a doubt.

---

* A serviceable edition, it is believed, of the uncanonical writings was published by the author of this work in 1852, containing the substance of all that had then appeared, under the following title :—
Codex Apocryphus Novi Testamenti. The uncanonical gospels and other writings referring to the first ages of Christianity; in the original languages: collected together from the editions of Fabricius, Thilo, and others. By the Rev. Dr. Giles, late fellow of C.C.C. Oxford, 2 vols, 8vo, London, D. Nutt, 270, Strand, 1852.
Those, however, who wish to have the latest critical editions of these writings, will choose the following, edited by the two able theological critics, Tischendorf and Hilgenfeld.
Evangelia Apocrypha, &c. edidit Constantinus Tischendorf, &c., Lipsiæ, 8vo, 1863.
Acta Apostolorum Apocrypha, &c., edidit Constantinus Tischendorf, &c., Lipsiæ, 8vo, 1851.
No edition of *Epistolæ Apocryphæ* has yet appeared.
Apocalypses Apocryphæ, &c., additis Evangeliorum et Actuum Apocryphorum Supplementis, &c., edidit Constantinus Tischendorf, &c. Lipsiæ, 8vo, 1866.
To these volumes of Tischendorf must be added the following, containing all that remains of other uncanonical writings.
Evangeliorum secundum Hebræos, secundum Petrum, secundum Ægyptios, Matthiæ Traditionum, Petri et Pauli Prædicationis et Actuum, Petri Apocalypseos, Didascaliæ Apostolorum Antiquioris quæ supersunt, Addito libro qui appellatus est: "Duæ Viæ vel Judicium Petri," &c., edidit Adolphus Hilgenfeld, Lipsiæ, 8vo, 1866, forming the fourth part of his "Novum Testamentum extra Canonem Receptum."
A translation of several of these writings was published by W. Howe, 8vo, London, 1820, and a Mr Cooper has since published another version of some of them.
† The present Bishop of Winchester, Dr Harold Browne.

CHAPTER VI.

THE NEW TESTAMENT WHOLLY WRITTEN IN GREEK—THE GREEKS UNKNOWN TO THE HEBREWS UNTIL ALEXANDER THE GREAT—SYRIA AND ANTIOCH—EGYPT AND ALEXANDRIA—HEBREW STILL SPOKEN, NOT GREEK—JOSEPHUS LEARNT GREEK WITH DIFFICULTY—EVIDENCE OF COINS.

FROM what has been advanced in the first of these volumes, the reader will probably have concluded that the Old Testament consists of literary remains which the leading men of the Jewish nation collected together to form the basis of their religion and their legislation. Nor does this view differ from the received opinion about those early records; for all admit that the sources of these writings must be assigned to very different dates during the long period of fifteen hundred years between the age of Moses and that of Christ. We have now to examine the books of the New Testament, taking for our starting-point the equally acknowledged fact that these books too, although all produced within a much shorter period of time, have the character at present of being separate writings, collected together to form a similar groundwork for the Christian religion, if not also for that national legislation in which they have since borne a part. For the latter purpose, it is true, their authority has been weakened by time, but their sanction is still valued in practice even by those who in theory reject their authority.

In comparing the two volumes which form our Bible, we discover a remarkable diversity in the fact that the older volume written for the Jewish people, relating to the Jewish history, and having Jewish writers for its authors, has been handed down to us, as we might expect, in the Hebrew or Jewish language, whereas the later volume, written (so it is said) by Jewish authors and relating events which passed among the Jewish people, has come down to us in a language wholly foreign to the Jews, and as far as we know as unintelligible to the mass of that people as any of the continental languages of modern Europe would be in the streets of London. In this particular it must be admitted there is a great divergency between the two volumes which now are united and form the Christian canon.

But there is another particular in which these two volumes appear more in harmony, and their agreement under this head seems to owe its origin to the wish on the part of those who compiled the later volume, to produce a canon similar, as far as was possible, to the earlier volume of the Jews. If the venerable Pentateuch describes the earliest and almost prehistoric narrative of the Hebrew origin, so do the Gospels give us the first accounts of the source from which Christianity is derived. As Joshua, Judges, and the other historical books give us a narrative of what was done to extend and confirm the Jewish nation in their settlement of the promised land, so may the Acts of the Apostles be looked upon as confirming the Christian faith and extending it to the various nations of the world that lay within a reasonable distance from its source. The same view suggests a comparison of the Psalms and other moral or devotional writings under the Old Dispensation, with the Epistles which appear in the New Testament as addressed to various nations with whom the writers are supposed to have been in communication. And lastly, the Revelation of St John the Divine seems to bear a similar relation to those prophetical works which complete the canon of the Hebrews. This comparison, if intentional on the part of those who put together the Christian books, cannot fail to have some bearing on our present subject, for it is not the practice of these who are propagating a new doctrine in the midst of adversaries to form a canon or code of laws for the regulation of life, but rather to be active in recommending by precept and example the theory and the doctrines which they teach. And yet, even if we admit the later origin to which the symmetrical arrangement of the books would lead us, we may well hesitate before we admit that the process of imitation has been carried to the length which the most eminent of German critics has advocated in his comparison of the Old Testament with the New. If, as he argues, the facts of the Gospel history are myths framed out of the imagination of the first Christian Church, so as to form parallelisms throughout with the various miraculous and other facts recorded in the older Testament, the Christian doctrines, however good in themselves, lose the authority which they now possess from the fact that those doctrines were actually exhibited in practice to the world in the beautiful life and character of their first teacher. We therefore need go no further in our speculations on this subject, however interesting in itself, than to admit that the later volume of our religion seems to have been compiled in form somewhat to imitate its Jewish precursor, and so we may proceed to the more weighty observation that the language in which the New Testament has come down to us seems to present a strong objection to the theory that it was written by Jewish authors, or for the use either wholly or partly of the Jewish people. That it is not a contemporary record of the events which it relates would follow as a natural corollary to this argument, if it were shown that the language in which it is written could not have been used by its presumed authors, nor understood generally by those for whose edification it was written.

This then is the point to which our attention must first be directed, to inquire why the early records of Christianity have come down to us in Greek, a language which, as far as we know, none of their writers were either able to speak as their native tongue or likely to have learnt in the course of their early education; and this is a difficulty which cannot be explained and has not yet met with a satisfactory solution, on the supposition that those who appear as actors in the history found in the Christian books, were also the writers of those books in which their own history is recorded. In the previous volume of this work it has been shown that Hebrew was still spoken at Jerusalem in the time of Christ, and the reader who refers to that volume (p. 341) will see that the arguments there brought forward tell strongly in favour of the conclusion that Hebrew was then the language of the Jewish nation, of Palestine generally, of our Lord himself and of his Apostles. It may then be asked how it is that this inference, drawn not only from the facts which have been cited in its favour, but also from its antecedent probability, and also from the jealous nationality of the Jews, who cherished with the utmost care all their old traditions, is wholly incompatible with the assertion that the Christian Scriptures were given forth to the world in Greek, a foreign language, within a few years after the events therein recorded had taken place, or were written professedly by Jews. And it is still less likely that the books which have come down to us could have been written by those Jews to whom they have been ascribed. For the first Christians, and especially the twelve Apostles, were taken from the lowest classes of the people, who by no possibility can be supposed to have been acquainted with literary composition even in their own language, but much less so in Greek, which they could have heard spoken only by those who were in the civil or military service of the empire.

But it has been said in explanation of the remarkable

fact now under consideration that the language of all the East was at that time Greek, or that at all events Greek was spoken by every one who had the least claim to a position in society removed above the level of the lowest classes. If this were true, the ancient world might indeed justly claim that superiority over the moderns, which the fancy of some writers, perhaps more in the spirit of amusement than of truth, has sometimes been pleased to assign to it. But the supposition is as much negatived by facts, and by the tenour of all those passages which have been quoted from the New Testament, as it is by the improbability that, when the means of spreading knowledge among the people were infinitely less than now, the difficult knowledge of a foreign tongue should have made so great a progress as that which is suggested in the case now before us. It may not be foreign to the purpose if we trace the connection which history records as having existed between the Hebrews and the western nations at various times from the Exode to the time of Christ.

From the whole tenour of Biblical history it is evident that the Hebrews had little or no intercourse with the nations of Europe or indeed with any other people than the Syrians in the north, the Babylonians or Assyrians on the east, and the Egyptians on their south-western border. They were indeed almost wholly shut out from the sea-coast by the intervention of the Tyrians, the Sidonians, and the Philistines, who still were in existence down to the latest period of the Jewish commonwealth, until all of them were included in the larger monarchies of Cyrus and of Alexander the Great, by whom the numerous little communities of Asia and Palestine were swallowed up. It is not then to be wondered at that we read nothing certain of the Greeks by name in all the Old Testament; for the word Javan, supposed by some to designate Greece and the Greeks, and to be the Hebrew equivalent for the Ionians, one of the four races into which the Greeks were divided, occurs in six places* only of the Hebrew text, and in passages so short and vague of meaning that conjecture alone and the doubtful testimony of Josephus have identified it with the name of Greece.

Rejecting then the consideration of this word Javan, to which nothing but the imagination of different writers has

---

* Genesis, x, 2: Isaiah, lxvi, 19: Ezekiel, xxvii, 13: Daniel, viii, 21: Joel, iii, 6: and Zechariah, ix, 13.

given a meaning that bears upon our present investigation, we must not omit to mention certain words, which the Bible presents to us in a Hebrew form, but which bear so remarkable a likeness to corresponding Greek words that it is difficult to ascribe their introduction into the Hebrew language to any other than a Grecian source.

1. The first of these is the proper name *Lamech*, which occurs in Genesis, iv, 18: and v, 25. The original Hebrew consists of three letters which may be represented in English by *L m ch*; the vowels of course are to be supplied from the knowledge of the language which those who spoke it by birth could hardly fail to possess, and the word bears a remarkable likeness to the Greek word Λάμαχος; the origin of which is in harmony with Grecian, but by no means whatever can be referred to, Hebrew etymology.

2. The second instance occurs in the word *Ada* the wife of Lamech; and it is remarkable, as Professor Ewald points out, that both these names occur in the inscriptions which have been found in Pisidia and the neighbouring district, and they are found in no other passage of the Hebrew Bible, nor in any correlative form which would lead to the conclusion that they were of native origin.

3. We proceed to the forty-ninth chapter of Genesis, verse 5, where we have a word which may be represented in English letters *m ch r th i* (or y) *he m*. In this word, it is said, may be detected the Greek μάχαιρα a sword: and,

4. The same combination of letters occurs in the First Book of Chronicles (xi, 36), where introducing the proper vowels we read *Chepher ha Mecherati*, which our version, following the Greek Septuagint and the Latin Vulgate, renders "Hepher the Mecherathite;" but which others interpret "Hepher the Swordsman"—armed with the *machæra*, a Grecian weapon.

Whatever may be the truth about these words, so little is known on the subject, that we may limit ourselves here to the remark that, according to Schlegel (*Ramayana*, i, 2, p. 169), and Gorresio (vol. vi, p. 443), quoted by Dr. Donaldson in his Christian Orthodoxy (p. 235), the word *Javan* was not adopted by the eastern nations as the name of Greece until after the time of Alexander the Great. It is also believed by those who have been more curious about these points than is needful for us to be at present, that David, at the end of his reign, employed mercenaries from Crete; and this is entirely in harmony with the fact that Cretans, according to Herodotus (i, 173), colonized Lycia in

Asia Minor, where also there was a tribe called Solymi ; and both Carians and Cretans seem to have been disposed to migrate and found colonies or serve abroad as mercenaries even more readily than the other tribes of Greece, all of whose inhabitants, increasing beyond the means of subsistence which their narrow territory furnished, were always ready to leave their homes and settle wherever sufficient inducements could be found.

"The Greek idiom," says Deutsch in his Literary Remains (p. 299), "is generally supposed to have added next to nothing to the Shemitic before the time of Alexander." But the conquests of that great Macedonian king had the effect of breaking through the barrier which until then had kept the Jews from intercourse with the Greeks. The account indeed which Josephus gives of the interview between the victorious Macedonian and Jaddua the high priest, has been regarded by most critics as highly coloured by the Jewish historian, and by others is rejected altogether as a fiction ; but it is certain that the isolation of the Jewish nation ceased from that time, and that they were soon afterwards brought into subjection first under Ptolemy King of Egypt and afterwards by Antiochus King of Syria. The persecutions, to which they were exposed under the latter monarch, are too well known from the Maccabean history found in the Apocrypha attached to the authorized version of our Bibles, to require that we should dwell on them at present ; but the existence of those books shows that the Greek language now began to be used in the composition of writings which have Jewish transactions for their subject. It has too hastily been inferred from this that Hebrew, their native tongue, was now less an object of care and attention than in previous periods of their history; but this inference may be easily refuted, if our theory is correct that the later portions of the Jewish Scriptures are not earlier than the time when the Macedonian conquests were completed. It was certainly during the last period of the Jewish history that the greatest respect was shown to those books which were written in their native tongue, and it is well known that the Jews from the first, like Protestant Christians in modern times, have excluded from their canon every book which was written in Greek or Latin or any other language than their own.

But the solution of this question lies upon the surface : the empire of Alexander was dissolved into its naturally component parts. The kingdom of Egypt, which had been powerful under Amasis, was revived under the Ptolemies, and Syria, including Babylonia and other provinces which being inland were naturally liable to disruption such as so often happens to countries away from the sea, became again a powerful kingdom under the dynasty of Antiochus. Thus Judæa, lying between the two, resumed its neutral character with even greater eventual success than when it vacillated formerly between the Pharaohs and the Babylonian or Assyrian kings. This position however had much influence on the literature and religion of the Jews; and fully accounts for their separation from this time into two distinct and possibly rival classes. The kings of Syria for a time reduced the Hebrew nation into subjection to their sceptre, but those kings had also to contend with the two growing empires of Rome and Parthia. About a hundred and forty years after the death of Alexander, the Jews again free, entered into a treaty with the Romans against the Syrian king Demetrius Soter, and indeed there was hardly a moment in which they had repose from the aggressions of their Syrian neighbours. On the other hand Egypt, more favourably situated and having the sea, the desert, and the strong fortress of Jerusalem to separate them from the large rival empires which were contending for mastery, seems on the whole eventually to have shown much favour to the Jews, and to have encouraged that extensive settlement of them in the Grecian city of Alexandria which is so prominent at the time of the Christian era. It is to the dynasty of the Ptolemies that the Septuagint translation of the Old Testament is ascribed, and probably is due, whilst the Apocryphal books, attached to it as an appendix, probably owe their origin to the same source. Most of them are indeed thought by Jerome and others to have been written originally in Hebrew, in which case the Greek translation only of those books may still be regarded as due to the reigns of the Ptolemies, under whom Grecian literature in general was so highly favoured. At all events the testimony of Josephus excludes those books from the Jewish canon, and the whole history of the Jews who dwelt in Jerusalem itself forbids us to believe that anything alien to their native language and native customs would be tolerated among them.

But the proximity of Greek neighbours would not wholly exclude words of Greek origin from entering into their language and becoming naturalized among them. Such were those names of musical instruments occurring in the third chapter of Daniel, which coincide so remarkably with Greek names, that it is difficult to maintain for them a separate origin. Thus 'harp,' κίθαρις in Greek, is represented in the Hebrew text of Daniel by the letters K I T H R S; 'dulcimer,' in Greek *symphonia*, becomes in Hebrew S U M P H N I A; 'sackbut' is *sambuke* in Greek, and in Hebrew S B K A; 'psaltery,' in Greek *psanterion* (Macedonian dialect for *psalterion*), is P S N T R I N in Hebrew. If one of these words alone were found in the Hebrew text, it might be thought one of those casual coincidences of which so many examples may be adduced in the comparison of languages; but the four words above cited, if we bear in mind the Hebrew vowels which must be supplied, show so great a similarity and almost identity both in speech and writing, and they all flow so etymologically from Greek roots, that it is difficult to impugn the conclusion at which we have arrived.

If then there was a Greek as well as a Hebrew element in the Jewish nation and its literature from the time of Alexander or somewhat later to that of Christ, it seems to follow that the Greek element prevailed chiefly at Alexandria.

A rival of this Egyptian city however was the Syrian city of Antioch, situated in the most delicious climate and most fertile plain of Asia. We are informed by Josephus (*Antiq.* XII, iii, 1) that the Jews in this city were at first admitted to the same privileges as the Greeks, and in the time of Chrysostom, the Christians, including Jews no doubt, numbered a hundred thousand, or nearly half the inhabitants of the city. But in the interval of so many hundred years that intervene between King Seleucus who favoured the Jews, and the time of Chrysostom, when the Christian community was so firmly established, the Greeks in Antioch were on terms far from friendly with the brave people who so strenuously maintained their independence against all the attempts of the Syrians to subdue them. It is an established fact that no Greek writings have come down to us that can be ascribed to Jewish authors, and were composed in the city of Antioch, unless the Christian books beginning with our Canonical New Testament, and followed by at least some of the numerous Apocryphal writings still extant, can be shown to have had their origin in the beautiful city of Seleucus.* That this probably was the case is

---

* "Christianity found its way at a very early period into Syria, and its

mostly the subject of this work, but our object now is to prove that Jerusalem or Judæa at all events was not the place where these books were written, and that the authors to whom they are commonly ascribed could not possibly have been Jews.

Reverting however to the theory that Greek had superseded Hebrew in Palestine generally and even in Jerusalem its capital, or at all events that it was well understood by men of every class, we cannot wisely pass over the evidence which Josephus, "the learned and warlike Jew," furnishes on this subject. In the last chapter of his work on the "Antiquities of the Jews" occurs the following passage, as rendered from the original Greek in Whiston's English translation.

I am so bold as to say, now I have so completely perfected the work I proposed to myself to do, that no other person, whether he were a Jew or a foreigner, had he ever so great an inclination to it, could so accurately deliver these accounts to the Greeks as is done in these books. For those of my own nation freely acknowledge that I far exceed them in the learning belonging to the Jews; I have also taken a great deal of pains to obtain the learning of the Greeks, and understand the elements of the Greek language, although I have so long accustomed myself to speak our own tongue, that I cannot pronounce Greek with sufficient exactness: for our nation does not encourage those that learn the languages of many nations, and so adorn their discourses with the smoothness of their periods; because they look upon this sort of accomplishment as common, not only to all sorts of freemen, but to as many of the servants as please to learn them.

The same writer gives further supplementary evidence to the same effect in his "Treatise against Apion" (i, 9) and not only to the same effect, but also proving that the Jews generally knew nothing of any language but their own, and that Josephus was the only man in the Roman camp before Jerusalem during the siege who understood the numerous Jews who deserted out of the city. This passage also is too interesting to be omitted, and is here given in full.

---

capital Antioch became naturally a centre for missions into countries still remaining heathen. Greek undoubtedly was the dominant language at Antioch, but Syriac continued to be that of the people in the country districts—certainly across the Euphrates in Mesopotamia, where Christianity had found an entrance for some time; for there are evident signs of the existence of a Christian literature there so early as the second century. The necessity for a version of the Gospels in the vernacular would soon be felt, and to this we are indebted for the earliest Syriac version."—Tischendorf translating from Bleek.

As for myself I have composed a true history of that whole war, and all the particulars that occurred therein, as having been concerned in all its transactions; for I acted as general of those amongst us who are named Galilæans,* as long as it was possible for us to make any opposition. I was then seized on by the Romans and became a captive. Vespasian also and Titus had me kept under a guard, and forced me to attend them continually. At the first I was put into bonds; but was set at liberty afterward, and sent to accompany Titus when he came from Alexandria to the siege of Jerusalem; during which time there was nothing done which escaped my knowledge; for what happened in the Roman camp I saw and wrote down carefully; and what information the deserters brought [out of the city] I was the only man that understood them. Afterward I got leisure at Rome; and, when all my materials were prepared for that work, I made use of some persons to assist me in learning the Greek tongue, and by these means I composed the history of those transactions.

Josephus elsewhere tells us more than once that he was employed to act as interpreter between the Romans and the rebellious Jews. It would seem impossible to draw any other inference from these extracts than that which has been so often repeated—that Hebrew and not Greek was the language of the Jews in the time of Christ, and that the books of the New Testament, at whatever period of our era they may have been written, being written in Greek, a language unknown to the Jews, were written probably by Greeks.

It remains only to add to what has been here said the evidence of certain monuments the most lasting and convincing that human workmanship ever yet has produced—the almost imperishable testimony of coins and medals. That coined money was unknown to the Israelites is admitted by all who have examined or written upon the subject, nor is this inference weakened by any of the passages in the Old Testament, in which the words, money, gold, and silver, repeatedly occur. We read in Genesis, xiii, 12, that Abraham was "rich in cattle, in silver and in gold:" but in a later chapter of the same book (xxiii, 16) we read that he weighed the silver with which he bought the cave of Machpelah from Ephron the son of Zoar. In the reign of David the same use of bullion, estimated by

---

* The inhabitants of Galilee must be here meant: it would be hazardous to suggest that Josephus was at the head of a Christian band, although the Christians are called Galilæans by more than one heathen writer.

weight, is still existing, and though the two passages, in which the transaction alluded to is related, are hopelessly conflicting one with the other, yet they may be cited as furnishing the same conclusion that coined money was not then in use among the Hebrews.

II *Samuel*, xxiv, 24. And the king said unto Araunah, Nay, but I will surely buy it of thee at a price: neither will I offer burnt offerings unto the Lord my God of that which doth cost me nothing. So David bought the threshing floor and the oxen for fifty pieces of silver.

Compare with this the account given in the First Book of Chronicles, xxi, 24.

And King David said unto Ornan, Nay, but I will buy it for the full price: for I will not take that which is thine for the Lord, nor offer burnt offerings without cost. So David gave to Ornan for the place six hundred shekels of gold.

These two accounts, handed down separately by divergent tradition, combine only to prove that, whilst gold and silver were used and valued as a medium of commerce among the Hebrews as among almost all other nations, they derived their value from their weight, and not from any emblem or inscription impressed upon them.

We may pass over the ring-money, thought to be meant by the Hebrew term which our version translates "ear-ring of gold," but which the Septuagint renders by "tetradrachm of unstamped gold," thereby giving the idea that such rings could be used as money, and state shortly that no Jewish coins have ever been found bearing an earlier date than that of Simon the Maccabee son of Mattathias who first successfully withstood the armies of Antiochus and paved the way for the last period of independence which the Jewish nation enjoyed.

It must not however be supposed that no coined money was circulated until they had their own national mint in the middle of the second century before the Christian era. During the captivity, and afterwards whilst they formed part of the Persian empire, the Jews used the Persian money, mostly Darics, so called from Darius the King of Persia, whilst in the time of Alexander the Great Grecian money would naturally be introduced. It is true that we read of talents in the time of Ezra (viii, 25), but that name in all countries, where it was used, denoted money the value of which was ascertained by weight and not by the number of coined pieces. Nor is there any impropriety in the inference that, as no earlier Jewish coins have been found, none ever were in existence; for we have never failed to find numerous pieces of money lost and buried in the earth wherever such pieces have been used as the medium of commerce in any nation of the ancient world. It was about the year B.C. 139 that Antiochus VII, surnamed Sidetes, sent letters to Simon High Priest and Prince of the Jews, in which the following sentence is found, as we read it in the First Book of Maccabees (xv, 6), "I give thee leave also to *coin money* for thy country with thine own stamp." This permission of Antiochus, hardly needed by those to whom it was given—for the power of Syria was declining, whilst that of Judæa was growing—explains the appearance for the first time of coins marked with inscriptions in the Hebrew language and in a character different from that in which Hebrew words are now written, but without doubt that which, as we find from all the inscriptions, Jewish, Phœnician, and Carthaginian, that have come down to us, prevailed among the Jews during the later period of their nationality.

A few of the legends and emblems occurring on these coins, on the authority of Madden's able History of the Jewish Coinage, may here with propriety be introduced.

1. A copper coin: OBVERSE *Shkl Ishral* (Shekel of Israel), round a cup with the A over it, denoting the first year of Simon's reign or coinage. REVERSE *Jrushlm kdshh* (Jerusalem the Holy) round a triple flower.

2. A copper coin: OBVERSE *Chzi hshkl* (Half-shekel) round a cup with A over it. REVERSE *Jrushlm kdshh* (Jerusalem the Holy) round a triple flower.

3. A third copper shekel, struck in the second year of Simon, has the same emblems and inscription but exhibits a slight variation by spelling Jerusalem on the Reverse *Jrushlim* instead of omitting the *yod* before the final *m*.

These examples from so late a period before our era seem to refute most thoroughly the theory that the Hebrew nation had forgotten their original language. No ancient people are known to have struck coins in any other than their native tongue, and, though we need not wonder that a national mint was unknown to such semi-barbarous races as those which inhabited Palestine in the earlier ages, yet that, when freed from Persian, Macedonian, and Syrian rulers in an age which had advanced in every kind of knowledge, they should have issued national money of their own in the

Hebrew tongue, can only be explained by the inference that Hebrew was the language both of their public business and of their social life.

But it cannot be ignored and need not be a matter of surprise, that some among the Jews looked with favour towards the Greeks who were their neighbours and enjoyed a higher system of civilized life than themselves. Judas Aristobulus, who ruled among the Jews in the year B.C. 106, was called *Philhellen* from his love of the Grecian people, and in the time of Alexander Jannæus appear coins with bilingual inscriptions, Hebrew and Greek, some of which, preserved in the British Museum, bear traces of Greek letters under the more recent Hebrew writing.

But we may hasten on to more conclusive evidence that the Jews, whenever an opportunity occurred of asserting their national independence, asserted also the nationality of their language. Although coins struck in Greek or Latin under the dominion of the Roman emperors were the circulating medium in Judæa down to the reign of Nero, yet in the four years from A.D. 66 to A.D. 70, when the revolted Jews held possession of Jerusalem until it was taken by Titus, Hebrew coins again appear, some with the inscription *Eleazar Hakkohen* "Eleazar the High Priest," and others inscribed *Shenath Achath Ligullath Israel* "First year of the redemption of Israel."

Nor does the revolt of the Jews, in the reign of Trajan under Simon Bar-cochab, furnish other evidence than what has already been brought forward. The leader of the rebellious Jews circulated Roman coins, with Hebrew inscriptions stamped over the original Latin, of which specimens are still preserved, and others bearing the words in Hebrew characters *Lacheruth Jerusalem* "The deliverance of Jerusalem" connected with the name *Simon*, i.e. Simon Barcochebas, to whom that momentary deliverance was ascribed.

It would seem needless to prolong this argument; for the evidence already produced seems to prove conclusively that Hebrew and no other language was spoken and written not only in the time of Christ, but also in the first half of the second century after Christ, when Hadrian, taught by the revolt of Barcochebas that half measures would never quell the rebellious spirit of the Jews, built upon the ruins of Jerusalem another city named *Ælia Capitolina*, from which all Jews were excluded, and where only Christians or Pagans were allowed to dwell.

But the character, and not only the language, in which these coins were struck, is also of much importance to our present purpose. The difference between the form of Hebrew letters found in these inscriptions and the square letter which prevails in all the manuscripts now remaining has caught the notice of all those who have taken any interest in this subject. The Phœnician inscriptions, which have been published and illustrated in the learned work of Gesenius (*Scripturæ Linguæque Phœniciæ monumenta, Lipsiæ, 4to,* 1837) confirms the opinion that the present square letter of the Hebrew manuscripts has been introduced, perhaps gradually, and brought to its present state of perfection at a much later period, in the same way as the set and regular form of Greek and Latin letters has been developed out of the straggling characters of a more early date.

There is however one letter in the Hebrew alphabet which apparently has changed its shape since the books of the New Testament were written. In the Gospel according to St Matthew (v, 18) we read:

For verily I say unto you: Till heaven and earth pass, one jot or one tittle shall in no wise pass from the law till all be fulfilled.

Now the word here rendered *jot* is *iota*, the Greek name of the letter *i*, which, as it is now written, is the smallest letter in the alphabet; and the word rendered tittle is the Greek *keraia*, which denotes the apex, point, or extremity of any thing. Both these words are here used to denote the smallest particle of a thing. But in the time of Christ, as before, and for more than one hundred years later the letter *yod*, of which *iota* is the Greek equivalent both in sound and sense, was one of the largest letters of the Hebrew; it consisted of three strokes instead of one, like the Greek *iota*, and would not certainly have been selected by a Hebrew in the first century, although it might have been by a Greek writer nearly 200 years after Christ, to denote the smallest particle of the law that was not to pass away, till all things spoken by our Lord had been fulfilled.

I conclude this chapter by two extracts from the able work on the Hebrew coins, which has been already quoted, and from which much assistance has been derived to my present subject, and which will show that the Jews still adhered in more recent times, as they had formerly, whenever a favourable time allowed them, to their ancient language.

In September, 1853, some Jewish catacombs were discovered at Venusa, upon some of the niches of which some inscriptions in *Hebrew*, Latin, and Greek are either roughly painted or scratched. Twenty-four of the inscriptions as yet found are in Hebrew. The Latin and Greek inscriptions are mis-spelt, but the *Hebrew* ones are more correct. It has also been noticed that at Lavello there were also found some *Hebrew Inscriptions* in the last century, and other *Hebrew catacombs* were discovered in 1854 at Oria (p. 319).

The author of the same work speaks in a note of some other Hebrew inscriptions, found at Rome, and thought by M. de Vogüé, who has described them in the *Revue Archéologique* for March 1864 (p. 200), to belong to A.D. 70, on the ground that Hebrew ceased to be spoken after the capture of Jerusalem by Titus. But, according to Mr. Madden,

This assumption is evidently of little weight, for it is certain that the Hebrew language and alphabet were employed by the Jews in sepulchral and other inscriptions from the earliest period at which they are found through successive centuries downwards, as evidenced by the inscriptions at Rome (assigned by M. de Vogüé himself to the second century), the bowls from Babylon, and the monuments from Aden.

CHAPTER VII.

HEBRAISMS FEW OR NONE IN THE NEW TESTAMENT—NO CONNECTION BETWEEN ITS WRITERS AND THE JEWS WHO REMAINED IN JUDÆA—ITS STYLE AND LANGUAGE CLOSELY COPIED FROM THE SEPTUAGINT.

THE exclusive character of the religion and the polity of the Jews resulted mainly from the circumscribed nature of their country and the isolation in which they were placed. Their language also partook of this isolation, and in fact almost disappeared from their literature from the time when the Greek kingdoms of Egypt and Syria interfered either as allies or as enemies in the affairs of Palestine. If any other Hebrew works were ever written during the century and a half which immediately precedes the Christian era, none of them now remain; nor is it certain that those works which now are extant in the Arabic, Syriac, Coptic, and Ethiopic dialects were ever represented by a Hebrew original, although it has been a favourite object of some modern theological critics to supply the place of missing Hebrew documents by Syriac and other works, stated without authority to have been *probably* translated from the Hebrew. A volume of such writings has been edited by Drs Cureton and Wright, and furnishes some curious information respecting the times at which they were written, but they supply nothing which enables us to connect them with the older Hebrew literature, and the remarks which Dr Westcott has made on the subject seem sufficiently appropriate to sanction the following extract.

> The *Ancient Syrian Documents*, edited by Dr Cureton and Dr W. Wright (London, 1864), do not throw any new light upon the Syrian canon. The writings themselves cannot maintain the claim to Apostolic antiquity which has been set up for some of them. In their present form they contain numerous anonymous references to the substance of the Gospels. . . . . . The strange passage (p. 56) :—" One of the Doctors of the Church hath said : The scars, indeed, of my body—that I may come to the resurrection from the dead :" appears to be derived from Gal. vi, 17 ; Phil. iii, 11. Some Evangelic passages are given in what may be a traditional form. Thus we read (p. 20) that the Lord said : " Accept not any thing from any man, and possess not any thing in this world." (Cf. Matt. x, 7-10.) . . . . A general review is given of the writings of the Apostles, with the exception of St Paul. . . . The omission of St Paul is made the more remarkable by the fact that in the distribution of the various countries among the Apostles no land is assigned to St Paul, (Rome, Spain, and *Britain*, are given to St Peter,) though he is afterwards mentioned casually in the same paragraph (p. 35). WESTCOTT, *Canon of the N. T.* 3rd edition, Lond. 1870, p. 223.

The partial destruction of Jerusalem by the arms of the Roman Titus occurred early enough after the Crucifixion to remind the followers of our Lord that the abomination of desolation spoken of by Daniel the Prophet had really stood in the Holy Place, and that it was now the time to verify their faith in the words of their Master by fleeing to the mountains and taking such other modes of escape as chance or opportunity might offer. But the desolation which the arms of Titus brought upon the Holy City, was not final. A Jewish community was still found in Jerusalem—for the city still sheltered a large number of inhabitants sixty years later, and it was only the persistence in rebellion, for which they were so famous, that brought on them, from the vengeance of Hadrian, a still more severe extermination than from his predecessor Titus. But the city then received the Roman name of Ælia, and its church probably was rather of the Latin than the Greek character. The desolation to which the Holy Land had for many years been subject, rendered it difficult to find inhabitants for Hadrian's new city, and the plan of forming there a Roman colony was the result, as it had been the usual practice in such cases. Latin coins still remain struck in the reign of Commodus bearing the inscription COL. ÆL. CAP. COMM. P. F. and the Latin language was no doubt spoken and well understood there, as it was even at Constantinople in the reign of Constantine the Great, until the Greek resumed its natural influence and became, with great tendency to corruption, again the prevalent dialect of the Eastern Empire. Among these changes the Jews retained much of their national character, and the opinion that there was from the first a Jewish element of Christianity kept up at Jerusalem, somewhat distinct from that which St Paul preached in Asia Minor, derives strong confirmation not only from what we read in the Acts of the Apostles, and from the accounts of the Apostle James found in Eusebius and Josephus, but also from the fact that fifteen bishops, all circumcised Jews, are said to have presided over the church of Jerusalem down to the reign of Hadrian. Thus the Hebrew tongue still continued in the same isolated position which it had occupied from the times of remote antiquity, and no evidence whatever can be adduced to connect the books of the New Testament in any way with either Hebrew writers or with the Hebrew tongue. They are entirely of Greek origin, and as such contain few Hebraisms either of idiom or of single words.

It has however been customary to quote certain words as used in a sense somewhat different from their original meaning, and pointing to a Hebrew origin. A few instances of such words will show the nature of the case. It is said that the words *debts* and *debtors* used in the Lord's Prayer and elsewhere can only by Hebrew usage be understood as synonymous with sin and sinners ; *bride* was used to denote *a daughter in law ; tongue* denotes a nation ; *lip* represents *speech ; to drink a cup to the dregs* means to *go through suffering to the end ;* the word *bowels* stands for the feeling of *compassion ;* and many other examples are given of the same kind, as occurring in numerous passages throughout the whole of the New Testament. But those who compare these books with the Septuagint translation of the Hebrew Bible must acknowledge that the language of the Gospels, Acts, Epistles, and Revelations finds the most exact counterpart in the older volume. It has always been allowed by scholars that the quotations from the Old Testament which occur in the New, are taken almost verbatim in every case from the Septuagint translation, and the labours of Mr Grinfield, the result of which is set forth in his Hellenistic edition of the Greek Testament (4 vols Lon. 1843), have made it clear that not only the quotations but almost every phrase and every idiom found in the later volume has its counterpart, as if written by the same hand and dictated by the same thought, in the Greek volume of the Septuagint. Neither is there the slightest indication in the various books of the New Testament, that its writers were aware of there being any Hebrew Bible at all. We read in the Gospel the words of our Lord " Search the Scriptures," but every word which He quoted from the Scriptures is found in the Greek Septuagint, and the only marks of there being any Hebrew language in existence are those which have already been given in our previous volume (p. 342). In all those places the writer uses language which shows that his readers were unacquainted with Hebrew, and indeed the way in which the various writers spell the Hebrew words which they quote shows that they used each his own system of Greek equivalents, and that the language from which they quoted was only beginning to decline rather than that it had been superseded by the Greek in which they wrote. That the expression *Eli, Eli, lama sabachthani*, quoted in the Gospel according to St Matthew, and rendered in our version 'My God, my God, why hast Thou forsaken me,' may be considered as identical with the Hebrew original in the Twenty-second Psalm, cannot be impugned by the various modes of spelling, *Eloi &c.* seen in the Gospel according to St Mark, as indicating a different dialect; for the recent collation of the three most ancient MSS, given in page 16 of this volume, shows that in two of these MSS the Sinaitic and the Vatican texts of St Matthew agree with St Mark in reading *Eloi*, instead of *Eli*, whilst all the three MSS, in the Gospel of St Mark, differ from one another in the mode of spelling, and one of them spells the last of the words with *z* instead of *s*, thereby refuting the theory of those who regard *z* as indicative of the pure Hebrew and *s* of a Syro-Chaldaic origin.

That the style of the New Testament is wholly modelled on that of the Septuagint has not escaped the notice of those who have devoted their attention exclusively to the subject, but the inference that the books of one canon were addressed to Greeks including of course Jews who had become Greeks since the subversion of the Jewish state, and were written by Greek authors, has either not suggested itself to the minds of those students, or at all events has not been expressed in the works which they have written on the subject. On the contrary, instead of bringing the copy to the level of the Septuagint its prototype, they have endeavoured to raise the prototype to the level occupied by its copy; and some of them have not hesitated to ascribe to this Greek version that inspiration which few critics in modern times are willing to allow even to its Hebrew original. Thus the author of the *Apology for the Septuagint* (p. 80) writes:

> The version of the Seventy is not to be regarded merely as the first and most important of all versions of the Old Testament, whether ancient or modern; but as constituting a great historical fact or epoch in the plan of the Christian dispensation.

And the author of *New Testament Quotations*, before mentioned, copies these words, and adds:

> It was made in the wonderful providence of God, in order to prepare the way for the calling of the Gentiles. The whole New Testament is founded on it; most, if not all, of the doctrinal terms of the Gospel are derived from it; and, had not such a translation been published and received a proper time before our Saviour's advent, the composition of the New Testament would, humanly speaking, have been impossible. An idea of the vast extent to which Septuagintal phraseology is employed in the New Testament may be gained from the immense mass of citations, allusions, and parallels of thought and expression—"thousands and tens of thousands of incidental resemblances"—collected in the learned and most valuable works of the Rev. E. W. Grinfield.

From these passages, combined with the arguments previously adduced and others hereafter to be brought forward, it is my opinion that the New Testament was compiled out of documents, after the total dispersal of the Jews in the reign of Hadrian, at a time when Hebrew no longer designated a nation, when the dialect of those who lived dispersed in the different countries of the Roman empire was corrupted by mixing with the speech of the countries where they dwelt, and the Targums or paraphrases furnished greater facilities than the original text for understanding the ancient Scriptures, to exiles, who living among Greeks, adopted for the business of their daily lives the language of those among whom they sojourned.

CHAPTER VIII.

LATINISMS IN THE NEW TESTAMENT.

WE have seen in the last chapter that a strong argument against the contemporary character of the New Testament is derived from the fact that the writings which pass under that name have come down to us in Greek—a language not spoken by its supposed writers, if those writers were Jews, the disciples of our Lord, who were the only contemporaries able from their knowledge of the events to record His history. A similar argument may be derived from the various Latin words which are found in all the books of the New Testament. It is well known that at the time of Christ's birth the nation of the Jews was still to a certain extent independent.

The Gospel history informs us that Herod the Great, in whose reign Christ is said to have been born, was succeeded on the throne by his son Archelaus. This king reigned only a few years, when he was deposed for mal-administration, and his dominions reduced to the form of a Roman province. The Crucifixion of Jesus Christ took place about twenty years after the abolition of the Jewish monarchy, and it may be admitted that numerous officials speaking the Latin language would be found residing not only in Judæa but throughout all Asia, and discharging various duties belonging to the offices which they held under the Roman governor. We fail to see in the narratives of the New Testament any signs of amalgamation between the two peoples. On the contrary the nationality of the Jews was never more rampant than during the last fifty years of its existence, before it was on the point of perishing for ever. It is unlikely that a nation so stubborn should have prided itself less in its ancient language than in the various institutions, some of them trivial enough, which, as we see in our books, met with all the care and attention of which they were capable. If it is improbable that the Jews adopted the Greek as their vernacular language, according to an absurd theory which some professing to be critics have maintained, it is still less probable that their writers should have been very studious of the Latin, which was the language of their conquerors, or that they would have interspersed their writings with so many Latinisms both of single words and of complete sentences. A catalogue of many such Latin words will no doubt interest the reader, and, as it illustrates the present argument, it is here subjoined with the Greek words, which correspond to the Latin, showing the closest likeness and almost an identity with one another.

LATIN.	GREEK.	REFERENCE.
Assarium	*Assarion*,	Matthew, x, 29 : Luke, xii, 6.
Census	*Kensos*,	Matthew, xvii, 25.
Centurio	*Kenturion*,	Mark, xiv, 39, 44, 45.
Charta	*Chartes*,	II John, 12.
Colonia	*Kolonia*,	Acts, xvi, 12.
Crypta	*Krupte*,	Luke, xi, 33.
Custodia	*Kustodia*,	Matthew, xxvii, 65.
Denarius	*Denarion*,	Matthew, xxii, 19.
Euroaquilo	*Euruhulon*,	Acts, xxvii, 14.
Exitus	*Exodos*,	Luke, ix, 31; II Peter, i, 15.
Flagellans	*Fragellosas*,	Matthew, xxvi, 26.
Flagellum	*Fraggêlion*	John, ii, 15.
Forum	*Foron*,	Acts, xxviii, 15.
Grabatus	*Krabbatos*,	Mark, ii, 4.
Legio	*Legeon*,	Mark, v, 19.
Libertinus	*Libertinoi*,	Acts, vi, 9.
Linteum	*Lention*,	John, xiii, 4.
Litra	*Litra*,	John, xii, 3.
Macellum	*Makellon*,	I Cor. x, 25.
Membrana	*Membrana*,	II Tim. iv, 13.
Miliare	*Milion*,	Matthew, v, 41.
Modius	*Modios*,	Matthew, v, 15.
Pœnulum	*Phailonen*,	II Tim. iv, 13.
Prætorium	*Praitorion*,	Matthew, xxvii, 27.
Quadrantes	*Kodrantes*,	Mark, xii, 42.
Rheda	*Rheda*,	Apoc. xviii, 13.
Satum	*Saton*,	Matthew, xiii, 33.
Semicinctium	*Semihinthion*,	Acts, xix, 12.
Sicarius	*Siharios*,	Acts, xxi, 38.
Spiculator	*Spekoulator*,	Mark, vi, 27.
Sudarium	*Soudarion*,	Luke, xix, 20.
Taberna	*Taberne*,	Acts, xxviii, 15.
Titulus	*Titlos*,	John, xix, 19, 20.

Almost all these words are found in Latin authors, and manifestly took their origin among the Latins: few of them occur in any other Greek books than the New Testament, where however they abound,—in perfect conformity with the theory that the Latin language was well known in the second century, and furnished numerous words and phrases which would enter largely into the writings of the tributary nations, among whom it penetrated.

But a more startling theory was suggested by the author of *Palæoromaica*, a man whose learning was of the highest order, even if the result of his labours is less convincing. According to the suggestion thrown out in his erudite and modest work, our existing New Testament betrays marks of having been translated from a Latin original, and that too in many passages by an ignorant translator, who in rendering certain passages has suffered his ear to mislead him by a similarity of sound suggesting meanings wholly different from those which the original Latin words would convey. This, he remarks, would account for many expressions, either barbarous and of unknown etymology, or else tending to draw away the understanding of the reader to alien and often erroneous interpretations. A few examples of his line of argument will suffice as a mark of respect to a work which cannot be altogether ignored, although the judgment of the world has not hitherto been influenced by a theory so improbable and unexpected.

1. In the First Epistle of St Peter, v, 5, we meet with the words τὴν ταπεινοφροσύνην ἐγκομβώσασθε, the last of which occurs in no other Greek book now existing. Our authorized version renders this, "Be clothed with humility:" but the writer of Palæoromaica thinks that the barbarous word ἐγκομβώσασθε is no other than the Latin word *incumbite*, and that the Latin text from which it was taken, was *in humilitatem incumbite*, "Be earnest for humility."

2. A second example is given from Mark, xii, 4, where the English text 'wounded him in the head' is represented in Greek by the single word ἐκεφαλαίωσαν, which is derived from the noun *kefale* 'head,' and might be rendered in English by the corresponding preterite tense 'headed,'—not 'beheaded,' for it is added that they 'sent him away shamefully handled.' But the Greek word occurs in no other book, and the suggestion is that it was brought to the mind of the Greek translator by some kind of rhyming likeness— very slight at all events in this case—to the Latin word *expulerunt* 'they cast him out.'

3. A much stronger example in support of the theory of a translation from the Latin is furnished by the words *nardou pistikes* in the account which is given in the Gospel of the anointing of our Lord. I shall quote the criticism on this in the words of its author.

In Mark, xiv, 3, we are told that the woman who anointed Our Lord brought a box νάρδου πιστικῆς, which in the same passage of the Vulgate is rightly given *Nardi spicati* [*spicatæ*]. This word *pistikes* is quite unknown; and many critics, who had not the slightest notion that the Gospels were composed in Latin, (or at least that our present Greek text is a version from that language,) have yet been of opinion that *pistikes* is a mere corruption from the Latin. " Critics (says Dr Campbell) have been divided about the exact import of this term. Some have thought that it has arisen from the Latin name *Nardus spicatus*, the latter part of which denoting the species of the plant has *by some accident* been corrupted into *pistikes*." This *accident*, of a conversion of Latin words into Greek ones, is very common in our Greek Vulgate, and has happened once more to this very word in *John*, xii, 3, where the phrase *Nardou pistikes* again occurs. . . The [Latin] Vulgate, which in *Mark*, xiv, 3, rightly reads *Nardi spicati*, is in *John*, xii, 3, *Nardi pistici*. . . . . This latter word is still more barbarous and unmeaning than *pistikes* is in Greek. . . . . Nothing seems to be more probable than that the *Nardi pistici* [*John*, xii, 3] of the Latin Vulgate is merely a transcript of the *Nardou pistikes* of the Greek, and that this latter was derived from the *Nardi spicatæ* of a more ancient exemplar. *Palæoromaica*, p. 191.

4. In Mark xii, 38, we read 'Beware of the Scribes,' and this in the Greek text is *Blepete apo ton grammateon*, which may be literally rendered, ' Look ye from the Scribes,' more fully ' Look ye to it,' i.e. ' See that ye get no evil from the Scribes.' Here our critic thinks that the Latin original was *Devitate*, that the prefix *de* was rendered by the Greek *apo*, and that *vitate*, mistaken for *videte*, gave rise to the Greek βλέπετε which now appears in the verse we are considering.

To save the reader's time and yet to give a fair illustration of the theory which the author of this learned work (p. 229) propounds, I subjoin a list of Greek words, written as before in Italic letters, with the corresponding Latin words from which he supposes them to have been bungled.

Akmen, in Matthew, xv, 16, from *acumen*.
Di' hemeran, in Mark, ii, 1, from *demorari*.
Ektromati, in 1 Cor. xv, 8, from *extremitate*.
Enotisasthe, in Acts, ii, 14, from *annotate*.
Exoutheneo, in 1 Thessal. v, 20, from *extenuo*.
Epainos, in Rom. ii, 29, from *penis*.
Epifosco, in Luke, xxiii, 54, from *offusco*.
Efie, in Mark, i, 34, and xi, 16, from *sivit*.

Hairetizo, in Matthew, xii, 18, from *arrideo*.
Haploteti, in II Cor. ix, 13, from *amplitudine*.
Hodegeo, in Rev. vii, 17, from *adduco*.
Klesis, in I Cor. vii, 20, from *classis*.
Koinon, in Heb. x, 29, from *cænum*.
Koite, in Heb. xiii, 4, from *coitus*.
Loidorian, in I Peter, iii, 9, from *ludibrium*.
Metanoian, in Heb. vi, 1, from *mutationem*.
Meteorizo, in Luke, xii, 29, from *metuor*.
Parektos, in II Cor. xi, 20, from *peractus*.
Perpereuomai, in I Cor. xiii, 4, from *perperam*.
Pterugion, in Matt. iv, 5, and Luke, iv, 9, from *porticum*.

It can scarcely be expected that the reader will from these examples hastily accede to the suggestion that the books of the New Testament were originally written in Latin—ignoring in fact the difficulties which lie in the way of this inference from the distance between Rome and the country of Palestine to which the first elements of Christianity must be traced. But the abundance of Latin words and phrases found in the Gospels and other books indicate, not obscurely, the influence which the Latin language in the second century of our era exercised over the Oriental and even over the Hellenic race. This influence was felt more in the new communities and colonies which the Romans had founded or conquered in Asia and Africa, than in Greece itself. The schools of Athens and other Grecian cities had maintained their independence and literary fame for many centuries: their language surpassed that of the Romans beneath whom they had bent, even in the estimation of the Romans themselves, and we do not find that their idiom or their phraseology was corrupted by the mixture of Latin except where technical and official terms were required to express things which had no counterpart in their own social or political systems. Latinisms do not abound in the writings of Plutarch and others who lived and wrote in the second century of our era. But in the Asiatic provinces of the Roman empire, where men of so many and dissimilar tongues came together and where the Romans would see the necessity of supporting their authority by every means which prudence could suggest, there would naturally be a strong body of Latin or Roman officials, mixed no doubt with Greeks, and also a military force, capable of checking those sudden outbreaks of revolution within or attacks from without, to which Eastern peoples have in all ages of the world been liable. These remarks apply to Antioch still more than to Alexandria; for in Egypt the Roman power surrounded by deserts was less likely to be disturbed by foreign invasion, but Antioch lay on the high road to the East, and more than once in its history suffered from the contests for empire which took place between Rome and the great Asiatic monarchies. If, as we know to have happened, the Apostles and other Jews, besides foreigners perhaps who had learnt Christianity at Jerusalem, at a very early period of our era introduced the new religion into the Greek metropolis of Syria, and made it the centre from which the missions of St Paul and others radiated among the various tribes and nations of Asia Minor, it is not unreasonable to suppose that Christian writings might emanate from such a centre and that the phraseology might embody many words and expressions taken from the language of the ruling dynasty intermixed with the Greek which was spoken universally among the upper classes of the people.

In support of our assertion might be cited the inscription placed over the cross on which our Lord was crucified. That there were many Grecian soldiers, merchants, and others, for whom their language might be necessary to understanding the accusation for which Jesus was crucified, may without difficulty be conceded, even if we assert that the native Hebrew was amply sufficient for the mass of the population. But the addition of Latin to the inscription would hardly have been needful, unless that language also had gained such a footing in the East that it was thought proper to supply those who spoke it with the same information about the great events which had lately taken place.

Notwithstanding however that this fact coincides with probability to establish the assertion that Latin was well known at all the centres of government throughout the Roman empire, a remarkable and most improbable statement has been put forward by the learned Cambridge Professor of Divinity, which would imply that, whilst the Latin tongue had reached to every country of the known world, it had ceased almost to exist at Rome, like a stream which by over-expansiveness has been dried up at its source. The important bearing which this view if true would have upon ancient history, demands that the passage be extracted in full.

At first [says Dr Westcott] it seems natural to look to Italy as the centre of the Latin literature of Christianity, and the original source of that Latin Version of the Holy Scriptures which in a later form has become identified with the Church of Rome. Yet however plausible such a belief may be, it finds no support in history. Rome itself under the emperors was well described as a 'Greek city;' and Greek was its second language.* As far as we can learn, the mass of the poorer population—to which the great bulk of the early Christians everywhere belonged—was Greek either in descent or in speech. Among the names of the fifteen bishops of Rome up to the close of the second century, four only are Latin,† though in the next century the proportion is nearly reversed. When St Paul wrote to the Roman Church he wrote in Greek; and in the long list of salutations to its members with which the epistle is concluded, only four genuine Latin names occur. Shortly afterwards Clement wrote to the Corinthians in Greek in the name of the Church of Rome; and at a later date we find the bishop of Corinth writing in Greek to Soter the ninth in succession from Clement. Justin, Hermas, and according to the common opinion Tatian,‡ published their Greek treatises at Rome. The Apologies to the Roman emperors were in Greek. Modestus, Caius, and Asterius Urbanus, bear Latin names, and yet their writings were Greek. Even further west Greek was the common language of Christians. The churches of Vienne and Lyons used it in writing the history of their persecutions; and Irenæus, though 'he lived among the Gauls,' and confessed that he had grown unfamiliar with his native idiom, made it the vehicle of his Treatise against Heresies.§ WESTCOTT, *Canon, &c.*, p. 224.

In describing Rome as a Greek city at the time of the Christian era, it would have been as well if Dr Westcott had given some authority from ancient authors for so bold an assertion. The names and works of Virgil, Horace, Ovid, Livy, Juvenal, Tacitus, Pliny, and many more, rise up in condemnation of such an assertion. The early Christians everywhere belonged to the lowest classes, and eleven out of those fifteen obscure persons, who have been dignified with the name of Roman bishops, may have been Greeks, for the Christian religion, as it is presented to us, has its root in the Greek tongue, and was propagated by Greek missionaries. None of the early Christian writers were Jews; none were Latins. Ignatius, Hermas, Polycarp, Justin Martyr, Irenæus, Origen, and almost every minor writer quoted in our numerous ecclesiastical catalogues, were Greeks by country, by birth, or by native tongue, and

---

* Cf. Wiseman, III, p. 366 f. Bunsen's *Hippolytus*, II, 123, S 99.
† Bunsen, *l. c.* says "two, Clement and Victor:" but probably Sixtus (Xystus, Euseb. *H. E.* IV, 4; cf. VII, 5) and certainly Pius should be included in the number.
‡ Otto, *Prolegg.* xxxv. Lumper, *Hist. Patrum*, II, p. 321.
§ *Contra Hær.* I, Pref. 3.

all their writings have come down to us in no other language than the Greek. The churches of Vienne and Lyons may have written the short tract which Dr Westcott calls the history of their persecutions, because it was a document destined to be sent to Eastern countries, nor is it remarkable that Irenæus a Greek should become a bishop in Gaul; but it would be remarkable if Greek were in such general use in Gaul, as is stated in the extract which has been cited, and yet that Irenæus should complain that, owing to his having lived so long among the Gauls, he had become unfamiliar with his native tongue. I cannot resist the belief that the first missionaries of Christianity were actuated by the same motives which still influence those who preach the Gospel among the heathen. "The labourer is worthy of his hire," says our Lord, and already in the Gospel history, his discourses tend to show that his followers were to draw their subsistence from the heathen to whom they preached. The Greek race has always been remarkable for the readiness with which they throw themselves into any foreign enterprise. The early Christians, Greeks for the greater part, would find a rich harvest of converts in those barbarous regions to which they are said to have carried the Gospel, and they would be endowed with abundant reward from the ignorant natives among whom they settled. In the sixth century Sanctus Ægidius migrated from Athens to the same country as Irenæus four centuries before, and was so largely endowed that Raymond Count of Toulouse and his descendants were satisfied to bear the equivalent title of Raymond Count of St Giles.

CHAPTER IX.

CHRISTIANITY NOT MENTIONED BY JOSEPHUS OR PHILO—NOTICE OF THE OTHER HEBREW WRITINGS—TARGUMS—MISHNA AND GEMARA—TALMUD.

THE seventh year after the Crucifixion of Jesus Christ is remarkable for the birth of Josephus, who is often spoken of by historians as the learned and warlike Jew. A short sketch of his life has been given in the first volume of this work; and nothing more needs to be said on the eventful character of his career. About the same time, whilst Josephus was still a boy, flourished Philo Judæus, a philosopher of Alexandria, half Jew half Greek, and author of numerous writings still extant, mostly treatises on the Jewish law, and imbued with the spirit of the Platonic philosophy, which for nearly two centuries had flourished in the Egyptian capital. The history of Philo has little connection with our present subject. He was probably between 20 and 30 years old when Christ was crucified, and he went on a public embassy to Rome in the reign of Claudius Cæsar, but was refused admittance into the Emperor's presence. He has left upwards of thirty treatises on various subjects connected with the Bible, and it is clear that he looked upon the books of Moses as allegories and not as real histories. The chief of his works, indeed, were written to prove this, and it is reasonable to believe that he wished, like Josephus, to smooth away the miracles contained in those books, and so to commend them the more successfully to the enlightened judgment of the Greeks.

That two voluminous writers, whose collected works fill several volumes, should have lived so near the time of the Christian history, one of them being actually contemporary with Christ, and probably about the same age, is a fact fraught with much interest to our subject, as likely to furnish some test by which the accuracy of the sacred narrative might be tried. Great therefore is our disappointment at finding nothing in the works of Philo about the Christians, their doctrines or their sacred books. About the books indeed we need not expect any notice in these works, but about the Christians and their doctrines his silence is the more remarkable, seeing that he was about sixty years old at the time of the Crucifixion, and living mostly in Alexandria, so closely connected, as we are told, with Judæa and the Jews, could hardly have failed to know something of the wonderful events that had taken place in the city of Jerusalem, unless, as is probable, the explanation of this lies in the comparative obscurity which enveloped the first years of the Christian era, but which ecclesiastical writers have never been ready to admit.

The works of Josephus furnish three extracts which require to be more carefully noticed, as they have in all ages of the Christian era been the subject of discussion among the learned, and even in the present day are supported by a few who are unwilling to give up the testimony which they are thought to furnish in favour of the early history of our religion.

About this time was Jesus, a wise man, if at least it be right to call him a man : for he was the doer of wonderful works, a

teacher of men who receive with pleasure the things which are
true, and he gained over to himself many Jews and many of
the Grecian [race]. He was the Christ [ὁ Χριστος οὗτος ἦν]. And
when Pilate, on the information of the first men among us, had
punished him on the cross, those who loved him from the first did
not cease to love him. For he appeared to them again the third
day alive; the divine prophets having spoken both these and
numberless other wonders about him. The tribe of Christians, so
named from him, have not ceased to exist until the present time.
JOSEPHUS, *Antiquities*, XVIII, iii, 3.

Those who are best acquainted with the character of
Josephus and the style of his writings, have no hesitation
in condemning this passage as a forgery interpolated in the
text during the third century by some pious Christian, who
was scandalized that so famous a writer as Josephus should
have taken no notice of the Gospels or of Christ their subject. But the zeal of the interpolator has outrun his discretion, for we could scarcely hope to find this notice of
Christ among the Judaizing writings of Josephus. It is
well known that this author was a zealous Jew, devoted to
the laws of Moses and to the traditions of his countrymen.
How then could he have written that *Jesus was the Christ?*
Such an admission would have proved him to be a Christian
himself, in which case the passage under consideration, too
long for a Jew, would have been far too short for a believer
in the new religion, and thus the passage stands forth contrasting inharmoniously with everything around it. If it
had been genuine, we might be sure that Justin Martyr,
Tertullian, and Chrysostom would have quoted it in their
controversies with the Jews, and that Origen or Photius
would have mentioned it. But Eusebius, in his Ecclesiastical History, i, 11, is the first who quotes it, and our
reliance on the judgment or even the honesty of this writer
is not so great as to allow of our considering everything
found in his works as undoubtedly genuine.

But the writer, who first placed this narrative in the text
of Josephus, like all interpolators, did not see that its concluding sentence destroys its authenticity altogether. The
sect of Christians, he says, was still in existence when he
wrote. There can be no doubt of that fact. They abounded
still in Jerusalem and at Rome, where they were regarded
somewhat as a sect of the Jews. But not many years after
the death of Josephus they were found in almost every part
of the Roman empire, so that his cool assertion that the sect
still existed about the year 60 A.D. must be taken as wholly

inapplicable to the age in which Josephus wrote, and cannot possibly have formed part of his work. Nor is it without weight that a writer so ambitious of obtaining honour among the Greeks and Romans, would have hesitated to speak with such pointed and pithy commendation of a sect which was almost universally despised, and which gained its ultimate position in the world solely by its rapid growth—so wholly irreconcilable with the sublime indifference with which he despatches his notice of the sect to whose founder he nevertheless has ascribed miraculous deeds and the power of having risen from the dead.

Besides this extract there is another short notice of Christ, which, in the words of Paley, is "allowed by many, though not without considerable question being moved about it." The main point of the narrative is very brief; but it is best to give the context from the beginning of the chapter.

Cæsar sends Albinus as eparch [governor] into Judæa, when he learnt that Festus was dead. But the emperor took away the high-priesthood from Joseph, and gave to the son of Ananus, who was also called Ananus, the succession to the office. The elder Ananus is said to have been a most lucky man: for he had five sons, and it happened that they all were God's high-priests, whilst himself also had before enjoyed that dignity for a very long time, which never was the case with any other of our high-priests. But the younger Ananus, whom we just named as having been appointed to the high-priesthood, was of a very bold and enterprising character: he followed the sect of the Sadducees, who are severe in their judgments beyond all the other Jews, as we have already shown. Ananus, then, being such a man as I have described, thinking that he had met with a fitting opportunity, seeing that Festus was dead, and Albinus was still on his journey, appoints a sanhedrim [meeting] of judges, and bringing before it [the brother of Jesus who is called Christ, named James] and some others, accused them of having broken the law, and gave them over to be stoned.—JOSEPHUS, *Antiquities*, xx, ix, 1.

καθίζει συνέδριον κριτῶν, καὶ παρα-
γάγων εἰς αὐτὸ [τὸν ἀδελφὸν Ἰησοῦ
τοῦ λεγομένου Χριστοῦ, Ἰάκωβος
ὄνομα αὐτῷ] καί τινας ἑτέρους, ὡς
παρανομησάντων κατηγορίαν ποιησά-
μενος, παρέδωκε λευσθησομένους.

The words enclosed in brackets, *the brother of Jesus*, &c., are probably an interpolation* in the text, introduced, like

---

* Mr Hartwell Horne, in his "Introduction &c." says of this passage, "the authenticity of which has NEVER been disputed or suspected," which

the preceding, by some dishonest copyist in order to set aside the unfavourable consequences deduced from the silence of Josephus. Many reasons may be given for looking upon the words in question as an interpolation. I shall, however, be content, at present, to rest the case upon internal evidence ; reserving until a future chapter the consideration of the relationship between Christ and James —for there is a remarkable obscurity on this point, in all the texts of the New Testament, where it is noticed. The internal evidence of the words before us is against their authenticity. For if the longer passage quoted from Josephus be rejected as spurious, the few words now before us are incomplete : they clearly refer to a more full account of Jesus which had preceded. If, however, we admit the former extract as genuine, the latter is inconsistent with it ; for, in the former, Jesus is called '*the* Christ,' as if well known and equivalent to 'the Messiah': but in the latter he is simply 'called Christ,' a name having no spiritual signification, and importing nothing more than an ordinary surname. It is extremely improbable that Josephus would use the term *the Christ*, without further explaining its signification ; it is equally improbable that he would have used the surname *Christ*,† without showing that it originally had a spiritual derivation : but it is doubly improbable that he would have used both expressions, for the same individual, without stating that it indicated the Messiah whose coming the Jewish people were daily expecting. It would be very possible, also, to raise a question about the name *Christ* itself, if such inquiries were the main subject of this work ; for its etymology though evident, does not denote its origin. Suetonius and Lucian have Χρηστος CHRESTUS *good*, which is a different word from Χριστος CHRISTUS *anointed*, the Greek term for MESSIAH, the Hebrew name by which the expected prophet of the Jews was pointed out. These inquiries would be interesting, but must not detain us from our purpose, which is,—not to examine the evidences on which the history of Christianity is founded, but to ascertain at what stage of its progress this history was written. The authenticity of the passages quoted from Josephus does but slightly affect this question. If it be admitted that his

---

is hardly consistent with Paley's remark, quoted in a former note, "not without considerable question being moved about it."

† The theory of Dr Middleton about the Greek article cannot be allowed as applicable to a subject which required such a clear specification of meaning.

notice of Christ is genuine, it is certain that we find nowhere in his works any mention of the Christian books.

In contrast with this notice of Christ is another passage found in Josephus respecting John the Baptist, about which I am not aware that any suspicion of spuriousness has ever been entertained.

It seemed to some of the Jews that Herod's army was destroyed by God, thus taking deserved vengeance for the death of John surnamed the Baptist. For Herod slew him, though he was a good man and exhorted the Jews to cherish virtue, and whilst practising uprightness towards one another, and piety towards God, to have recourse to baptism: for that their baptism would be acceptable to him, not if they made use of it for the setting aside of their sins, but for purity of body, that is if the soul also had been previously purified by righteousness. And when the rest of the people gathered themselves together—for they were excited to a great degree by hearing his words—Herod, fearing his great power of persuading men, lest it might lead to a revolt —for they seemed likely to do every thing by his counsel—deemed it much better, before any new thing should proceed from him, to seize him and put him to death, than, after some change had been wrought, to repent when he had fallen into trouble. And so he [John], on account of Herod's suspicion, was sent in bonds to the before-mentioned castle of Machærus, and there put to death.* But the Jews thought that Herod's army was destroyed in vengeance for his death arising from God's anger being kindled against Herod.—JOSEPHUS, *Antiqq.* XVIII, v, 2.

Here would have been a good opportunity for the writer to allude to the connection between John the Baptist and Christ—if, at least, he was acquainted with the life and mission of both those teachers. But a good reason is supplied by Josephus himself, in the memoir of his own life, why he should have been acquainted with the teaching of John the Baptist, but not with that of Christ. For, in his search after truth, Josephus joined for a time the sect of the Essenes, to which John the Baptist, from the remarkable similarity of their doctrines, seems to have belonged, and so had an opportunity of learning the nature of their teaching: whilst on the other hand, as he afterwards left them and

---

* It is almost needless to point out—were it not that readers in general do not pay much attention to the minute details of what they read—that the Gospel account of John's imprisonment can hardly be reconciled with the account here given from Josephus.

joined the Pharisees, the enemies of Christ, it is not likely that he ever knew of the Christian doctrines, or, certainly, that he would mention Christ as the Messiah that was to come.

The paragraphs here quoted are the only ones in the works of Josephus which bear upon the history found in the four Gospels, and the silence of Josephus leads to the inference that Christianity had not begun to attract the notice of the world during his life; that is, prior to about the 90th year of the Christian era.

But besides the rather voluminous works of Philo and Josephus, there are other writings which have come down to us, it is said, from a very early age of Christianity. These pass under the names of Targums, Mishna, Gemara, and Talmud. The *Targums* have already been named in the first volume of this work, as furnishing no evidence to the date when the book of the Old Testament was compiled. They are indeed free translations or paraphrases of the Hebrew Scriptures into the more modern dialect which began to be spoken not after the Babylonish but after the Roman captivity, later than the time of Christ. But neither does any one of the Targums allude in the slightest degree to the Christian books, to the Christian religion, or to its founder, although the earliest of these is reasonably thought to have been written 150 years after the Crucifixion. They no doubt owe their existence to the pious labours of the Jews who took refuge and founded a national school at Babylon, or who even remained at Jerusalem amid all the vicissitudes which befell their country and its capital during the first two centuries since the birth of Christ. Nor is this out of harmony with the equally established fact that there was even from the first a rival school of Hellenistic or Græcizing Jews both at Alexandria and at Antioch, and traces of their rivalry are found even in the New Testament itself, as far at least as Antioch is concerned, for whilst the capital of Syria is often named as the centre of Christian missions and other doings, Alexandria is named only as the native country of certain foreigners whose business lay more in the path of commerce than of religion.

The *Mishna* is a work of a very different kind from the foregoing. It contains the civil and canonical law of the Jews, as compiled in the second century of our era; and may be considered to represent the traditions and practices of the Pharisees in the time of our Saviour. Modern commentators have made much use of it to illustrate and

explain the narratives and allusions of the New Testament.*
It has been pretended by the Jews that the traditions contained in the Mishna were given to Moses on the Mount, and handed down through Aaron and the prophets to the time of Rabbi Judah who died about the year A.D. 139, but it is not needful to show the weak basis upon which such a tradition rests.

The Mishna is not the only work dating from the earliest half of the Christian era, and containing Jewish customs, opinions, and traditions. There are two commentaries on its text, called *Gemara*, one of which was compiled at Jerusalem, of unknown date, perhaps soon after the Mishna, but certainly before the fifth century, and the other at Babylon compiled a hundred or more years later, and full of fables. When the text found in the Mishna and the commentary of the Gemara accompany one another, the whole work is called the Talmud, distinguished further as the Babylonian or the Jerusalem Talmud according as the Mishna or text is accompanied by the particular Gemara or commentary which had its origin in either of those Eastern cities. The extent of these relics of a decaying people is somewhat alarming to those who propose to study them. The Mishna alone occupies six folio volumes, the Gemara twelve, and the two editions of the Talmud, wherein both the former are combined, extend each to several folio volumes, and consequently present great difficulties in the way of the general student. Neither of these works has the slightest allusion to our present subject—the origin and authorship of the Christian Scriptures, although the Mishna has one of its chapters headed *De cultu peregrino*, " Of foreign worship." The omission is thought by Dr Paley to prove nothing, for, says he, " It cannot be disputed but that Christianity was perfectly well known to the world at this time." This must depend upon the date at which the Mishna was written. If before the appearance of the Christian books, we cannot expect a mention of those books in the pages of the Mishna: if after the Gospels were published to the world, we should expect that a volume of so high a character which has attracted the admiration of the world would not have escaped notice by the editor of the work now under consideration. Strange however beyond measure, and highly suggestive to the thoughtful, where no data exist on which

---

* The German commentator Koppe, in his edition of the New Testament, gave an abridgment of all former writers on this subject.

to build conclusions, are the parallels between maxims found in the Talmud and those which occur in our Gospels. The reader is referred to the Literary Remains of Emmanuel Deutsch for further information on the subject, and he will no doubt be surprised at the note with which the learned author concludes his article on this obscure but interesting subject.

With regard to the striking parallels exhibited by them [*the sentences quoted in the text*] to some of the most sublime dicta of the Gospels, we disclaim any intention of having purposely selected them. It is utterly impossible to read a page of the Talmud and of the New Testament without coming upon innumerable instances of this kind, as indeed they constantly seem to supplement each other. We need not urge the priority of the Talmud to the New Testament, although the former was redacted at a later period. To assume that the Talmud has borrowed from the New Testament* would be like assuming that Sanskrit sprang from Latin, or that French was developed from the Norman words found in English.—DEUTSCH, *Lit. Remains*, p. 54.

CHAPTER X.

TESTIMONY OF THE EARLY GREEK AND LATIN WRITERS, SUETONIUS, TACITUS, PLINY THE YOUNGER, SENECA, EPICTETUS, MARCUS AURELIUS, LUCIAN—STORY OF PEREGRINUS—LETTER OF HADRIAN—CHARACTER OF THE EGYPTIANS IN THE SECOND CENTURY.

FROM Josephus and Philo, who are the only Jewish writers contemporary with Christ and his Apostles, we turn to the Gentiles, by which name are meant the Grecian and Roman authors who lived during the first two centuries of the Christian era. We have seen that perhaps not even the existence of the Christian faith, much less that of its written records, was known to either of the two only literary Jews of that period. But the case of the classical writers of Greece and Rome is different: these were certainly aware that there was a sect of men calling themselves Christians, but they were ignorant that the Christians had any religious books among them. To extract from all the classical

---

* The reader who is unwilling to believe that the writers of the Gospels have copied from the Talmud, are at liberty to suppose that the maxims found in both were copied from the "Sayings of the Lord," which certainly must have been earlier than either the Gospels or the Talmud.

writers, who lived between A.D. 30 and A.D. 200, would be the most satisfactory mode of making the reader acquainted with the history of our religion as far as the Greeks and Romans are concerned, after the termination of the apostolic age: but, for our present purpose and with one exception, such a minute examination of these writers is superfluous. For though the remains of Grecian and Latin profane literature, which belong to the first and second centuries of our era, are enough to form a library of themselves, they contain no allusion to the New Testament, and consequently the testimony which they render is of little moment to the question concerning that book, though it fully proves that the Christians were very numerous even at that early period.

But we may not dismiss these authors altogether without consideration: for a negative testimony may be derived, even from those descriptions which are adduced from them to prove the early existence and rapid spread of the Christian religion.

The Latin writers, who lived between the time of Christ's crucifixion and the year A.D. 200, are Seneca, Lucan, Suetonius, Tacitus, Persius, Juvenal, Martial, Pliny the Elder, Silius Italicus, Statius, Quintilian, and Pliny the Younger, besides numerous others of inferior note. The greater number of these make mention of the Jews but not of the Christians. In fact, Suetonius, Tacitus, and the younger Pliny appear to be the only Roman writers who mention the Christian religion or its founder. Their testimony is decided as to the great increase of Christianity at the end of the first century.

Suetonius, speaking of the transactions of Nero's reign, says:

Affecti suppliciis Christiani genus hominum superstitionis novæ et maleficæ.—*Nero*, 16.	The Christians, a set of men of a new and mischievous superstition, were visited with punishment.

These words seem to imply that the Christians were punished as magicians—an opinion confirmed by several passages in authors of the early ages. Suidas, a much later writer, tells us that one of the Christian martyrs cried out in his dungeon, " You have loaded me with fetters as if I were a profane man and a sorcerer!" Pliny the Elder also (xxx, 1) seems to consider the Jews, wholly or in part, magicians.

In the lives of Tiberius and Domitian by Suetonius occur the extracts which here follow:—

Externas ceremonias Ægyptios Judaicosque ritus compescuit, coactis qui superstitione ea tenebantur, religiosas vestes cum instrumento omni comburere. Judæorum juventutem per speciem sacramenti in provincias gravioris cœli distribuit: reliquos ejusdem gentis, vel *similia sectantes*, urbe submovit sub pœna perpetuæ servitutis nisi obtemperassent. —*Tib.* 36.

He[Tiberius] checked foreign ceremonies Egyptian and Jewish rites, compelling those who were held by that superstition to burn their religious vestments with all their gear. The Jewish youth he dispersed under the appearance of military service in provinces where the climate was severest: others of the same nation or who held the same observances he removed from the city under pain of being made slaves for life if they disobeyed.

Præter cæteros Judaicus fiscus acerbissime actus est: ad quem deferebantur, qui vel *improfessi Judaicam viverent vitam*, vel dissimulata origine imposita genti tributa non pependissent. —*Dom.* 12.

The tax on the Jews was rigorously exacted beyond the others: it included those who in their lives resembled the Jews though not professedly, or who dissembling their nationality had not paid the tribute imposed on their nation.

In these passages it is suggested, seemingly on good grounds, that by *similia sectantes* and *improfessi Judaicam vitam* are meant the Christians, who were always confounded with the Jews by the profane writers, from inability to see the subtle differences which existed between them.

In another passage, also, the same author briefly alludes to Christ—at least it would appear so; though the ideas of the writer are very confused, and his knowledge of the subject very scanty. He seems to have supposed that Christ, or Chrest as we read in the Latin manuscripts of his work, had placed himself at the head of a seditious movement, not in Jerusalem, but in Rome.

Judæos impulsore Chresto assidue tumultuantes Roma expulit. *Claud.* 25.

He expelled from Rome the Jews who were continually making disturbances at the instigation of Chrestus.

That Christ is here meant, it is most obvious to conjecture, but it would not be right to conceal the fact that Chrestus was the name of a Roman citizen at that time, as will appear from two of the most indecent epigrams that ever were penned (vii, 55; and ix, 27) by the poet Martial.

The poets Lucan and Juvenal mention the Jews but not the Christians. The latter indeed, in *Sat.* i, 155, alludes to the manner in which certain victims were tied to a stake and burnt to death, but there is nothing to indicate who those victims were.

The other poets of this age, Statius, Silius Italicus, and Persius, do not name the Christians at all, and Quintilian (III, vii, 21) speaking of the "author of the Jewish superstition," evidently speaks of Moses, and not, as some have thought, of Christ.

The next writer is Tacitus, who was contemporary with Suetonius: they both wrote about the year 100. The account which Tacitus gives of the Christians is as follows:

Ergo abolendo rumori Nero subdidit reos, et quæsitissimis pœnis affecit, quos, per flagitia invisos, vulgus CHRISTIANOS appellabat. Auctor nominis ejus Christus, Tiberio imperitante, per procuratorem Pontium Pilatum supplicio affectus erat. Repressaque in præsens exitiabilis superstitio rursus erumpebat, non modo per Judæam, originem ejus mali, sed per urbem etiam, quo cuncta undique atrocia aut pudenda confluunt celebranturque. Igitur primo correpti, qui fatebantur, deinde indicio eorum, multitudo ingens, haud perinde in crimine incendii, quam odio humani generis, convicti sunt. Et pereuntibus addita ludibria, ut ferarum tergis contecti laniatu canum interirent, aut crucibus adfixi, aut flammandi, atque, ubi defecisset dies, in usum

Nero, therefore, to put an end to the report, laid the blame, and inflicted the most exquisite punishments, upon those, whom, being hated for their crimes, the vulgar called Christians. The author of that name was Christ, who, in the reign of Tiberius, had been punished by Pontius Pilate the procurator. This deadly superstition, having been checked for the present, broke out again, not only throughout Judæa, the origin of that evil, but also throughout the city [of Rome] whither all atrocious and shameful things flow together from all quarters and are put in practice. Those, therefore, who confessed, were first seized, and then, by their information, a great multitude were convicted, not so much on the charge of arson, as for hatred of mankind. Their deaths also were aggravated by insult; for they were wrapped in the skins of wild beasts, and torn to pieces by dogs, or else were crucified, or destined to be burnt, and so, when the day

nocturni luminis urerentur. Hortos suos ei spectaculo Nero obtulerat, et circense ludicrum edebat, habitu aurigæ permixtus plebi vel curriculo insistens. Unde quanquam adversus sontes et novissima exempla meritos, miseratio oriebatur, tanquam non utilitate publica, sed in sævitiam unius, absumerentur.—*Ann.* xv, 44.

was over, they served as a light to enlighten the night. Nero had offered his gardens for that spectacle, and exhibited the circensian games, mingling with the people in the dress of a charioteer, or standing in a chariot. Wherefore, though they were guilty, and had deserved the worst punishments, yet pity was felt towards them, as if they were put to death, not for the public good, but to gratify the cruelty of one man.

The most important testimony, however, concerning the early Christians is that of Pliny the Younger, who was some years younger than Tacitus and Suetonius. He was proconsul of Pontus and Bithynia, and found the number of Christians in those provinces increase so rapidly, that he was puzzled how to act towards them, and consulted the emperor Trajan on the subject. The letters which passed between them have been preserved.

CAIUS PLINIUS TRAJANO IMPERATORI SALUTEM.—Solemne est mihi, domine, omnia, de quibus dubito, ad te referre. Quis enim potest melius vel cunctationem meam regere, vel ignorantiam instruere? Cognitionibus de Christianis interfui nunquam: ideo nescio, quid et quatenus aut puniri soleat, aut quæri. Nec mediocriter

hæsitavi, sitne aliquod discrimen ætatum an quamlibet teneri nihil a robustioribus differant; deturne pœnitentiæ venia, an ei, qui omnino Christianus fuit, desîsse non prosit;

C. PLINY TO THE EMPEROR TRAJAN, HEALTH.—It is customary with me to refer to you, my lord, all matters about which I entertain a doubt. For who is better able either to rule my hesitation or to instruct my ignorance? I have never been present at the inquiries about the Christians: and therefore cannot say for what crime or to what extent they are usually punished, or what is the nature of the inquiry about them. Nor have I been free from great doubts whether there should not be a distinction between ages, or how far those of a tender frame should be treated differently from the robust: whether those who repent should not be pardoned, so that one who has been a Christian, should not derive advantage from having ceased

nomen ipsum, etiamsi flagitiis careat, an flagitia cohærentia nomini, puniantur. Interim in iis, qui ad me tanquam Christiani deferebantur, hunc sum sequutus modum. Interrogavi ipsos, an essent Christiani: confitentes iterum ac tertio interrogavi, supplicium minatus: perseverantes duci jussi. Neque enim dubitabam, qualecunque esset, quod faterentur, pervicaciam certe, et inflexibilem obstinationem debere puniri. Fuerunt alii similis amentiæ: quos, quia cives Romani erant, adnotavi in urbem remittendos. Mox ipso tractatu, ut fieri solet, diffundente se crimine, plures species inciderunt. Propositus est libellus sine auctore, multorum nomina continens, qui negarent se esse Christianos, aut fuisse, quum, præeunte me, deos appellarent, et imagini tuæ, quam propter hoc jusseram cum simulacris numinum adferri, thure ac vino supplicarent, prætera maledicerent Christo: quorum nihil cogi posse dicuntur, qui sunt revera Christiani. Ergo dimittendos putavi. Alii ab indice nominati, esse se Chris-

to be one: whether the name itself, of being a Christian, should be punished, or only crimes attendant upon the name. In the mean time, I have laid down this rule in dealing with those who were brought before me for being Christians. I asked whether they were Christians: if they confessed, I asked them a second and a third time, threatening them with punishment: if they persevered, I ordered them to be led off. For I had no doubt in my mind, that whatever it might be which they acknowledged, obduracy and inflexible obstinacy at all events should be punished. There were others guilty of like folly, whom I set aside to be sent to Rome, because they were Roman citizens. In the next place, when this crime began, as usual, gradually to spread, it showed itself in a variety of ways. An indictment was set forth without any author, containing the names of many, who denied that they were Christians or ever had been; and, when I set the example, they called on the gods, and made offerings of frankincense and wine to your image, which I, for this purpose, had ordered to be brought out together with the images of the gods; moreover they cursed Christ: none of which acts can be extorted from those who are really Christians. I consequently gave orders that they should be discharged. Again: others, who had been informed against, said that they were Christians, and afterwards de-

tianos dixerunt, et mox negaverunt: fuisse quidem, sed desîsse; quidam ante triennium, quidam ante plures annos, non nemo etiam ante viginti quoque. Omnes et imaginem tuam, deorumque simulacra venerati sunt: ii et Christo maledixerunt. Adfirmabant autem, hanc fuisse summam vel culpæ suæ, vel erroris, quod essent soliti stato die ante lucem convenire: carmenque Christo, quasi Deo, dicere secum invicem: seque sacramento non in scelus aliquod obstringere, sed ne furta, ne latrocinia, ne adulteria committerent, ne fidem fallerent, ne depositum appellati abnegarent: quibus peractis morem sibi discedendi fuisse, rursusque coeundi ad capiendum cibum, promiscuum tamen, et innoxium: quod ipsum facere desîsse post edictum meum, quo secundum mandata tua hetærias esse vetueram. Quo

magis necessarium credidi, ex duabus ancillis, quæ ministræ dicebantur, quid esset veri, et per tormenta quærere. Sed nihil aliud inveni, quam superstitionem pravam et immodicam, ideoque, dilata cognitione, ad consulendum te decurri.

Visa est enim mihi res digna consultatione, maxime propter

nied it: that they had been so once but had ceased to be so; some three years ago, some longer than that, and some even twenty years before: all of them worshipped your image and the statues of the gods; they also cursed Christ. But they asserted that this was the sum total of their crime or error, whichever it may be called, that they were used to come together on a stated day before it was light, and to sing in turn, among themselves, a hymn to Christ, as to a god, and to bind themselves by an oath, not to any thing wicked, but that they would not commit theft, robbery or adultery, nor break their word, nor deny that any thing had been entrusted to them when called upon to restore it. After this they said that it was their custom to separate, and again to meet together to take their meals, which were of a common and of a harmless nature: but that they had ceased even to do this since the proclamation which I issued according to your commands, forbidding such meetings to be held. I therefore deemed it the more necessary to inquire of two servant-maids, who were said to be attendants [deaconesses?] what was the real truth, and to apply the torture. But I found that it was nothing but a bad and excessive superstition, and I consequently adjourned the inquiry, and consulted you upon the subject. For it seemed to me to be a matter on which it was desirable to take advice, in consequence of the

periclitantium numerum. Multi enim omnis ætatis, omnis ordinis, utriusque sexus etiam, vocantur in periculum, et vocabuntur. Neque enim civitates tantum, sed vicos etiam atque agros superstitionis istius contagio pervagata est: quæ videtur sisti et corrigi posse.

Certe satis constat, prope iam desolata templa cœpisse celebrari, et sacra solemnia diu intermissa repeti, passimque venire victimas, quarum adhuc rarissimus emtor inveniebatur.

Ex quo facile est opinari, quæ turba hominum emendari possit, si fiat pœnitentiæ locus.— PLIN. *Ep.* 97.

TRAJANUS PLINIO SALUTEM. Actum quem debuisti, mi Secunde, in excutiendis caussis eorum, qui Christiani ad te delati fuerant, sequutus es. Neque enim in universum aliquid, quod quasi certam formam habeat, constitui potest. Conquirendi non sunt: si deferantur et arguantur, puniendi sunt: ita tamen, ut, qui negaverit se Christianum esse, idque re ipsa manifestum fecerit, id est, supplicando diis nostris, quamvis suspectus in præteritum fuerit, veniam ex pœnitentia impetret.

Sine auctore vero propositi libelli, nullo crimine locum ha-

number of those who are in danger. For there are many of every age, of every rank, and even of both sexes, who are invited to incur the danger, and will still be invited. For the infection of this superstition has spread through, not only cities, but also villages and the country; though it seems possible to check and remedy it. At all events it is evident that the temples, which had been almost deserted, have begun to be frequented, and the sacred solemnities which had been intermitted are revived, and victims are sold everywhere, though formerly it was difficult to find a buyer. It is therefore easy to believe, what a number of persons may be corrected, if the door of repentance be left open.

TRAJAN to PLINY, HEALTH.— You have acted very properly, my Secundus, in inquiring into the case of those, who were brought before you for being Christians. For it is impossible to lay down any universal rule bearing a set form. The Christians are not to be sought out: but if they are brought up and convicted, they must be punished: yet in such a way that, if any one denies he is a Christian, and proves what he says by some deed, such as making offerings to our deities, though he may be open to suspicion about the past, yet he should be pardoned in consequence of his repentance. But indictments put forth anonymously cannot be admitted in the case of any crime. For

bere debent. Nam et pessimi exempli, nec nostri seculi est.— PLIN. *Ep.* 98.

this would be a most dangerous precedent, and wholly incompatible with the age in which we live.

The philosopher Seneca lived in the latter half of the first century after Christ. His writings, which are tolerably numerous, do not allude to the Christians: though, from more than one passage we may gather that he was acquainted with the Jewish nation. In his 95th epistle, § 47, we read,

Accendere aliquem lucernam sabbathis prohibeamus : quoniam nec lumine dii egent, et ne homines quidem delectantur fuligine.

Let us forbid a man from lighting a candle on the sabbath day; for the gods do not want a light, and neither do men take pleasure in smoke.

In Epistle 108, § 22, we read as follows:

In Tiberii Cæsaris principatum juventæ tempus inciderat: alienigena tum sacra movebantur: sed inter argumenta superstitionis ponebatur quorundam animalium abstinentia.

My youth was cast in the reign of Tiberius Cæsar: foreign religious rites were at that time much talked of: among their different kinds of superstition was abstinence from the flesh of certain animals.

In this extract Seneca may be thought to allude to both Jewish and Christian ceremonies, especially by what he says of abstaining from the flesh of certain animals. And it has also been thought that Seneca was personally acquainted with St Paul; for they both lived at the same time; and we learn from the Acts of the Apostles that Paul dwelt two whole years in his own hired house, and received all that came in unto him, preaching the kingdom of God, and teaching those things which concern the Lord Jesus Christ, *no man forbidding him.* The possibility of such an acquaintance between the philosopher and the preacher led to the fabrication of thirteen letters, said to have passed between them: but these letters, which are still extant,[*] are too dull to have been written by St Paul and Seneca, and have been justly set aside as neither authentic nor valuable.

The foregoing extracts furnish all the evidence which can be gained from the Latin writers on the subject of Chris-

---

[*] They are found in *Codex Apocryphus Novi Testamenti*, 2 vols 8vo, Lond. apud D. Nutt, 1852.

tianity down to the latter half of the second century of our era.

The Greek classic writers, who lived between the time of Christ's crucifixion and the year 200, are those which follow; Epictetus, Plutarch, Ælian, Arrian, Galen, Lucian, Dionysius of Halicarnassus, Ptolemy, Marcus Aurelius, (who though a Roman emperor wrote in Greek,) Pausanias, and many others of less note. The allusions to Christianity found in most of their works are singularly short, and lead to the belief that the religion was still confined to the poor, of whom, we have our Lord's assurance, the kingdom of Heaven was mostly to consist. Yet we must bestow a few remarks upon the Greek authors whose names have been enumerated; for they throw a certain light over the early progress of Christianity, and one of them, I believe, furnishes valuable information towards discovering the time, the place, and the writers, to whom the volume of the New Testament is mostly due.

Epictetus, the Stoic philosopher, speaks of the Christians under the name of Galilæans, and ascribes to them an intrepidity of character which he sets down as madness.

Is it possible that a man may arrive at this temper, and become indifferent to these things from madness or from habit AS THE GALILÆANS?

Fifty years later than Epictetus lived Marcus Aurelius, the well-known emperor, who, amid the cares of royalty, found time to indulge in the delights of learning. In his philosophic treatise *Concerning himself*, we find the following words, not very complimentary to the Christians, but clearly indicating their existence and the position they occupied in the reign of the younger Antonine.

Such is that soul which, if it must be separated from the body, is at once ready, either indeed to be extinguished, or be dissipated or remain whole: but so that this readiness must come from one's own judgment, not by mere determination [ψιλὴν παράταξιν] as the Christians, but after having deliberated, and with dignity, and so as also to persuade another man, but not in a tragic manner. (xi, 3.)

But the most remarkable notices of the Christians occur in the works of Lucian of Samosata, the author of numerous dialogues and discourses, still extant, and written in a style not unworthy of the best age of Grecian literature. The character of their author has been unjustly assailed by modern bigots, who have ascribed to him a violent hatred against the Christians. This charge is wholly unsupported by the notices of Christianity that occur in his writings. He certainly speaks of the Christians in a slighting and perhaps disdainful manner, but that is no more than we should expect. Tacitus, Suetonius, and other ancient writers did the same. The doctrines of the early Christians were neither understood nor even known by the Greeks and Romans generally, whilst their opposition to all the established institutions and their denunciation of all the prevailing worship and of all the deities then held in honour, was thought to savour not only of intolerance, which the Romans so much disapproved, but of a rebellious and revolutionary spirit which the magistrates were determined to repress.

It is not to be wondered that the writers of those days, giving no credit to any of the existing forms of worship, but maintaining all alike as means of securing public tranquillity, should have treated with contempt a new religion which sought to subvert all the others, whilst its adherents belonged mostly to the lowest classes of society, and were thought to be introducing a communistic system tending to revolutionize and bring to a level every class of society. Lucian therefore speaks of them with contempt but not with hatred, and as far as we know of him, although aware of their existence, yet he never sought to make himself acquainted with their doctrines or social habits. It is true that we know very little of his life; no more indeed than what he says of himself in the seventy-six dialogues of which he appears as the author.

He was born at Samosata, a city lying on the western bank of the Euphrates in Commagene a district of Syria, which at one time was a separate kingdom and at another formed part of the Roman empire. The date of Lucian's birth cannot be fixed with accuracy, but it was probably in the reign of Hadrian, about the year A.D. 120, which date is in tolerable harmony with all the notices he gives of himself in various parts of his works. He followed the profession of rhetoric until he was forty years old, and during the early part of his life travelled about a good deal in Ionia. As a rhetorician he practised at Antioch, as we are informed by Suidas, and it is this fact, from which we infer that he was well acquainted with that city, its inhabitants and its literature, that makes his testimony so important on the subject of early Christianity, seeing that the disciples are said in the Acts of the Apostles to have been called Christians first in Antioch.

After Lucian had given up rhetoric, he probably returned to his native country, and no doubt had by that time acquired the knowledge of the Greek tongue which enabled him to write in so elegant a style those works which have come down to our own times. His account of the life of Peregrinus furnishes some interesting particulars about that impostor's connection with the Christians, and it is not the least interesting fact in the life of Lucian that he was present, about the year A.D. 165, at the Olympic games, when that notorious man sought by burning himself to obtain the fame which he had not been able thoroughly to secure by any other means.

The first extract from Lucian applicable to our present subject is taken from his Philopatris. The dialogue here lies between Triephon and Critias: the former says to his friend,

Why so downcast, Critias? &c.

CRITIAS. O Triephon, I have been hearing a great and inexplicable discourse, involved in many ways, and I am still thinking of the nonsense, and I am stopping my ears, lest perchance I hear it still. . . . .

. . . .

TRIEPHON. I see that you are revolving [in your mind] a subject which is neither trifling nor easily to be made light of; but certainly one of those which cannot be talked about. . . . . But get rid of the trouble, and discharge the trash, lest you suffer from it. . . . .

. . . .

TRIEPHON. Let us go, Critias. I fear lest what you have heard is witchcraft. . . . .

CRITIAS. I swear by the heavenly Jupiter, this shall not be used towards you.

TRIEPHON. You frighten me still more, now that you swear by Jupiter: for how will he be able to defend you, if you break your oath? I am sure you know all about this Jupiter of yours.

. . . .

CRITIAS. Then we should perhaps swear by Apollo. . . .

Triephon objects to Apollo also, and in succession to Mercury, Mars, Venus, and Minerva. Here they turn off from the subject, and speak of the Gorgon's head, which Perseus cut off and fixed on the shield of Minerva.

By the Unknown God at Athens, [says Critias] she was a virgin until her head was cut off. . . . . . .

CRITIAS. What think you then of Juno, the wife and sister of Jupiter?

TRIEPHON. Speak not of her for her most abominable adultery—her who was suspended by her feet and hands from heaven.

CRITIAS. And by whom shall I swear?

TRIEPHON. The god who rules aloft, great, immortal, heavenly, Son of the Father, Spirit proceeding from the Father: One out of Three, and Three out of One: These consider as Jove; look on him as God.

CRITIAS. You are teaching me arithmetic; and the oath is arithmetical. You are arithmeticizing, like Nicomachus the Gerasenian. For I know not what you say, one-three, and three-one. Do you allude to the tetrad of Pythagoras, or the ogdoad, or the triakad?

TRIEPHON. Say nothing of those earthly matters, that should be for ever buried in silence: we have not now to follow the traces of spiders. I will teach you all, and who was the earliest of all, and what is the system of the universe. For I was once what you are now: but when the Galilæan [*St Paul*] lighted upon me, that bald-headed, long-nosed man, who trod the air into the third heaven, and became acquainted with such beautiful things, and renewed us with water, he guided me into the footsteps of the blessed, and rescued us from the wicked places, and I will make you also a man in reality, if you will only listen to me.

CRITIAS. Tell me then, most learned Triephon, for I am quite alarmed.

TRIEPHON. You have read the poems of Aristophanes the dramatist, [called] the "Birds"?

CRITIAS. Certainly.

TRIEPHON. Something of this kind was written by him, "There was at first Chaos, and Night and black Erebus, and wide Tartarus: but earth, nor air, nor heaven existed."

CRITIAS. You say well: what was there then?

TRIEPHON. There was light imperishable, invisible, incomprehensible, which dispels the darkness and which did away with this [chaotic] deformity, by the word alone spoken by him, as he who was slow of tongue has left it in writing. He fixed the earth on the waters, spread out the heaven, formed the fixed stars, and arranged their course; which stars you worship as gods. He adorned the earth with flowers, and brought mankind into being out of things which were not. And he is now in heaven looking on the just and the unjust, and writes in a book their deeds, and will recompense all men on the day which he has appointed.

CRITIAS. And what has been spun by the Fates for all men, do they write that also? . . . .
. . . .
Say no more about the Fates even though you may have been

taken up with your master and been taught the ineffable mysteries. . . . .

But tell me: Do they write down the deeds of the Scythians also in heaven?

TRIEPHON. All, if at least there be a Chrestos [good man] among the nations.

CRITIAS. From what you say, there are many scribes in heaven to write out all this.

TRIEPHON. Speak respectfully; say nothing in ridicule of the good God, but becoming a catechumen, be persuaded by me if you wish to live for ever. . . . . Your gods have become a mere game to all sensible men. . . .

CRITIAS. I will take your god then—no harm shall happen to you. . . . .

TRIEPHON. Come then tell me about that wonderful thing. . .

CRITIAS. By the son [proceeding] from the father, that shall not happen to you.

Critias now relates to his friend what he had heard from the assembly at which he had been present, and which undoubtedly was an assembly of Christians as held in those early times.

Say no more, *says Triephon*, do not prolong such trash . . . . Leave these people alone, beginning with the prayer from the Father and adding at the end the song of many names.

Concerning the dialogue from which these extracts are taken, it is but right to say that some modern critics have doubted whether it is a genuine work of Lucian. It was the opinion of Gesner that a later Lucian wrote it in the time of Julian, when the apostasy of that emperor made it less dangerous than at any preceding time to turn into ridicule the practices and tenets of a new religion, that was rapidly taking possession of the great majority of mankind.

A second extract is from the dialogue entitled Alexander, wherein the author treats with just severity the character and adventures of a magician bearing that name. He makes the pretender say to his deluded followers:

Pontus was full of atheists and Christians, who tried to spread the basest calumnies about him; and he bade his followers stone them, if they wished to have the favour of God.—*Alex.* 35.

A third extract from the "Death of Peregrinus," gives us all that can be gained out of the works of Lucian on our present subject. The author relates the previous history and crimes of this talented but wicked man, how he killed his father and was saved by flight from the punishment due to his misdeeds.

Consigning himself to exile, he took to flight, and wandered about from one country to another. At this time it was that he learnt the wonderful philosophy of the Chrestians, having kept company with their priests and scribes* in Palestine. And what was the end of it? In a short time he showed them to be mere children, for he became a prophet, a leader of their processions, the marshaller of their meetings, and every thing in himself alone.

Καὶ τῶν βίβλων τὰς μὲν ἐξηγεῖτο καὶ διεσάφει· πολλὰς δὲ αὐτὸς καὶ συνέγραψε, καὶ ὡς θεὸν αὐτὸν ἐκεῖνοι ἡγοῦντο, καὶ νομοθέτῃ ἐχρῶντο, καὶ προστάτην ἐπέγραφον.

And of their books he explained and cleared up some, and wrote many himself: and they deemed him a god, made use of him as a legislator, and enrolled him as their patron.

They still worship that great man who was crucified in Palestine, because he introduced this new worship into life. For this, then, Proteus was seized and thrown into prison, which circumstance also gave him no little importance from that moment, both in the working of wonders, and in thirst for popularity, of which he was very fond. When he was put in prison, the Christians, looking upon it as a misfortune, moved every thing in their endeavours to rescue him. But when this was impossible, every other kind of attention was shown to him, not leisurely but with all their zeal. At early dawn might be seen waiting about the prison old women, certain widows, and orphan children. But those of them who were in authority, also, corrupting the guards, slept in the prison with him. Then elegant suppers were carried in for him, and they held there their sacred conversations, and the good Peregrinus (for he was still so called) was named by them a new Socrates. Moreover there came to him persons from some of the cities of Asia, sent by the Christians, out of their common stock to assist him, to join in advising him, and to comfort the man. But it is wonderful what alacrity they show, whenever such a thing happens, in the common cause. For in a very short time they are lavish of every thing they have: and Peregrinus, on the plea of his imprisonment, then received so many things from them, that he made no small revenue from this source. For those unlucky people have brought themselves to the belief, that they shall be wholly immortal, and live for ever; for which reason also the most part of them despise life, and willingly give themselves up. In the next place, their first lawgiver has persuaded them that they are all brethren one of another, when, having once

---

* Lucian here perhaps confounds the Christians with the Jews.

transgressed the law, they have denied the gods of the Greeks, and worship that sophist of theirs who was crucified, and live according to his laws. They therefore despise all things alike, and look upon all things as common, having received such doctrines without any very exact belief. If then any man, who is a magician, or good artist, and knows how to manage matters, goes among them, he immediately becomes rich in a short time, and laughs at those foolish people.

The governor of Syria, being a man who took pleasure in philosophy, treated Peregrinus with mildness; for perceiving his madness, and that he would even die to leave behind him a reputation on that account, he set him free, not thinking him worthy of punishment. But he, returning to his own country, found the ferment about his father's murder still alive, and many persons ready to accuse him. The greatest part of his possessions had been plundered through his absence, and nothing remained but the land, to the value of fifteen talents: for the whole of the property, which the old man left, was in value about thirty talents, not five thousand, as the ridiculous Theagenes stated. For this is a sum which all the city of the Parianians, with five other neighbouring cities, including their men and cattle, and all their goods, would not fetch. But the accusation and the charge against him was still hot, and it was probable that before long some one would stand forward against him. The people at large were most excited against him, from sorrow that a good old man, according to those who had seen him, should have been so impiously murdered. But only see the contrivance which this cunning Proteus adopted to meet all this, and how he escaped the danger. His hair was now long, and he had on a rough cloak: a staff was in his hand, and he had altogether a very tragic appearance. In this guise, then, he went before the people, and said that he would give up to them as public property, all that his good father had left him. The people, being mostly poor men, and eager to receive distributions, no sooner heard this than they shouted out he was a philosopher and a patriot, equal to Diogenes and Crates: but his enemies held their peace. If any one attempted to recall to mind the murder he had committed, he was immediately stoned.

16. Peregrinus then went out a second time on his wanderings, having plenty of provision for his journeys from the Christians, by whom he was escorted as if by guards, and had every thing in great plenty: and in this way he supported himself for some time. But afterwards he gave some offence to them also,—he was seen, I believe, eating some of the meats which are forbidden among them—and being at a loss what to do when they no longer visited him, he thought it best to recant, &c.

The writer of the dialogues from which these passages are taken lived till the end of the second century; and

Peregrinus the subject of the last extract lived some years earlier. He threw himself into the fire at the Olympic games in the year A.D. 165, and Lucian tells us that he witnessed this remarkable deed. Peregrinus must then have joined the Christians some years previously, and in all probability, the books of the New Testament were, about the year 150, being compiled out of documents and traditions, which had come down from the time of the first disciples. It might be dangerous, and yet possible, to suppose that some of our canonical scriptures were included among the writings which are here indicated as owing their origin to the Christians at Antioch, although we have some reason to doubt that any of them were among the "many" which Peregrinus wrote himself. The expressions used by Lucian give us the idea of a process of writing books as being then practised, perhaps on an extensive scale. We know from other sources that the second century was most productive in Gospels, Acts of apostles, Epistles, and Revelations. A large number of such works still remain, as appears by the catalogue of seventy given in a former chapter, and some of them, for aught we know, may have been written by Peregrinus, during the time that he frequented the Christian meetings, and made himself famous for his versatile acquirements.

The account given of Peregrinus and the "books," forbids us to limit the term to the apostolical writings which now form the canon of the New Testament. If those books had been then in existence, and received for canonical, we can hardly believe that Peregrinus could have gained credit for writing others, which, like the brazen shields of Numa, would in after ages make it difficult to distinguish between the genuine and the false.

Yet although it is probable that, at this very time, or about the middle of the second century, the books of the New Testament were written, it is not necessary to suppose that they possessed the authority of the Church, but shared with other writings, some of which are still in existence, the attention of Christians, according as each was believed to contain facts of Christ's history worthy to be read by believers. It is tolerably well ascertained that those now included in our canon were to a great extent selected from the others which are now called apocryphal, and that these last were set aside as comparatively worthless.

But besides the more classic writers here quoted, there are several passages in the biographies of the Roman emperors, by Julius Capitolinus, Lampridius, and others, writers of what is termed the Augustan History. Both Jews and Christians are mentioned in these biographies, which extend from the beginning of the second to the latter part of the third century after Christ. None of these works however contain the slightest allusion to the Christian Scriptures, or to any of those apocryphal books which certainly before the end of that period were in circulation together with the books of our present canon. And yet we find it recorded in those works that more than one Roman emperor paid great respect to the name of Christ, and more than one meditated to enroll him among the public recognized deities of the empire. It is not necessary to quote all these books of the Augustan History, yet some of them require to be here noticed. Spartianus tells us in his life of Hadrian that

> This emperor so hated the people of Antioch, that he wished to separate Syria from Phœnicia, that Antioch might not be called the capital of so many states. The Jews also at that time commenced war, because they were forbidden to practise circumcision. *Ibid.* xiv.

Let us now change the scene from Antioch to Alexandria, in the reign of the same emperor and about the year A.D. 130—from Antioch the city of luxury, of elegance, and of literary repose, to Alexandria, the turbulent and commercial capital of Egypt; of which the emperor Hadrian seems to think rather meanly if we may trust the report of Vopiscus who wrote the life of Saturninus, and quotes a letter from Hadrian to his friend Servianus as illustrating the state of Egypt at that time. The preliminary remarks of Vopiscus are not more flattering than the letter itself.

Sunt enim Ægyptii, ut satis nosti, viri ventosi, furibundi, jactantes, injuriosi, atque adeo vani, liberi, novarum rerum usque ad cantilenas publicas cupientes, versificatores, epigrammatarii, mathematici, haruspices, medici. Nam sunt Christiani, Samaritæ, et quibus presentia semper tempora cum enormi libertate displiceant. Ac	For the Egyptians are, as you know well enough, windy fellows, furious, boastful, unjust, and moreover vain, without restraint, and eager to make a revolution even to singing songs in public, versifiers, epigrammatists, astrologers, soothsayers, and medical men. For they are Christians, Samaritans, and men, who, giving themselves immense liberty, are always dissatisfied with the present times. And,

ne quis mihi Ægyptiorum irascatur, et meum esse credat quod in literas retuli, Hadriani epistolam ponam ex illis Phlegontis liberti ejus proditam, ex qua penitus Ægyptiorum vita detegitur.

lest any of the Egyptians should be angry with me and think that what I have reduced to writing is my own, I will give the letter of Hadrian taken out of the books of Phlegon his freedman, from which the life of the Ægyptians is thoroughly laid open.

[HADRIANUS AUGUSTUS SERVIANO CONSULI SALUTEM!]

Ægyptum, quam mihi laudabas, Serviane carissime, totam didici levem, pendulam, et ad omnia famæ momenta volitantem. Illic qui Serapem colunt Christiani sunt et devoti sunt Serapi qui se Christi episcopos dicunt, nemo illic archisynagogus Judæorum, nemo Samarites, nemo Christianorum presbyter, non mathematicus, non aruspex, non aliptes. Ipse ille patriarcha quum Ægyptum venerit, ab aliis Serapidem adorare, ab aliis cogitur Christum. Genus hominum seditiosum, vanissimum, injuriosissimum; civitas opulenta, dives, fæcunda, in qua nemo vivat otiosus. Alii vitrum conflant, aliis charta conficitur, alii linifiones, omnes certe cujuscunque artis et videntur et habentur. Podagrosi quod agant habent, habent [cesi quod agant habent] cæci quod faciant, ne chiragrici quidem aput eos otiosi vivunt. Unus illis deus nummus est: hunc Christiani, hunc Judæi, hunc omnes venerantur et gentes.

[HADRIAN AUGUSTUS TO SERVIANUS THE CONSUL, HEALTH!]

Egypt, which you used to praise to me, my dear Servianus, I have found to be wholly trifling, inconstant, and ready to move at every impulse of public talk. There are there Christians who worship Serapis, and devoted to Serapis are those who call themselves bishops of Christ. There is in that country no chief of a Jewish synagogue, no Samaritan or Christian presbyter, who is not also an astrologer, an augur, or a trainer of athletes. The very patriarch himself, when he has come to Egypt, is compelled by some to worship Serapis, by others Christ. They are a race of men most seditious, vain, and given to wrong-doing: the city is well-to-do, rich, and prolific; no one there lives idle. Some blow glass; others make paper; others are linen-cloth weavers: at any rate they all have both the appearance and the repute of belonging to some craft or other. Men with gouty feet have something to do; the blind have some occupation, and even men with gouty hands do not live idle amongst them. Money is their only god; Christians, Jews and all, both indi-

Et utinam melius esset morata civitas, digna profecto quæ pro sui fœcunditáte, quæ pro sui magnitudine totius Ægypti teneat principatum. Huic ego cuncta concessi, vetera privilegia reddidi, nova sic addidi ut præsenti gratias agerent. Denique ut primum inde discessi, et in filium meum Verum multa dixerunt, et de Antinoo quæ dixerint comperisse te credo. Nihil illis opto, nisi ut suis pullis alantur, quos quemadmodum fœcundant, pudet dicere. Calices tibi allassontes versicolores transmisi, quos mihi sacerdos templi obtulit, tibi et sorori meæ specialiter dedicatos; quos tu velim festis diebus conviviis adhibeas. Caveas tamen ne his Africanus noster indulgenter utatur.— VOPISCUS, *Saturn.* vii, viii.

viduals and tribes, worship that. I wish their state had better morals, worthy to take the lead of all Egypt according to its prolificness and its greatness. I have conceded everything to this city, I have restored its ancient privileges, and added new ones, so that they thanked me when I was among them. Lastly, as soon as I had gone away, they both said many things against my son Verus, and what they have said about Antinous, I think you have found out. I wish them nothing more than to feed on their own chicken, which they make prolific in a way that I am ashamed to tell you. I have sent you some shifting cups that change colours, which the priest of the temple gave me, meant especially for you and my sister. I wish you to bring these out on holidays at your feasts. Take care however that our friend Africanus does not use them too freely.

These extracts furnish no argument in favour of Alexandria, as the place where the books of the New Testament first came into existence, and the date at which the letter of Hadrian was written is nearly the same at which Antioch was the scene of Christian writers compiling and revising their sacred books. It is believed that the arguments which every phase of this subject presents, will confirm the theory that the volume of the New Testament is of Grecian and not of Jewish origin, and was put together mostly at Antioch in or about the middle of the second century of our era.

CHAPTER XI.

THE TESTIMONY OF THE APOSTOLICAL FATHERS, BARNABAS, CLEMENT, HERMAS, IGNATIUS, AND POLYCARP.

THOSE modern theologians, who have written on the evidences of the Christian religion, lay much stress upon the testimony of five writers, Barnabas, Clement, Ignatius, Polycarp and Hermas, who are said to have been contemporary with the twelve Apostles, and under whose names are still extant certain short compositions, mostly epistles, and these are said to furnish the strongest evidence to the existence and identity of the Gospels in the first century of the Christian era, and of the history in them contained. If any such writings still exist and have really come down to us from so early a date, they must naturally be of the utmost importance and interest to every member of the Christian community. Unfortunately the authentic remains of those early times are few in number, of doubtful origin, and often obscure in meaning. It was to be expected that those, who were busy in the active task of preaching and teaching a doctrine of such benevolent and universal import, would have little time for writing, in an age too when reading and writing must have been luxuries confined to the few, when writing materials were scarce and dear, when the nation, to which the new faith was first offered, lay beyond the pale of Grecian and Roman literature, and when the rapid success which it met with entailed upon the preacher the necessity of fresh exertion by widening the field over which his labours were extended. It is not then surprising that the Christian books, supposed to have been written before the year 100 of our era, should have been largely criticised, or that doubts have been entertained whether parts or even the whole of certain writings have not been improperly ascribed to those early times.

It is chiefly against the letters of Ignatius that these doubts have been entertained. Some of them have been described as forged and spurious; but such terms seem too harsh to be without hesitation applied to these writings.

It is charitable to believe that the Christians as a body did not make it a system to fabricate and pass off under the name of Ignatius or of any other apostolic teacher writings which might lead to falsehood and other lamentable results in a church which has pre-eminently truth for its groundwork, and it is charitable to believe, even if it is not quite possible to prove, that if none of these treatises were written within the period assigned to them, yet that they may have been compiled out of earlier remains, however loosely so, by some Christians of a later but still early age, and assigned at first conjecturally, and then directly, although erroneously, to the authors whose names they bear.

The works which have been written on this question are almost as numerous as those which concern the age, authorship, and authenticity of the Gospels themselves, but the general issue of the inquiries which have been instituted, has been unfavourable to the antiquity of these works as remains of writers who were contemporary with the Apostles, but favourable to the theory that they are productions of the latter half of the second century. That was the time when so many Christian writings came into existence, and all the records of our religion were sedulously sought out, because tradition was then becoming faint, original and even secondary witnesses had gone off the stage, and the great increase of the Christian community gave birth to extended curiosity about its early history, whilst it furnished greater safety to those who employed themselves in its service.

It will follow as a necessary inference from these remarks that we must examine with great minuteness the treatises now under our notice, because they are the only writings now remaining that have been ascribed to the first century of the Christian era; and, as their authors are said to have had familiar intercourse with the Apostles themselves, we might expect to find in them explicit mention of every thing which the Apostles themselves had written. The point at which I am here aiming, must not be misunderstood. If the four Gospels and other books were written by those who had been eye-witnesses of Christ's miracles, and the five apostolical fathers had conversed with the Apostles, it is not to be conceived that they would have omitted to name the actual books themselves which possessed so high authority and would be looked up to with so much respect by all the Christians. This is the only way in which their evidence could be of use to support the authenticity of the New Testament as being the work of the Apostles; but this is a testimony which the five apostolical fathers fail to supply. There is not a single sentence, in all their remaining works, in which a clear allusion to the New Testament is to be found. It is in vain that their evidence to the facts of

Christianity has been cited by Archdeacon Paley and other advocates of their contemporary character. This is not the point at issue. Few persons will be found to dispute the main facts of Christ's history, but many contend, and with truth, that the accounts of them, which have come down to us in the New Testament, were not put together as we now have them, until many years had elapsed—a sufficient time, in short, to explain the vagueness with which some of the facts are recorded, and even the contradictions which lie between the narratives of the same event as given by the four evangelic histories.

A short account of the apostolical fathers, the opinions of various modern writers about them, and notices of the form in which they have been published to the world, will not be thought out of place by those who reflect that besides the canonical books, these are thought by some to be the earliest documents of our religion.

I. *Barnabas.*

The first work to be here mentioned, is a "Catholic Epistle" ascribed to Barnabas, who is named in the Acts of the Apostles as the companion of St Paul. The candid reader will, I think, agree with me, that its chief value is derived not from any merit it possesses but from this supposed authorship. A summary of the life of Barnabas, gathered from the New Testament, will throw some light on the subject of the epistle ascribed to him.

Acts iv, 36, 37.—"And Joses, who by the apostles was surnamed Barnabas, (which is, being interpreted, The son of consolation,) a Levite, and of the country of Cyprus, having land, sold it, and brought the money, and laid it at the apostles' feet."

— ix, 26, 27.—Barnabas introduces Saul, after his recent conversion, to the Apostles at Jerusalem, A.D. 37.

— xi, 22-30.—Barnabas, having been sent by the brethren to Antioch, fetches Paul thither from Tarsus, and with him conveys contributions to the famishing Christians in Judæa, A.D. 44.

— xiii, 1-14, 28.—Paul and Barnabas make a tour through Asia, and return to Antioch, A.D. 46.

— xv, 2, &c.—Barnabas and Paul are sent to Jerusalem, and are present at the council of the Apostles, A.D. 51. See also Galat. ii, 1-9.

— xv, 22-39.—Barnabas sets out with Paul on a second

tour through Asia, but they quarrel and part from one another, A.D. 53.

After A.D. 53 Barnabas is not again named in the New Testament, but from the First Epistle to the Corinthians, ix, 6, it is inferred that he worked with his hands and was not married, whilst in Galat. ii,13, he seems to have imitated Peter in dissembling for fear of the Jews. Again, Marcus, his sister's son, appears in company with St Paul in A.D. 62, see Coloss. iv, 10; from which it has been inferred that Barnabas himself was then dead. See also I Pet. v, 13; and II Tim. iii, 11. Alexander, a monk of Cyprus, of the 8th or 9th century, assigns his death to A.D. 53-57, for which assertion he may have had the authority of some older writing now no longer extant. A doubt has been raised with respect to the identity of Barnabas with Barsabas, both named in the Acts (i, 23): and critics have differed on this subject, but our data are so slight, that it is impossible to arrive at a satisfactory conclusion. Those who reflect on the obscurity which always attends the first operations of missionaries and religious teachers in our own times, will not wonder that the operations of the first Christians mostly were discussed in their own private meetings and scarcely formed a topic for the great historians and public writers of the age.

The first ancient author who names Barnabas is Clement of Alexandria (A.D. 200), who seven times quotes passages which seem to have been taken from the existing epistle (Strom. II, 6, 7, 15, 18, 20, v, 8, 10.) Origen, who was the pupil of Clement, also names Barnabas as being the author of an epistle, and the passages which he quotes are still found in that which passes under the name of Barnabas. We may therefore conclude that this tract was written before the time of Clement or Origen, without determining the question whether it really was the work of the apostolic Barnabas or not.

Neither is it important to dwell upon the notices found of Barnabas or of his epistle in the works of Eusebius and Jerome: for the whole subject was already patent and public in their times, and, though succeeding ages have overlaid primitive Christianity with numberless fictions and falsehoods which create a great impediment to the cause of truth, yet no act of commission or of omission occurring since the time of Jerome has caused half so much difficulty to the ecclesiastical students as the obscurity in which the Christian history is involved previous to the time of Eusebius.

The history of Peregrinus, related by the heathen writer Lucian, gives us a vivid picture of the state of things at Antioch about the year 150. Christian books were then revised, and new ones written.* Can we doubt that many books of uncertain character were then introduced, if not by fraud, yet by the ignorance and errors of well-meaning but uneducated persons, members of the Christian community?

Of the epistle which remains under the name of Barnabas, different opinions have been held by different writers. Its authenticity has been maintained by Dupin, "Bibl. des Auteurs, &c." I, 6, &c.; Nourry, "Appar. ad Bibl. M. Patt." I, dissert. 3; Galland, "Bibl. vet. Patt." I, Proleg. p. 29, &c.; Henke, "De Epist. q. Barn. tribuitur, Authentia," Jen. 1827; Roerdam, "De Authentia Ep. Barn." Hafn. 1828; and Franke, "Guerike et Rudelbach Zeitschrift für luth Theol." 1840, fasc. 2. It has been deemed spurious by Menard, "Edit. of Barnabas;" Tentzelius, "Fabric. Bibl. Eccl." p. 42, sec. 10; Natalis Alexander, "Hist. Eccl." sec. I, c. 12, art. 8; Remi Ceillier, "Hist. Gener. des Auteurs," &c. I, p. 498, &c.; Ittigius, "Select. Cap. Hist. Eccl." sec. I, tom. I, p. 20; Mosheim, "Comment. de Rebus Christ. ante Const. Mag.," p. 161; Lumper, "Hist. Theol. Crit." I, p. 150; Hugius, "Zeitschrift für das Erzbisthum Freiburg," Fasc. 2, p. 132, Fasc. 3, p. 208, &c.; Ullmann, "Studien u. Kritiken," t. I, p. 381; Neander, "Kirchengesch." t. I, 3, p. 733; "Mynster, "Studien u. Kritiken," II, 323; Winer, "Bibl. Realwoerterbuch s. v. Barnabas," and Hefele, "Das Sendschreiben des Apostels Barnabas," &c. Tub. 1840, cap. 3, pp. 147-195, and in his edit. of Barnabas.

Those who defend the genuineness of this epistle, plead especially the notices of it which occur in such early writers as Origen and Clement of Alexandria, but the arguments which may be adduced on the other side of the question seem too strong to be refuted, and they lead to the conclusion that the work was written about the year 140, in that obscure interval between the apostolic age and the appearance of those great writers, Justin Martyr, Tatian, Clement and Origen, with whom ecclesiastical literature may be said to have begun.

The epistle of Barnabas is not mentioned by any later author from the time of Nicephorus, Patriarch of Constantinople in A.D. 828, down to the seventeenth century. The

---

* See p. 82, &c. of this volume, and also my Heathen Records to the Jewish Scripture History, London, 1856.

first modern writer who noticed it was Sirmond, who found a copy of it in an ancient MS [Codex Turrianus], soon after which, three other MS copies were discovered, belonging to the Vatican library, Cardinal Colonna, and Andrew Schott. Hugh Menard then found a Latin version of it in a Corbey MS earlier than the ninth century. A transcript of this Latin version and of the MS of Schott passed from Salmasius to Isaac Vossius, and from Vossius to Archbishop Usher, who had it printed at Oxford, A.D. 1643; but the whole impression was consumed by a fire which burnt several houses in that city.

In 1645 Luke D'Achery published an edition of it, which had been prepared by Menard, but was broken off by his death in 1644.

Vossius published it again in 1646 at Amsterdam, having collated a Florence, a Vatican, and other manuscripts. Since that time have appeared the editions of Cotelerius, Galland, Russell, Jacobson and Hefele, all comprising more or less completely the whole of the five apostolical writers, Barnabas, Clement, Hermas, Ignatius and Polycarp.

In all the Greek texts of this epistle the first four chapters and part of the fifth are wanting: these portions are found in the Latin version only.

II. *Clement of Rome.*

The second of the apostolical fathers, Clement, surnamed "of Rome," to distinguish him from Clement of Alexandria, who lived an hundred years later, is supposed by Origen, "In Joan." i, 29; Eusebius, "Hist. Eccl." iii, 15; Epiphanius, "Hæres." 27, n. 6; Jerome, "De Viris Ill." c. 15, and others, to be the same Clement who is named in St Paul's Epistle to the Philippians, iv, 3. Others however have held a different opinion, and their doubts derive great support from the fact that Irenæus, who has said much in praise of Clement, seems not to have clearly indicated that these two were one and the same.

It is the opinion of Hefele, that Clement was a citizen of Philippi, who was converted by St Paul, and remained at home to teach his countrymen, when St Paul left that city. In support of this opinion it may be observed that St Paul had no other companions in his journey to Philippi than Silas, Timotheus, and Luke [Acts xvi], that the Scriptures mention Clement in one passage only, as living at Philippi, and he is mentioned in terms precisely similar to those in which other persons are named, who certainly were inhabitants of that town.

In the Homilies and Recognitions falsely ascribed to Clement, his father is said to have been one Faustinus, descended from the family of the Roman Cæsars, and this absurd fable is copied in the "Liber Pontificalis" or Book of the Roman Pontiffs, in the Roman Breviary, and in the works of Eucherius bishop of Lyons.

It is agreed by all that Clement was bishop of Rome, or rather of the Christian congregation in Rome; but it is doubtful in what order he succeeded after Peter. Some say, with Jerome, "De Viris Ill." c. 15, that he was the fourth bishop, having been preceded by Linus and Anacletus; whilst others make him to have been the immediate successor of St Peter. When we reflect on the scantiness of our information about the most important facts connected with Christianity in times so early, I think we may fairly be sceptical as to even the names of such humble persons as those who preached the Christian doctrines in the first century at Rome. The office of bishop was not then accompanied with that splendour which now makes it so brilliant: nor is it likely that those who were bent on teaching and practising humble-mindedness, should feel the least care about the order of precedence in which they stood one to another (a point so important among their successors) or about handing down their names to future ages. All they did was done, we cannot doubt, in secret, and their heavenly Father, as he had promised, and as they no doubt believed, would reward them not by the praise or memory of men, but in that kingdom of heaven to which they had aspired. As a matter of historical minutiæ, it may be observed that Augustine, "Ep. 53 ad Generos." Optatus, "Lib. ii," and the author of the Apostolical Constitutions, vii, 46, place Clement as the successor to Linus, whereas Irenæus, "Adv. Hæres." iii, 3, apud Euseb. "H. E." v, 6; Eusebius, "Hist. Eccl." iii, 13, 15, 34; and Jerome, "De Viris Ill." 15, place Cletus, otherwise called Anacletus, between the two. Both views of the question have been held by the later fathers of the Church, and discussed in various modes, but the subject is too unimportant to occupy our time at present.

The First Epistle of Clement to the Corinthians is said by Eusebius to have been written for the purpose of introducing peace and concord among them, after they had quarrelled among themselves; but no traces of it occur in any writer until the year 1628, when Cyril Lucar, Patriarch of Constantinople, sent as a present to King Charles I, the magnificent Alexandrian manuscript, now deposited in the British Museum, and containing the Greek Septuagint Old Testament, the Greek New Testament, and Clement's Epistle to the Corinthians, together with a portion of another, described in the table of contents prefixed to the manuscript, as a Second Epistle to the Corinthians by the same writer. From the text furnished by this unique manuscript, both of these epistles were published by Patrick Young the king's librarian at Oxford, 1633, again at Cambridge 1718 by Wotton, and by Cotelerius, Jacobson and Hefele in their respective editions of the Apostolical Fathers.

It remains to review the arguments by which some have endeavoured to impugn, whilst others have defended the authenticity of these writings.

The First Epistle is thought to have been known to Polycarp, in whose epistle occur some passages thought to have been copied from it.

Irenæus also, " Adv. Hær." iii, 3, 3, gives a description of the Epistle which agrees with what is now found in the Alexandrian manuscript.

Clement of Alexandria quotes many sentences which are still found in the present text. See " Strom." i, 7: iv, 17: v, 12: vi, 8.

The same may be observed of Origen, " De Princ." ii, 3, n. 6: " In Ezec." c. 8: " In Joan." i, 29; Eusebius, iii, 16, 38; Cyril of Alexandria, " Catech." 18, c. 8; Epiphanius, 27, n. 6; and Jerome, " De Viris Ill." c. 15: " Comm. in Is." xiv, 52, 13: " In Ep. ad Eph." i, 2, 2: ii, 4, 1. It is true also, on the other hand, that some ancient writers, as for instance Basil, " De Spir. S." 29, no. 72, have quoted passages which are not found in our present epistle; but as the Alexandrian manuscript has lost a leaf after chapter 57, it is possible that those passages were taken from that part of the work which was written on the missing leaf.

It has been held by some that, however the Epistle generally may be authentic, yet certain passages, about the Phœnix in c. 25, the word *layman* in c. 40, and the antiquity of the Church at Corinth in c. 47, together with the abundance of epithets scattered over parts of the work, prove it to have been interpolated at a later date. These objections have been replied to by others with more or less success; and some modern writers have come to the conclusion that at least the First Epistle of Clement is a genuine relic of the apostolic age, and even that it was written to the Corinthians about one or two years before the destruction of Jerusalem.

Very different however is the case of the second epistle ascribed to Clement. The first who mentions such a document is Eusebius, iii, 38, who acknowledges that its authenticity is doubtful. Jerome and Photius also, among the ancients, denied its authenticity, whilst, among the moderns, Wotton, Simon, Grabe, and others have found in the tract itself sufficient internal evidence to justify the conclusion that it is a composition of a later age, though, from its being found in the Alexandrian manuscript, we must infer that it was thought to be genuine in the fifth century of our era, when that manuscript is supposed to have been written.

Resuming the whole question of Clement's Epistles, we may observe that their insertion in the Alexandrian manuscript cannot be accepted as a proof that one is genuine, if the other, also found there, is an acknowledged forgery; and secondly that whereas Origen, Irenæus, and Clement of Alexandria, at the end of the second or the beginning of the third century, first mention and quote either of these epistles, it is within that period of 200 years from the birth of Christ that we must look for proofs, whether writings are genuine or spurious. We may readily admit that even both of Clement's Epistles were in existence before the time of Origen, Irenæus or Clement of Alexandria, and still be far from proving that either of them was the work of the immediate follower of the Apostles. We know from the dialogues of Lucian, that, in the first half of the second century, the Christians were occupied in collecting written records, and we may believe the report of that satirical writer, that their well-meaning exertions were sometimes baffled by their own simplicity and the knavery of pretended converts.

III. *Hermas.*

The "Shepherd" of Hermas stands on a different basis from the other writings of the apostolical fathers, in that it exists only in a Latin text. This is generally understood to be a translation from a Greek original. The work is found in the Sinaitic MS of the New Testament together with the Epistle of Barnabas.

The most remarkable fact about it would be that it was read publicly in the churches, as divinely inspired and scarcely inferior to the books that were accounted canonical:

were it not that this is no more than has been said of other books, having, if possible, still less pretension.

It has been by some ascribed to the Hermas who is named in St Paul's Epistle to the Romans, xiv, 14. The canon of Muratori ascribes it to another Hermas, brother of Pius II bishop of Rome.

There are still fragments of the "Shepherd" in Greek, which is said to have been the original language, and to have been circulated from Rome in the second century. The few passages of the Greek which remain were collected by Fabricius in his "Codex Novi Testamenti," iii, 738, and have also been printed by Grabe in the first volume of his "Spicilegium." The Latin text was first edited by Faber, Paris, 1513. It appears in almost all the editions of the Fathers, and was also printed with the Epistle of Barnabas at Oxford, 12mo, 1685.

This work is of no more value, perhaps of less, than any of the other remains of the Apostolical Fathers, although according to Jerome ("De Script. Eccles." 10) it was once held in great esteem in those countries where Greek was the vernacular language.

IV. *Ignatius.*

Of Ignatius surnamed Theophorus, a Greek word implying that he had God always with him, or in his thoughts, we have no authentic records in any early writer. Eusebius relates (iii, 22) that he succeeded Evodius, who had been appointed by the Apostles themselves, in the government of the Church of Antioch. In a tract called Acts of the Martyrdom of Ignatius, it is related that Ignatius was condemned to be cast to the wild beasts by Trajan, whilst he was stopping at Antioch on his march against the Parthians, and that he was consequently conveyed to Rome, where the sentence was put in execution. The venerable man—for he was then perhaps eighty years old—after a tedious voyage, arrived at Smyrna, where he conversed with Polycarp, and wrote four epistles, to the Ephesians, the Magnesians, the Trallians, and the Romans. He next stopped in the Troad, where he is said to have written three other epistles, to the Philadelphians, the Smyrnæans, and Polycarp. On his arrival at Rome, he was cast to the lions, and his bones, gathered from the area of the amphitheatre, were carried back to Antioch and preserved with great care by the Christians of that city. These facts and others are found in the Acts of his Martyrdom, before mentioned.

Doubts have however been raised concerning this story, from the difficulty of making the visit of Trajan to Antioch coincide with the condemnation of Ignatius. The Acts of his Martyrdom fix it expressly to the ninth year of Trajan, that is from Jan. 26, A.D. 106 to Jan. 26, A.D. 107: and his execution to the tenth year of the same emperor. But Lloyd, Pearson, Grabe, and several other writers have shown that Trajan did not visit Antioch until the year 114; and to remove this difficulty Tillemont, in his "History of the Emperors," endeavoured to show that Trajan twice visited Antioch, once in 106 and again in 114. On the other hand it has been suggested that it was not the emperor himself, but the proconsul, who condemned Ignatius to the lions, because the words of Eusebius, the Paschal Chronicle, Jerome, and others, do not allow us to put off the martyrdom so late as the year 114 of the Christian era.

In this conflict of opinion, without expressing at the moment any doubt on the general tenour of the history, we may reasonably call in question the accuracy of its details, when we find such difficulty in reconciling the alleged circumstances of his life with the acknowledged history of those times. Those who reflect on the known clemency and mild government of Trajan will hesitate to believe that he personally sentenced an old man to so cruel a death for no other crime than being a Christian; those who have read his rescript to Pliny on the very subject of dealing with Christians, will be startled at such ruthless practice as detailed in the Acts of Ignatius's Martyrdom, so wholly at variance with the precepts which Trajan had laid down; and thirdly, those who duly appreciate the exaggerations to which all such personal narratives are liable, and in which ecclesiastical history abounds, will not be disinclined to believe that the history of Ignatius and his sufferings has been highly coloured by those through whose hands the narrative has passed. That exaggeration has been rife in the record of his martyrdom, I do not doubt; for what can be more dramatic and unreal, than that the old man, a prisoner, should be allowed to break his journey into stages for the purpose of writing seven epistles advocating the very doctrines for which he was to suffer, addressed to persons of whom he knew little or nothing, and above all, to the Romans, among whom he was going? Criminals condemned to death are not generally allowed to convert their conveyance to the place of execution into a triumphal entry, nor would the cruelty of his judge have so utterly stultified itself as to allow such apparently unrestrained communication with his friends, or, in a word, have treated with such honour and respect one whom he must either have despised as a contemptible fanatic or have constrained as a dangerous revolutionist. These considerations create in the mind a difficulty in receiving all the details of Ignatius's history; and they are in harmony with an opinion long since expressed by others that the number of Christian martyrs in the early ages, instead of being large, was remarkably small, and that, though the rigid Roman may have punished rebellion against the laws, yet he magnanimously overlooked, whenever it was possible, all such questions as seemed to concern religion only, for which the Roman constitution allowed freer scope than any code of laws either before or since.

Of the fifteen letters ascribed to Ignatius, eight have long since been rejected as of no authority whatever—I hesitate to say as forgeries: for truth never gains by ascribing dishonest motives or dishonest action, where a more lenient judgment may, even with the slightest reason to support it, be pronounced. The remaining seven epistles were accounted genuine by most critics, although disputed by some, previous to the discoveries of Mr Cureton, which have shaken and indeed almost wholly destroyed the credit and authenticity of all alike.

Of the seven, then, still for a time admitted as perhaps genuine, there are two copies in circulation. The text of one of these is longer than the other, and contains passages which have apparently been expanded by the addition of words which tend to support certain ecclesiastical tenets, and in consequence of this, the longer text has been almost universally rejected, though Schmidt and Netzius have endeavoured to show that the longer copies have been expanded, and the shorter ones abbreviated, with no evil intent, from a common prototype. Meier also has even attempted to show that the longer text is the most ancient, in spite of such expressions as "*the rest of the clergy*" found in the longer copy of the Epistle to the Philadelphians, ch. 4; for it is notorious that in the time of Ignatius and even for many years after, the orders of the Church inferior to deacons, and which still exist in the Roman communion, were not yet introduced.

Three of these letters occur only in a Latin version, and were printed at Paris at the end of the *Quadrilogus*, 4to, 1495. In 1498, Jacobus Faber Stapulensis published eleven others at Paris. In 1536 Symphorianus Champerius Lugdunensis published as many as fifteen in Latin; after which the Greek text of twelve appeared, Dillingæ, 1557, and again, Tiguri, 1559, edited by Gesner with a Latin version.

All the foregoing were from manuscripts containing the longer text of the epistles, but in 1646 Isaac Vossius published the shorter, usually considered the more genuine text, at Amsterdam, from a Medicean manuscript of the eleventh century, whilst Usher, archbishop of Armagh, published an edition of the same at Oxford, 1644, from a Cambridge MS, and another belonging to the bishop of Norwich, and corresponding in text most closely with the edition of Vossius. In 1689, Ruinart published at Paris, in his "Acta Sincera Martyrum," the Epistle to the Romans which was wanting in the Medicean MS, and consequently in the edition of Vossius. In 1709 appeared the excellent Oxford edition of Smith, and, since then, the various editions of the apostolical fathers, Cotelerius's folio edition containing all, both the genuine, the interpolated, and the spurious, whilst the 8vo volumes of Jacobson and Hefele give the text of those seven only which were accounted genuine.

The first writer who impugned the genuineness of all Ignatius's epistles alike was Daillé, who, in 1666, published "De scriptis quæ sub Dionysii Areopagitæ et Ignatii Antiocheni nominibus circumferuntur," in which he asserts that these letters were forged many years after and falsely ascribed to Ignatius. Soon after the publication of this work appeared the elaborate work of Bishop Pearson, "Vindiciæ Ignatianæ," &c. Cantab. 1672; a new edition has been published at Oxford in two vols, 8vo, 1852. In opposition to Pearson arose Larroquan, Basnage, Oudin, and others, who were principally led to impugn the authenticity of the epistles by the frequent allusion to bishops and hierarchical ordinances, which were probably introduced at a later period into the Church. But the authenticity found defenders in Nourry, Ceillier, and Lumper: whilst again, in more recent times, Baur, Schwegler, and Hilgenfeld have published their opinion that all the epistles now remaining were written about the middle of the second century, and attributed to Ignatius by some dishonest zealot, to forward the cause of episcopacy and the ecclesiastical system.

The opinion of Hefele is in favour of the authenticity of the seven, and in his fourth edition of "Patres Apostolici," he replies to Mr Cureton, who, in the interval had made an important discovery of a very ancient manuscript containing three only of the Ignatian epistles, and these omitting certain passages, hitherto found in even the shortest text of every Greek manuscript.

The first volume which Mr Cureton published on this subject, bears this title:

The ancient Syriac version of the epistles of Saint Ignatius to Saint Polycarp, the Ephesians, and the Romans: together with extracts from his epistles, collected from the writings of Severus of Antioch, Timotheus of Alexandria, and others, edited with an English translation and notes. Also the Greek text of these three epistles, corrected according to the authority of the Syriac version. By William Cureton, M.A. London: Rivingtons. Berlin: Asher and Comp. MDCCCXLV.

The editor of this book, not without some appearance of reason, concludes that, as his manuscript dates from a very early period of the Christian era, the three letters of Ignatius, of which it contains a Syriac translation, did not at that time contain those passages which do not appear in the translation, and inclines further to the belief that these three epistles are the only genuine ones of the whole collection that before passed under the name of Ignatius. This conclusion had been already impugned in the "English Review" and elsewhere, on the supposition that the Syriac version was an epitome as well as a translation, when Cureton published a reply in a complete edition of all the epistles, with this title:

Corpus Ignatianum: a complete collection of the Ignatian epistles, genuine, interpolated, and spurious; together with numerous extracts from them, as quoted by ecclesiastical writers down to the tenth century; in Syriac, Greek, and Latin: an English translation of the Syriac text, copious notes and introduction, by William Cureton, M.A.F.R.S. chaplain in ordinary to her majesty the queen. London 1849.

In preparing this volume for the press the editor made use of a third manuscript agreeing in its contents with the other two from which he had published his former volume. In consequence of this agreement between the manuscripts Mr Cureton adheres to his former opinion that the text of Ignatius has been interpolated, rejecting the explanation that the Syriac version had been abridged from the original Greek for the private use of some pious or ascetic monk.

His words, from page ix of the work, are quoted by Hefele:

Is there, therefore, any thing in the three epistles themselves which would tend to show that, in their present form, [that is in the Syriac version] they are an epitome, of monkish and ascetic origin? The Epistle to the Romans consists almost entirely of arguments, which Ignatius urges upon those to whom he was writing, in order to induce them to refrain from making any effort to reverse the decree of Trajan, and to save him from the death to which he was condemned. Now it is a well-known fact that monasticism and asceticism, in their simplest and purest form, chiefly derived their origin from the desire which some converts to Christianity felt to avoid persecution, and consequent martyrdom, for the profession of their faith, by retiring to those wild and sequestered spots, where they might escape the observation of their Pagan persecutors. Moreover, I am not aware that in any subsequent ages such an earnest desire for the crown of martyrdom, as that evinced by Ignatius in the Epistle to the Romans, has ever been considered so peculiarly appropriate to the aspirations of monkish asceticism, that we should reasonably expect a Syrian monk to retain this epistle for his own "pious use," in preference to any of the others which he has rejected.

Another extract from the same volume may suffice:

The Epistle to the Ephesians contains an acknowledgment on the part of Ignatius for the kind attentions which they had shown to him, an exhortation to them to imitate the good example of their bishop, and advice how they should comport themselves toward their opposers, in returning kindness for injuries and meekness for railing. The Epistle to Polycarp also gives further advice as to relative duties in common life; and likewise adds some instructions respecting matrimony, with an admonition to wives to love their husbands, and to husbands to cherish their wives. These surely could not have been peculiarly appropriate to the "pious use" of a monk, whose very name indicates that he has quitted the busy world, renounced the holy tie of matrimony, and, consequently, could not stand in need of any of those instructions which relate peculiarly to a state with which he has no concern.

The remainder of this subject may be got rid of in few words. The opinion of Cureton has been supported by Chevalier Bunsen in two publications, both issued at Hamburg, 1847: whilst Dr Petermann, in a new edition of the Epistles of Ignatius, Lips. 1849, has endeavoured to show that there is an earlier Syriac version, not mutilated, as are the MSS of Cureton, but agreeing accurately with the full text of the Greek MSS. The views of Bunsen have been espoused by Dr Ritschl, Weiss, and others, but this phase of the controversy has on the whole tended to throw doubt on all the epistles alike. Baur and Hilgenfeld—for the Germans have this subject of controversy almost wholly to themselves—deny the authenticity of all alike, which on the other hand has been as vehemently maintained by Denzinger and Uhlhorn.

It is needless to observe that in this variance of opinion, some have tried to steer a middle course by holding that the epistles are genuine in the groundwork, but have been interpolated. A wiser course will probably be to accept them as compositions of the early part of the second century, and therefore as useful in adding light, however little, to a period that is generally so dark.

V. *Polycarp.*

Of Polycarp, the fifth Apostolical Father, we have no information earlier than the time of Irenæus, who tells us, "Adv. Hæres." iii, 3, that he had been "taught by the Apostles, and associated with many who had seen Christ." Eusebius, "Eccl. Hist." iii, 36, says that he was bishop of Smyrna, to which Tertullian, "De Præs." 32, and Jerome, "De Viris Ill." 17, add that he was successor in that see to St John the Apostle.

We learn the sequel of his history from the Acts of his Martyrdom, combined with what Irenæus says of him. He went to Rome, where, we are told, various opinions were already entertained concerning the celebration of Easter, and Polycarp, it appears, advocated the opposite view of the question to that which Pope Anicetus held. The discussion which ensued between them ended like many other similar argumentations: neither party could convince the other, and they separated in a manner becoming the disciples of Christ, without breaking the bond of love that united them. It is however to be regretted that Polycarp did not maintain the same forbearance towards others who differed from him; for, if we may believe Irenæus, when Marcion requested Polycarp to look upon him, the venerable bishop, forgetting that charity and love are the very groundwork of the Christian religion, said to him in reply, "I look on thee as the first-born of Satan!"

The year in which Polycarp suffered martyrdom, cannot be ascertained: some fix it at 147, others 161, 167, and even so late as 178.

We learn from Irenæus that Polycarp left behind him several epistles: one only however now bears his name, inscribed to the Philippians. Its authenticity has been questioned by Daillé, Semler, Röster, Schwegler, Hilgenfeld, the centuriators of Magdeburg, and others, and defended by Nourry, Pearson, Mosheim, Tillemont, Ittig, Lücke, Möhler, Uhlhorn, and Hefele.

It was first published in Latin, Paris, 1498, by Jac. Faber Stapulensis, and at Douay, 1633, in Greek and Latin by P. Halloiscius. Later editions are those of Usher, Lond. 1647, and Smith, 1709: and in the collections of Patres Apostolici by Cotelerius, Jacobson, and Hefele.

Having thus then traced the history of the writings which appear under the name of the Apostolical Fathers, we may resume the thread of our argument, first pointing out more fully the difference between the external character of a book and the truth of the facts which it relates, and here may be cited the author of the "Evidences of Christianity," whose remarks are important in reference, still more to the age immediately following in close connection with the age of Christ than to any other later period.

That the original story, the story delivered by the first preachers of the institution, should have died away so entirely as to have left no record or memorial of its existence, although so many records and memorials of the time and transaction remain; and that another story should have stepped into its place, and gained exclusive possession of the belief of all who professed themselves disciples of the institution, is beyond any example of the corruption of even oral tradition, and still less consistent with the experience of written history: and this improbability, which is very great, is rendered still greater by the reflection, that no such change as the oblivion of one story, and the substitution of another, took place in any future period of the Christian era. Christianity hath travelled through dark and turbulent ages; nevertheless it came out of the cloud and the storm, such, in substance, as it entered in. Many additions were made to the primitive history, and these entitled to different degrees of credit, many doctrinal errors also were from time to time grafted into the public creed; but still the original story remained, and remained the same. In all its principal parts, it has been fixed from the beginning.

That the treatises ascribed to Barnabas, Clement, Ignatius, Polycarp and Hermas are based upon the same story as the books of the New Testament, is not to be denied. The events related in the history of Christ passed current in tradition among the Christians long before they were set down in writing: and the sayings of Christ were no doubt treasured up like household jewels by his disciples and followers. Why, then, may we not refer the quotations of Christ's words, occurring in the Apostolical Fathers, to an origin of this kind?

It is evident, from authorities which we shall soon have to produce, that these were *Memorials*, or *Memoranda* (Ἀπομνημονεύματα) of the Apostles, widely circulated at a very early period, and that there was also a collection of the *Sayings** *of the Lord* (Λόγια τοῦ Κυρίου) equally well known. If then these five fathers have quoted facts of our Lord's history or any of his sayings, but have not mentioned any book in which they are contained, it is reasonable to believe that they quote from those writings which are known to have existed, and not from others of which no trace can be found until after the period at which those fathers lived. If we examine two or three of these quotations the supposition just stated will expand into reality. In the epistle ascribed to Barnabas, we read:

Lest, as is written, we be found "Many called, but few chosen." *Chapter* iv.

But when he [Christ] chose his own apostles, who were about to preach his gospel, and who were lawless beyond every kind of sin,—that he might show how he came not "to call the righteous but sinners to repentance,"—he then displayed himself to be the son of God. *Chapter* vii.

Here are not necessarily allusions to either of the four Gospels which we now have, but only to remarkable apophthegms of our Lord, which may have been current universally among the Christians, long before they were perpetuated in the Gospels. The same may be said of every sentence found in any of the Apostolical Fathers, which on first sight might be thought to be a decided quotation from one of the Gospels according to Matthew, Mark, Luke or John. It is impossible to deny the truth of this observation; for we see it confirmed by the fact that the Apostolical Fathers do actually quote Moses, and other Old Testament writers by name, "Moses hath said," "Moses says," &c. in numerous passages; but we nowhere meet with the words "Matthew

---

* "The Sayings ascribed to our Lord by the Fathers and primitive writers, and incidents in his life narrated by them otherwise than found in Scripture by J. T. Dodd, B.A. late junior student of Christ Church, Ox. and Lond. Sm. 8vo, 1874."

hath said in his Gospel," "John hath said," &c. They always quote, not the words of the evangelists, but the words of Christ himself directly, which furnishes the strongest presumption, that, though the sayings of Christ were in general vogue, yet the evangelical histories, into which they were afterwards embodied, were not then in being.

To recur to Barnabas, there are other peculiarities found in the existing epistle, which are hardly reconcilable with what is related of him in the Acts of the Apostles. Such are the notice of the Sabbath in Chapter 15, circumcision in Chapter 9, and the abolition of the Jewish law in Chapters 4 and 14. And lastly: the whole of the epistle is so thoroughly beneath mediocrity, both for sentiments and style, that its authenticity as a production of a contemporary and that so celebrated an apostle would have rather a sinister than a beneficial influence on the subject of primitive Christianity. Its genuineness as a production of the second century gives it the value of an historical document, but as a relic of the first century it cannot exercise any useful influence on the cause with which it is connected.

But this subject will be hardly complete without similar extracts from the other Apostolical Fathers; and first of Clemens Romanus. In Chapter xii of his Epistle, we read:

Pity that ye may be pitied.
Forgive that it may be forgiven to you.
As ye do, so it shall be done to you.
As ye give, so shall it be given to you.
As ye judge, so shall it be judged to you.
As ye are good, so shall good be done to you.
With what measure ye mete, in the same it shall be meted to you. *Chap.* xii.

These sentences form only one in the Epistle of Clement, and do not occur in any one place of the four Gospels, where their equivalent is to be found only by combining together parts of the following texts: Matt. v, 7: vi, 14: vii, 2, 12; Luke vi, 31, 36, 37, 38; and neither of the fragments thus united into one, employs the same words to express the same thought, as those words which occur in St Clement's Epistle.

Woe to that man;
It were better for him if he had not been born,
Than to offend one of my elect:
It were better that a mill-stone should be put on him, and he should be drowned in the sea,
Than to offend one of my little ones.

To make up this apparent quotation (in Chapter xlvi) it is necessary to combine, or at all events to compare Matthew xviii, 6: xxvi, 24: and Luke xvii, 1-2.

In the Shepherd of Hermas are no quotations from the New Testament, nor any words which might be thought to refer to it. Neither has it any quotations from the Old Testament: although there is a reference to an apocryphal work of which nothing otherwise is known.

The Lord is nigh to those who turn to him, as is written in Eldad and Modat who prophesied in the wilderness to the people. *Shepherd*, Vis. ii, 3.

In the Book of Numbers, xi, 26, it is true, Eldad and Modat are named as prophets, who prophesied to the people. From Ignatius the following extracts will be sufficient.

Be thou wise as a serpent in all things and harmless as the dove.—" Ep. to Polycarp," ii.
For if the prayer of one and of a second has such strength, how much more so both that of the bishop and of all the church? —" Ep. to Ephesians," v.
For every one whom the master of the house sends to his own household, we ought to receive him as him that sent.—" Ep. to Ephesians," vi.
These men are not my father's planting.—" Ep. to Trallians," xi.
He who receiveth let him receive.—" Ep. to Smyrnæans," vi.

With these extracts may be compared the following texts from the Gospel according to St Matthew, and it will be seen how little they can be considered as verbal quotations, and how much they look like mere references to maxims and sayings which at that time were current, by tradition, and perhaps in various memoranda also, among the early Christians: MATT. x, 16: xviii, 19; x, 40: xv, 13: xix, 12.

And the following from Polycarp tend in the same direction and support the same inference.

Judge not that ye be not judged.
Forgive and it shall be forgiven to you.
Pity that ye may be pitied.
In what measure ye mete, it shall be meted to you again.
Blessed are the poor and they which are persecuted for righteousness' sake: for theirs is the kingdom of heaven.— "Epistle," ii.

These five maxims form only one sentence in Polycarp's Epistle; but they occur, partly in the same, and partly in different words, in Matthew's Gospel, v, 3, 7: vi, 14: vii, 1, 2. They are all found, with variations both of word and thought, in the Sermon on the Mount, but do not help us in determining whether that sermon was delivered at one time, as we now have it in the Gospel of St Matthew, or whether it was compiled out of discourses delivered at different times, and afterwards condensed for convenience of use into one continued address.

But there is another fact connected with this subject which leads to the same conclusion. The Apostolical Fathers, like several other Christian writers, quote sayings of Christ and facts of his history which are not found in our Gospels. If we suppose Barnabas to have quoted, as above, from our Gospel according to St Matthew, from what source did he take the following, which also appears in the seventeenth chapter of his treatise?

Those who wish to see me, and to touch my kingdom, must be contrite and suffering and so take hold of me.

Clement also, in Chapter xlvi of his Epistle, quotes what follows:

It is written: Cleave to holy men; for those who cleave to them shall be made holy.

Now these words do not occur in any part of the New Testament, and many other instances of uncanonical quotations are found in all the Apostolical Fathers. Aware of the importance of this fact, some have endeavoured to explain it by alleging that passages *of similar meaning* are to be found in the New Testament. This explanation however is not satisfactory: for if Barnabas had the New Testament before him, why did he not make use of it by wording his quotations with accuracy? We must not lower our religion or its early teachers by ascribing to them a mode of acting which, on all other subjects, would expose them to contempt. Nor is it necessary to do so; for there is no proof that our New Testament was in existence during the lives of the Apostolical Fathers, who therefore could not make citations out of books which they had never seen.

The foregoing remarks have been made more or less on the supposition that the writings which remain under the names of Barnabas, Clement, Hermas, Ignatius, and Polycarp, were really written by persons who bore those names, and that those persons not only lived in the first century, but were intimate with the Apostles and their companions.

But such admission is, unhappily, more than the cause of truth will warrant. The writings of the Apostolical Fathers labour under a more heavy load of doubt and suspicion than any other ancient compositions either sacred or profane. In former times, when the art of criticism was in its infancy, these writings were ten times as extensive as they are now, and they were circulated without the slightest doubt of their authenticity. But, as the spirit of inquiry grew, and the records of past times were investigated, the mists which obscured the subject were gradually dispersed, and the light of truth began to shine where there had previously been nothing but darkness. Things which had chained and enslaved the mind for ages, dissolved and faded into nothing at the dawn of day, and objects that once held the most unbounded sway over the belief, proved to be unreal beings, creatures of superstition, if not of fraud, placed like the lions in the path of the pilgrim, to deter him from proceeding on the way that leads to the heavenly city of truth.

I have said that the writings of the Apostolical Fathers were once ten times as bulky as at present. The assertion does not pass due bounds: for under that title were once included the works of Dionysius the Areopagite, mentioned in the Acts of the Apostles, and occupying two large folio volumes. When these works, consisting of religious dissertations, had for many hundred years passed as authentic throughout all Christendom, and had even been painfully translated into Latin by Rufinus the celebrated presbyter of Aquileia, a sudden shock was given to the feelings of those who believed in these mysterious volumes. Truth laid its wand upon them and they disappeared from the sight, leaving to their author the narrow limits of fame which he occupies in the Acts of the Apostles—limits beyond which he should never have been compelled to go: for, as an enlightened man and one of the first to recognize the truth of Christianity, his reputation has more brilliancy than all the theological treatises in the world, even if authentic, could bestow. The works of Dionysius the Areopagite were found out to be forgeries, put together, perhaps, by some pious but ill-principled devotee, who thought that the paucity of writings in the first century of the Christian era was a defect, which might better be supplied by fraud than the void be suffered to remain. With the works of Dionysius nine-tenths of primitive Christian writings lost all claim to authenticity: and about 250 pages, as given in the edition of Hefele, were now all that remained of what had once been ascribed to the pens of the contemporaries of the Apostles. But the process of exhaustion was not yet ended. The Shepherd of Hermas, a weak and spiritless train of allegories, and all that remained of their supposed author, soon followed the forged writings of the Areopagite. The Shepherd also was declared to be a forgery, or at all events to have been written by another Hermas who lived many years later, and not the contemporary of the Apostles. This fact is now no more disputed than in the case of Dionysius: no one ventures to say that the work of Hermas is genuine, —unless, perhaps, some solitary and credulous critic rebuilds upon a blind faith the edifice which the free use of reason had demolished.

With Hermas, 130 more pages of testimony disappeared, and the enemies of the authenticity rejoiced in the destruction made in the ranks of their opponents.

But the defenders of the early Christian writers were not dismayed by the process which had thinned their ranks. There were four Apostolical Fathers remaining of the six; and the credit of these could not be shaken. The victory was still theirs, with the compact body of evidence which these four undoubted witnesses supplied. Let us notice the issue, which awaits an examination of the four remaining Apostolical Fathers. It is hard to find words in which to relate the sentence that has already been passed on the Epistle of Barnabas. Hefele, the enlightened and orthodox editor of these writings, has passed the following judgment upon it.

No one will deny that the testimonies are in favour of its authenticity. Nevertheless, we are induced for grave reasons to deny that it is the production of the Apostolic Father.

1. If it had been considered authentic by the ancients, it would have been read in the churches, as Augustine said of the apocryphal writings ascribed to Andrew and John : " If written by them, they would have been received by the church."

2. The epistle was written after the destruction of Jerusalem, as may be conjectured from Chapter 16. But, as we have shown above (Lit. 1), there is no doubt that Barnabas was then dead.

3. In Chapter 5, the Apostles are called " lawless beyond every kind of sin ;" which I think Barnabas, who had been the companion of the Apostles, would hardly have uttered. Such hyperbolical expressions rather suit a rhetorician of the second century.

4. The marvels related in Chapter 10 about the hare, the

XI.]   APOSTOLICAL FATHERS NOT GENUINE.   111

hyæna, &c. savour of some allegorizing trifler rather than of an apostle.

5. Barnabas, who had travelled over all Asia Minor, and lived many years at Antioch in Syria, ought to have known the falsehood of that which is stated in Chapter 9, that the priests of the idols, and all the Syrians were circumcised.

6. There are numerous allegorical trifles, particularly in Chapters 5-11, which could not have been written by him, who, for the vivacity of his eloquence, was called by the Apostles Barnabas, THE SON OF CONSOLATION.

7. There are some errors in Chapters 7 and 8, respecting the Jewish sacred rites, which could not have been committed by Barnabas, who was a Levite, and had dwelt long at Jerusalem.

8. Numerous other inconsistencies are found in the same epistle, &c.

A similar train of reasoning has led Hefele to ascribe the epistle of Barnabas to some writer who lived in the early part of the second century. We need not repeat those reasons, but it is important to remark that, if the work be correctly ascribed to that later period, its making no mention of the four Gospels would equally show that the canon of the New Testament was not even then formed; nor indeed is this inconsistent with our view of those histories. There is no evidence that they existed earlier than the middle of the second century, for they are not named by any writer who lived before that time.

The sentence pronounced upon Barnabas leaves little more than a hundred pages for all that remains of the works of Polycarp, Clement of Rome, and Ignatius. But the work of elimination is not yet ended. Hefele passes the following judgment upon them also.

The authenticity of Polycarp's Epistle has been called in question by the Centuriators of Magdeburg, by Dallæus and others, and defended by Nicolas de Nourry, &c.

We agree to the opinion of Grabius, and Möhler, that the so-called second epistle of Clement was one of the homilies falsely ascribed to him, &c. Wocher thinks it was written by Dionysius bishop of Corinth. But Grabius considers it a spurious work of the middle of the third century.

Fifteen epistles pass under the name of Ignatius . . . . . Of these, eight, by the unanimous decision of the learned, are pronounced to be spurious!

Thus not one of these primitive writers has escaped suspicion. The three survivors, Polycarp, Clement and Ignatius, present a feeble phalanx, quite incompetent to maintain

the communication between A.D. 60, the date of Paul, and
A.D. 150, when Justin Martyr and others are said to continue the process of tradition: and, as we have seen, not one
of these has been allowed to pass unquestioned. A heavy
blow has, within the last few years and since the judgment
of his editor above mentioned, been dealt on Ignatius the
most important even of these. His works, long disputed
because they contained passages supporting certain ecclesiastical ordinances, and in the opinion of many pointing to a
more recent date when those ordinances were better established, had given much labour to Pearson and others to
defend their authenticity. We have seen that in the ancient
MSS brought to Europe from the east, and published by
the Rev. W. Cureton, many of the disputed passages are not
found!

In this way the testimony of the Apostolical Fathers is
reduced within a very small compass. Humbled from the
high office of speaking in the cause of truth, they have to
fight for their own existence. From two folios, they have
dwindled to about the quantity of matter which would fill
fifty pages of the present volume, and still, in this form, they
give no indication that, in their day, the books of the New
Testament were in being. What conclusion may we then
draw from these reasonings? That the four Gospels, in their
present form, were not compiled before the beginning or the
middle of the second century; that consequently they are
not strictly contemporary, however early, records of the
Christian history; that we do wrong in abiding by the
letter when it is quite evident that we have nothing to do
but with their spirit: that adventitious authority adduced in
their support is unnecessary and prejudicial: that they are
to be judged by their own doctrines alone; and that they
derive no more support or illustration from the writings of
the Apostolical Fathers than the sun can receive additional
brilliancy from a wax-taper or a farthing rushlight.

CHAPTER XII.

Papias quoted by Irenæus and Eusebius.

BEFORE we proceed to examine the remains of Justin Martyr, and Irenæus, and numerous minor writers who lived in the second century, it will be convenient to name one of these, of whom undue use has been made to establish what the few fragments which are still extant, seem rather to refute and cancel. I am speaking of Papias, who is quoted by Eusebius in Book iii, chapters 36 and 39, of his "Ecclesiastical History;" and we learn from his authority that Papias was bishop of Hierapolis about the year 100 A.D. and was well skilled in all manner of learning, and well acquainted with the Scriptures—*i.e.* of the Old Testament.

Archdeacon Paley, in his "Evidences of Christianity," brings forward Papias to prove that the books of the New Testament, which we now have, were in existence and publicly known to the world at the time when Papias lived. These are the words of Paley:

> Papias, a hearer of John, and companion of Polycarp, as Irenæus attests, and of that age, as all agree, in a passage quoted by Eusebius, from a work now lost, expressly ascribes the respective Gospels to Matthew and Mark; and in a manner which proves that these Gospels must have publicly borne the names of these authors at that time, and probably long before; for Papias does not say that one Gospel was written by Matthew and another by Mark; but, assuming this as perfectly well known, he tells us from what materials Mark collected his account, namely from Peter's preaching, and in what language Matthew wrote, namely in Hebrew. Whether Papias was well informed in this statement, or not; to the point for which I produce this testimony, namely, that these books bore these names at this time, his authority is complete.

Before we proceed to comment upon these words, let us examine the whole chapter, in Eusebius's "Ecclesiastical History," where almost all that we know of Papias is found.

Of the writings of Papias.

The writings of Papias are said to have been five in number, which are also entitled "Description of our Lord's Oracles." Irenæus also mentions these as the only things written by him: his words are something thus (ὧδέ πως λέγων):

"Papias also, who was the hearer of John and a companion of
"Polycarp, an ancient man, witnesses these things in writing in
"the fourth book of his works. For there are five books compiled
"by him."

These are the words of Irenæus. Papias himself, however, in the preface of his works, shows that he was by no means a hearer and witness of the holy Apostles, but teaches us that he received the things of the faith from those who were known to them [the Apostles]. He says:

"But I will not hesitate to combine with my interpretations
"to you whatever things I formerly well learnt from the elders and
"well remembered, maintaining the truth about them. For I did
"not take pleasure like most men in those who spoke the most,
"but in those who taught the truth; not in those who quoted the
"commands of others but those who [delivered] the commands
"given by our Lord in the faith and the truths that came from it.
"But if by chance any one came who had followed the elders,
"I examined the words of the elders, what said Andrew, or Peter,
"or Philip, or Thomas, or James, or John, or Matthew, or any
"other of the Lord's disciples? and what Aristion and the elder
"John, our Lord's disciples, say. For I did not consider that what
"came out of books would benefit me so much as what came from
"the living and abiding voice."

In this passage we may dwell one moment on the fact that the name of John is there twice mentioned. The former of them he classes with Peter and James, and Matthew and the other apostles, plainly indicating the evangelist. But the other John, diverting his narrative, he includes among those others who were over and above the number of the Apostles, placing him after Aristion. He also plainly names him as elder. So that by these words is shown to be true the statement of those who have said that there were two who bore the same name in Asia, and that there were two monuments in Ephesus, each of which is still said to be that of John. These things are worthy of consideration. For it is probable that the second, if one is not disposed to allow that it was the first, saw the revelation which passes under the name of John. But Papias, of whom we are now speaking, acknowledges that he received the words of the Apostles from those who followed them: and he says that himself was a hearer of Aristion and of the elder John. He at least mentions them often by name, and in his writings gives their traditions. So far then may what I have said be not said fruitlessly. But it is worth while to add to the sayings of Papias which have been related, other sentences of his, in which he records some other marvellous things, as having come to him by tradition. The story of Philip the Apostle having stopped with his daughters at Hierapolis, has already been related. But how Papias tells us that he was in their company and heard a wonderful narrative from Philip's daughters, I will now particularize. He relates the resurrection of a dead man that took place where he was; and again another miracle that happened to Justus surnamed Barsabas, how he drank a rank poison and by the grace of the Lord suffered no harm. This was the Justus, whom, after the resurrection of our Lord, the holy Apostles set up with Matthias and prayed over them, for the drawing of lots to fill up their number in the stead of the traitor Judas; as the book of the Acts thus describes it:

"And they appointed two, Joseph called Barsabas, who was "surnamed Justus, and Matthias: and they prayed and said."

Other things also hath the same [Papias] set forth as having come to him by unwritten tradition, both some strange parables of our Saviour, and teachings of his, and some other mythical things. Among which also he says that there will be a thousand years [MILLENNIUM] after the resurrection from the dead, when Christ will reign bodily upon this earth. This idea I suppose he formed, from having received the apostolical descriptions, not understanding the things which were said by them mystically by way of examples. For he appears to have been a very little-minded man, if we may conjecture from his works; except in the judgment of the greatest part of ecclesiastical writers who came after him, to whom he was in part the cause of their having the same opinion as himself, and who sheltered themselves under the antiquity of the man, such as Irenæus, and others if there be any, who showed that they held the same opinions. But in his own writings he delivers also other descriptions of our Lord's sayings which he got from Aristion already mentioned, and traditions of the elder John: to which we refer those who are desirous of knowing more about them: at present we find it necessary to add to those sayings of his which have been already explained, a tradition respecting Mark who wrote the Gospel, which is thus worded:

"And this the elder said. Mark became the interpreter of "Peter, and wrote accurately as many as he remembered, not "indeed in a regular order, of the things which were said or "done by Christ. For he was neither a hearer nor a follower of "Christ. But afterwards, as I said, he followed Peter, who "delivered his teachings as necessity served, but did not make a "regular arrangement of our Lord's words: so that Mark made "no error, thus writing some things as he delivered them from "memory. For he took forethought of one thing, not to leave "out anything of what he heard, or to make a mistake about "anything therein."

These things are related by Papias about Mark. But about Matthew these are his words:

"Matthew, then, in the Hebrew dialect wrote the oracles: and each person interpreted them as he was able."

The same man uses testimonies from the former epistle of John and likewise from that of Peter. He sets forth, also, another history, concerning the woman, who was charged with many sins before our Lord, and which is contained in the Gospel according to the Hebrews.

It is clear from this account of Papias given by Eusebius, who lived about A.D. 320, that not one of Paley's assertions about him is correct. The evidence, indeed, which we have is mostly at second-hand: Eusebius and Irenæus differ in their accounts: the latter says that Papias was a hearer of John; Eusebius denies this, and proves by the testimony of Papias himself that he was not contemporary with the Apostles but received the rudiments of the faith from an intermediate generation. Neither does Papias "expressly ascribe the respective Gospels to Matthew and Mark." On the contrary, he tells us that Matthew wrote a gospel in the Hebrew language; and there is no proof that the Greek Gospel, now extant, is a translation from a Hebrew original. This explanation rests purely upon conjecture, and cannot be supported by any argument whatever. In the absence of positive proof, we may be allowed to indulge in a harmless conjecture, but not to use that conjecture as a certainty, or to build an inference and a theory upon so weak a foundation.

The notice of St Mark bears a sense still more opposed to that which Paley has attributed to it. Papias tells us that Mark gathered up the various stories which dropped from the mouth and memory of St Peter, and did not make a regular arrangement of our Lord's words, but "writing some things as he [Peter] delivered them." This shows that the Gospel according to St Mark, which we now have, is not the work which was compiled by St Mark: for ours is a "regular arrangement of our Lord's words," written in a regular order, and not a collection of anecdotes, written down promiscuously, as they fell from the mouth of Peter. It is highly probable that all the four Gospels now in existence were compiled out of such fragments and short narratives as had been gathered from the first Apostles, and handed down by tradition: but there is no evidence to show that the four Gospels were, any of them, written by the Apostles themselves.

Little more needs to be said about Papias. Granting, for the moment, that he alludes pointedly, in the extracts quoted from Eusebius, to those very Gospels which we still have, bearing the names of Matthew and of John: why has Paley passed over in silence the Gospel of the Hebrews, which Papias mentions with quite as much respect as those of Matthew and Mark? The argument proves too much ; for, if the words of Papias show the early existence of the canonical Gospels, they also show that the uncanonical ones were equally ancient ; and if Papias alone were our authority, would leave us in a great state of embarrassment how to distinguish the true ones from the false.

CHAPTER XIII.

Justin Martyr—Irenæus—Clemens Alexandrinus.

THE second century of our era opens with a generation of men, who had, in all probability, never conversed with the disciples and first followers of our Lord, from whom they were separated by an interval of seventy years. It is not to be denied that an intermediate race, who had associated with St Paul, may have connected the Apostles with the age of which we are about to speak. But this has no bearing upon the question of the Gospel histories. If, during the seventy years which passed between the Crucifixion, A.D. 30, and the year 100, it cannot be shown that these identical works were actually in existence, but merely that the doctrines and the sayings of Christ, which they contain, were current in tradition only, it is a moral certainty that such deviations as we actually find between one Gospel and another, in relating the same fact, would assuredly take place. The total absence of all allusion to Matthew, Mark, Luke, and John, in the Apostolical Fathers, who alone are said to have been prior to A.D. 100, justifies us in saying that those Fathers were not aware of there being such books as the four evangelical histories: but the fact of their existence is inseparable from that of their being well known to those fathers ; we cannot for an instant suppose that those men could have been ignorant of writings so vitally important to their religion, in comparison with which everything else was as nothing in their sight.

Neither would the recent occurrence of the Christian

miracles, and their currency in tradition, call off the attention of the public, much less of their teachers, from the writings in which all those miracles were related by eye-witnesses. We find, on the contrary, by our own experience, that the freshness of an event gives vogue to the most trivial history in which it is related, so much so that the general estimate of it derives a colouring from the mode in which it is first published to the world in writing, and loses many of the traits by which it was marked in the reality. It is, therefore, from the most weighty reasons which the case will admit of, that we come to the conclusion already stated, that the Gospels were not yet reduced to the form which they now bear, at the beginning of the second century of our era.

If we pursue the investigation further than this date, the same striking peculiarity, which is so evident in the writers of the first century, forces itself on our notice at the beginning of the second. Reference is still made, not to any book in which Christ's doctrines are to be found, but to the doctrines as floating on the wings of tradition, or perhaps even found in short narratives of a fragmentary character.

In the second century we have a large number of writers whose names with a few fragments only remain, and these will recur to our notice in the next chapter. At the end of the same period lived Irenæus and Clement of Alexandria, from whose writings it appears that our present Gospels had been published to the world and were already, with few deviations from our present canon, well known and extensively circulated.

It is much to be regretted that the indiscreet zeal of the early Christians, or the cupidity of copyists—for the true origin of the evil has not been clearly ascertained—should have led to the fabrication of so many writings, ascribed to men of talents and piety, that difficulties spring up before us at almost every step, and envelope the works of the early fathers in a cloud of doubt and mystery almost impenetrable. This evil, which in the case of the Apostolical Fathers led to its own remedy by the ill-judged length to which its authors carried their audacity, becomes, in the second century, more limited in its dimensions and therefore the more uncertain and dangerous in its results.

The process of elimination, which gradually reduced the so-called writings of the first century from two folio volumes to fifty slender pages, would, in the case of profane works, have prepared the inquirer for casting from him the small remnant, even if not fully proved to be spurious—for there is no other case in record of so wide a disproportion between what is genuine and what is not. When nine-tenths of a book has been set aside as worthless, it has seldom been thought worth while to deal with equal delicacy towards the remainder. Like the Æsopic fable, which tells us that the innocent often suffers for his companionship with the guilty, so, also, human tribunals are less charitable about those whose character is doubtful when found in company with notorious and convicted offenders.

The evil, we have observed, follows us into the very middle of the second century; for of the writings ascribed to Justin Martyr and to Irenæus more than half are acknowledged either forgeries, or at all events not authentic. This will be evident from the following list of them.

The latest and best edition of Justin Martyr's works is by Otto, 3 vols, 8vo, Jenæ, 1848. The first volume contains the *Opera Indubitata* or *Undoubted Works* of Justin, which are these:

1. Apologia Major, ad Antoninum Pium—Greater Apology, addressed to Antoninus Pius.
2. Apologia Minor, ad Senatum Romanum—Lesser Apology, addressed to the Roman Senate.
3. Dialogus cum Tryphone Judæo—Dialogue with Trypho the Jew.

Volume II contains the *Opera Addubitata* or *Doubtful Works*:

1. Oratio ad Gentiles—Address to the Gentiles.
2. Cohortatio ad Gentiles—Exhortation to the Gentiles.
3. De Monarchia—On Monarchy.
4. Epistola ad Diognetum—Epistle to Diognetus.

Volume III contains the *Opera Subditicia* or *Spurious Works*:

1. Expositio Rectæ Fidei—Exposition of the True Faith.
2. Epistola ad Zenam et Serenum—Epistle to Zena and Serenus.
3. Confutatio dogmatum quorundam Aristotelis—Refutation of certain dogmas of Aristotle.
4. Quæstiones et Responsiones ad Orthodoxos—Questions and Answers, addressed to the Orthodox.
5. Quæstiones Christianorum ad Gentiles—Questions from Christians to the Gentiles.
6. Quæstiones Gentilium ad Christianos—Questions from the Gentiles to Christians.
7. About twenty or thirty from other books, which have been lost.

This list shows that more than half of the works once ascribed to Justin Martyr are either doubtful or actually spurious. These must, then, be set aside altogether; for they were no doubt written long after the time of Justin, when his authority as an ancient father of the Church was great, and the pious but fraudulent wish to support its dogmas by the weight of his name may have tempted dishonest men to forge such writings—or, perhaps, the pecuniary value of his works allured the avarice of copyists to multiply works and to pass them off upon the world as his; or, by a more charitable judgment, these writings which are called doubtful, may have been written at a later date, and by similarity of name or from some other cause, have been ascribed to him whose name they now bear.

Let us then confine our remarks to those parts of Justin Martyr which are held to be genuine, and turn our attention to the mode in which these remains have been used to support the alleged authenticity of the Gospels, and their contemporaneousness with the facts which they contain.

In the "Evidences of Christianity," chapter IX, § i, 7, we find the following use made of Justin Martyr's works:

Although the nature of his two principal writings, one of which was addressed to heathens, and the other was a conference with a Jew, did not lead him to such frequent appeals to Christian books, as would have appeared in a discourse intended for Christian readers; we nevertheless reckon up in them between twenty and thirty quotations of the Gospels and Acts of the Apostles, certain, distinct, and copious: if each verse be counted separately, a much greater number, if each expression, a very great one.

We meet with quotations of three of the Gospels within the compass of half-a-page.—"And in other words he says, Depart from me into outer darkness, which the Father hath prepared for Satan and his angels," (which is from Matthew xxv, 41). "And again he said in other words, I give unto you power to tread upon serpents, and scorpions, and venomous beasts, and upon all the power of the enemy." (This from Luke x, 19.) "And before he was crucified, he said, The Son of Man must suffer many things, and be rejected of the Scribes and Pharisees, and be crucified, and rise again the third day." (This from Mark viii, 31.)

In another place, Justin quotes a passage in the history of Christ's birth, as delivered by Matthew and John, and fortifies his quotation by this remarkable testimony: "As they have taught, who have written the history of all things concerning our Saviour Jesus Christ; and we believe them." Quotations are also found from the Gospel of St John.

What, moreover, seems extremely material to be observed is, that in all Justin's works, from which might be extracted almost a complete life of Christ, there are but two instances in which he refers to any thing as said or done by Christ, which is not related concerning him in our present Gospels: which shows, that these Gospels, and these, we may say, alone, were the authorities from which the Christians of that day drew the information upon which they depended. One of these instances is of a saying of Christ, not met with in any book now extant.* The other, of a circumstance in Christ's baptism, namely, a fiery or luminous appearance upon the water, which, according to Epiphanius, is noticed in the Gospel of the Hebrews: and which might be true: but which, whether true or false, is mentioned by Justin, with a plain mark of diminution when compared with what he quotes as resting upon Scripture authority. The reader will advert to this distinction: "And then, when Jesus came to the river Jordan, where John was baptizing, as Jesus descended into the water, a fire also was kindled in Jordan; and when he came up out of the water, *the Apostles of this our Christ have written*, that the Holy Ghost lighted upon him as a dove."

All the references in Justin are made without mentioning the author, which proves that these books were perfectly notorious, and that there were no other accounts of Christ then extant, or at least, no others so received and credited as to make it necessary to distinguish these from the rest.

But, although Justin mentions not the author's name, he calls the books, "Memoirs composed by the Apostles and their Companions;" which descriptions, the latter especially, exactly suit with the titles which the Gospels and Acts of the Apostles now bear.

From this notice of Justin Martyr, the hasty reader might be led to infer that the books of the New Testament

---

* To which Paley adds the following note:—"Wherefore also our Lord Jesus Christ has said, In whatsoever I shall find you, in the same I will also judge you." Possibly Justin intended not to quote any text, but to represent the sense of many of our Lord's sayings. Fabricius has observed, that this saying has been quoted by many writers, and that Justin is the only one who ascribes it to our Lord, and that perhaps by a slip of his memory.

Words resembling these are read repeatedly in Ezekiel: "I will judge them according to their ways" (chap. vii, 3; xxxiii, 20). It is remarkable that Justin had just before expressly quoted Ezekiel. Mr Jones upon this circumstance founded a conjecture, that Justin wrote only "the Lord hath said," intending to quote the words of God, or rather the sense of those words in Ezekiel; and that some transcriber, imagining these to be the words of Christ, inserted in his copy the addition "Jesus Christ." Vol. i, p. 539.

were, at all events in Justin's time, perfectly well known and formed into a canon, as we now have them, to the exclusion of all other unrecognized gospels, of which a great number were even then or within a few years known to be in being. Here then at last, he would infer, must a limit be placed to those speculations which ascribed to them a later origin than the age of the Apostles themselves. The testimony of Justin Martyr who wrote his " Apology for the Christians " in A.D. 151, must remove all doubt that the four evangelic histories were already in his time the basis of Christian teaching and the exclusive record of Christ's life and miracles. Such also is the common opinion respecting the origin of the Gospels: taking for granted the report made by Lardner, and from him copied into the " Evidences of Christianity," few persons have ever compared the report with the original witnesses ; and never felt a misgiving that statements could, even unintentionally, be so perverted. Justin does not name a single writer of the eight, who are said to have written the books of the New Testament. The very names of the evangelists Matthew, Mark, Luke and John, are never mentioned by him—do not occur once in all his works. It is therefore not true that he has quoted from our existing Gospels, and so proves their existence, as they now are, in his own time. It is *possible* that they were then in being ; but, if so, they did not pass under the names by which they are now known, nor were they held in the same estimation as now: or they would certainly have been quoted, not vaguely, but specifically, by Justin Martyr. That they were " perfectly notorious," and Justin therefore has not named their authors, is a rhetorical flourish on the part of Paley: for Justin has not even named the books themselves, much less their writers. He has nowhere remarked, like those fathers of the Church who lived several ages after him, that there are *four Gospels*, of higher importance and estimation than any others, forming the Christian canon, and he probably would have been astonished to hear the arguments of some later fathers to prove, by the most irrelevant analogies, that four Gospels, and only four were necessary to maintain the Christian faith. All this was the growth of a later age, but is wanting in Justin Martyr, and we are thus led to the conclusion that our four Gospels had not then emerged from obscurity, but were still, if in being, confounded with a larger mass of Christian traditions which about this very time were beginning to be set down in writing. The age of Justin Martyr, we must remember, was the very age, in which the unscrupulous Peregrinus, whose history we have given from Lucian, professed himself a Christian, and beat the Christians at their own weapons,—expounded their books for them—wrote others himself, and ended by deserting their brotherhood as hastily as he had entered it. The age of Justin Martyr was the age when books would naturally begin to be written; for the obscurity of the first generation of Christians had given way to a more flourishing condition. The sect was emerging into importance, and as tradition would no longer preserve the truths of Christianity and the miraculous history of its founder, it behoved them to collect together these traditions and to store them up for the use of future times. A multitude of Gospels, Acts of different Apostles, Epistles, and Revelations then swarmed into life. Many of these have come down either wholly or in substance to our times; and Justin Martyr has actually mentioned facts and sayings of Christ which are found in such uncanonical gospels only. These assertions must now be substantiated by a more close examination of the works which are believed to be his genuine productions.

1. Justin Martyr never once mentions by name the evangelists Matthew, Mark, Luke, and John —This circumstance is of great importance; for those who assert that our four canonical Gospels are contemporary records of our Saviour's ministry, ascribe them to Matthew, Mark, Luke, and John, and to no other writers. But Justin Martyr, it must be remembered, wrote about A.D. 150, and neither he, nor any writer before him, has alluded, in the most remote degree, to four specific Gospels bearing the names of Matthew, Mark, Luke, and John; nor does any other writer until the end of the century bear any certain or even probable testimony to the authorship which is generally ascribed to our books.

2. Justin Martyr never, if we except an interpolated passage, mentions even any book called a gospel.—The four histories, which contain the life of Christ, have for sixteen centuries borne the name of Gospels—a word compounded of two old English words *good* and *spell*, and these literally represent in our tongue the Greek word *euangelion*, which during the same long period has been used to express the same idea in the original language. But the word itself is not of Christian origin, although its use has long been limited to the books which now bear that name. It occurs twice in Homer's "Odyssey" (xiv. 152. 166), where it is generally translated a "reward for good news," but it is doubtful whether

in these passages the word for reward is not to be understood, in which case *euangelion* would be an adjective, but in either case the word in the Greek and Roman writers implies an abstract quality and not a material thing. In this sense too it is to be understood in the early ages of Christianity, and in no other sense does Justin Martyr use this term. The truth of this observation may be shown by citing two passages in which the word occurs. The first of these is in the tenth chapter of his " Dialogue with Trypho the Jew," who used these words :—

I know that those precepts of yours in that which is called the Gospel (ἐν τῷ λεγομένῳ Εὐαγγελίῳ) are so wonderful and great, that we suspect it is not possible for any one to observe them : for I have made it my business to obtain a sight of them.

In the 100th chapter of the same Dialogue Justin says:

But he is described in the Gospel also as saying: " All things have been given to me by my Father, and no one knows the Father except the Son, nor the Son except the Father and those to whom the Son shall reveal him." He hath then revealed (ἀπεκάλυψεν) to us all things as many as we have understood (νενοήκαμεν)* through his grace from the Scriptures.

Here we have no mention of a book but only of the Christian Dispensation " called the Gospel," and in the last extract this interpretation is confirmed by the mention of the Scriptures: for not only in the time of Justin, but long afterwards this term was used to denote the Old Testament, and in almost all such cases the names of those who wrote those ancient Scriptures are expressly given, contrasting strongly with the quotations from the Gospel, which was long in circulation before the various records were collected into the four books which we now have, bearing the names of those Apostles, under whose authority these records were first circulated.

But there is a third passage in Justin Martyr which must not be passed over.

The apostles, in the Memorials made by them *which are called*

---

* The classical scholar will observe the difference of tense, which confirms the interpretation given in the text. Jesus " has lately been revealing " to us things which we had previously understood from the Scriptures of the Old Testament. The past tense in Greek denotes some previous definite time: the aorist represents the action as continuing during an indefinite period, even down to the present time.

Gospels (ἐν τοῖς γενομένοις ὑπ' αὐτῶν ἀπομνημονεύμασιν, ἃ καλεῖται Εὐαγγέλια), have handed down that Jesus instructed them thus: that having taken bread and given thanks, he said "Do this in remembrance of me."

Here for the first time we meet with the word *evangelia* in the plural number—a word until then restricted to the doctrines of Christianity, and therefore not admitting a plural number. The absence of any other similar passage in which our Gospels are so indicated, may have been the chief reason why Schleiermacher long ago pointed out that this is an instance of a gloss or side-note, which had crept into the text.

But the use of the word *Evangel* to denote the Christian Dispensation is illustrated by the use of a kindred term Evangelist to denote the person who preached or propagated that Dispensation: and here again we find that for a very long time this name was used to denote not those who wrote histories of Christ and of Christianity, but those who went about in the earliest ages of our religion to evangelize and preach its doctrines. Thus Philip is surnamed the Evangelist in Acts xxi, 8, and it is well known that he went about to preach the Gospel. The same no doubt is the meaning of the term in Ephesians iv, 11. where St Paul classifies the various ministers as Apostles, Prophets, Evangelists, Pastors, and Teachers. Nor is there any reason why the same interpretation does not apply to the Second Epistle to Timothy, iv, 5: "Do the work of an evangelist." It is clear, also, not only from these passages, but also from other later writings, that the term Evangelist was not restricted or even applied especially to Matthew, Mark, Luke, and John. Any one, whatever his position in the early Church, might become an evangelist by going about to preach the Gospel. Nor does the term seem to have been restricted to the four in much later times. Theodoret and Chrysostom define the term as applicable to travelling preachers, and Eusebius, speaking of Pantænus the philosopher, who, about the year 180 A.D. in the course of his ministry went as far as India, continues his narrative as follows:—

For there were even up to that time many Evangelists of the Word purposing to introduce a divine zeal of apostolic imitation for the increase and building up of the Divine Word.—*H. E.* v, 10.

The same historian tells us elsewhere that eighty years or more before Pantænus, the same process of evangelizing was carried on.

Setting out on foreign journeys, they fulfilled the work of evangelists, being ambitious to preach Christ to those who had still never heard at all of the faith and to deliver the writing of the divine Gospels.—37. . . . . . . But it is impossible for us to enumerate by name all who formerly according to the first succession of the Apostles became shepherds or even evangelists in the Churches throughout the world.—*H. E.* iii, 36.

3. Justin Martyr several times alludes to Memorials of the Apostles, Ἀπομνημονεύματα Ἀποστόλων, in general terms, without the slightest indication of their number, nature, or extent.—Six passages are here given in an English translation.

An angel of God brought to her the glad tidings, saying, "Behold, thou shalt conceive in thy womb by the Holy Spirit, and bring forth a son, and He shall be called Son of the Highest, and thou shalt call His name Jesus: for He shall save His people from their sins, as those have taught, who have recorded all things concerning our Saviour Jesus Christ."—*Vol.* i, p. 86, *ed. Otto.*

Compare with this Matthew i, 21, and Luke i, 31.

On the day called the day of the Sun a meeting in one place is held, of all who dwell in the cities or the country; and the memorials of the Apostles or the writings of the prophets are read, as long as there is time. Then when the reader has done, the president, in a speech, makes an admonition and exhortation to imitate these good men. Then we stand up all of us together and send forth prayers. And, when we have ended the prayer, as we said before, bread, and wine, and water are brought, and the president utters at the same time prayers and thanksgivings, as well as he is able, and the people give assent saying Amen, and the distribution and partaking of the things blessed is made to each, and is sent to those who are absent, by means of the attendants [DEACONS]. Those who are well off and willing give each at his own option what he chooses, and what is collected is placed before the president, who gives assistance to both orphans and widows, and to those who are left from illness or any other cause, and to those who are in bonds, and to strangers resident among them, and, generally, he becomes a guardian to all who are in need. We all in common come to the meeting on the day of the Sun, since it is the first day, on which God, having changed darkness and matter, made the world, and Jesus Christ our Saviour rose from the dead on the same day: for they crucified Him on the day before Saturn's day, and on the day after Saturn's day, which is the day of the Sun, appearing to His Apostles and disciples He taught these things which we have given out to you also for consideration.—Vol. i, p. 158.

For also when giving up His breath on the cross, He said, "Father, into Thy hands I commend my spirit," as also I learnt this also from the Memorials. For it is written in the Memorials that when urging His disciples to surpass the system of the Pharisees, or, if not, to be assured that they would not be saved, He said to them these words: " Except your righteousness shall exceed the righteousness of the Scribes and Pharisees, ye shall in no case enter into the kingdom of heaven."—Vol. i, p. 358.

Being with them he sang a hymn to God, as also is shown to have been done in the Memorials of the Apostles, &c. . . . . and that he changed the name of one of his disciples to Peter, this also is written in his Memorials, together with his also changing the names of two other brethren, sons of Zebedee, calling them Boanerges, that is, Sons of Thunder.—Vol. i, p. 361.

This last extract is peculiar for having not αὐτῶν *their* memorials, *i. e.* the memorials of the Apostles, but αὐτοῦ *his* memorials; and it is doubtful whether the memorials of Peter or of Christ are meant. The learned editor Otto says that, if six hundred manuscripts were in favour of the common reading αὐτοῦ, he would alter it to αὐτῶν. This bold style of criticism is certainly convenient for those who adjust facts to theories, but not for those who adapt their theories to facts. As αὐτοῦ and not αὐτῶν is the actual reading, we must infer that either Peter's memorials or Christ's memorials are here spoken of. If Peter's, no such book is now known to exist: if Christ's, the expression is too vague to designate the four canonical Gospels, and may refer to the uncanonical writings or to any other traditionary accounts.

The star then having appeared in the heaven at the time of his birth, as is written in the Memorials of his Apostles, the magi of Arabia, knowing him from this, came and worshipped him.— Vol. i, p. 362.

And because he was to rise from the dead on the third day after his crucifixion, it is written in the Memorials, that those of your nation questioning him, said, Show us a sign. And he answered to them, An evil and adulterous generation seeketh after a sign; and there shall no sign be given to them, but the sign of Jonas.—Vol. i, p. 362.

4. Justin Martyr has nowhere mentioned any of the Epistles, nor even once named Paul or any other of the Apostles, except John and the remark that Christ changed Simon's name to Peter, &c. This is a fact not to be overlooked: not even the Epistles, which bear the names of Paul, Peter, James, John, and Jude, nor any of their writers, are ever once mentioned by Justin Martyr. Is not this a sign that the distinctness, into which these works, with the names of their writers, have since then been

brought, is the result of a development which had hardly begun in the time of Justin Martyr? Even the change of Simon's name to Peter, so briefly noticed in the extract quoted in page 127, confirms this view of the gradual growth of our Gospels out of original memoranda and no doubt also of primitive traditions; for by describing Peter as one of the Apostles, Justin seems to suppose that without this explanation his readers would not know who Peter was.

5. Justin Martyr has, in a remarkable passage, named one John, to whom a revelation was made by God, in terms showing plainly that Justin Martyr knew no more about the canon of the New Testament than we do. As this is an important extract, the Greek is here given with the English in parallel columns.

Καὶ ἔπειτα καὶ παρ' ἡμῖν ἀνήρ τις, ᾧ ὄνομα Ἰωάννης, εἷς τῶν ἀποστόλων τοῦ Χριστοῦ, ἐν ἀποκαλύψει γενομένῃ αὐτῷ χίλια ἔτη ποιήσειν ἐν Ἱερουσαλὴμ τοὺς τῷ ἡμετέρῳ Χριστῷ πιστεύσαντας προεφήτευσε, καὶ μετὰ ταῦτα τὴν καθολικὴν καὶ, συνελόντι φάναι, αἰωνίαν ὁμοθυμαδὸν ἅμα πάντων ἀνάστασιν γενήσεσθαι καὶ κρίσιν. Ὅπερ καὶ ὁ Κύριος ἡμῶν εἶπεν, ὅτι Οὔτε γαμήσουσιν οὔτε γαμηθήσονται, ἀλλ' ἰσάγγελοι ἔσονται, τέκνα τοῦ Θεοῦ τῆς ἀναστάσεως ὄντες. (vol. 1, p. 282.)

And then among us also, a *certain man, whose name was John,* one of the Apostles of Christ, in *a revelation made to him*, prophesied that those who believed on our Christ would spend a thousand years in Jerusalem, and after this would be the general, and to speak briefly, the eternal resurrection and judgment of all men; which also our Lord has said, They shall neither marry nor be given in marriage, but shall be equal to the angels, being the children of the God of the resurrection.

Is this the language of a writer who regarded "*the Revelation not a revelation of St John the Divine*" as a portion of the holy word of God, distinct from all other revelations whatever? Does Justin Martyr speak of the favourite Apostle John in these unseemly terms as *a certain man,* "one John" as we might render it? The zeal of the commentators has here greatly damaged the books of the New Testament by asserting that the early fathers quoted them, especially in such disparaging terms as these! If our books of the New Testament were at that time in circulation, and known to the world as verbally inspired, their writers, especially one, whose name is so prominent as that of John, would hardly have been quoted in such words as Justin Martyr uses to describe the writer of the Revelation; for his language, instead of manifesting his respect for the writer and his book, only tends to show in what little esteem he held both the one and the other. But it is fair to add that even in the early days of Christianity it was doubted by many whether the Revelation which has been admitted into the canon was really the work of John the Evangelist or not.

6. Justin Martyr has in six instances—not two only, as Paley erroneously states—quoted sayings of Christ, or events of Christ's life, which do not occur in our Gospels, but were found in other uncanonical writings.

The six instances here follow:

1. For an ass's foal was standing at a certain entrance to a village, tied to a vine.—Vol. i, p. 82, *ed. Otto*.

That the foal was *tied*, is apparent from the canonical Gospel, but that it was tied to a *vine* nowhere appears in our books: Justin Martyr obtained this additional fact from some other source, perhaps from tradition.

2. For also, as said the prophet, mocking him, they placed him on a tribunal, and said, "Give judgment for us."—Vol. i, p. 90.

Our Gospels relate that the soldiers plaited a crown of thorns for Jesus, and placed a reed by way of sceptre in his hand: but they are silent about his being placed on a *tribunal* or judgement seat. Yet this additional act of mockery perhaps was related in some other of the numerous gospels not admitted into the canon.

3. Wherefore also our Lord Jesus Christ said, "In whatsoever things I shall apprehend you, in those also will I judge you."— Vol. i, p. 156.

This saying of Christ occurs nowhere in our Gospels, but was no doubt to be found somewhere or other, in Justin Martyr's time, or he would not have quoted it. Grotius and others think that it is taken from the Gospel according to the Hebrews.

4. The child then being born in Bethlehem, when Joseph had no place to put up at in that village, he put up in a cave near the village, and then, whilst they were there, Mary brought forth Christ, and placed him in a manger, where those who came from Arabia found him.—Vol. I, pt ii, p. 268.

In this extract we recognize a particular of Christ's history, related not by either of the canonical Gospels, but by the Protevangelium Jacobi, Historia Josephi, Evangelium Infantiæ, and Historia de Nativitate Mariæ, all apocryphal works,* not received by the Church.

5. And then when Jesus had gone to the river Jordan, where John was baptizing, Jesus having gone down into the water, both a fire was kindled in the Jordan, and when he came up from the water, the apostles of this same our Christ have written that the holy spirit lighted upon him like a dove.—Vol. I, pt ii, p. 306.

This kindling of a fire in Jordan is evidently a fact not to be gathered from the canonical Gospels: Justin Martyr read it in one of the numerous uncanonical works with which the early ages of Christianity abounded. It was found among others, in *Prædicatio Pauli,* "The Preaching of Paul," a work now lost ; in the Gospel of the Ebionites, mentioned by Epiphanius, *Hæres.* 30, § 13 ; and in the Sibylline Oracles, a work still extant, Lib. vii, 81-83.

6. To whom also he [John the Baptist] cried out, " I am not the Christ, but the voice of one crying: for there shall come he who is stronger than I, whose shoes I am not able to carry." And Jesus having come to the Jordan, and being thought to be the son of Joseph the carpenter, and appearing uncomely, as the scriptures foretold, and being thought to be a carpenter (for whilst he was among men he made these works of a carpenter, ploughs and yokes, teaching by means of them tokens of justice and an active life), the holy spirit also, for man's sake, as I said before, lighted on him in the shape of a dove, and a voice came at the same time from heaven, which also was spoken by David, as saying in his person what was about to be addressed to him by the Father, " Thou art my son ; this day have I begotten thee," meaning that he was then born to men, when their knowledge of him first began.—Vol. I, pt ii, p. 308.

That our Saviour was the son of a carpenter is known from our canonical Gospels, but that he himself worked at that trade is related in two of the uncanonical writings, namely the " Gospel of our Saviour's Infancy," and the " Gospel of St Thomas." In the latter, *ploughs* and *yokes* are especially named as the articles which he was occupied in making ; and it is possible that Justin Martyr quoted the fact from this very uncanonical gospel of St Thomas.

The quotations, which we have thus minutely examined,

---

* All these are to be found in the editions of Apocryphal writers named in page 32 of this volume.

lead us to believe that Justin Martyr draws from many sources, some of which are now no longer in being, and not from the four Gospels only. Indeed he appears not to have known that there were four and four only authentic records of our Saviour's teaching. This view will be confirmed if we find that the sayings of Christ which he quotes are not in exactly the same words as we read in our existing four Gospels. This is actually the case. In hardly a single instance does he quote the exact words which we find in Matthew, Mark, Luke, and John, but rather the same in substance; and in some cases we cannot find any single sentence in our four Gospels corresponding even in sense with the words of Justin Martyr, but are obliged to form a compound of words brought together from two or more of the canonical Gospels.

This seems to prove that Justin quotes the sayings from the current traditions of the day, and from a variety of memorials relating the deeds of Christ and his apostles. Nor is it to be wondered at that Christ's expressions should be remarkably similar in these different traditions and narratives, for they were peculiarly adapted for being remembered.

In the First Apology, said to have been addressed to the Roman emperor Antoninus Pius, Justin himself notices their short and pithy character:

Βραχεῖς δὲ καὶ σύντομοι παρ' αὐτοῦ λόγοι γεγόνασιν· οὐ γὰρ σοφιστὴς ὑπῆρχεν· ἀλλὰ δύναμις θεοῦ ὁ λόγος αὐτοῦ ἦν. APOL. I, § 14.

The sayings that came from him were short and concise: for he was not a sophist, but his word was the power of a god.

This peculiarity, it must be observed, rendered it easy for Christ's sayings to be preserved and handed down to posterity, as we find they were, with very little verbal disagreement, and yet disagreeing slightly, as we, in fact, read them, in the four Gospels, in Justin Martyr, and elsewhere.

I shall now copy word for word the first ten sentences of Justin Martyr, which seem to be taken from our four Gospels, and place in parallel columns the passages of similar import, from Matthew, Mark, Luke, and John, which Justin Martyr is said to have quoted. The object of this comparison will be to show that Justin Martyr gives us Christ's sayings in their traditionary forms and not in the words which are found in our four Gospels: it is evident that this argument addresses itself to the learned reader alone:

as the identity of quotation can be proved or disproved, not in a translation, but in the original language only.

1.

[Περὶ μὲν οὖν σωφροσύνης τοσοῦτον εἶπεν·] Ὅς ἂν ἐμβλέψῃ γυναικὶ πρὸς τὸ ἐπιθυμῆσαι αὐτῆς ἤδη ἐμοίχευσε τῇ καρδίᾳ παρὰ τῷ Θεῷ.

The same sentiment is found in Matthew, v, 28, but the words are different:

Πᾶς ὁ βλέπων γυναῖκα πρὸς τὸ ἐπιθυμῆσαι αὐτῆς, ἤδη ἐμοίχευσεν αὐτὴν ἐν τῇ καρδίᾳ αὐτοῦ.

Why did Justin Martyr write Ὅς ἂν ἐμβλέψῃ, when, if he had St Matthew's Gospel before him, he might with more ease and accuracy have written Πᾶς ὁ βλέπων? Why also has he omitted αὐτὴν and added παρὰ τῷ Θεῷ, if he might have cited the passage more correctly from St Matthew's Gospel, then lying before him? The solution is that he cites a well-known saying, current in tradition, and perhaps also in numberless brief documents handed down as records of what Christ had said and taught.

2.

Εἰ ὁ ὀφθαλμός σου ὁ δεξιὸς σκανδαλίζει σε, ἔκκοψον αὐτόν· συμφέρει γάρ σοι μονόφθαλμον εἰσελθεῖν εἰς τὴν βασιλείαν τῶν οὐρανῶν, ἢ μετὰ τῶν δύο πεμφθῆναι εἰς τὸ αἰώνιον πῦρ.

This passage is very like to Matthew, v, 29:

Εἰ [δὲ] ὁ ὀφθαλμός σου ὁ δεξιὸς σκανδαλίζει σε, ἔξελε αὐτὸν, καὶ βάλε ἀπὸ σοῦ· συμφέρει γάρ σοι, ἵνα ἀπόληται ἓν τῶν μελῶν σου, καὶ μὴ ὅλον τὸ σῶμά σου βληθῇ εἰς γέενναν.

But it is also like Matthew, xviii, 9:

Εἰ ὁ ὀφθαλμός σου σκανδαλίζει σε, ἔξελε αὐτὸν, καὶ βάλε ἀπὸ σοῦ· καλόν σοι ἐστὶ μονόφθαλμον εἰς τὴν ζωὴν εἰσελθεῖν, ἢ δύο ὀφθαλμοὺς ἔχοντα βληθῆναι εἰς τὴν γέενναν τοῦ πυρός.

And it bears an equal likeness to Mark, ix, 47:

Ἐὰν ὁ ὀφθαλμός σου σκανδαλίζει σε, ἔκβαλε αὐτόν· καλόν σοι ἐστὶ μονόφθαλμον εἰσελθεῖν εἰς τὴν βασιλείαν τοῦ Θεοῦ, ἢ δύο ὀφθαλμοὺς ἔχοντα βληθῆναι εἰς τὴν γέενναν τοῦ πυρός.

Yet, strange to say, it is not identical in words with either of the three.

3.

Ὅς γαμεῖ ἀπολελυμένην ἀφ' ἑτέρου ἀνδρὸς μοιχᾶται.

Matthew and Luke may be compared, but only to detect a difference:

Matt. v, 32. Ὅς ἐὰν ἀπολελυμένην γαμήσῃ, μοιχᾶται.

Luke xvi, 18. Πᾶς ὁ ἀπολελυμένην ἀπὸ ἀνδρὸς γαμῶν, μοιχεύει.

4.

Εἰσί τινες οἵτινες εὐνουχίσθησαν ὑπὸ τῶν ἀνθρώπων, εἰσὶ δ' οἱ ἐγεννήθησαν εὐνοῦχοι, εἰσὶ δὲ οἱ εὐνούχισαν ἑαυτοὺς διὰ τὴν βασιλείαν τῶν οὐρανῶν· πλὴν οὐ πάντες τοῦτο χωροῦσιν.

This is a paraphrase rather than a quotation of the following in St Matthew's Gospel.

Matt. xix, 12. Εἰσὶ γὰρ εὐνοῦχοι, οἵτινες ἐκ κοιλίας μητρὸς ἐγεννήθησαν οὕτω· καὶ εἰσὶν εὐνοῦχοι, οἵτινες εὐνουχίσθησαν ὑπὸ τῶν ἀνθρώπων· καί εἰσιν εὐνοῦχοι, οἵτινες εὐνούχισαν ἑαυτοὺς διὰ τὴν βασιλείαν τῶν οὐρανῶν. Ὁ δυνάμενος χωρεῖν, χωρείτω.

5.

[Εἶπε δὲ οὕτως·] Οὐκ ἦλθον καλέσαι δικαίους ἀλλ' ἁμαρτωλοὺς εἰς μετάνοιαν.

These words are found in three of the canonical Gospels:

Matt. ix, 13. Οὐκ ἦλθον καλέσαι δικαίους ἀλλ' ἁμαρτωλοὺς εἰς μετάνοιαν.

Mark ii, 19. Οὐκ ἦλθον καλέσαι δικαίους, ἀλλ' ἁμαρτωλοὺς εἰς μετάνοιαν.

Luke v, 32. Οὐκ ἐλήλυθα καλέσαι δικαίους, ἀλλ' ἁμαρτωλοὺς εἰς μετάνοιαν.

In this only instance is there a perfect agreement between the words of Justin and the Gospels, two of which, Matthew and Mark—not Luke exactly—give the same saying of Christ in the same words. A variety of thoughts here rush upon the mind. Are these three Gospels based upon a common document? If so, is not Justin Martyr's citation drawn from the same anonymous document, rather than from the three Gospels, seeing that he does not name them? If, on the other hand, Justin has cited them accurately in this instance, why has he failed to do so in the others? For no other reason than that traditional sayings are generally thus irregularly exact or inexact, and Justin, citing from them, has been as irregularly exact as they were.

6.

[Περὶ δὲ τοῦ στέργειν ἅπαντας ταῦτα ἐδίδαξεν.] Εἰ ἀγαπᾶτε τοὺς ἀγαπῶντας ὑμᾶς, τί καινὸν ποιεῖτε ; καὶ γὰρ οἱ πόρνοι τοῦτο ποιοῦσιν.

Matt. v, 46. Ἐὰν γὰρ ἀγαπή- σητε τοὺς ἀγαπῶντας ὑμᾶς, τίνα μισθὸν ἔχετε ; οὐχὶ καὶ οἱ τελῶναι τὸ αὐτὸ ποιοῦσι ;

Luke vi, 32. Εἰ ἀγαπᾶτε τοὺς ἀγαπῶντας ὑμᾶς, ποία ὑμῖν χάρις ἐστί ; καὶ γὰρ οἱ ἁμαρτωλοὶ τοὺς ἀγαπῶντας αὐτοὺς ἀγαπῶσι.

7.

Ἐγὼ δὲ ὑμῖν λέγω· Εὔχεσθε ὑπὲρ τῶν ἐχθρῶν ὑμῶν καὶ ἀγαπᾶτε τοὺς μισοῦντας ὑμᾶς, καὶ εὐλογεῖτε τοὺς καταρωμένους ὑμῖν καὶ εὔχεσθε ὑπὲρ τῶν ἐπηρεαζόντων ὑμᾶς.

Matt. v, 44. Ἐγὼ δὲ λέγω ὑμῖν, Ἀγαπᾶτε τοὺς ἐχθροὺς ὑμῶν, εὐλογεῖτε τοὺς καταρωμένους ὑμᾶς, καλῶς ποιεῖτε τοῖς μισοῦσιν ὑμᾶς, καὶ προσεύχεσθε ὑπὲρ τῶν ἐπηρεαζόντων ὑμᾶς καὶ διωκόντων ὑμᾶς.

Luke vi, 27. Ἀλλ' ὑμῖν λέγω τοῖς ἀκούουσιν, Ἀγαπᾶτε τοὺς ἐχθροὺς ὑμῶν· καλῶς ποιεῖτε τοῖς μισοῦσιν ὑμᾶς· εὐλογεῖτε τοὺς καταρωμένους ὑμῖν· προσεύχεσθε ὑπὲρ τῶν ἐπηρεαζόντων ὑμᾶς.

8.

[Εἰς δὲ τὸ κοινωνεῖν τοῖς δεομένοις καὶ μηδὲν πρὸς δόξαν ποιεῖν ταῦτα ἔφη.] Παντὶ τῷ αἰτοῦντι δίδοτε καὶ τὸν βουλόμενον δανείσασθαι μὴ ἀποστραφῆτε. Εἰ γὰρ δανείζετε παρ' ὧν ἐλπίζετε λαβεῖν, τί καινὸν ποιεῖτε ; τοῦτο καὶ οἱ τελῶναι ποιοῦσιν.

Matt. v, 42. Τῷ αἰτοῦντί σε δίδου καὶ τὸν θέλοντα ἀπὸ σοῦ δανείσασθαι, μὴ ἀποστραφῇς.

Luke vi, 30-34. Παντὶ δὲ τῷ αἰτοῦντί σε δίδου, καὶ ἀπὸ τοῦ αἴροντος τὰ σὰ μὴ ἀπαίτει... (v. 34.) Καὶ ἐὰν δανείζητε παρ' ὧν ἐλπίζετε ἀπολαβεῖν, ποία ὑμῖν χάρις ἐστί ; καὶ γὰρ οἱ ἁμαρτωλοὶ ἁμαρτωλοῖς δανείζουσιν, ἵνα ἀπολάβωσι τὰ ἴσα.

9.

Ὑμεῖς δὲ μὴ θησαυρίζητε ἑαυτοῖς ἐπὶ τῆς γῆς, ὅπου σὴς καὶ βρῶσις ἀφανίζει καὶ λῃσταὶ διορύσσουσι· θησαυρίζετε δὲ ἑαυτοῖς ἐν τοῖς οὐρανοῖς, ὅπου οὔτε σὴς οὔτε βρῶσις ἀφανίζει.

Matt. vi, 19-20. Μὴ θησαυρίζετε ὑμῖν θησαυροὺς ἐπὶ τῆς γῆς, ὅπου σὴς καὶ βρῶσις ἀφανίζει, καὶ ὅπου κλέπται διορύσσουσι καὶ κλέπτουσι· Θησαυρίζετε δὲ ὑμῖν θησαυροὺς ἐν οὐρανῷ, ὅπου οὔτε σὴς οὔτε βρῶσις ἀφανίζει.

10.

Τί γὰρ ὠφελεῖται ἄνθρωπος, ἂν τὸν κόσμον ὅλον κερδήσῃ, τὴν δὲ ψυχὴν αὐτοῦ ἀπολέσῃ ; ἢ τί δώσει αὐτῆς ἀντάλλαγμα ; Θησαυρίζετε οὖν ἐν τοῖς οὐρανοῖς, ὅπου οὔτε σὴς οὔτε βρῶσις ἀφανίζει.

Matt. xvi, 26. Τί γὰρ ὠφελεῖται ἄνθρωπος, ἐὰν τὸν κόσμον ὅλον κερδήσῃ, τὴν δὲ ψυχὴν αὐτοῦ ζημιωθῇ ; ἢ τί δώσει ἄνθρωπος ἀντάλλαγμα τῆς ψυχῆς αὐτοῦ ; Matt. vi, 20. Θησαυρίζετε δὲ ὑμῖν θησαυροὺς ἐν οὐρανῷ, ὅπου οὔτε σὴς οὔτε βρῶσις ἀφανίζει.

11.

Γίνεσθε δὲ χρηστοὶ καὶ οἰκτίρμονες, ὡς καὶ ὁ πατὴρ ὑμῶν χρηστός ἐστι καὶ οἰκτίρμων, καὶ τὸν ἥλιον αὐτοῦ ἀνατέλλει ἐπὶ ἁμαρτωλοὺς καὶ δικαίους καὶ πονηρούς.

Matt. v, 45. Ὅτι τὸν ἥλιον αὐτοῦ ἀνατέλλει ἐπὶ πονηροὺς καὶ ἀγαθοὺς καὶ βρέχει ἐπὶ δικαίους καὶ ἀδίκους.

Luke vi, 35. Γίνεσθε οὖν οἰκτίρμονες, καθὼς καὶ ὁ πατὴρ ὑμῶν οἰκτίρμων ἐστί.

12.

Μὴ μεριμνᾶτε δὲ τί φάγητε ἢ τί ἐνδύσησθε. Οὐχ ὑμεῖς τῶν πετεινῶν καὶ τῶν θηρίων διαφέρετε ; Καὶ ὁ Θεὸς τρέφει αὐτά. Μὴ οὖν μεριμνήσητε τί φάγητε ἢ τί ἐνδύσησθε· οἶδε γὰρ ὁ πατὴρ ὑμῶν ὁ οὐράνιος ὅτι τούτων χρείαν ἔχετε. Ζητεῖτε δὲ τὴν βασιλείαν τῶν οὐρανῶν, καὶ ταῦτα πάντα προστεθήσεται ὑμῖν. Ὅπου γὰρ ὁ θησαυρός ἐστιν, ἐκεῖ καὶ ὁ νοῦς τοῦ ἀνθρώπου.

To make up this passage in Justin Martyr, we are obliged to join together several from the Gospels of St Matthew and St Luke.

Matt. vi, 25. . . . . Μὴ μεριμνᾶτε τῇ ψυχῇ ὑμῶν, τί φάγητε καὶ τί πίητε· μηδὲ τῷ σώματι ὑμῶν, τί ἐνδύσησθε.
(31.) Μὴ οὖν μεριμνήσητε, λέγοντες· Τί φάγωμεν, ἢ τί πίωμεν, ἢ τί περιβαλώμεθα.
(32.) . . . Οἶδε γὰρ ὁ πατὴρ ὑμῶν ὁ οὐράνιος ὅτι χρῄζετε τούτων ἁπάντων. Ζητεῖτε δὲ πρῶτον τὴν βασιλείαν τοῦ Θεοῦ καὶ τὴν δικαιοσύνην αὐτοῦ· καὶ ταῦτα πάντα προστεθήσεται ὑμῖν.
(21.) Ὅπου γὰρ ἔστιν ὁ θησαυρὸς ὑμῶν, ἐκεῖ ἔσται καὶ ἡ καρδία ὑμῶν.

Luke xii, 22. . . . . Μὴ μεριμνᾶτε τῇ ψυχῇ ὑμῶν, τί φάγητε· μηδὲ τῷ σώματι, τί ἐνδύσησθε.
(24.) . . . Πόσῳ μᾶλλον ὑμεῖς διαφέρετε τῶν πετεινῶν ;
(29.) Καὶ ὑμεῖς μὴ ζητεῖτε τι φάγητε, ἢ τί πίητε, καὶ μὴ μετεωρίζεσθε.
(30.) . . . Ὑμῶν δὲ ὁ πατὴρ οἶδεν, ὅτι χρῄζετε τούτων. Πλὴν ζητεῖτε τὴν βασιλείαν τοῦ Θεοῦ, καὶ ταῦτα πάντα προστεθήσεται ὑμῖν.
(34.) Ὅπου γάρ ἐστιν ὁ θησαυρὸς ὑμῶν, ἐκεῖ καὶ ἡ καρδία ὑμῶν ἔσται.

13.

Μὴ ποιῆτε ταῦτα πρὸς τὸ θεαθῆναι ὑπὸ τῶν ἀνθρώπων, εἰ δὲ μή γε, μισθὸν οὐκ ἔχετε παρὰ τοῦ Πατρὸς ὑμῶν τοῦ ἐν τοῖς οὐρανοῖς.

Matt. vi, 1. Προσέχετε τὴν δικαιοσύνην ὑμῶν μὴ ποιεῖν ἔμπροσθεν τῶν ἀνθρώπων, πρὸς τὸ θεαθῆναι αὐτοῖς· εἰ δὲ μήγε, μισθὸν οὐκ ἔχετε παρὰ τῷ πατρὶ ὑμῶν τῷ ἐν τοῖς οὐρανοῖς.

14.

[Περὶ δὲ τοῦ ἀνεξικάκους εἶναι καὶ ὑπηρετικοὺς πᾶσι καὶ ἀοργήτους ἃ ἔφη ταῦτά εστι.] Τῷ τύπτοντί σοῦ τὴν σιαγόνα πάρεχε καὶ τὴν ἄλλην, καὶ τὸν αἴροντά σου τὸν χίτωνα ἢ τὸ ἱμάτιον μὴ κωλύσῃς.

Matt. v, 39-40. . . . Ὅστις σε ῥαπίσει ἐπὶ τὴν δεξιάν σου σιαγόνα, στρέψον αὐτῷ καὶ τὴν ἄλλην· καὶ τῷ θέλοντί σοι κριθῆναι, καὶ τὸν χιτῶνά σου λαβεῖν, ἄφες αὐτῷ καὶ τὸ ἱμάτιον.

Luke vi, 29. Τῷ τύπτοντί σε ἐπὶ τὴν σιάγονα, πάρεχε καὶ τὴν ἄλλην· καὶ ἀπὸ τοῦ αἴροντός σου τὸ ἱμάτιον, καὶ τὸν χιτῶνα μὴ κωλύσῃς.

15.

Ὅς δ' ἂν ὀργισθῇ, ἔνοχός ἐστιν εἰς τὸ πῦρ. Παντὶ δὲ ἀγγαρεύοντί σε μίλιον ἀκολούθησον δύο.

Λαμψάτω δὲ ὑμῶν τὰ καλὰ ἔργα ἔμπροσθεν τῶν ἀνθρώπων, ἵνα βλέποντες θαυμάζωσι τὸν πατέρα ὑμῶν τὸν ἐν τοῖς οὐρανοῖς.

Matt. v, 22. . . . . . ὃς δ' ἂν εἴπῃ, μωρέ, ἔνοχος ἔσται εἰς τὴν γέενναν τοῦ πυρός . . . . (41.) Καὶ ὅστις σε ἀγγαρεύσει μίλιον ἕν, ὕπαγε μετ' αὐτοῦ δύο. . . . . (16.) Οὕτω λαμψάτω τὸ φῶς ὑμῶν ἔμπροσθεν τῶν ἀνθρώπων, ὅπως ἴδωσιν ὑμῶν τὰ καλὰ ἔργα, καὶ δοξάσωσι τὸν πατέρα ὑμῶν τὸν ἐν τοῖς οὐρανοῖς.

16.

[Περὶ δὲ τοῦ μὴ ὀμνύναι ὅλως, τἀληθῆ δὲ λέγειν ἀεὶ, οὕτω παρεκελεύσατο·] Μὴ ὀμόσητε ὅλως· ἔστω δὲ ὑμῶν τὸ ναὶ ναὶ καὶ τὸ οὒ οὔ· τὸ δὲ περισσὸν τούτων ἐκ τοῦ πονηροῦ.

Matt. v, 34. Μὴ ὀμόσαι ὅλως. . . . . (37.) Ἔστω δὲ ὁ λόγος ὑμῶν, ναὶ ναὶ, οὒ οὔ· τὸ δὲ περισσὸν τούτων, ἐκ τοῦ πονηροῦ ἐστιν.

17.

[Ὡς δὲ καὶ τὸν Θεὸν μόνον δεῖ προσκυνεῖν, οὕτως ἔπεισεν εἰπών·] Μεγίστη ἐντολή ἐστι· Κύριον τὸν Θεόν σου προσκυνήσεις καὶ αὐτῷ μόνῳ λατρεύσεις ἐξ ὅλης τῆς καρδίας σου καὶ ἐξ ὅλης τῆς ἰσχύος σου, Κύριον τὸν Θεὸν τὸν ποιήσαντά σε.

Matt. iv, 10. Γέγραπται γάρ· Κύριον τὸν Θεόν σου προσκυνήσεις, καὶ αὐτῷ μόνῳ λατρεύσεις.

Mark xii, 30. Καὶ ἀγαπήσεις Κύριον τὸν Θεόν σου ἐξ ὅλης τῆς καρδίας σου, καὶ ἐξ ὅλης τῆς ψυχῆς σου, καὶ ἐξ ὅλης τῆς διανοίας σου, καὶ ἐξ ὅλης τῆς ἰσχύος σου· αὕτη πρώτη ἐντολή.

Luke x, 27. Ἀγαπήσεις Κύριον τὸν Θεόν σου ἐξ ὅλης τῆς καρδίας σου, καὶ ἐξ ὅλης τῆς ψυχῆς σου, καὶ ἐξ ὅλης τῆς διανοίας σου.

Justin quotes nearly two hundred of these sayings, but makes hardly a single clear allusion to all those circumstances of time or place, which give so much interest to

Christ's teaching, as recorded in the four Gospels. The inference is that he quotes Christ's sayings as delivered by tradition or taken down in writing before the four Gospels were compiled into their present form out of those primitive materials.

And this inference is strengthened by the fact that he cites no less than one hundred and ninety-seven times the authors of the Old Testament with the names either of themselves or of their books, and that he cites little more than half that number anonymously; but to have quoted two hundred sayings and maxims from the New Testament, without either name of the books where they occur or of the books themselves, only in such general terms as "Sayings of our Lord" (Λόγια τοῦ Κυρίου), and "Memorials of the Apostles" (ἀπομνημονεύματα τῶν ἀποστόλων), and that he quotes by name, as of equal authority, other books not included in our canon, suggests the natural inference that there was in his time current among Christians a Collection of our Saviour's Teachings and Sayings, together with a large number of Memorials, more or less accurate and complete, and that from these materials our present Scriptures of the New Testament were formed into a Canon by the early Church.

At the end of the second century lived Irenæus, of whom we know but little. He is supposed by Dodwell to have been born as early as A.D. 97, but Dr Lardner more reasonably places him about A.D. 178. He is said to have been Bishop of Lyons in Gaul about this time, and his principal work being a treatise against heresies seems to be a reason why the time at which he lived should be fixed as late as possible; for otherwise we are led to receive an unfavourable impression from the fact that heresies were already in existence so soon after the teaching of Christianity. The only work of Irenæus *Against heresies*, has come down to us in Latin and very mutilated, and, as it was written many years after the Apologies of Justin Martyr, there was ample time in the interval for the compilation of our Gospels, out of the authentic "Memorials of the Apostles," and the "Sayings of our Lord." Irenæus quotes all our four Gospels with the names of their writers, and states, from mystic reasons, why there could be four only. But it is worthy of remark that he speaks of other writings also: thus he mentions, as we learn from Eusebius, iii, 8, the "Memorials" of a certain apostolical presbyter, whose name however he does not give. And we may infer from certain passages in his work, that the text even of the four Gospels was not in his time as firmly settled in every particular as it is at present. Thus he says, in Book iv, chapter 6 of his work, that, notwithstanding the agreement of Matthew (iv, 27), Mark, and Luke, respecting the knowledge of God the Father through the Son, and of the Son through the Father, some who wished to be more learned than the Apostles ("qui peritiores apostolis volunt esse") had inverted the order of those words, in order to establish their own peculiar doctrines. Lastly, this author in the nineteenth chapter of his first book writes thus:

But in addition to these things they introduce an unspeakable number of apocryphal and spurious writings, which themselves have forged to the consternation of those who are foolish and who do not know the writings of the truth.

We have already seen that numerous writings were fabricated a little before the age of Irenæus, but as it is evident that the four Gospels were in his time distinguished from other writings, at all events by those who are generally accounted orthodox as opposed to others who were called heretics, it will not be necessary to dwell longer upon the writings of Irenæus.

The same also may be said of Clemens Alexandrinus who lived at the beginning of the third century. The canonical books, not differing much from what are now received, were well known in his time, although his writings, however otherwise interesting, do not add much practical utility in supporting the benevolent doctrines of the New Testament.

CHAPTER XIV.

Minor Writers of the Second Century.

The course of this inquiry has now brought us down to the early part of the second century, about eighty years later than the crucifixion of our Lord. Up to that date we find no mention made of the Gospels, of the Acts of the Apostles, or of the Epistles, which now enter into the canon of the Christian Scriptures. The works of Justin Martyr, as we have seen, fail to indicate that their author was acquainted with the books of which we are speaking. At the end of the second century, it is true, we have the works of Irenæus,

Origen, Tertullian, and a few others, and there can be no doubt that in their time the books of the New Testament had begun to be publicly known, and the greater part of them to be quoted under the names of the several writers to whom they are still commonly ascribed. But we may rightly infer, from an incidental remark made by Lucian in his "Life of Peregrinus" that about the middle of the second century, the Christians at Antioch were occupied in gathering together the records of their founder, of the Apostles, and of others who had assisted in establishing the new religion which they professed. The unscrupulous Peregrinus, as we are informed by Lucian, "explained and cleared up or interpreted some of their books, and wrote many himself." This was done in the city of Antioch, where Lucian the elegant writer of "Dialogues" still remaining then lived, and where also, it must be remembered, the disciples, as we read in the Acts of the Apostles, were first called* Christians. In the last century indeed we find that some of our ecclesiastical writers endeavoured to disparage the authority of Lucian as being an enemy, and a malicious enemy, to the Christian religion, but this accusation seems to be in every respect unfounded; we find in his writings nothing more than a certain superciliousness and contempt for the doctrines which the Christians held, and the low social position which they occupied.

We may now proceed to review the minor writers, who lived in the second century, and to see whether in the fragments of their writings which remain we can find any indication that they quoted from the existing text of our Scriptures, or that they were acquainted with any such books as being then in general circulation or as held to be authorized exponents of the Christian religion. Between twenty and thirty such writers are now to be noticed, besides two or three anonymous documents, and among so many we should expect to find some mention of those who wrote the books of the New Testament, or at all events some mention of the books themselves. The names of these writers here follow in alphabetical order.

1. AGRIPPA CASTOR† is quoted by Jerome, in his work

---

* It may be doubted how far the Greek word *chrematisai* is correctly rendered "were called" in this passage. It is a verb in the active voice, and its literal meaning is "to act, carry on business, &c.": it would be difficult in the English language to find a strict equivalent for the word.

† The remains of these minor writers, translated into English, are contained in a volume entitled "Writings of the Early Christians of the

De viris illustribus (xxi), as having written against Basileides, and also by Eusebius (iv, 7), as having written on the Gospel. This expression does not sanction the inference that he alludes to our four canonical writings ; but the English translator of Eusebius's Ecclesiastical History, either ignorant that "the Gospel" means only the dispensation so called, or wishing to convey an erroneous idea to the minds of his readers, has, by the addition of an *s*, turned the *Gospel* into the *Gospels*, as now found in the volume of the New Testament. The name of this writer indicates a Greek or Latin origin, and I fail to see how Dr Westcott, in his *Canon* (p. 85), infers his Hebrew descent "from the fact that he charged Basileides with teaching indifference in eating meats offered to idols," as if Jews only were forbidden and Greeks allowed to eat those meats.

2. APOLLINARIS. See Claudius.

3. APOLLONIUS, a Phrygian, is known to us only by the fragments of his works against heresies preserved by Eusebius. In one of these passages we read, " Our Lord says, Possess not gold nor silver, nor two coats," no doubt quoted from the Sayings of Jesus then (A.D. 180) still in general circulation.

4. ARISTIDES. Jerome tells us that he was an eloquent philosopher of Athens, who dedicated an apology for Christianity to the Emperor Hadrian. Nothing but a fragmental quotation remains of his writings.

5. ARISTON, of Pella, wrote a disputation between Jason and Papiscus, quoted by Eusebius, Jerome, Origen contra Celsum, and Maximus in his commentary on Dionysius the Areopagite, but not a line of his own writing has survived.

6. ATHENAGORAS. All we know of him from ancient writers is from Methodius, who quotes a single sentence, and from Philippus Sideta. The latter, as quoted by Dodwell, says, in his twenty-fourth sermon :—

Athenagoras was the first master of the Alexandrian schools in the reigns of Hadrian and Antoninus, to whom also he inscribed his " Oration" on behalf of the Christians: he professed the Christian religion, even whilst he wore the cloak of philosophy and was master of the academic school. Whilst he was meditating to write against the Christians, as Celsus did after him, and

---

Second Century, namely, Athenagoras, Tatian, &c." collected together and first translated complete by the Rev. Dr Giles, late fellow of Corpus Christi College, Oxford, 8vo, London, J. R. Smith, 36, Soho Square, MDCCCLVII.

was reading the Holy Scriptures in order to attack them more thoroughly, he was seized by the Holy Spirit, and, like the great Paul, instead of persecuting that doctrine which he was attacking, he became a teacher of it.

The only works of Athenagoras now remaining are: 1. *Apology for Christianity*, and 2. *Treatise on the Resurrection*. The time when he wrote, namely, about the year 180 after Christ, is learnt from the inscription of the former work to the Emperors Marcus Antoninus and Lucius Aurelius Commodus.

Athenagoras speaks of the Trinity in these terms:—

Who then would not wonder at hearing the name of atheists applied to us, who believe in God the Father, God the Son, and God the Holy Ghost, who show their power in unity and their distinctiveness in their practice?

He quotes two other passages which may have been taken from our Gospels, if then extant, but more probably and consistently with other evidence, taken from the " Sayings of our Lord."

1. What are the doctrines in which we are brought up? " I say unto you, Love your enemies; bless them that curse you, pray for them that persecute you: that ye may be the children of your Father, which is in heaven; for he maketh his sun to rise on the evil and on the good, and sendeth rain on the just and on the unjust."—Compare *Matt.* v, 44.

2. For, says our Lord, " Whoever looketh on a woman to lust after her, hath committed adultery with her already in his heart."—*Matt.* v, 28.

7. CANON OF MURATORI. This is a short fragment, often quoted by those who have written on either side of our present subject, which I shall here briefly notice. It is called the Canon of Muratori, from the name of the learned Italian scholar who discovered it, about the year 1740, in the Ambrosian Library at Milan. Muratori thought that the MS in which it occurred was written in the seventh or eighth century of our era, but some critics have ascribed the original document to the third, or even the second century. The text is exceedingly corrupt, and has evidently been copied by a scribe who knew nothing of the Latin language. Some, indeed, have said that it betrays marks of having been translated from a Greek original ; but the fragment is too short to allow a judgment, which can be only conjectural, on such a point as that. The " Canon," as

it has been termed, was first published in Muratori's "Antiquitates Italicæ Medii Ævi," iii, p. 851, and has been often copied into other works. It has lately been published at Oxford (1867), with notes by Dr Tregelles. It is not absolutely necessary to ignore this fragment, and if it has been copied from an authentic original, it would prove what no one can deny—that, about the year 180 A.D., the canon of the New Testament was generally acknowledged. Some indeed of the books therein contained were still disputed some hundreds of years later, but the Gospels, at all events, were without dispute canonical at the end of the second century. The zeal of Dr Westcott and others who defend the authenticity of this fragment, and also of those who, like the author of "Supernatural Religion," labour to destroy it, has probably led them into arguments which those who weigh them dispassionately may view as incomplete. I acknowledge my inability to decide on this question, nor is it important to arrive at any decision on such a point. It is against a conclusive judgment in its favour that we have it only in a Latin form, and in a Latin MS of the seventh or eighth century, and that it contains an improbable legend about St John. A corresponding argument in its favour is that no motive can be assigned for its fabrication, at so late a period, to prove what was already proved by the notices of our canon in Irenæus and Clement of Alexandria, namely, that in the last quarter of the second century our canonical books were known and acknowledged.

Those who are curious to inquire farther into the history and character of this document, are referred to the works on that subject which have been already mentioned. A few lines taken from its commencement, line for line with the original, will suffice to show its subject matter and the corrupt Latinity of its style.

> quibus tamen interfuit et ita posuit
> tertio euangelii librum secand lucan
> lucas iste medicus post ascensum xpi
> cum eo paulus quasi ut juris studiosum
> secundum adsumsisset numeni suo
> ex opinione concriset dnm tamen nec ipse
> duidit in carne.

8. CELSUS. Concerning this opponent of Christianity we know nothing more than the fact that he wrote against the authenticity of the Gospel history, and that Origen wrote five books, which still survive, in refutation of him. In this

work Origen says that Jesus is nowhere called a carpenter in any of the Gospels received by the Church, and as this is evidently a mistake on the part of Origen, for Jesus is called a carpenter in Mark vi, 3, it has been inferred by Dr Lardner that Celsus had certainly used that Gospel as his authority for stating such a fact. But this is, as the author of "Palæoromaica" well describes it, a "most lame and impotent conclusion;" for "Origen, in stating that Jesus is nowhere called a carpenter in any of the Gospels received of the Church, had plainly hinted that he was so called in apocryphal gospels, and that there Celsus had found it."

It is not improbable that the Celsus, against whom Origen wrote, is the same whose name occurs in some of Lucian's dialogues, and even there we find nothing about his life or his philosophical opinions. The nature of these is a subject of uncertainty with learned men to this present moment, and even the simplest circumstances of his history were unknown even to his inquisitive opponent. "Whatever may have been his character and his tenets, it is evident," says Dr Waddington, "even from the fragments of his work which are cited by his adversary, that he possessed great general powers of expression, especially of sarcasm and of rhetoric; that he was skilful in the selection of points for attack; and that he possessed too that wicked talent of perverting truth and insinuating falsehood, of suppressing largely and inventing discreetly, and confounding established facts with rumoured calumnies—which so commonly marks the distinguished controversialist." The work of Celsus has perished—it would indeed have been wonderful, if it had survived so many centuries of intolerance, when everything that opposed the prevailing belief was carefully destroyed, and all men were bent not so much upon the pursuit of truth as upon the maintenance, at all sacrifices, of their own opinions and of the existing order of things.

9. CLAUDIUS APOLLINARIS of Hierapolis inscribed a work in defence of Christianity to the Emperor Marcus Aurelius, and also wrote about Easter. Three short fragments of this work remain; one given by Eusebius, and two others in the Paschal Chronicle. The first of these concerns the absurd story of the Thundering Legion. The other two concern the dispute about the due celebration of Easter, and are found only in the Paschal Chronicle. But Eusebius, who treats very fully of this dispute, would certainly have quoted Apollinaris as having written on that subject, and no other writer until the seventh century, when the Paschal

Chronicle was compiled, has made the slightest reference to such a work. In that fragment Apollinaris says that some who have written on the subject of Easter quote Matthew in support of their doctrine.

We admit that the Gospel according to St Matthew may have been compiled before the year A.D. 180, but the Hebrew work of Matthew also may have survived up to that time, and the words of Apollinaris are vague as to the book referred to, even if the author of the Paschal Chronicle, 500 years later, has been accurate in his quotation, or even if, as we know has happened in other cases, he has not mixed his own words with those which he may have quoted vaguely in the third person from Apollinaris.

10. DIONYSIUS bishop of Corinth. Eusebius has preserved four fragments from eight epistles, of which he was the author. He briefly names St Paul, St Peter, and the Epistle of Clement, but not any of the books of the New Testament, nor does he leave us to infer that St Peter and St Paul ever wrote anything. His words are found in a letter addressed to the Romans, as follows:

Thus you also by such admonition have mingled together the planting of Romans and Corinthians, which originated from Peter and Paul. For both also having also planted us into our own Corinth, taught us alike, and alike also having carried their teaching into Italy, became martyrs about the same time.— EUSEB. v, 25.

11. HEGESIPPUS. This is one of the most important of the minor writers of the second century. He compiled in the reign of the Antonines a history, in five books, of Christianity from the time of Christ to his own time. The fragments which remain, as quoted by Eusebius, contain some interesting notices of the Apostles, especially of James the Just, and of his violent death in the Temple. He also speaks of the numerous heresies which distracted the Christian community, but does not make the slightest reference to written canonical books, or their authors.

12. HERMIAS is the author of a short work called "Derision of the Gentile Philosophers." It is not known when or where he lived. Cave places him in the second century, but the Benedictine editor of his work thinks he may with as great probability be ascribed to the third. He does not name the Gospels but quotes St Paul's Epistle to the Corinthians, which no doubt was well known in his time, but he shows remarkable ignorance where Corinth was.

Paul the blessed Apostle, my beloved brethren, writing to the Corinthians *who inhabit Laconian Greece*, spake saying, "The wisdom of this world is folly in the sight of God."

13. MELITO, bishop of Sardis, wrote, 1. On the Passover; 2. An Apology for Christianity addressed to Marcus Antoninus Verus; 3. Selections on the Old Testament; 4. On Christ's Incarnation, against Marcion; 5. Sermon on Christ's Passion; 6. Clavis, a Key to Scripture, in which almost every word is interpreted allegorically: besides other works from which a few extracts remain. None of these writings are now extant; for the Clavis published in Don Pitra's Spicilegium Solesmense, Paris, 1855, and occupying two large volumes of that collection, has not the slightest pretension to be the genuine work.

But in a letter preserved by Eusebius (iv, 26), the authenticity of which there is no reason to doubt, Melito gives a list of the books of the "Old Covenant," and it has been strangely contended by some that this expression implies the existence of a new Covenant. It certainly implies that the old state of things had passed away and was obsolete, and that a new state of things had succeeded, but not that a new book had been composed in distinction from the old book of which Melito enumerates the contents.

14. PANTÆNUS was a Stoic philosopher in the time of Severus and Caracalla. He is named by Eusebius, Clement of Alexandria, Maximus, and Jerome: but only two short unimportant fragments of his works remain.

15. PAPIAS. In a former chapter of this volume the few fragments which remain of Papias bishop of Hierapolis, as being earlier in time than Justin Martyr, have been extracted from the work of Eusebius in which they have been handed down to us. These fragments will recur to our notice in connection with the Gospels in a future chapter.

16. PINYTUS bishop of Gnossus. He is known only for his letter to Dionysius, of which Eusebius has preserved a fragment, but it contains nothing to our present purpose.

17. POLYCRATES, bishop of Ephesus, was the principal advocate of the Asiatic mode of celebrating Easter. He wrote to Victor bishop of Rome a synodical letter of which a long fragment has been preserved by Eusebius (v, 24). In this fragment he names "Philip one of the twelve apostles who sleeps in Hierapolis, and his two daughters, aged virgins: and his other daughter whose conversation was in the Holy Spirit [and who] sleeps in Ephesus. . . . .

John who leaned on the breast of our Lord, who became a priest bearing the plate and martyr and teacher, and sleeps in Ephesus. . . . Melito the eunuch, whose conversation was wholly on the Holy Spirit. . . ."

18. QUADRATUS bishop of Athens is quoted by Eusebius, and wrote an apology for the Christians addressed to Hadrian when he was sojourning for a time at Athens. The only fragment of his work is the following preserved by Eusebius (iv, 3):

> The works of our Saviour were always present; for they were real. Those who were healed, those who rose from the dead, who were not only seen when healed and when rising from the dead, but also being always present; and not only whilst our Saviour sojourned [among men], but also when he was gone, they remained for a long time, so that some of them have reached to our own times.

If any who had witnessed our Lord's miracles were alive about 120 A.D. (the date of Quadratus), this reference to the "living voice," which Papias preferred to what was written, furnishes an indirect testimony against the existence of a better and collective body of evidence such as our present New Testament would supply.

19. RHODON was of Asiatic origin, and a disciple of Tatian at Rome under Commodus and Severus. Some fragments of his work against Marcion remain, but they do not notice any of our canonical books or writers.

20. SERAPION was made bishop of Antioch in the eleventh year of Commodus, and wrote against the Montanists, the Gospel of Peter, &c. He speaks of the work ascribed to this Apostle as follows:

> We, brethren, receive both Peter and the other Apostles like as we do Christ, but the writings falsely inscribed with their names we as experienced men disclaim, knowing that we have not acknowledged such. For I, when I was among you, thought that you all adhered to the true faith; and when I had not gone through the Gospel put forth by them in the name of Peter, I said, "If this is all that seems to cause you discouragement, let it be read." But now that I have learnt that their mind finds a covering for itself in a certain heresy from the words spoken by me, I will hasten again to go to you. . . . EUSEB. vi, 12.

21. SIBYLLINE ORACLES. Among the legendary characters known to the Greeks and Romans, were ten women, supposed to be prophetesses, and designated by the name of

Sibyls. No mention is made of them by any purely Hebrew writer, although their legends were certainly current in the East before the later Hebrew books were written. Nor are they, indeed, named in any of the Greek and Latin uncanonical books which were written whilst the Jews were still independent. Josephus is the first writer who mentions them, and in such terms that he would seem to admit their authority.

Speaking of this tower [Babel] and of the varied language of mankind, the Sibyl speaks thus. "When all men were of the "same tongue, some of them built a very high tower, as if they "would by means of it get up to heaven. But the gods sent "winds and upset the tower, and gave to each his own language, "and it happened on account of this that the city was called "Babylon."

These lines are still found in the Sibylline Oracles which remain, and it is a natural inference that they were found in some such work in the time of Josephus. But it is only of late years that a full collection of these oracles has been given to the world, and it appears that no complete manuscript copy has yet been discovered. They exist, it seems, piecemeal, as if additions had been made to them at different times and in different parts of the world. This fact is a strong argument in favour of their having been interpolated, and it is rendered conclusive by the nature of certain passages which evidently have been introduced since the Christian era, and which assume the character of prophecies intended to prepare mankind for the introduction of Christianity. It is indeed probable that the whole body of these oracles was re-written in the first century of our era, or at all events about the middle of the second century, for they are quoted as books of authority by some of the writers whose names have been passed in review before us in these pages.

Thus Justin Martyr, about the year 150 A.D. names the Sybil, and Theophilus, thirty years later, does not hesitate to style her a prophetess, and quotes her as an authority in his work addressed to Autolycus.

The Sibyl among the Greeks, who was a prophetess among other nations also, inveighs against mankind at the beginning of her prophesy, in these words:

" Ye mortal fleshly men, who nothing are,
" How quick ye swell, seeing no end of life!

" Nor fear nor care for God who looks down on you,
" Most highest, who knows, sees, witnesses all things,
" Nurturer and Creator, who in all
" His spirit placed, making it guide for all men,
" One God who reigns alone, great, unbegotten,
" Omnipotent, unseen, alone sees all,
" But is not seen by any human flesh."

Athenagoras also, in his Apology for Christianity (§ 30), quotes a few lines from the Sibyl, adding that she is mentioned by Plato ; but he does not assign to her the name of a prophetess, nor is it needful to copy what he quotes. But great has been the audacity of those who have either made insertions in the original copy of the Sibylline Oracles, or have forged the whole collection, as will be seen from the following lines, which refer to the miracles of our Saviour and his co-operation with God the Father in creating the human race :—

The Almighty spake ; " My son, let us two make
" A mortal race impress'd from our own likeness.
" I now by hand, and thou by word hereafter
" A common work produce in our own form."
He mindful of these words shall come to judgment,
His counterpart join to a virgin mother,
Illume with water through the hands of priests,
Do all things by his word, heal all disease,
Calm the winds by his word, the raging sea
Quell 'neath his feet, treading in peace with faith ;
And from five loaves with one fish of the sea
Shall in the desert feed five thousand men,
And taking up the fragments which remain,
Twelve baskets fill to be the people's hope.

Orac. Sibyl. Paris, 1841, vol. i, p. 278.

It is the opinion of an able commentator on the Old Testament, De Wette (ii, 491), that in the later period of the Jewish independence there was a great tendency of literature towards apocalyptic visions, and that from this cause prophecies were forged and made to apply to the events of real history, and dated back to ancient times and attributed to ancient authors. The same commentator, supported by the judgment of his English translator, likens the Sibylline Oracles to the book of Daniel, and the fourth book of Ezra, which is our apocryphal second book of Esdras, and he places the later portion of Isaiah in the same class, as bearing a striking resemblance to the third book of the

Oracles (156-271, and 319-746), for that both "announce the destruction of all the kingdoms of the world, especially the Egyptian and the Roman; they threaten Antiochus Epiphanes with destruction; the order of nature is to be changed; and the people of God, under the guidance of kings sent by him, are to extend his dominion over the whole world."

Whatever may have been the origin or the development of these bold fictions, there is no doubt that the authenticity of many valuable works, not excepting the Scriptures either of the Old or New Testament, would be reasonably suspected by the heathen world, when mixed up with the forgeries which were published in their defence, and when such works as the Sibylline Oracles were obtruded on them as of equal authority with the "genuine inspirations of heaven."

One brief remark, however, may suffice to complete our account of these forged Sibylline works. They do not name either the New Testament or any one of its writers, and it would appear from two words which occur in the First Book, line 382, εὐαγγελίης διάθημα, the "dispensation of the Gospel," where εὐαγγελίου διαθήκην would equally have satisfied the metre, that even the dispensation at that time was not limited to the exact descriptive words which a few years later would have been deemed essential.

22. TATIAN was an Assyrian by birth, became a convert to the new religion, and was a disciple of Justin Martyr. What we know of him is derived mostly from Eusebius, who also quotes additional particulars from Irenæus. We learn from these two authors that Tatian was a sophist, and taught various branches of literature among the Greeks, comparing it with that of the Hebrews. Eusebius says that he belonged to the class of Encratites, and that he founded a sect called Severians from one of their number whose name was Severus. His only remaining work is an *Oration* against the Greeks, in which he says nothing about our canonical Scriptures; but he is quoted by Irenæus (III, xxiii, 8), as referring to the words of St Paul, "In Adam all die."

Jerome, in the preface to his Commentary on the Epistle to Titus, says that Tatian rejected some of St Paul's Epistles, but thought the one addressed to Titus to be undoubtedly genuine.

23. THEOPHILUS. The only remaining work of this writer is his "Three books addressed to Autolycus." He is named by Eusebius as the sixth bishop of Antioch, and is

thought by some to be the Theophilus to whom the Gospel of St Luke and the Acts of the Apostles were inscribed. The time when he lived is fixed, to a certain extent, by his bringing down his chronology at the end of his treatise to the death of Aurelius Verus, A.D. 169.

Theophilus quotes the Sibylline books, the Stoics, Epicurus, and other heathen writers, besides Moses, Solomon, and the books of the Old Testament, but does not name the Gospels. He does however quote from St John, without naming the work from which he quotes, the passage with which our present Gospel according to St John begins. His words are these—

The Holy Scriptures teach us, and all those who received the Spirit, of whom John says, "In the beginning was the Word, and the Word was with God, and the Word was God."—*Ad Autolycum*, ii, 22.

Here there is no mention of a gospel, and the words Holy Scriptures mean the Old Testament, and this testimony of Theophilus is given about 180 years after the Christian era. Is it not clear that the words are quoted from the Memorials of St John, notwithstanding that about this time we all admit that those "Memorials," together with the "Sayings of our Lord," were being brought together and compiled, or even had already been compiled into the present Gospel according to St John? And lastly, it is worthy of remark that Theophilus at this time was bishop of Antioch, where I conceive the consolidation of the Gospel histories to have been made.

24. To this list of writers may be added certain *presbyters* or elders, whether so called from their age or from their office in the Church, who are quoted by Irenæus, Clement of Alexandria, and Eusebius. Nothing more is known about them, and in the few lines which remain of their writings, nothing occurs bearing on our present subject.

25. The *Church and Council of Cæsarea*. A short fragment remains in Eusebius (v, 25) of a synodical letter addressed by this council, through Irenæus, to Victor, bishop of Rome, about the celebration of Easter.

26. From the *Council of Lyons*, from the *Churches* of *Lyons* and *Vienne*, and from the *Martyrs of Lyons*, letters have been preserved by Eusebius (v, 1-4, 24) as having been written either wholly or in part by Irenæus, and addressed to the bishop of Rome ; but no notice of our canonical books is found in them. Only the synodical letter

from the Council of Lyons names Polycarp as having associated "with John the disciple of our Lord and the other disciples."

From these notices, brief in proportion to the little which remains of these writers, no evidence can be derived to reverse the opinion which has already been formed on our present subject.

CHAPTER XV.

INTERNAL EVIDENCE CONCERNING THE FOUR CANONICAL GOSPELS—§ 1. MATTHEW—§ 2. MARK—§ 3. LUKE—§ 4. JOHN.

HAVING, in the preceding chapters, examined the historical evidence derived from without, bearing upon the authorship and date of the books of the New Testament, we must now turn to the books themselves, if perchance they may supply from within any indication of the age when they were written. This mode of proceeding is sanctioned by the authority of all critics: for, in all ages, there have been instances of books that have been proved genuine or spurious by the application of this test only. It is even admitted among all men, that there is no other test so sure, to distinguish the true from the false: for truth must be harmonious and consistent with itself, but error—not to say *intentional* error or forgery—will betray itself by inconsistencies, contradictions, and a general want of harmony between its various parts. It cannot be too often repeated, that our concern is not, mainly, with the facts which are related by the four evangelists, but simply with the mode in which those facts are related—not to prove that the Gospel histories are untrue, but that many matters of detail are not in such strict harmony as to allow us to suppose that they were written by eye-witnesses, guided in every word and about every fact by divine inspiration. A work which truly possessed such a claim would, by the necessity of the case, be free from blemish and defy criticism. It would compel the faith alike of friends and of foes. But this is not a picture of the evangelical histories, even in the judgement of their most partial commentators. The notes and explanations with which the simplicity of the Gospels has often been overwhelmed, are unworthy of the text which they are intended to illustrate.

They vacillate from one point to another, that they may reconcile things which do not allow of being reconciled: they apply to the interpretation of the Bible a mode of criticism that would be rejected if applied to the profane histories of Greece and Rome. And they do this to support a theory which cannot be maintained, which has been the cause of all the opposition that the Christian writings have ever had to encounter. Let it be maintained that those books are the writings of the disciples of Christ, acting under verbal inspiration, and we are at a loss to explain the imperfect accounts, discrepancies of statement, and other peculiarities in which those books abound. But admit that they are the works of pious men living more than 100 years after the time when the events which they relate happened, let it be granted that the Gospels were compiled when tradition, becoming faint, could no longer transmit those events, and it is clear that inaccuracies in modes of speech, discrepancies in dates and details, and such other difficulties,* many of which occur in the four Gospels, will dwindle into nothing: we admit with reverence the divinely-inspired and benevolent doctrines taught by our great Master, and recorded in these books by those who worthily succeeded to the office of the first teachers, and who have left for our use the most perfect records of their religion which they on the one hand were able to deliver, and we on the other have been able to receive.

We will now proceed to inquire what internal evidence the New Testament furnishes, bearing upon the question, in what age the books of the New Testament were composed? The external evidence has been considered in the previous chapters; so far, at least, as is necessary to establish the conclusion that the four Gospels, bearing the names of Matthew, Mark, Luke, and John, do not appear to be contemporary records: for, if they were not in being during the 120 years immediately following after the crucifixion of our Lord, it is certain that they could not have been compiled into their present form by any writers who were themselves witnesses

---

* "The history of the New Testament," says Dr Lardner, [vol. i, p. 136,] "is attended with many difficulties." This remark suggests a variety of thoughts, which crowd upon and almost overwhelm the mind. Were the Gospels written by our Lord's apostles, to be the only source from which his followers are to draw their Christian morals and to regulate their course of life—and is their history still "attended with many difficulties"? No remark can be more injurious to Christianity than this admission on the part of one who has always been named as among its most able defenders.

of those events. To establish the same inference, indeed, a less space than 120 years would, ordinarily, be sufficient, but the circumstance of the great age ascribed to St John, Polycarp, and others, by ecclesiastical writers, contrary to all general probability, makes it necessary to comprise a longer space of time in the review of authors who are said, or may be supposed, to name the Gospels and their authors.

Having then failed to find any notices of the four Gospels in works earlier than the date of Irenæus, we will now first examine whether any allusion is made to the Apostles as having written or handed down to posterity any records at all of the wonderful things which they had witnessed in their life-time, and then review certain passages in each of the four Gospels, which do not seem to harmonize with one another, or with the opinion that the works in which they occur were written by those to whom they are ascribed. Here we shall find abundant evidence to convince us that what the Apostles or their immediate disciples left behind them, although containing the same doctrines and subject matter, was different in form from that which our New Testament now contains. We must here consider the existing four Gospels with reference to the apostles to whom they are ascribed, and see how far they harmonize with existing notices of what those apostles left behind them in writing. For, if it should appear that the disciples of our Lord did actually leave any writings behind them, or were thought to have done so, and those writings seem to be of a different character from our existing Gospels, the identity of the four will be disproved by the same process.

Now the gradual stages by which the world became possessed of our four Gospels is recorded by Eusebius in the third book (§ 24) of his "Ecclesiastical History." After informing us that only two of our Lord's disciples delivered in writing, and that of necessity, an account of his life and teaching, the historian proceeds as follows:—

Matthew, having before preached to the Hebrews, when he was about to go to others also, left in writing in the language of his country the Gospel which is *according to him*, thus supplying by writing the void which his absence occasioned to those from whom he was sent away. And whereas Mark and Luke had already delivered the Gospels which are *according to them*, they say that John, having during the whole time used unwritten preaching, at length came to write it, from some such cause as this. When the three [Gospels] previously written had been already given out to all as well as to himself, they say that he received them, bearing witness to their accuracy, but that the only thing wanting to the narrative was a description of the things done by Jesus at the beginning of his preaching. And this is the truth.

§ 1. *Matthew.*

We shall have occasion presently to recall this passage, and to consider how far the work ascribed to St John may be considered as supplementary to the other three, but in the first place the Gospel according to St Matthew must be brought to notice, that we may see how far it agrees with that which is ascribed to St Matthew by Eusebius and Papias, whom he quotes, as having been written by that Evangelist in the Hebrew tongue. On this point it may be said without hesitation that there is nothing to show the identity of our present Gospel with that which is said to have been written at an early period for the use of the Jews. The words quoted by Eusebius from Papias have been already given at page 116:—

Matthew, then, in the Hebrew dialect wrote the Sayings [λόγια]: and each person interpreted them as he was able.

If St Matthew wrote his Gospel in Hebrew, why has the original perished? The existing Greek text is either a translation of the Hebrew, or it is a separate work. But it cannot be a translation, for many reasons.

1. Because there is not the slightest evidence on record of its being a translation.

2. Because it is unreasonable to believe that an authentic work—written by inspiration—would perish or be superseded by an unauthenticated translation—for all translations are less authentic than their original.

3. Because there are many features in our present Gospel according to St Matthew, which are common to the Gospels of St Mark, St Luke, and even St John; which would lead to the inference that the latter are translations also.

4. Besides, there is nothing in the Gospel of St Matthew, as regards its style or construction, that would lead to the inference of its being a translation, any more than all the other books contained in the New Testament. Most of them bear marks of having been put together out of previous materials, and these materials are very likely to have been found in the Hebrew, Syriac, or any other of the various dialects which existed then, as they exist now, derived from the original Arabic, and used over the wide

range of Arabia, Palestine, Syria, and other conterminous parts of Asia. That such an account of the Life and Acts of Jesus might reasonably proceed from the pen of Matthew a tax-gatherer, for his very office would denote that he was familiar with the art of writing and the practice of the pen, is not improbable, and that this original record should have perished, is also not an unprecedented event, but that it should be superseded by a translation is not a theory hastily to be received. The original might indeed survive, as Mr Greswell remarks in his second Dissertation on the Harmony of the Gospels (i, 104), "for a time in Judæa—as long perhaps as the succession of Hebrew bishops was kept up in the Jewish Church, and consequently the Hebrew or mother Church could still be externally distinguished from the Gentile. But this was not longer than the eighteenth of Hadrian, within little more than sixty years from the first destruction of Jerusalem." But a more fatal objection lies against the theory that our existing first Gospel is a reproduction in Greek of an original work that had been first composed in Hebrew. Papias, whom Eusebius quotes, does not tell us that St Matthew wrote any gospel at all. His words are "Matthew wrote the Sayings (*ta logia*) in the Hebrew dialect and each person interpreted them as he was able." The Sayings is a well-known term applied to the brief and sententious teaching of Jesus, and a collection of these certainly existed before the compilation of the four Gospels. Such a collection is quoted perhaps two hundred times by Justin Martyr, who was not aware that they had been embodied with the Memorials so as to form Gospels as we now have them. Neither is there any ground for saying that St Matthew's Hebrew work was translated into Greek. Papias says that each person *interpreted*, not *translated* the Sayings. This also is intelligible: in our Gospels we have the acts and almost the daily life of Jesus, or at all events the particular occasions on which his Sayings were delivered, and this explains their meaning and their application. But the Sayings themselves reduced to writing by St Matthew (if the tradition be true) would be left to the private interpretation of all who read them without the aid which we now have from the History in which they are embodied. The Greek word *hermeneus* denotes one who explains or expounds a subject quite as often as one who interprets a foreign language, and it can hardly be supposed that every individual reader would make a translation of the work for his own use—a process which would entail great useless labour on those who undertook to study it, even if their means and appliances for doing so were seconded by the necessary ability which such a task would require. This, however, is not the only difficulty we meet with. It was not till the end of the second century that Pantænus discovered in India or Ethiopia the Hebrew work of St Matthew which had been conveyed to India, as we may infer, by the Apostle Bartholomew more than a hundred years before, and meanwhile was unknown to more western Christians. It is clear from what has been here quoted that no sound conclusion connecting the Hebrew which has perished with the Greek which has survived can be deduced, and for these reasons we conclude that the Hebrew "Gospel of St Matthew," which perhaps no one has seen since Pantænus who brought it from India,* and the Greek "Gospel according to St Matthew," are separate and independent works.

§ 2. *Mark.*

The second of our Gospels is said to have been written by St Mark, although its title in all manuscripts and editions

---

* Eusebius gives us the following account of Pantænus:—"At that time [about B.C. 180], there presided in the school of the faithful at that place [Alexandria] a man highly celebrated on account of his learning, by name Pantænus. For there had been from ancient time erected among them a school of sacred learning, which remains to this day; and we have understood that it has been wont to be furnished with men eminent for their eloquence and the study of divine things; and it is said that this person excelled others of that time, having been brought up in the Stoic philosophy; that he was nominated or sent forth as a missionary to preach the Gospel of Christ to the nations of the East, and to have travelled into India. For there were yet at that time many evangelists of the word, animated with a divine zeal of imitating the Apostles, by contributing to the enlargement of the Gospel, and building up the Church; of whom this Pantænus was one; who is said to have gone to the Indians, where it is commonly said he found the Gospel of Matthew, written in the Hebrew tongue, which before his arrival had been delivered to some in that country who had the knowledge of Christ, to whom Bartholomew, one of the Apostles, is said to have preached, and to have left with them that writing of Matthew, and that it was preserved among them to that time. This Pantænus, therefore, for his many excellent performances, was at last made president of the school of Alexandria, where he set forth the treasures of the divine principles both by word of mouth and by his writings."—Eccl. Hist. v, 9.

St Jerome, as quoted by Dr Lardner, vol. i, p. 391, says of him: "Pantænus, a philosopher of the Stoic sect, according to an ancient custom of the city of Alexandria, was, at the request of ambassadors from India, sent into that country by Demetrius, bishop of Alexandria, where he found that Bartholomew, one of the twelve Apostles, had preached the coming of our Lord Jesus Christ, according to the Gospel of Matthew, which he brought back with him to Alexandria, written in Hebrew letters."

is The Gospel according to St Mark. But the work mentioned by Papias as quoted by Eusebius, even if it could be called a gospel at all, seems to have been wholly different, and the account which they give of it is not applicable to the work which we now have. For the "Gospel according to St Mark" professes to give a continuous history of Christ's life, as regularly as the other three Gospels, but the work noticed by Papias, as may be seen from the fragment recited in page 115 of this volume, was written by Mark "not indeed in a regular order," but as much as he remembered of what Christ did and said. And Papias adds that Mark made no error, but wrote down accurately such things as Peter delivered from memory. In this case also the same Greek word *hermeneutes* is used to designate St Mark's relation to St Peter: the former became a follower and, as we say, *exponent* of the latter, but there has seldom if ever been any suggestion made by any of the commentators that the Gospel according to St Mark was ever translated from a lost original. Such an opinion would not however be wholly untenable, if it be true that our second Gospel was written at Rome, and that Mark was, as his Latin name *Marcus* would imply, by birth a Roman. To this however an important objection may be raised. Eusebius, quoting from Irenæus, tells us (*Hist. Ecc.* v, 8) that Mark the disciple and interpreter of Peter delivered to us in writing the things preached by Peter, after the *exodus* of Peter and Paul who had founded the Church at Rome. It has been a question whether these two Apostles were dead or had only departed from Rome. But in either case we are involved in great difficulties, for Eusebius tells us (ii, 24) that Annianus succeeded Mark as bishop of Alexandria in the 8th year of Nero's reign, which would correspond with the 61st year of the Christian era, when it would appear from the former statement that Mark was still at Rome, and Paul, consistently with the narrative in the Acts of the Apostles which makes him to have passed at least two whole years in that city, could not have left it before A.D. 63. Whether therefore we interpret the exodus as denoting the death or only the departure of the two Apostles, we do not escape the inconsistent statements that Annianus succeeded to Mark as bishop of Alexandria in A.D. 61, and that Mark wrote his Gospel at Rome after the death or departure of St Peter and St Paul in A.D. 63. It appears also from other passages in the Ecclesiastical History of Eusebius, to be almost certain that St Mark never was in Rome at all.

If it be admitted, as suggested in page 60 of this volume, that the early Christians were actuated, laudably it may be allowed, by mixed motives to display the zeal, which undoubtedly influenced them, in propagating the true religion, yet we can hardly go to the length which our early Christian writers would lead us, in their description of those missions. It may be doubted whether many leaders of the new sect would be thought worthy of deportation to Rome; and it does not seem reasonable to accept the accounts of Eusebius and others, who ascribe a sort of ubiquity to the Apostles and other early preachers of Christianity. If it is difficult to reconcile the two apparently conflicting accounts of St Mark above noticed, how shall we escape from the embarrassment which is thrown in our way by another account which Eusebius gives us as follows?

The first [Gospel] is written *according to* Matthew, the same that was once a publican, but afterwards an apostle of Jesus Christ, who published it for those who believed from out of Judaism, written in Hebrew letters. But the second is that according to Mark, who made it as Peter instructed him, whom also he acknowledged in his Catholic epistle (i, v, 13) as his son in these words saying, "The Elect *church* in Babylon saluteth you, and Marcus my son."

This passage has caused great embarrassment to all the commentators; who have failed to find that the solution of the difficulty is connected with the true estimate of the accuracy which is to be attributed to the historian who records it. Eusebius, who quotes the salutation sent by Peter from Babylon as undoubtedly due to Mark the Evangelist, has equally stated that St Mark was with Peter and Paul at Rome, and with equal plainness, as we have seen, stated that he died at Alexandria and was succeeded by Annianus in the episcopate of that city. A fourth passage occurs in the work of the same ecclesiastical historian (ii, 16) as follows:

They say that this Mark, being the first that went to Egypt, preached the Gospel, which indeed he also composed, and first established churches in Alexandria itself: and so great a multitude of those who there believed, both men and women, at the first outset, through their severe philosophical discipline, that Philo has deemed their pursuits, their meetings, their entertainments and all their other conduct of life, worthy to be noticed in his writings.

The embarrassment in which the reader is involved by these brief notices of St Mark and the work which he is said

XV.]   LUKE'S GOSPEL.   159

to have originally written, needs no augmentation from the fact that his name Marcus would show that he was a Roman: for there were many Greeks with Roman names and *vice versa* in those days. Nor, if written at Rome, is it surprising that the Gospel should be written in Greek; for the first promulgation of Christianity was effected by Greek missionaries, and the first converts at Rome were most probably Greeks also. The embarrassment here alluded to is mostly caused by the obscure language of Papias as quoted by the historian Eusebius. His constant reference to the "elder" and the "elders" does not sanction our attaching any authority to what remains of his works concerning the Gospel which now exists "according to" Mark, and the doctrines therein contained.

§ 3. *St Luke.*

The third of our canonical Gospels entitled according to St Luke, and commonly ascribed to him as its writer, differs from the others in having a form of dedication prefixed, from which we learn that it was compiled for the use of one Theophilus: which name occurs both in this dedication, and in another like it prefixed to the Acts of the Apostles. The purpose for which the dedication is here brought forward is to correct the grave errors which occur in the translation of it found in the authorized version of our Bible. I use the term grave errors, because the words, by which the Greek is translated, may lead the English reader to the belief that the author claims the credit of being a contemporary writer, whereas the Greek expressly declares that the author has accurately followed the accounts which had been handed down to his time by others who had been eye-witnesses of the facts. This is an important difference between the writer's real meaning and that which is attributed to him by those who follow an erroneous translation. The reader may judge from what follows whether this statement is correct.

AUTHORIZED VERSION.	CORRECTED TRANSLATION.
1. Forasmuch as many have taken in hand to set forth in order a declaration of those things which are most surely believed among us,	1. Forasmuch as many have taken in hand to set forth in order a NARRATIVE of those things, which HAVE BEEN BROUGHT TO FULFILMENT IN US,
2. Even as they delivered them unto us, which from the beginning were eye-witnesses, and ministers of the word;	2. Even as THEY, WHICH from the beginning were eye-witnesses and ministers of the word, have HANDED DOWN to us,

3. It seemed good to me also, having had perfect understanding of all things from the very first, to write unto thee in order, most excellent Theophilus,	3. It hath seemed good to me also, FOLLOWING ALL ACCURATELY FROM THE BEGINNING, to write unto thee in order, most excellent Theophilus,
4. That thou mightest know the certainty of those things, wherein thou hast been instructed.	4. That thou mightest know the certainty of those things, wherein thou hast been instructed.

There are here three mistranslations. The writer of this Gospel does not say that he is going to write about things "which are surely believed among us," but things, "which have been brought to fulfilment or completion (πεπληροφορημένων) in us." Neither was it himself and his contemporaries, "which from the beginning were eye-witnesses and ministers of the word," but others "who handed it down to him and his contemporaries." Again, the writer had not "perfect understanding of all things from the first," but he "followed or traced down (παρηκολουθηκότι) all the accounts of others from the first." If these statements do not show that he disclaims a contemporary character, and writes only at second-hand, then is there no rule for receiving literary evidence, but words may be turned to any meaning that may best suit the purpose of those who use them.*

Having then pointed out the preliminary errors which stand in the way of the English reader of this Gospel, we

---

* Dr Westcott, in his work on the Canon, suggests that the Greek verb translated "have attempted" may be translated "attempt," indicating that Luke's Gospel was written at the same time with the others which were less authentic. Let me remind him that the aorist denotes a past event which continues down to the present time, but never indicates positively any time at all. In this respect the English language corresponds with the Greek. We say *I did* a thing at some definite time, I *have done* it indefinitely, indicating a time that extends down to the present moment. If any one maintains the accuracy of the " assuredly believed," let him be informed that a man may be "filled with belief" as in Ep. Rom. iv, 21, whereas a thing cannot be "filled with belief" but is brought to fulfilment, as in II Tim. iv, 17, also it ought to be translated. The word also which is erroneously rendered "having had perfect knowledge of all things from the first," has in fact a totally different meaning. The word is used constantly, both by sacred and profane writers, to denote one who follows either a person or a doctrine, history or theory. See I Tim. iv, 6: II Tim. iii, 10: II Maccabees ix, 27: Justin M. Dial. c. T. p. 33 D; also Dioscorides Prolog. ad lib. vi; Lucian de Consc. Hist. § 6: Xenophon, Eq. viii, 14; Dem. cclxxxv, 21: Epict. II, xvi, 3. To these remarks it may be added that Theophilus was a man in some authority when the Gospel was dedicated to him, and that this must have been many years after he had been instructed or as the early Church expresses it had become a catechumen.

have only to observe further that not only the short preface, but the whole narrative of John the Baptist's birth and parentage, recorded in this Gospel alone, has met with severe criticism and been explained by the supposition, for which no ample and conclusive evidence has been produced, that the narrative which follows the preface in the Gospel according to St Luke, comprehending the genealogy and the account of Zacharias, are later additions made for some specific purpose and possessing less authority than the remainder of the Gospel. Those who have adopted this view refer to the Protevangelium Jacobi, one of the uncanonical gospels, but perhaps as ancient as those which form our canon. As there were conflicting accounts concerning the death of John the Baptist, described in page 65 of this volume, so also is there an incompleteness concerning the circumstances which accompanied his birth. The account given in the Protevangelium Jacobi is as follows:

But Herod sought for John and sent his attendants to Zacharias saying, "Where hast thou hidden thy son?" But he answered them saying, "I am a minister of God and serve in the temple of the Lord: I know not where my son is." And the attendants departed and told Herod all these things: and Herod being angry said, "His son is to be king of Israel," and he sent to him again, saying, "Speak the truth; where is thy son? for thou knowest that thy blood is under my hand." And Zacharias said, "I am a witness [martyr] of God, if thou sheddest my blood: for the master will receive my spirit, because thou sheddest innocent blood on the vestibule of the temple of the Lord." And about the time of dawn Zacharias was slain, and the sons of Israel knew not that he was slain. *Protev. Jac. p.* 44, ed. Tischendorf.

The devout believer in the truth of the Christian history, however prepared to admit errors or mistakes of detail incidental to everything proceeding from the pen, will need no arguments to induce him to question if not to reject accounts which materially affect the authority of our books; but error can only be detected and truth vindicated by the production of all the evidence which the case allows. As regards the death of Zacharias related in the above-named uncanonical gospel, the narrative has been connected with that passage of St Matthew's Gospel in which allusion is made to a certain Zacharias son of Barachias as slain between the temple and the altar. This event must have happened during or not long before our Saviour's time, for the victim of this murder is named as the last of those which were due to the unholy and rebellious spirit of the Jews, and the story more fully related in the Protevangelium Jacobi, was evidently well known, for it is referred to in St Luke's Gospel also (xi, 51) without any of those attendant circumstances which the uncanonical gospel supplies. It cannot however be denied that those who come for the first time to the knowledge of this narrative are naturally at a loss to know why St Luke, if he wrote those details which are recorded in his Gospel, should have omitted to relate the tragical event which followed so soon after; nor can it be wondered at that the German critic Ewald has doubted the authenticity of the chapter in which the miraculous birth of John the Baptist is recorded. In this doubt the reader will concur perhaps so far as to question the antiquity of the document, whilst he may still give credit to the truth of the facts.

§ 4. *John.*

The Gospels according to Matthew, Mark and Luke, are remarkably alike, both in the sequence of facts, the style of the composition, and in the identity of their words and language. This circumstance has attached to them the name of "Synoptical Gospels" in contradistinction to that according to John, which differs wholly in its historical arrangement and in its style, although in numerous passages it is identical in words and language with the other three. The transition from them to the fourth Gospel involves the passage from one world of thought to another; nor can any familiarity with the general teaching of the Gospels, or wide conception of the character of the Saviour suffice to destroy the contrast which exists in form and spirit between the earlier and the later narratives.* A few observations

---

* This is the judgement of Dr Westcott in his Introduction to the Study of the Gospels, page 249. He more fully develops the "contrast" in what follows:—"The Synoptic Gospels contain the Gospel of the infant Church; that of St John the Gospel of its maturity. The first combine to give the wide experience of the many: the last embraces the deep mysteries treasured up by the one. All alike are consciously based on the same great facts, but yet it is possible, in a more limited sense, to describe the first as historical, and the last as ideal; though the history necessarily points to truths which lie beyond all human experience, and the *ideas* only connect that which was once for all realized on earth with the eternal of which it was the revelation." If this be so, the contrast, spoken of in the text above, is still more striking than it is there described to be, and it becomes still more difficult to recognize two histories, if the divergence, even in the purpose for which they were written, is so remarkable.

on some of the peculiarities of this Gospel are all that is necessary at present. The other matters which require to be noticed, will recur in the comparison to be more fully instituted with reference to the harmonies and discrepancies which exist between all the four works in which the life and deeds of our Saviour are related.

We learn from the words of Papias, given in page 114, that there were two Johns, one of whom is named the elder, but Papias does not say that either of them had left anything in writing either of the nature of a Gospel or otherwise. The reader is left to form his own judgement on this point, and is at liberty to form it according to any one which he may prefer of the various opinions that have been given upon that subject. Again, we read in the Acts of the Apostles (iv, 13), that the rulers of the Jews and others, some of whom were kinsmen of the high priest, having examined Peter and John because they had preached the resurrection of the dead, marvelled at their boldness, perceiving that they were *unlettered and ignorant* men. As regards this statement which is probably true, for it is not likely that Jewish fishermen would possess much learning, it is certainly remarkable that the Gospel according to St John is written in much purer Greek than that of the other three, nor must it be forgotten that no sufficient explanation has been given for the fact that a fisherman of Galilee should be able to write in Greek at all. It is of course to be understood that any difference of style in a foreign language on the same subject is not readily noticed by the English reader, and this is especially the case with the authorized version of the New Testament, the language of which is, in every part of it, somewhat removed from the style of the present day, and in which also the various translators would seek as much as they were able to use similar language, so as to produce for the use of the English Church an uniform and harmonious work. It may further be remarked that, whereas Annas the high priest and Caiaphas were present at the inquiry related in the Acts, the prisoners Peter and John appear to have been wholly unknown to the tribunal before which they are summoned. But at the examination of our Lord himself recorded in the fourth Gospel (xviii, 16) we read that John—for all admit that he was that other disciple there named—being known unto the high priest, "spake unto her that kept the door, and brought in Peter." It has also been suggested that the writer of this Gospel by exalting the character and acts of

John, whilst he depreciates those of Peter, has betrayed himself to be that John, whose position he has sought to exalt. To inquire how far the fact is so would bear with little weight upon our present argument. Nor is it necessary to prove in the case of the fourth Gospel that a Jew could not have been its author; for the expression so constantly occurring about the "feasts" and other customs of the Jews (ii, 6, 13: v, 1: vi, 4: vii, 2: &c.) would hardly have been used if the writer had been a Jew himself.

It is of more importance to discuss, however briefly, a question which has in all ages been agitated concerning the last two verses of the twentieth and also the whole of the twenty-first chapter, with which the Gospel according to St John concludes. The former of these chapters ends thus:

30. And many other signs truly did Jesus in the presence of his disciples, which are not written in this book. 31. But these are written, that ye might believe that Jesus is the Christ, the son of God; and that believing ye might have life through his name.

These two verses, notwithstanding the adverse judgement of a few German critics, seem to form a fit termination to the history in which they are found. It is not easy however to pass a similarly favourable opinion on the twenty-first chapter of the Gospel, which seems rather to be an appendix attached afterwards than to have been a portion of the original work. "After these things Jesus showed himself again, &c." is the connection between this appendix and the preceding narrative which seemed to have been brought to a conclusion. It is however unimportant to determine whether this was written by St John at the same time as what goes before or by him at a later period of his life: for our argument is that St John is not the writer of any part of the work, unless perhaps of individual passages which he may have left in writing, and which have been embodied by those whose aim it was to collect the Memorials of all the Apostles and as many as could be got together of the "Sayings," or Oracles as they are also called, "of our Lord" Jesus Christ. It will be observed that of the three Synoptical Gospels, in one only, that according to St Matthew, is there a notice, and that a very slight one, of Jesus appearing in Galilee after his resurrection from the dead.

Then the eleven disciples went away into Galilee into a mountain where Jesus had appointed them.

There Jesus gave them brief instructions to teach and to baptize, and the history there ends. But in the Gospel according to St John, the history is resumed and, although some say the style of the language is different, yet the tenour of the facts related is certainly similar to that which had been wound up at the end of the previous chapter. There is also a peculiar feature of this appendix which has caught the attention and exercised the critical ingenuity of numberless critics. In verse 21 of this chapter Peter, speaking of the disciple whom Jesus loved, asks Jesus, "What shall this man do?" To this somewhat vague question, Jesus answers, "If I will that he tarry till I come, what is that to thee? Follow thou me." The answer would have been as obscure as the question, if we did not know from other sources that for many years the Christians believed that Christ would come again soon and establish on earth what he, and John the Baptist before him, had preached as the kingdom of heaven. After this, three more verses are added and the book concludes.

23. Then went this saying abroad among the brethren, that that disciple should not die: yet Jesus said not unto him, He shall not die; but, If I will that he tarry till I come, what is that to thee? 24. This is the disciple which testifieth of these things, and wrote these things: and we know that his testimony is true. 25. And there are also many other things which Jesus did, the which, if they should be written every one, I suppose that even the world itself could not contain the books that should be written. Amen.

Similar to this is the statement in the thirty-fifth verse of the nineteenth chapter, which refers to the soldier piercing the side of Jesus.

And he that saw it bare record, and his record is true: and he knoweth that he saith true, that ye might believe.

The two statements here compared were no doubt written by the same author, and it is obvious to infer that he is quoting the authority of the disciple whom Jesus loved, possibly St John as tradition had delivered it down, but, if he meant to say that he was himself that disciple, he has adopted a more singular mode of expressing his meaning than any other author either before or since his time.

Having premised these observations on the Gospels and the authors to whom they are ascribed, we will proceed to examine the history therein contained, and to compare the testimony of the four concerning the salient points of our Lord's life and actions, and thence to obtain such evidence as may be the result on the question whether they have been rightly ascribed to those authors or not.

CHAPTER XVI.
Genealogies of Christ, in the Gospels according to St Matthew and St Luke.

IN the Gospels according to St Matthew and St Luke are given genealogies of Christ, showing his descent, in the former from Abraham, the great ancestor of the Hebrews, in the latter from the first man, Adam. The catalogue, given in Luke's Gospel (iii, 23-38) is in accordance, for the earlier part from Adam to Abraham, with the list of names found in the book of Genesis; and from Abraham downwards to David, it agrees with the genealogy given in St Matthew's Gospel (i, 2-6), and both agree with the genealogy of the Old Testament, in either the Septuagint version or the Hebrew original. But the descent of Jesus, after the time of David, is told so discrepantly in the two Gospels, that it is absolutely impossible to reconcile them. In this portion of the genealogy, from David to Christ, the two accounts are inadmissible for these five reasons:

1. They do not agree with one another.
2. They do not agree with the genealogy found in the Old Testament.
3. They are not supported by probability.
4. The genealogy of St Matthew is not consistent with itself.
5. They impugn the doctrine of the Church, that the Christ was to be the descendant of King David.

The inference to be deduced from these serious discrepancies will be that the genealogies were drawn up later than the time of Christ, not by contemporary writers, who might perhaps have ascertained the truth, but by later writers, after the dispersion of the Jews into other countries, when the destruction of records and registers had made it difficult to ascertain the exact lineage of the family of Christ.

1. The first of the discrepancies will be evident from an inspection of the following table, in which the several

XVI.] THE GENEALOGICAL TABLES. 167

pedigrees from David to Christ are given in three parallel columns.

OLD TESTAMENT	MATTHEW	LUKE
David = Bath-sheba	David	David
Solomon Nathan	Solomon	Nathan
Rehoboam	Roboam	Mattatha
Abijah	Abia	Menan
Asa	Asa	Melea
Jehoshaphat	Josaphat	Eliakim
Jehoram	Joram	Jonan
Ahaziah or Azariah		Joseph
or Jehoachaz	Ozias	Juda
Joash		Simeon
Amaziah		Levi
Uzziah or Azariah		Matthat
Jotham	Joatham	Jorim
Ahaz	Achaz	Eliezer
Hezekiah	Ezekias	Jose
Manasseh	Manasses	Er
Ammon	Amon	Elmodam
Josiah	Josias	Cosam
Eliakim or Jehoiakim		Addi
Jeconiah	Jechonias	Melchi
		Neri
Salathiel	Salathiel	Salathiel
Pedaiah		
Zorobabel	Zorobabel	Zorobabel
	Abiud	Rhesa
	Eliakim	Joanna
	Azor	Juda
	Sadoc	Joseph
	Achim	Semei
	Eliud	Mattathias
	Eleazar	Maath
		Nagge
		Esli
		Naum
		Amos
		Mattathias
		Joseph
		Janna
		Melchi
		Levi
	Matthan	Matthat
	Jacob	Heli
	Joseph	Joseph
	Christ	Christ

On comparing these lists, we find that between David and Christ there are only two names which occur in both Matthew and Luke—those of Zorobabel and of Joseph the reputed father of Jesus. In tracing the list downwards from David there would be less difficulty in explaining this, at least to a certain point, for Matthew follows the line of Solomon, and Luke that of Nathan—both of whom were sons of David. But even in the downward line, on reaching Salathiel, where the two genealogies again come into contact, we find, to our astonishment, that in Luke he is the son of Neri, whilst in Matthew his father's name is Jechonias. From Zorobabel downwards, the lists are again divergent until we reach Joseph, who in St Luke is placed as the son of Heli, whilst in St Matthew his father's name is Jacob.

As an explanation of this difficulty we find in a note attached to the genealogy by St Luke in the Bible published by the Society for Promoting Christian Knowledge, the following passage:

It is seen that the genealogy of our Saviour, here given by St Luke, is entirely different, as far as David, from that given by St Matthew, chap. i. Among the various methods of explaining this, which have been proposed, the most probable is, that whereas St Matthew traced the genealogy through Joseph the husband of his mother, so St Luke here traces it through Mary his mother. It is certain that Heli was not the natural father of Joseph, for St Matthew expressly tells us, that "Jacob begat Joseph": it is therefore inferred that Heli was the father of Mary, and only father-in-law of Joseph. But it was never usual with the Jews to mention the names of females in their genealogies; on this account, Mary is not mentioned here by St Luke, but is only intimated or included, when the line is commenced from her father Heli. The true purport of this genealogy becomes more evident, if we consider, as seems to be intended, the word Jesus to be understood at every step. Thus it is to be supplied, Jesus, as was supposed, the son of Joseph, Jesus the son of Heli, Jesus the son of Matthat, &c.—Jesus the son of Seth, Jesus the son of Adam, Jesus the son of God. A style of genealogy precisely similar to this is used by Moses at Gen. xxxvi, 2, "Aholibamah the daughter of Anah, the daughter of Zibeon," &c.

Thus it appears that St Luke composing his gospel for the use of the Gentiles, and intending to prove that Christ was the seed of the woman, necessarily reckons by the line of his mother, Mary the daughter of Heli. St Matthew, on the other hand, intending to deduce his legal descent from David and Abraham, reckons by the line of Joseph the espoused husband of Mary through whom the legal descent was to be carried.—DR LIGHTFOOT.

It is difficult to look upon this extract seriously, or to believe that such a line of argument could ever have been put forward to explain what is really a great difficulty to all those who believe that the two Gospels in question were written by two contemporaries, and one of them a disciple, of our Lord. If we suppose Luke to *say* that Joseph was the *son* of Heli, and to *mean* that Mary, Joseph's wife, was the *daughter* of Heli, we are at liberty to give to words whatever meaning may best suit our own convenience, and the critical art, by which so many truths have been saved from oblivion, may be cast aside as no longer of any benefit to mankind. But there is nowhere any indication that Mary was the daughter of Heli, or that the Jews omitted "women in their genealogies." The utmost that can be said on this point is that the Jews, like the English, traced their descent if possible through the male line ; and in the case cited from Genesis xxxvi, 2, where is the evidence that Anah was not a female as well as a male appellation among the Jews? The passage cited is in itself a proof of this fact. The words "Aholibamah . . . the daughter of Zibeon," occurring in serious prose—not poetry—indicates that females were named occasionally in Jewish genealogies, and also that Anah, at least in this instance, was the name of a woman. But to recur more closely to our subject: the genealogies of Matthew and Luke are so different that it is impossible both can be true ; and it is not a sufficient reply to this objection to state that the writers wrote one thing, and meant another: there is no evidence that Jewish writers ever called a man the son of his wife's father, without some indication of their doing so.

2. But the genealogies do not differ less from that which is found in the Old Testament than they do from one another, as may be seen from the tables given above. That of St Luke does not so easily admit of being tested by this comparison ; for Luke traces the lineage of Christ through Nathan, another son of David, whose family and descent do not occur at all in the Old Testament. Yet even here, on the only point where it is possible to compare the two, they are found to differ : for Salathiel and Zorobabel, the only intermediate links which occur both in the Old Testament and in Luke, are placed in the older genealogy as grandfather and grandson, whilst in Luke they stand in the relation of father and son ; besides which Salathiel appears in Luke as the son of Neri, whilst in the Old Testament his father's name is Jechonias. Luke also mentions Resa as the son of

Zorobabel, but no such name occurs in the Old Testament of any such person. As the Old Testament genealogy is the more ancient, being in fact the original authority, it is clear that the genealogy given by St Luke must be set aside as inaccurate, because refuted by the evidence of an original and more authentic document. The genealogy of St Matthew, following the line of Solomon, as does that of the Old Testament, admits of a more ready comparison between the two ; and here also we find a perfect harvest of divergences.

First, as to the number of generations: the Old Testament gives twenty-two, St Matthew only seventeen from David to Zorobabel. Secondly, though the names for the first eight generations, from David to Jehoram, are as nearly alike as, perhaps, the Greek and Hebrew idioms will admit, yet a serious discrepancy immediately occurs ; for before Ozias, the eighth member of St Matthew's list, we have three names, Ahaziah, Joash and Amaziah, given in the Old Testament, and altogether omitted in St Matthew. The same Gospel genealogy also omits Eliakim after Josiah, and Pedaiah between Salathiel and Zorobabel.

The question then arises, How are these difficulties to be surmounted? and the dilemma which arises is simple: one of the two accounts must be erroneous ; but, as the Old Testament is the original authority, from which all later Jewish writers must have drawn their information, if they wished their histories to be received for truth, it follows that St Matthew's Gospel, as well as that of St Luke, have been inaccurately copied from the original sources. This leads us to believe that the writings, in which such mistakes are found, were composed when the means of arriving at the truth had been removed out of the way, which is equivalent to saying that these writings are not contemporary with the events which they describe.

3. But the third objection, which lies to the reception of these genealogies, is that they offend against probability ; for whilst the Gospel of St Matthew has twenty-eight generations from David to Christ, both inclusive, St Luke has forty-three generations for the same period. Now, the interval between David and Christ, 1050 years, divided by twenty-eight in the one case and by forty-three in the other, gives thirty-four years to a generation according to St Matthew, and twenty-four according to St Luke. The former estimate is much too long; no instance can be found in the history of the world, of twenty-eight generations, each of thirty-four years' duration. The objection does not apply to

the other Gospel, for twenty-four years is perhaps a reasonable duration to allow to each member in so long a pedigree.

4. A fourth objection to the genealogy of St Matthew is that it is inconsistent with itself: for, although the writer sets out with the statement that the pedigree from Abraham to Christ exhibits three periods, each of fourteen members or forty-two altogether, yet the names given in the list amount to forty-one only, even if we include those of Abraham and of Christ. This cannot have arisen from the error of a copyist; at least not within the last 1600 years, for Porphyry, one of the early opponents of Christianity, has mentioned the omission. It is true that some manuscript copies of the New Testament still exist, in which the number is made to amount to forty-two, by the insertion of an additional name, Jehoiakim, between Josias and Jechonias; but, unfortunately for this mode of correction, it has the effect of augmenting the second period of names from fourteen to fifteen, and still leaves the third period, from Jechonias to Jesus, where only thirteen names occur, imperfect as before.

Some persons have attempted to account for the discrepancy by supposing that the writer has counted some of the names in his list twice, so as to include them in two of the separate periods of fourteen. It would be a waste of words to refute so puerile an idea; and it is more to the point to suppose that the writer was led by a fanciful view of his subject, to divide the genealogy into three periods, for the sake of convenience, and neglected the slight difference between the actual number and that which he arbitrarily adopted. This may be admitted without much danger to the truth of the history—if it be supposed that the writer lived at a time when he could trifle with a serious subject—but not if that writer was one of the twelve disciples, inspired by God to declare to future ages the marvellous deeds which they had witnessed in the life and actions of Jesus their master.

5. Still more serious is the fifth objection, which lies against both the genealogies alike, connected it is true with a doctrine of the Church, but brought forward here for its historical significance only, and not for the purpose of supporting or weakening any doctrine of the Church at all. It is the belief of Christians that Jesus was the son of Mary by the Holy Ghost, in which case he would have a human mother but not also a human father. Mary however was of the tribe of Levi and therefore not descended from King David. Moreover she is not named in either genealogy, and her husband Joseph who is named, although descended from

King David, was not the father of Jesus. What then becomes of the genealogies, both of which represent Joseph as the father of Jesus, and do not mention his mother Mary? It is no solution of this difficulty that St Luke adds the words "as was supposed" to his statement that Jesus was the son of Joseph; for the writer does not even name Mary as entering into the genealogy at all; and St Matthew does not make the omission less remarkable by concluding his list of names with the words "Jacob begat Joseph the husband of Mary, of whom was born Jesus, who is called* Christ."

Amongst others who have taken in hand the solution of this discrepancy in the history, the Reverend Edward Greswell, certainly one of the most learned and diffuse of commentators, has given us the following account of the matter.

If Joseph was really the father of our Lord, the genealogy of Joseph, according to the flesh, would be the genealogy of our Lord, in the same respect—and it would be superfluous to search for any other. But if Joseph was not really the father of our Lord, that is, if the Christian doctrine of the Incarnation be scriptural and true—a doctrine, which St Matthew also confirms as plainly as St Luke—the genealogy of Joseph, according to the flesh, could in no wise be the similar genealogy of Christ. Now the genealogy, which is given by St Matthew, is obviously the genealogy of Joseph, according to the flesh: the use of the assertion "begat" between its several links, from first to last, admits of no other conclusion. If so, it could not be the genealogy of Christ in the natural sense. But it might still be his genealogy in some other sense—as reputed, for instance, the son of Joseph —that is, as naturally the son of the wife of Joseph [!]. It might be, therefore, his genealogy in a civil or political sense. Accordingly the same Evangelist, who so clearly propounds it as the natural genealogy of Joseph, does by no means propound it as the natural genealogy of Christ; for, when he is arrived at the name of Joseph, instead of continuing, as he had begun, and had proceeded all along until now—Ἰωσὴφ δὲ ἐγέννησε τὸν Ἰησοῦν —he changes his language in a striking manner—Ἰακὼβ δὲ ἐγέννησε τὸν Ἰωσὴφ, τὸν ἄνδρα Μαρίας ἐξ ἧς ἐγεννήθη Ἰησοῦς ὁ λεγόμενος Χριστός —It is evident, then, that he intended the previous line to stop short with Joseph—or not to pass on to Christ, except as the son of Mary, whose husband was Joseph. Nor is this all; but, if

---

* The word is here λεγόμενος, which does not mean called by a definite name like ὀνομαζόμενος, but so called by report, as we read in Liddell and Scott's Greek Lexicon, "τὸ λεγόμενον, absol. *as it is said, as the saying goes*, Lat. *quod perhibent* . . . ὁ λεγόμενος *the so-called.*"

the words be rightly translated, it is further implied by them, that Joseph did not become the husband of Mary until after the birth, or at least the conception, of Christ: And Jacob begat Joseph, the husband of Mary, of whom had been born, or had been conceived, Jesus who is called Christ. That this is a possible meaning of ἐγεννήθη, I have no hesitation in affirming.

It is almost needless to reply to these remarks of my late learned tutor and friend. A few words will be sufficient. Whatever may be the possible meaning of the word which we render "was born," it certainly has no other signification in the passage before us than that which is given to it in the authorized translation of the Bible. But if it had the meaning which is "affirmed to be possible," we might ask with reason why the genealogy of Joseph should be given at all, seeing that our Lord was born of Mary before her marriage with Joseph and was therefore in every respect unconnected with him or his family. A more reasonable explanation might be deduced from some observations on the first two chapters of St Matthew's Gospel by Dr Donaldson in his learned work on "Christian Orthodoxy," p. 277:

We agree, too, with Professor Norton (*Genuineness of the Gospels*, i, pp. 204, sqq.) that the translator and editor must have added some passages, which could scarcely have formed a part of the original Gospel. For example, there is every reason to believe that the first two chapters were derived from another source, and that the original Gospel began, like that of St Mark, with the preaching of John the Baptist. Other probable interpolations or additions are the following: the account of the repentance and death of Judas (xxvii, 3-10); the statement that many saints rose from the dead at our Saviour's crucifixion (xxvii, 52, 53); the reference to the sign of Jonah (xii, 40); and the doxology of the Lord's Prayer (vi, 13).

I refrain from touching further on the doubtful authenticity of the first two chapters of St Matthew's Gospel which contain the genealogy, or of the other passages which have been called in question by various critics. We are at present regarding the whole of this and the other Gospels as compilations from the original documents, namely the Memorials of the Apostles and the Sayings of our Lord, drawn up soon after the middle of the second century, when the living memory of the remarkable event therein recorded had become faint by the lapse of more than an hundred years.

CHAPTER XVII.

THE TWO ACCOUNTS OF THE ANNUNCIATION.

THE careful reader of the gospel history cannot fail to observe an incompleteness in the narratives of all the four evangelists, which gives them the appearance of contradicting one another, and has led their opponents to condemn them prematurely and in many instances unfairly. To this extreme they have been led, perhaps, in some cases, by the unreasonable conduct of indiscreet partisans whose admiration of the Gospels will not hear of their being incomplete or in any way defective. The truth is often found to lie half-way between extreme controversialists, even when the sacredness of the Gospel is assailed on the one hand, or defended on the other.

The history of the annunciation of the birth of Christ, as related by St Matthew and St Luke, will be found to be attended with a difficulty which requires to be noticed. The two accounts are here subjoined.

MATT. i. 18-25.	LUKE i. 26-38.
18. Now the birth of Jesus Christ was on this wise: When as his mother Mary was espoused to Joseph, before they came together, she was found with child of the Holy Ghost. 19. Then Joseph her husband, being a just man, and not willing to make her a publick example, was minded to put her away privily. 20. But while he thought on these things, behold, the angel of the Lord appeared unto him in a dream, saying, "Joseph, thou son of David, fear not to take unto thee Mary thy wife: for that which is conceived in her is of the Holy Ghost. 21. And she shall bring forth a son, and thou shalt call his name JESUS: for he shall save his people from their sins." 22. Now all this was done, that it might be fulfilled which was spoken of the Lord by the prophet, saying, 23, "Behold a virgin shall be with child, and shall bring forth a son, and they shall call his name	26. And in the sixth month the angel Gabriel was sent from God unto a city of Galilee, named Nazareth, 27. To a virgin espoused to a man whose name was Joseph, of the house of David: and the virgin's name was Mary. 28. And the angel came in unto her, and said, "Hail, thou that art highly favoured, the Lord is with thee: blessed art thou among women." 29. And when she saw him, she was troubled at his saying, and cast in her mind what manner of salutation this should be. 30. And the angel said unto her, "Fear not, Mary: for thou hast found favour with God. 31. And, behold, thou shalt conceive in thy womb, and bring forth a son, and shalt call his name JESUS. 32. He shall be great, and shall be called the Son of the Highest: and the Lord God shall give unto him the throne of his father David : 33.

Emmanuel, which being interpreted is, God with us." 24. Then Joseph being raised from sleep did as the angel of the Lord had bidden him, and took unto him his wife: 25. And knew her not till she had brought forth her firstborn son: and he called his name JESUS.

And he shall reign over the house of Jacob for ever; and of his kingdom there shall be no end." 34. Then said Mary unto the angel, "How shall this be, seeing I know not a man?" 35. And the angel answered and said unto her, "The Holy Ghost shall come upon thee, and the power of the Highest shall overshadow thee: therefore also that holy thing which shall be born of thee shall be called the Son of God. 36. And, behold, thy cousin Elizabeth, she hath also conceived a son in her old age: and this is the sixth month with her, who was called barren. 37. For with God nothing shall be impossible." 38. And Mary said, "Behold the handmaid of the Lord: be it unto me according to thy word." And the angel departed from her.

The points in these narratives which arrest our attention are manifold:

1. Either these are two different accounts of the same thing, or two separate annunciations were made, the one to Joseph, and the other to Mary. But either of these suppositions is attended with a difficulty. If they are two accounts of the same transaction, it is evident that they do not agree together; and we must explain the variation by supposing that tradition had gradually altered the features of the story, before it was at length set down in writing. If, however, there were two annunciations, it is obvious to remark that one of them seems to have been superfluous; for the announcement made to Mary, that she should conceive by the agency of the Holy Ghost, would render it unnecessary that the same announcement should be made to Joseph also. Not so—will doubtlessly be the reply—it was necessary that so important a fact as the conception of Mary by the Holy Ghost should be borne out by a heavenly communication made both to the husband and to the wife. If so, why was not the communication made to Joseph at the same time as to his wife? The angel appeared to Mary before she had conceived, but he did not show himself to Joseph until his nuptials with Mary had been solemnized, and then, before they came together, the husband discovered the condition of things. It is evident that two or three months must have passed since the conception, and it also appears that Joseph found out the fact for himself—and that Mary did not com-

municate it to him. This is not what we should have expected, nor what propriety seems to require. The heavenly message which Mary had received, followed by a change in her condition, that would naturally lead to suspicion and even scandal among her friends, would have extorted a confession of the truth; but to leave it to be found out by her husband, on the celebration of their wedding, would be neither prudent nor becoming.

In some of the uncanonical or apocryphal gospels the history of the annunciation is related with many additional particulars; for instance, that Mary's silence, previous to Joseph's discovery of her condition, arose from her having wholly forgotten the announcement made to herself; but this is simply absurd, for her condition would daily have reminded her of it. If we listen to another of the apocryphal gospels, Mary did actually communicate to Joseph what had passed; but in this case, if he had believed her, the later announcement made to himself would have been superfluous, and, on the other hand, if he did not believe her, the message previously delivered to Mary must as clearly have failed of its effect. Thus there are difficulties lying in our path, whichever view of the case we may prefer. Upon the whole, the weight of probability is in favour of the first-named interpretation—that St Matthew and St Luke relate the same annunciation with different features. To this conclusion it is no objection that it infers a discrepancy between the two evangelists; for such a discrepancy is sufficiently explained by the fading character of tradition, which always gives divergences to different accounts of the same transaction, until they are consigned to writing and admit of being thoroughly compared and tested. It is a fair argument against our accepting these separate annunciations, that neither of the evangelists has related both. It is rather remarkable that two only of them have alluded at all to so striking an intervention of the Almighty; but that two such interventions took place is less credible, when we find that neither of those two evangelists was acquainted with more than one.

CHAPTER XVIII.

DIFFERENT VIEWS ENTERTAINED BY THE FOUR EVANGELISTS CONCERNING THE DURATION OF CHRIST'S MINISTRY.

A COMPARISON of the four Gospels as to the general plan of the history which they contain, leads to the discovery of a very important divergency existing between them, respecting the duration of time occupied by the events therein related. On this point they do not all differ from one another; for the first three agree tolerably well in their general outline, and have for this reason been called Synoptic; but the chronology of John's Gospel is remarkably at variance with all the others.

According to the first Gospel, Christ, after his baptism and temptation in the wilderness, for which he had gone expressly out of Galilee into Judæa, immediately returns to Galilee and performs a series of cures, miracles, and other actions which occupy the whole of the evangelist's narrative as far as the end of the eighteenth chapter. In chapter xix, verse 1, he is related to have gone into Judæa beyond Jordan, and in the first part of chapter xxi, we have the visit to Jerusalem which led to his crucifixion. He there spends the day generally in the temple and retires to pass the night at Bethany.

The scheme of the second Gospel is in harmony with the foregoing. All the earlier part of it is occupied with Christ's teaching in Galilee, and at chapter x, verse 1, we read that he set out on his visit to Jerusalem.

The Gospel of St Luke does not differ from the two preceding. Eighteen chapters are occupied with Christ's teaching in Galilee, and in the first verse of chapter xix, we read that he went up to Jerusalem, passing through the town of Jericho.

Very different, however, is the historical basis of the Gospel according to St John, which represents Jesus first as showing himself to John the Baptist near the Jordan: "The next day John seeth Jesus coming unto him, &c." (i, 29). But in chapter ii, verse 1, we are told of the marriage at Cana of Galilee, and we should be at a loss to account for so long a journey performed in one day, if we were certain that the third day means the day after the interview with John.

Immediately after the account of this his first miracle, he goes to Capernaum, where he stops "not many days," and then we read in chapter ii, verse 13 :

> And the Jews' passover was at hand, and Jesus went up to Jerusalem.

Here he had the interview by night with Nicodemus, and in chapter iii, verse 22, we read :

> After these things came Jesus and his disciples into the land of Judæa; and there he tarried with them and baptized.

In the interval however between these two texts it is not said that Jesus had left Judæa, so that it appears superfluous information to tell us that he again came into it. But it was on this visit, if not that John the Baptist baptized Jesus, yet that he himself began to baptize, as appears also from chapter iv, verse 1-3, where we are told that he left Judæa, and for what reason.

> When therefore the Lord knew how the Pharisees had heard that Jesus made and baptized more disciples than John (though Jesus himself baptized not, but his disciples), he left Judæa, and departed again into Galilee. . . . . 46. So Jesus came again into Cana of Galilee, where he made the water wine.

On this journey it was necessary to pass through Samaria, and then occurred the interview at the well with the woman of that country. Whilst Jesus was talking with her, his disciples "were gone away into the city to buy meat" (iv, 8). But up to this time we have heard of only three disciples, Simon Peter, Andrew and Philip ; and yet the manner in which they are here named, without any allusion to the smallness of their number, being in fact precisely similar to the manner in which they are named elsewhere, supports the theory that this Gospel does not deal with events in a strictly chronological order, but relates them as they occurred to the mind of the writer, as a vehicle for the sayings and teaching of Jesus, which are so abundant in this work.

Having arrived in Galilee (iv, 43), he did not long remain there ; for we learn from chapter v, verse 1:

> After this there was a feast of the Jews; and Jesus went up to Jerusalem.

Here he cures the infirm man at the pool of Bethesda, and discourses about himself and John the Baptist, and we next find him again in Galilee, but nothing is told us of the manner or circumstances under which he went thither.

After these things Jesus went over the sea of Galilee, which is the sea of Tiberias. And a great multitude followed him, because they saw his miracles which he did on them that were diseased. And Jesus went up into a mountain and there he sat with his disciples (vi, 1).

In the next verse, vi, 4, we are told that " the Passover a feast of the Jews was nigh."

It is not, however, said that Jesus went up to this Passover; though shortly after he again goes up to Jerusalem, unknown to his disciples, whom he had led to suppose that he did not mean to attend the feast. We read this in chapter vii, verses 2-9, 10.

Now the Jews' feast of tabernacles was at hand . . . . 8. Go ye up unto this feast: I go not yet unto this feast; for my time is not yet full come. . . . 9. When he had said these words unto them, he abode still in Galilee. 10. But when his brethren were gone up, then went he also up unto the feast, not openly, but as it were in secret.

At chapter x, verse 22, we read:

And it was at Jerusalem the feast of the dedication and it was winter, And Jesus walked in the temple in Solomon's porch.

From which it would seem that Jesus passed the whole interval between the two feasts at Jerusalem—at least there is no notice of his having left it—between the feast of tabernacles and the feast of dedication.

At chapter x, 40-1, it is related that the Jews

Sought again to take him, but he escaped out of their hand, And went away again beyond Jordan into the place where John at first baptized; and there he abode.

It must have been here—namely, at Bethabara—that he received from Martha and Mary the message that their brother Lazarus was sick, and here that he abode two days longer before he went to raise him from the dead. According to chapter xi, verse 7, he said, " Let us go into Judæa again," and we then have the account of his return into Judæa out of Peræa, and his journey to Bethany for the purpose of recalling Lazarus to life. He subsequently retires " unto a country near to the wilderness, into a city called Ephraim," from fear of the Jews who had formed a design to kill him. From this place he returned to Bethany, six days before the final passover at which he was put to death (xii, 1).

The general character of the chronology of the four Gospels may be briefly stated as deduced from the above outline. The first three Gospels evidently lay the scene of Christ's teaching in Galilee, whilst the Gospel of St John places it principally in Judæa and in Jerusalem. So remarkable a discrepancy has not escaped the notice of the commentators and harmonists, and various modes have been adopted to reconcile the four narratives, so as to form a chronological basis for the history of our Lord's teaching and for the duration of his ministry. According to the first three Gospels, Christ's public life lasted only one year, at the end of which he went up to Jerusalem and was crucified. But, according to St John's Gospel, his ministry would appear to have lasted as many years as there occur passovers. This point, however, is not so easy to ascertain, for in some of the passages just quoted from St John's Gospel, where a feast is mentioned, it is uncertain whether the feast of the passover or some other feast is spoken of. It is, therefore, only by the most minute investigation of particular events that the commentators have endeavoured to form a system, and unhappily the results they have arrived at, do not speak favourably of the process by which they have been deduced; for whilst some have come to the conclusion that the whole period of Christ's ministry lasted two years, others have extended it to four and even to five years.

It appears that, during the first three centuries of our era, no one suspected the ministry to have lasted more than one year, but when the work of Eusebius appeared in the early part of the fourth century, and theology began to assume the form of a science, this, like every other subject, was examined and canvassed in a variety of ways, until there arose that great diversity of opinion which has since prevailed. That well-known ecclesiastical historian tells us (iii, 24) that the first three Gospels relate only what Jesus did and taught during the one year which elapsed after the imprisonment of John the Baptist, and that St John supplies the deficiency by relating what Jesus did before that time in Judæa, Jerusalem and elsewhere. To those who examine carefully the history as it is found in all the four Gospels, the explanation given by Eusebius will in no particular recommend itself. They say indeed that it was from the scarcity of copies of the New Testament and the difficulty of bringing together and comparing the four Gospels, that the world so long acquiesced in the first opinion; but also that St John's Gospel was then less known than it afterwards became. This argument however is dangerous to the antiquity of St John's Gospel; for, if not known, might not the enemies of its authenticity argue its non-existence? This, it is true, would be to draw an inference from imaginary premises; for there is no proof that the Gospel of St John was less known before the time of Eusebius than the other three Gospels. It is safer therefore to set aside all these opinions and inferences, and to be guided by a view of the Gospels themselves, and not by Eusebius or any other authorities; for the Gospels are open to us as to them, and are indeed more accessible to us than they were in the fourth century, when copies of them were exceedingly dear and scarce.

The first three Gospels plainly exhibit the events of only one year or little more; to prove them erroneous or defective in so important a feature as this, would be to detract greatly from their value—rather to nullify their authority—at least if we suppose them the work of the Apostles, who had witnessed the mighty works of Christ, and having seen him die upon the cross, were inspired by God to write a faithful account of his ministry. We cannot however convict them of such inaccuracy; for the whole tenour of their narratives points to the speedy termination of Christ's career, and that he only visited Jerusalem at the passover which coincided with his crucifixion. Could it be believed that so long a time as three, four, or five years would have produced no more sensible effect among so stubborn a people as the Jews? Such wonderful cures and miraculous deeds would have filled the whole world, if they had been continued for so long a time; and persons would have come from distant countries to see so wonderful a prophet—as the queen of Sheba came of old to see the wisdom and the riches of Solomon, or as pilgrims have gone in our days, from the farthest part of Europe, to witness the childish exhibitions which the Romish priests have from time to time set forth to deceive the unwary. Nothing however of this sort is recorded; and we justly infer from it that the ministry of Christ was short, as we read in the first three Gospels, and extended to little more than the period of one year.

This opinion is confirmed by certain indications, occurring in other parts of the history. Thus at Matthew xxi, 10, where Christ's triumphal entry into Jerusalem is recorded, we read:

And when he was come into Jerusalem, all the city was moved, saying, "Who is this?" And the multitude said, "This is Jesus the prophet of Nazareth of Galilee."

Would this questioning have taken place, if Jesus had often made visits to Jerusalem, and been well known there? The multitude who answered the question, and who knew Jesus, consisted of those "who had come to the feast,"—St John indicates this in chapter xii, verse 12.

On the next day much people that were come to the feast, when they heard that Jesus was coming to Jerusalem, took branches of palm trees, and went forth to meet him and cried, "Hosanna: blessed is the King of Israel that cometh in the name of the Lord."

It was then the strangers who knew Jesus, in Galilee perhaps, that recognized him, not the people of Jerusalem. The inhabitants of the city knew him not and therefore asked "Who is this?" But if St John's narrative is chronological, the people of the city also would have known him as well as the strangers who came up to the feast.

How then is the original divergency between the first three Gospels and that of John to be explained? If Matthew, Mark, and Luke cannot be convicted of error, must we accuse John of having falsified the fact of history? As there is no appearance of an intention to mislead in his narrative, is it possible that the writer was himself ignorant of the truth, and can merely be handing down to us the accounts which he had received from others? If so, the writer or compiler of this Gospel, as we now have it, was not contemporary with those facts—not to have known whether Christ's teaching occupied the space of one or of four years, or, at least, not to have stated this clearly for the benefit of his readers, shows clearly that the writer could not have been that John, Christ's beloved disciple, who was present at all the most important passages of his master's life, and who must have been able to settle this and every other doubt that might arise. This inference is the less to be avoided, if we admit, as is currently reported, that St John writes to supply the deficiencies of the former evangelists, and yet, so far from rectifying a most serious error, he has perpetuated a discussion, which, if we follow received opinions, is now farther from being cleared up than ever.

There is, however, a mode of explaining this difficulty also. The Gospel of St John is even still more unchronological in its order than the other three: and its general character, having rather doctrine than history in view, authorizes our supposing—what is indeed evident in almost every part of it—that the various facts which it records are placed as subordinate to Christ's teaching, and as suited the peculiar view of the writer. The fragmentary character, also, of all the four Gospels, showing that they have all been copied from tradition or from separate traditional anecdotes, would also have the effect of giving an unchronological and divergent appearance to the accounts of four separate compilers.*

CHAPTER XIX.

UNCERTAINTY ABOUT THE PLACE OF CHRIST'S BIRTH.

RESPECTING the time and place of Christ's birth, the evangelists St Mark and St John are altogether silent; for they begin their histories with the preaching of John the Baptist, and the appearance of Christ among those who throng to the banks of the river Jordan to be partakers of his baptism. St John does not name the place from which Jesus came for this purpose, but Mark is more explicit:

Mark i, 9. And it came to pass in those days, that Jesus came from Nazareth of Galilee, and was baptized of John in Jordan.

This tallies exactly with the general idea, common to all the evangelists, that Christ resided in Nazareth during the early part of his life. But residence at a place does not imply that a person was also born there; as is shown in the history before us: for two of the evangelists, St Matthew and St Luke, relate that Christ was born at Bethlehem, a village about six miles from Jerusalem. It is, indeed, very surprising that all the four evangelists have not related the fact of his birth at Bethlehem; for, as it was essential to the Messiah that he should be a Jew, and of the seed of David, it might be objected to the Gospels of St Mark and St John—if these were the only histories of Christ in existence

---

* A minute and almost exhaustive examination of the question concerning the duration of Christ's ministry is found in Fynes Clinton's "Fasti Romani," vol. ii, p. 227 (ed. Oxford, 4to, 1850).

—that having been born in Galilee, he might possibly not be a Jew at all.

Now the general reader is apt to regard Judæa, Samaria, and Galilee as three districts of the same land, like three counties of England; it may therefore be proper to explain the real nature of the connexion, which is not quite the same as in the case of the English counties.

We read in the "Annals of Tacitus," xii, 54, that in the year 32, two years after Christ was crucified, Cumanus a Roman had the government of Galilee, and that the inhabitants of the country waged a predatory war with their neighbours the Samaritans, who were under the government of Antonius Felix. This circumstance shows that there was at that time no common national feeling between the two states. The general tenour of the Gospels leads also to the same inference, that the Samaritans, and therefore also still more the Galileans, were aliens, and not included among God's chosen people. In fact, they were in the time of Christ a different people altogether, though it is true that they occupied the territory which had formerly belonged to the tribes of Issachar, Naphthali, Zebulon, Asher, and part of Dan. But the country was almost depopulated in the wars with the Babylonians, and had again been peopled by settlers of all nations. Strabo enumerates among its inhabitants Arabians, Egyptians, and Phœnicians; and, though they had, according to Josephus, two hundred and four cities and towns in their country, and were a very industrious people, yet the Jews treated them with contempt, and their language, although originally Hebrew, was a mixed dialect different from that which was spoken by the Jews at Jerusalem, as appears in the denial of Peter, who was instantly recognized by his speech. In accordance with these facts, we find that the Jews held the Galilæans in great contempt, and when told of the supposed birthplace of Christ, they asked, whether any good or any prophet could come out of Galilee and Nazareth.

Thus, then, we are justified in expressing some surprise that neither St Mark nor St John has alluded to the fact of Christ's having been born at Bethlehem, as a ready refutation of those who might contend that he was not a Jew at all.

St Matthew and St Luke, however, *have* recorded that Christ was born at Bethlehem; but it will be evident from an impartial perusal of their separate narratives, that the points of view, from which these two contemplate the birth at Bethlehem, do not coincide: for whilst St Matthew supposes that Christ's parents had always lived at Bethlehem before the flight into Egypt, St Luke tells us that they lived at Nazareth, and only went to Bethlehem for a short visit during which Mary gave birth to Jesus. The narratives of Matthew and Luke here follow.

MATTHEW ii, 1-23.

Now when Jesus was born in Bethlehem of Judæa in the days of Herod the king, behold, there came wise men from the east to Jerusalem, 2. Saying, Where is he that is born King of the Jews? for we have seen his star in the east, and are come to worship him.

3. When Herod the king had heard these things, he was troubled, and all Jerusalem with him. 4.

LUKE ii, 1-52.

And it came to pass in those days, that there went out a decree from Cæsar Augustus, that all the world should be taxed. 2. (And this taxing was first made when Cyrenius was governor of Syria.) 3. And all went to be taxed, every one into his own city.
4. And Joseph also went up from Galilee, out of the city of Nazareth, into Judæa, unto the city of David, which is called Bethlehem; (because he was of the house and lineage of David): 5. To be taxed with Mary his espoused wife, being great with child. 6. And so it was, that, while they were there, the days were accomplished that she should be delivered. 7. And she brought forth her first-born son, and wrapped him in swaddling clothes, and laid him in a manger; because there was no room for them in the inn.

. . . .

21. And when eight days were accomplished for the circumcising of the child, his name was called JESUS, which was so named of the angel before he was conceived in the womb. 22. And when the days of her purification according to the law of Moses were accomplished, they brought him to Jerusalem, to present him to the Lord; 23. (As it is written in the law of the Lord, Every male that openeth the womb shall be called holy to the Lord;) 24. And to offer a sacrifice according to that which is said in the law of the Lord, A pair of turtledoves, or two young pigeons.

25. And, behold, there was a man in Jerusalem whose name was Simeon, &c.

[*Here follows the narrative of Simeon and Anna in the Temple.*]

MATTHEW ii, 1-23.

And when he had gathered all the chief priests and scribes of the people together, he demanded of them where Christ should be born. 5. And they said unto him, In Bethlehem of Judæa: for thus it is written by the prophet, 6. And thou, Bethlehem, in the land of Juda, art not the least among the princes of Juda; for out of thee shall come a Governor, that shall rule my people Israel. 7. Then Herod, when he had privily called the wise men, enquired of them diligently what time the star appeared. 8. And he sent them to Bethlehem, and said, " Go and search diligently for the young child: and when ye have found him, bring me word again, that I may come and worship him also." 9. When they had heard the king they departed: and, lo, the star, which they saw in the east, went before them, till it came and stood over where the young child was. 10. When they saw the star, they rejoiced with exceeding great joy.

11. And when they were come into the house, they saw the young child with Mary his mother, and fell down, and worshipped him; and when they had opened their treasures, they presented unto him gifts: gold, and frankincense, and myrrh. 12. And being warned of God in a dream that they should not return to Herod, they departed into their own country another way.

13. And when they were departed, behold, the angel of the Lord appeareth to Joseph in a dream, saying, "Arise, and take the young child and his mother, and flee into Egypt, and be thou there until I bring thee word: for Herod will seek the young child to destroy him." 14. When he arose, he took the young child and his mother by night, and departed into Egypt: 15. And was there until the death of Herod: that it might be fulfilled which was spoken of the Lord by the prophet, saying, Out of Egypt have I called my son.

16. Then Herod, when he saw that he was mocked of the wise men, was exceeding wroth, and sent forth, and slew all the children that

LUKE ii, 1-52.

MATTHEW ii, 1-23.	LUKE ii, 1-52.
were in Bethlehem, and in all the coasts thereof, from two years old and under, according to the time which he had diligently enquired of the wise men. 17. Then was fulfilled that which was spoken by Jeremy the prophet, saying, 18. In Rama was there a voice heard, lamentation, and weeping, and great mourning, Rachel weeping for her children, and would not be comforted, because they are not. 19. But when Herod was dead, behold, an angel of the Lord appeareth in a dream to Joseph in Egypt, 20. Saying, "Arise, and take the young child and his mother, and go into the land of Israel: for they are dead which sought the young child's life." 21. And he arose, and took the young child and his mother, and came into the land of Israel. 22. But when he heard that Archelaus did reign in Judæa in the room of his father Herod, he was afraid to go thither: notwithstanding, being warned of God in a dream, he turned aside into the parts of Galilee: 23. And he came and dwelt in a city called Nazareth: that it might be fulfilled which was spoken by the prophets, He shall be called a Nazarene.	39. And when they had performed all things according to the law of the Lord, they returned into Galilee, to their own city Nazareth. 40. And the child grew, and waxed strong in spirit, filled with wisdom: and the grace of God was upon him. 41. Now his parents went to Jerusalem every year at the feast of the passover. 42. And when he was twelve years old, they went up to Jerusalem after the custom of the feast. 43. And when they had fulfilled the days, as they returned, the child Jesus tarried behind in Jerusalem: and Joseph and his mother knew not of it. 44. But they, supposing him to have been in the company, went a day's journey; and they sought him among their kinsfolk and acquaintance. 45. And when they found him not, they turned back again to Jerusalem, seeking him. 46. And it came to pass, that after three days they

LUKE ii, 1-52.
found him in the temple, sitting in the midst of the doctors, both hearing them, and asking them questions. 47. And all that heard him were astonished at his understanding and answers. 48. And when they saw him, they were amazed: and his mother said unto him, "Son, why hast thou thus dealt with us? behold, thy father and I have sought thee sorrowing." 49. And he said unto them, "How is it that ye sought me? wist ye not that I must be about my Father's business?" 50. And they understood not the saying which he spake unto them.
51. And he went down with them, and came to Nazareth, and was subject unto them: but his mother kept all these sayings in her heart. 52. And Jesus increased in wisdom and stature, and in favour with God and man.

The evangelists here agree in fixing the birth at Bethlehem; but St Matthew supposed that town—and not Nazareth—to be the place where Joseph and Mary had previously resided; or he would not have related that they feared to return into Judæa, and were so led to take up their abode at Nazareth, which was not in Judæa. If St Matthew had known Christ's parents to have commonly resided at Nazareth, and that they were only on a visit or forty days at Bethlehem, he would not have thought it required an explanation, why Jesus should be called a Nazarene, nor has the application of the word Nazarene, here made, been satisfactory to a large number of those who have commented on this part of the history. St Luke apparently knew that the family of Joseph were ordinarily inhabitants of Nazareth, and he therefore does not think it necessary to give any other reason for Christ's being so called.

CHAPTER XX.

UNCERTAINTY ABOUT THE TIME OF CHRIST'S BIRTH—ANACHRONISM OF THE CENSUS—CHRIST BORN BEFORE A.D. 1.

CONCERNING the *time* of Christ's birth there are even greater doubts than about the place; for, though the four evangelists have noticed several contemporary facts, which would seem to settle this point, yet on comparing these dates with the general history of the period, we meet with serious discrepancies, which involve the subject in the greatest uncertainty.

The data which the Gospels furnish for ascertaining the chronology are these:

1. The taxing [more correctly enrolment or census] stated by St Luke to have been the cause of Mary's visit to Bethlehem, where her son Jesus was born.

And it came to pass in those days, that there went out a decree from Cæsar Augustus that all the world should be taxed, And this taxing was first made when Cyrenius was governor of Syria (ii, 1).

2. The fifteenth year of the reign of Tiberius, marked, as St Luke tells us, by the following synchronisms:

Now in the fifteenth year of the reign of Tiberius Cæsar, Pontius Pilate being governor of Judæa, and Herod being tetrarch of Galilee, and his brother Philip tetrarch of Ituræa and of the region of Trachonitis, and Lysanias the tetrarch of Abilene, 2. Annas and Caiaphas being the high priests, the word of God came unto John the son of Zacharias in the wilderness. 3. And he came into all the country about Jordan, preaching the baptism of repentance for the remission of sins (iii, 1-3).

At verse 23 of the same chapter, we read, that at the same time Jesus himself began to be about thirty years of age.

From these data, we should infer that Christ was born fifteen years before the emperor Tiberius came to the throne, and that the census alluded to by the writer took place in the same year. To the former part of this inference, we have nothing to object at present; the statement that Jesus was thirty years old, fifteen years after the death of Augustus, implies that he was born fifteen years before the decease of that emperor; and no concurrent events are related, which enable us to dispute the truth of the account.

The writer however of St Luke's Gospel is not correct in stating that a census or taxation, decreed by Cæsar Augustus, and executed by Cyrenius, or as he is called in Latin Quirinus, furnished occasion for Mary's visiting Bethlehem, where her son Jesus was born, fifteen years before the death of the emperor Augustus. There is no mention in history of any census, or assessment of the whole Roman empire for the purpose of taxation, or indeed for any other purpose, as having been made at that time; and even if such a taxation had been made, it would not have extended to Judæa, which was still an independent country, under its king Herod the Great, and was not reduced to the form of a Roman province until ten years afterwards. Nor is there any proof that Lysanias was tetrarch of Abilene.

Is it then to be supposed that the account which St Luke's Gospel gives us of a census, is a forgery on the part of the writer, and that no such enrolment or mission of Cyrenius ever took place? Far from it—it is only necessary to suppose that the writer has committed an anachronism—not a forgery: for it is related by Josephus that Cyrenius did actually go into Judæa on a mission of the kind referred to by the evangelist about the year A.D. 10, and consequently ten years later than the birth of Christ. The affair is related by Josephus (*Antiq.* XIII, i, 1), in these words:

> Cyrenius, a man of those who assemble in the senate, who had both discharged the other magistracies, and had gone through all so as also to have been consul, and who was in other respects great in estimation, came with a few attendants to Syria, having been sent by Cæsar to give justice to the nation, and to take an account of their substance. Coponius also a man of the equestrian order, is sent with him to hold supreme authority over the Jews.
>
> But Cyrenius also came into the country of the Jews, which had been made an appendage to Syria, both to make a valuation of their substance, and to administer the property of Archelaus. But the people, although at first bearing ill their obedience to pay tribute, refrained from making any further opposition, by the persuasion of their chief priest Joazar, who was the son of Boethus. Overcome by the arguments of Joazar, they gave in a valuation of their property, nothing doubting.

There can be little doubt that this is the mission of Cyrenius which the evangelist supposed to be the occasion of the visit of Christ's parents to Bethlehem. But such an error betrays on the part of the writer a great ignorance of the Jewish history and of Jewish politics; for, if Christ was born in the reign of Herod the Great, no Roman census or enrolment could have taken place in the dominions of an independent king. If, however, Christ was born in the year of the census, not only Herod the Great, but Archelaus also his son was dead. By no possibility can the two events be brought together; for even after the death of Archelaus Judæa alone became a Roman province; Galilee was still governed by Herod Antipas as an independent prince, and Christ's parents would not have been required to go out of their own country to Jerusalem for the purpose of a census which did not comprise their own country Galilee. Besides which, it is notorious that the Roman census was taken from house to house, at the residence of each, and not at the birth-place or family *rendezvous* of each tribe.

Nor is there any proof that Lysanias was the governor of Abilene at this time. The only Lysanias mentioned in history as tetrarch of Abilene died many years before, and no mention is made of any son who bore that name. It is suggested by those who doubt the accuracy of St Luke's Gospel that he ignorantly makes Lysanias still alive, being deceived by the fact that the country was still called the Abilene of Lysanias, in honour perhaps of its former governor. It is in vain that harmonists and commentators have attempted to reconcile these conflicting accounts. There is no need of any other explanation than the partial obscurity of the history at the time St Luke's Gospel was written. This view does not weaken the estimation in which every sensible man will hold both that and the other three Gospels, which were written to perpetuate the benevolent sentiments and doctrines of Jesus, but not to teach us chronology. It matters not what was the circumstance that led the holy family to Bethlehem: all we know about it is, that it certainly was not the census, which did not happen until ten years afterwards, and which, if it had been in harmony as regards the time, would still have presented numberless difficulties, forbidding us to accept it in the manner which the evangelist has described.

But, notwithstanding these patent difficulties in the narrative, the Camden Professor of Ancient History, in a Lecture delivered at Oxford before the Christian Evidence Society, has endeavoured, as he thinks successfully, to vindicate the exact truth of the Gospel History in this account of the census, so that in this and in every other particular "the historical character of the New Testament (to use his own words) is, I think I may say, in the eyes of all sober historical critics established."

The answer, which the Professor makes to the charge of inaccuracy, is as follows.

The words of St Luke [ii, 2] cannot possibly mean that Cyrenius was governor at the time of the taxing; had it been St Luke's intention to express this, the verse would have run thus: "This taxation was made when Cyrenius was governor of Syria," and not "This taxing was first made, &c." "First," that is, which is manifestly the emphatic word of the sentence, would have been absent from it. Evidently, therefore, St Luke's words must bear some other meaning. They may signify "*this* taxing was made before Cyrenius was governor," and so before that better known taxing which he ordered. This is an allowable translation of the passage. Or they may mean, and I think they do mean, "this taxing was first completed—first took full effect —when Cyrenius was governor;" that is to say, the taxing ordered by Augustus, and commenced under Herod the Great, was interrupted (as it may easily have been, since the Jews were very bitter against it) and the business was first accomplished under Cyrenius. This is a sense which the Greek verb translated in our version " was made" sometimes has.

It seems hardly necessary to reply to criticism which— not for grammatical reasons, but to avoid the historical inference flowing from it—denies the accuracy of a translation that has passed current for several hundred years as well expressing the meaning of the Greek original, and borne out in terms still stronger by the Latin Vulgate. It is possible, however, to express the Greek still more literally and to support its meaning by the unmistakeable testimony of the Latin.

GREEK : This taxing [more correctly enrolment] was the first of Cyrenius governor of Syria. LATIN: This description first was made by the president of Syria.

Of the two translations substituted in the place of that which is generally received, the first, " although allowable," is rejected as unsatisfactory by the Professor himself, who will no doubt see that the declinable adjective, which we translate *first*, cannot have the meaning of the comparative *before* except between two names of persons or two names of things. The only two passages in the New Testament (John i, 15-30 ; and xv, 18) where it occurs with the apparent meaning of *before*, fulfil the conditions here pointed out, and it is not clear that in the last of those places the word *first* is equivalent to the adverb at all. Our Lord may be supposed to identify himself with his followers, and to say: "If the world hate you, ye know that it hated me first of you."

Of the second translation suggested by the Professor less still can be said in favour than of the first. For there is no idea of completion whatever implied in the verb ἐγένετο, which generally means that a thing happened or took place, but in numerous instances has more reference to the beginning of an event than to its end. The literal meaning of the verb is to grow or be produced, and in such a sense it occurs in Matthew xxi, 19, "Let no fruit grow (γένηται) on thee for ever." Still less worthy of refutation is the remark that the taxing named in the Gospel was interrupted by the Jews and therefore only completed ten years afterwards. Nothing is said of any disturbance; on the contrary everything passes off smoothly in the Gospel narrative, and when the Holy Family "had performed all things according to the law of the Lord, they returned into Galilee, to their own city Nazareth." *

As regards the difficulty about Lysanias, Professor Rawlinson quotes an inscription found near Baalbec on a memorial tablet or statue "to Zenodorus (son of the tetrarch Lysanias) and to Lysanias, her children," and suggests that it was the widow of the elder Lysanias and mother of the second Lysanias who set it up. This inscription would certainly indicate that there was a second Lysanias son of the former, but not that Lysanias the son was also tetrarch of Abilene. It would indeed rather tend to prove that the son was never governor of that or any other province. For we read in the "Antiquities" of Josephus, xv, x, i, that "one Zenodorus had hired the house of Lysanias," but the writer does not say that Zenodorus was the son of Lysanias, although he relates the rapine and other deeds which Zenodorus enacted in his office as tetrarch of the country now spoken of. His misdeeds attracted the notice of Augustus, but, as he died a natural death soon afterwards, these were not inquired into. Seeing however that his father Lysanias (if he was his father) was put to death by Mark Antony, B.C. 35, on a charge of introducing the Parthians into the

---

* "The two numbers in St Luke, the 15th year of Tiberius and thirty years of age for Jesus at the Baptism, are irreconcilable with each other." Clinton's *Fasti Romani*, vol. ii, page 237: to which the reader is referred for a full statement of the difficulties which surround this subject.

empire, and that one of the sons Zenodorus also appears to have given offence to the imperial government, it is far from likely that the second Lysanias should be made tetrarch after the punishment of his father and the imputed misconduct of his brother whilst successively at the head of the administration in those provinces.

There is another circumstance of some moment connected with the time of Christ's birth, which confirms our view, that the Gospels were not written until the events which they contain had become obscured by time. So important an occurrence as the intervention of the son of God to redeem and instruct mankind, might seem a likely subject to engage the attention of the world, and to occupy the pens of numerous writers to hand down to posterity every minute particular of so solemn a theme. To expect that nothing would be doubtful or unsettled about a person so exalted would be wholly natural and consistent with reason. That such an expectation would be in every way reasonable was admitted from the very beginning of the Christian Church: for not only do we date our time from the exact year in which Christ is said to have been born, but our ecclesiastical calendar has determined with scrupulous minuteness the day and almost the hour at which every particular of Christ's wonderful life is stated to have happened. All this is implicitly believed by millions; yet all these things are among the most uncertain and shadowy that history has recorded. We have no clue to either the day or the time of year, or even the year itself in which Christ was born. Every thing about him is unknown, save the morality which he has taught us, and that short space of his life termed his "Ministry," when, as the Gospels tell us, he went about doing good, and had not where to lay his head. Notwithstanding the seeming accuracy of our Gospels, which tell us that in the "fifteenth year of the reign of the emperor Tiberius—Jesus began to be about thirty years old," yet there has always been a doubt in the Church, whether a mistake of four years has not been made in fixing the first year of the Christian era. When we reflect that the present mode of calculating time was not adopted until 500 years of our era had already passed, it will not be wonderful that there should be some difficulty in recovering dates that had for so long a time been neglected. But all such probabilities as these are based upon the supposition that the history is similar to other histories, and the whole question, of a *human*, not of a *divine*, nature. For that which comes from God, suffers no obscuration by lapse of time—to Him especially is applicable that legal maxim, which we apply to our kings—*nullum tempus occurrit regi*. If the Gospels, written by his immediate inspiration, have once for all declared that his Son was born in the fifteenth year before the death of the emperor Augustus, that Herod the Great was still alive, and that a census of the whole Roman world was made in that year, we may be sure that all these points will be found to concur at the beginning of the year Anno Domini 1, so that no doubt may be raised or incredulity be entertained!

But, unhappily, there has been a doubt about the concurrence of these things; until it is at last allowed that those events do not concur at all, and that our present calculation of years since the birth of Christ is erroneous. It is true that no practical evil can result from this error; for a conventional harmony between the years following A.D. 1, and those preceding that date has long been established. According to our best system of chronology, the birth of Christ is fixed at December 25 or Christmas Day at the end of the year 1 before Christ, so that, by neglecting the short space of time, six days, which remain to complete the year B.C. 1, we consider Christ's birth to coincide with the end of the year B.C. 1, and the beginning of the year A.D. 1. It is also agreed, that the year A.D. 1 shall coincide with the following dates:

1. The 1st year of the 195th Olympiad.
2. The consulship of Caius Cæsar and Lucius Æmilius Paulus.
3. The 32nd year of the reign of the Emperor Augustus.

By this mode of synchronism, we find that so many years have passed down to the present time—not since the birth of Christ, but since the time conventionally fixed on as the end of B.C. 1 and the beginning of A.D. 1.

There can be no doubt that this system had its origin in too implicit a reliance on the words of the Gospel, "In the fifteenth year of the reign of the emperor Tiberius, Jesus began to be about thirty years old": for, since it has been usual to examine the grounds upon which history is founded —a process not so general in the days of Dionysius Exiguus, who introduced the present mode of dating—we have discovered, that at the time fixed for the birth of Christ, king Herod the Great had been dead nearly four years. By the same discovery also it was evident, either that the history of Christ's persecution by Herod the Great is erroneous, or else, that in the fifteenth year of Tiberius, Jesus began to be—not about *thirty* but about *thirty-four* years of age.

The ecclesiastical historian, Sulpicius Severus, has observed, in his "Chronicle" (ii, 29):

Christ was born in the consulship of Sabinus and Rufus, on the 8th day before the calends of January, *i.e.* Dec. 25, B.C. 1.

According to the observations made above, this would be correct: and we might be content to find that an unimportant error had been satisfactorily remedied. But other ancient writers are not found to be in agreement with Sulpicius on the one hand, or with the received system of chronology on the other.

Cassiodorus, who lived in the sixth century, says:

Caius Lentulus and Marcus Messala. In their consulship, our Lord Jesus Christ, the son of God, is born in Bethlehem, in the 41st year of the reign of Augustus.

The consulship of Caius Lentulus and Marcus Messala fell on the 3rd not the 4th year before A.D. 1: and Cassiodorus is supported in this account by Clement of Alexandria, who says, in his "Stromata," vol. 1, p. 340 B:

From the time when the Lord was born until the death of Commodus, were in all, 194 years, 1 month, and 13 days.

Commodus was slain A.D. 192, Dec. 31, so that our Lord's birth fell in B.C. 3.

But, unfortunately, the ecclesiastical historian Eusebius agrees with neither of the writers already cited, nor with the received chronological arrangement. In his "Ecclesiastical History," i, 5, he writes:

This was the 42nd year of the reign of Augustus, but of the subjection of Egypt and the death of Antony and Cleopatra, the 28th year.

"Eusebius," observes Mr Clinton in his "Fasti Hellenici," (vol. iii, p. 258), "like Josephus, 'Ant.' xviii, 2, 2, reckoned the years of Augustus from the death of Cæsar." He therefore places the birth of Christ in the year B.C. 2.

Epiphanius, also, in his work "On Heresies," liber 1, tom. 1, p. 48 B, says that the Saviour was born in the 42nd year of the emperor Augustus.

Zonaras also and Orosius agree in placing the birth of Christ at the end of the second year before the beginning of our era.

Again, Tertullian, in his work "Against the Jews," chapter 8, makes a calculation which fixes the birth of Christ both to the year B.C. 1 and B.C. 3, in the same sentence.

We shall see that Christ was born in the 41st of the reign of Augustus dating from the death of Cleopatra. Augustus survived the birth of Christ 15 years.

The particulars of this notice do not agree together. "41 + 15 = 56 years," as Mr Clinton observes, "do not express the interval." If Tertullian placed the Nativity fifteen years before the death of Augustus, he placed it in the year A.D. 1. But there is an error in the text of Tertullian: the reign of Augustus cannot be dated from the death of Cleopatra, which happened only 30 years before Christ. It has therefore been proposed to substitute *Cæsaris* for *Cleopatræ*, but as Cæsar was slain 43 years before A.D. 1, in this case Tertullian places the Nativity in B.C. 3. Thus in the same sentence he gives conflicting dates.

Lastly; the evidence of an old Roman calendar, *Fasti apud Norisium*, may be brought for placing the birth of Christ, not at the beginning, but at the end, of the first year of our era:

Cæsar and Paulus. In this consulship, Christ was born on the 8th day before the calends of January—*i.e.* Dec. 25, A.D. 1.

From a consideration of all these different opinions, it may safely be inferred that it is impossible to determine the exact truth. All the writers here named have, no doubt, taken the statements of the Gospels as the groundwork of their different systems of chronology; but, when we reflect that the statements of the Gospels are inconsistent with themselves and involve a dilemma, we are necessarily led to the inference that they are erroneous in one or other of the conflicting points—either Christ was thirty-four, not thirty, years old in the fifteenth year of Tiberius, or he was not born until four years after the death of Herod the Great. I leave it for those who worship the letter of the Gospels and neglect or undervalue their spirit, to say which alternative they will choose.

CHAPTER XXI.

FLIGHT INTO EGYPT—MURDER OF THE INNOCENTS, &c.

THE same two evangelists who have related that Christ was born at Bethlehem in the days of Herod the king, have gone further into details concerning what took place at Bethlehem and Jerusalem, followed by the massacre of the Innocents and the flight into Egypt; but these writers do not agree together, and cannot be reconciled in any other way than by supposing that one of them was ignorant of some facts with which the other was acquainted. Thus St Luke tells us, in the passage which has been given from his Gospel in a former page (187), that when Mary had made the usual offering for her purification in the temple, forty days after the birth of Jesus, the holy family immediately returned to Nazareth their usual place of residence. But if so, what becomes of the visit of the magi, and the flight into Egypt? There is no room for this to have taken place; for if the flight into Egypt and the tarrying there until the death of Herod are to be understood as following immediately after the birth, in that case Mary did not go to Jerusalem to present Christ in the temple. If, on the other hand, the offering in the temple is the first event after the birth, and the flight into Egypt followed, it is equally certain, that St Luke is wrong in saying that "when they had performed all things according to the law of the Lord, they returned into Galilee, to their own city Nazareth."

The solution of this dilemma is to be found not by laboriously endeavouring to prove that two years intervened between events, which the writers have related, in the same breath, as following closely one upon the other, but by admitting that the Gospels, like all other writings, are liable to error, that the writers of the different Gospels have put together all such separate narratives of particulars as came within their reach or seemed worthy of admission into their respective works. According to this view, we may infer—*must* indeed infer, for there is no reasonable alternative—that the writer of the Gospel according to Luke was not aware of the flight into Egypt, and therefore connects the return of Christ with his parents to Nazareth as immediately following the presentation in the temple, and the other incidents which took place during their short visit to Jerusalem and Bethlehem.

But our examination of this part of the narrative must not be limited to the divergency between the Gospels according to St Matthew and St Luke. We must take into consideration what St Mark's Gospel also records, or omits to record, on the same period of the Christian history. Our second Gospel then begins with the preaching of John the Baptist in the wilderness, and then, having described his appearance and the subject of his preaching, it brings Jesus to our notice for the first time as follows, in the 9th verse of the first chapter.

And it came to pass in those days that Jesus came from Nazareth of Galilee, and was baptized of John in Jordan.

On his coming up out of the water, the Spirit of God descends upon him, accompanied by a voice from heaven, recognizing his title to be the Son of God, and he is impelled by the same Spirit to go into the wilderness where he is tempted by the devil. Thus the Gospel of St Mark begins with the preaching of John the Baptist and the baptism of Jesus by John in the river Jordan. In this particular the fourth agrees with the second Gospel; whilst the third agrees with the first in prefixing two chapters, the one concerning Christ's birth at Bethlehem with the flight into Egypt, the murder of the innocents and the events therewith connected, the other concerning the birth of John the Baptist and the miraculous agency which preceded and followed that event. It may be remarked that, if we pass over these preliminary chapters, the testimony of the four Gospels is in almost perfect harmony, as the comparison of their statements in the next chapter (p. 207) will clearly show. But there has always been great doubt about the originality of the first two chapters of St Matthew's Gospel, and the same doubt may possibly be entertained concerning those which are prefixed to the Gospel of St Luke. It is more than probable that fresh facts connected with our Saviour's life may from time to time have come to the knowledge of those who copied the Gospels afresh, and that these facts were inserted in the new editions which in those days could owe their origin to no other instrument than the pen. It is notorious that such a doubt was entertained in very early times to the chapters prefixed to St Matthew's Gospel, and the concurrence of all the four in their mode of introducing

Christ's history, when these preliminary chapters have been removed, makes it possible to suggest a similar explanation concerning the Gospel of St Luke ; whilst the supplementary narrative concerning Zacharias, previously quoted from an uncanonical gospel in page 161 of this volume, shows that possibly the whole history of John the Baptist's infancy has not been recorded in the books which form our canon.

Proceeding then to the narrative concerning what is commonly termed the Massacre of the Innocents, we find no account of this event in either of the last three Gospels. It is related by St Matthew alone, and so clearly connected with the flight into Egypt that the accuracy of both narratives must rest upon the same basis.

It would be the extreme of scepticism to doubt the genuineness of the passage in the history of Josephus in which the name of John the Baptist is mentioned, and it is well known that baptism is a rite that has been practised by other sects than the Christians. In the work of the Jewish historian it is stated, as quoted in page 65 of this volume, that John the Baptist was put to death by Herod from a cause not the same as that which is given in the Gospels, but it would appear, if we believe the uncanonical gospel ascribed to St James, that Herod sought to destroy the Baptist, when he was a child, and that, failing to find the son, he wreaked his vengeance on the father Zacharias.* The most cursory reading of the uncanonical narrative would suggest that Herod's desire to find the youthful Baptist proceeded from the same motive which led him to inquire after the infant Christ, and the murder of the Innocents is said to have been the mode which Herod adopted to secure the death of one whom he regarded as his future rival for the sovereignty of Judæa. The zeal however of our ecclesiastical historians has, in this as in other instances, outrun their discretion. The calculation that a very large number of children, amounting even to several thousands, as stated on

---

* The main point of this narrative derives support from the authority of Origen, who says that the father of John the Baptist was killed in the Temple, but the editor of the Dictionary of the Bible, admitting that "many of the Greek fathers have maintained that this is the person to whom our Lord alludes," adds that "there can be little or no doubt that the allusion is to Zacharias, the son of Jehoiada (II Chron. xxiv, 20, 21)"—so easy does it appear to defend the authenticity of our Scriptures, if it is allowed to reject the authority both of Origen and of the uncanonical gospel, which confirm the present text, and to alter that text in those particulars which seem to introduce a difficulty into their own method of interpretation. See also Dr Lightfoot's citations from the Jerusalem Talmud, *Taanith*, fol. 69, and the Babylonian *Sanhedrim*, fol. 96.

the authority of Voltaire, may be set aside with contempt, but we must not neglect certain passages in credible histories, which tell us that Herod the Great committed many atrocious acts, none of which would be so atrocious or so likely to cause his own destruction, as the murder of fourteen thousand children "from two years old and under," in order that the youthful Saviour and King might perish with the rest. It can hardly be believed that even fifty infants, as suggested by the author of the "Introduction to the Critical Study of the Scriptures," could be slain by the arbitrary decree even of so cruel a king as Herod, and yet not be noticed by any contemporary or subsequent historian, but it is well known that Herod was a cruel king and that he perpetrated many acts which have been handed down to our times and have earned for him the execration of ages. But even in Herod there were qualities of a higher tendency, and of a certain magnificence that has everywhere and at all times been reckoned as a counterpoise however insufficient to the darker traits of the character of a prince. Josephus tells us that

Some there are who stand amazed at the diversity of Herod's nature and purposes; for when we have respect to his magnificence, and the benefits which he bestowed on all mankind, there is no possibility for even those who have the least respect for him to deny, or not openly to confess, that he had a nature vastly beneficent.—*Antiq.* XVI, v, 4.

But the historian does not hesitate to denounce the same monarch as brutally cruel, even to his own family; in proof of which has been quoted the death of his two sons, Alexander and Aristobulus, who were accused of rebellion and conspiracy against their father, on evidence which, whilst it does not exonerate them from the charge of insubordination and disobedience, yet was insufficient to render them liable to be put to death.

The execution of these young men is referred to by Strabo who lived and wrote his Geographical Accounts of various countries not many years later.

Some of his sons he himself put to death, and the others as he was dying he left as his successors, giving them each a part. But Cæsar also honoured Herod's sons and his sister Salome, and her daughter Berenice. His sons, however, were not fortunate, but fell under accusations; and one of them remained in exile, taking up his residence among the Allobrigian Gauls, and the others with difficulty, and by paying great court, obtained permission to return, when tetrarchies were given to both of them. —STRABO, xvi, 3.

It would seem dangerous to imagine, had it not been believed to be a fact, that the execution of Herod's sons was connected with the murder of the children at Bethlehem, and a certain significance may be attached to the suggestion by a passage from the Latin author Macrobius, whose words are these:

Quum [Augustus] audîsset inter pueros quos in Syria Herodes rex Judæorum *intra bimatum** jussit interfici filium quoque ejus occisum, ait: "Melius est Herodis porcum esse quam filium."—MACROB.*Saturn.* ii, 4.

When he [Augustus] had heard that among the boys, whom Herod king of the Jews commanded to be slain *within the age of two years*, his son also was put to death, he said: "It is better to be Herod's swine than his son."

If these words be duly weighed, it is difficult to arrive at a thorough identification of the events which some writers have too hastily sought to connect together and to ascribe to the same motive. We learn from the Gospel narrative, that to secure the dynasty of Herod by the death of a child who was destined to extinguish it, all the children of the same age were ordered to be put to death. But if this be true, it is hardly to be believed that the life of his own son, even if still a child under two years of age, would be sacrificed also, and it is scarcely possible that the execution of the two young princes Alexander and Aristobulus can be traced to the same circumstances or included in the same category as the murder of the children at Bethlehem, related in the Gospel of St Matthew. The accounts therefore of these events must remain as we find them in the Scriptural narrative, and must be judged on their own merits, unsupported and unimpugned by any evidence which friends or foes to the Gospel may endeavour to elicit from the writings or suggestions of any later writers.

---

* *Intra bimatum*, within the age of two years. It is likely that these words were added to the text of Macrobius by some reader, from no dishonest motive, but because he hastily imagined that this circumstance, *i.e.*
* Herod's cruelty, was identical with the murder of the children at Bethlehem.

CHAPTER XXII.

RELATION OF JOHN THE BAPTIST'S MINISTRY TO THAT OF CHRIST.

THE most remarkable prophet or teacher among the Jews before the appearance of our Saviour upon earth, was John the Baptist. The history of his miraculous conception, birth, and mode of life until the beginning of his public preaching, is related by St Luke alone, who concludes his narrative with these words:

80. And the child grew, and waxed strong in spirit, and was in the deserts till the day of his showing unto Israel.

Josephus alone, of all the profane ancient historians, has mentioned John the Baptist. The passages of his history where this notice occurs, have already been given in page 65 of this volume. They present a variation from the Gospel narrative, but both accounts are probably imperfect. Whilst the evangelist ascribes Herod's command that the Baptist should be beheaded, to the oath which he had sworn to his daughter-in-law, and the malice of his offended wife, Josephus attributes it to a political motive—the fear lest John might raise a sedition among the people. It is easy to see that, the fact being undoubted, the motive assigned for its commission may have varied according to the peculiar circumstances of the case. Whilst John's followers saw nothing but religious persecution, the politician may have seen nothing but precaution, political though unjust, in the cruel orders of the king. Nay, it is not impossible that the secret enmity instigated by his wife, may have been veiled by the more plausible appearance of regard for the public tranquillity; or, in another point of view, that real solicitude for the tranquillity of his government may have lurked beneath his apparent readiness to gratify Herodias, ratified by the obligation of the oath which he had sworn.

In the scarcity of information respecting this remarkable ascetic we turn to the profane writers to gather what they have left us concerning the class to which the Baptist belonged.

The poet Juvenal mentions an order of priests called Baptæ or Baptists, dedicated to the service of the goddess Cotytto:

Cecropiam soliti Baptæ las- The Baptæ, used to tire [with
sare Cotytto: [*Sat.* ii, 92].   their petitions] the Athenian
                                 Cotytto.

Some have named Thrace as the soil from which the worship of the goddess Cotytto was imported into Greece. But, generally, the Grecian gods and religious ceremonies came from Egypt and Phœnicia; nor is it difficult to imagine that Thrace may have received from those countries the orgies, which were afterwards transmitted to Greece and Rome. At any rate, it is worthy of observation, that the Baptæ of the Romans are not mentioned by the more ancient classics, but only by those who lived about the time of the Christian era.

The idea of using water as emblematic of spiritual washing is too obvious to allow surprise at the antiquity of this rite. Dr Hyde, in his treatise on the Religion of the ancient Persians, chapter xxxiv, p. 406, tells us that it prevailed among that people. The passage, translated from the original Latin, here follows.

They do not use circumcision for their children, but only baptism or washing for the inward purification of the soul. They bring the child to the priest into the church and place him in front of the sun and fire, which ceremony being completed they look upon him as more sacred than before. Lord says that they bring the water for this purpose in bark of the Holm-tree: that tree is in truth the Haum of the Magi, of which we spoke before on another occasion. Sometimes also it is otherwise done by immersing him in a large vessel of water, as Tavernier tells us. After such washing or baptism, the priest imposes on the child the name given by his parents. . . .

Afterwards, in the 15th year of his age, when he begins to put on the tunic, the sudra [a kind of cloak], and the girdle, that he may enter upon religion, and is engaged upon the articles of belief, the priest bestows upon him confirmation, that he may from that time be admitted into the number of the faithful, and may be looked upon as a believer himself.

The Manichæans, a Christian sect who followed the doctrines of Mani, are said by Beausobre to have administered baptism to children, conformably to the custom of the Persian Magi, "from which he, Mani, deviated as little as he possibly could." BEAUS. *liv.* 9, *chap.* 6, *sect.* 16.

We have positive evidence from Tertullian that the rite of baptism was used among the Gentiles in his time. He says in his treatise *De Baptismo, cap.* 5:

They are certainly dipped at the Apollinarian and Eleusinian solemnities, and they presume that they do this for the purpose of regeneration and impunity for their perjuries. . . .
At certain sacred rites of one Isis and Mithra they initiate themselves by dipping.

It has been thought that baptism was prevalent among the Jews also, long before the beginning of the Christian era. This is a subject which has not been very satisfactorily cleared up. Though there is no sure evidence disproving the existence of the rite, yet the evidence which is supposed to establish the opposite view is not so conclusive as could be wished. We have seen from Josephus that John was surnamed the Baptist, because he baptized those who came to him. This seems to indicate that baptism was not usual among the Jews, and yet it seems to presuppose that the rite was not altogether unknown. In the days of Justin Martyr, about A.D. 150, it is thought to have been practised among them; and the following passages from his works are supposed to bear reference to it.

For, this circumcision is not necessary to all, but to you alone; that, as I said before, you may suffer those things which you now justly suffer. For neither do we adopt that useless baptism, the baptism in cisterns; for there is no communion between this baptism and that of life. *Dial.* xix.

Let us glorify God, all ye assembled nations, because he hath also looked on us: let us glorify him through the king of glory, through the Lord of powers. For he hath been well pleased also with the gentiles, and receives sacrifices more willingly from us than from you. What account should I any longer make of circumcision, seeing that I have been borne witness to by God? What need of that baptism is there to one who has been baptized with the holy spirit? In saying these things, I think that I shall persuade even those who have very little sense. *Dial.* xxix.

But these passages are remarkably indecisive; and, even if they should be thought to point to a baptismal ceremony among the Jews, yet those who practised it may have belonged to the sect of the followers of John the Baptist, who certainly continued for some time to be distinct from the Christian community. See Acts xviii, 25.

In the absence of more explicit evidence concerning the practice of baptism among the Jews, we turn to a remarkable passage in St Paul's first epistle to the Corinthians, xv, 29, where the question is asked "What shall they do which are baptized for the dead, if the dead rise not at all?" To this question no answer is given, and no explanation of any such custom is found in the earliest Christian writers, and as the best interpretations which have been hazarded are, to say the least, wholly incompatible with the words of the text and also repugnant to every modern feeling, we are left to acquiesce in the literal meaning of the words, which imply that those who had died unbaptized might be still placed under the protection of the Christian covenant by any surviving friends who undertook to appear for them at the baptismal font. "A brother or a catechumen," says the Chevalier Bunsen in his work on Hippolytus (vol. iii, p. 196), "who could prove that a deceased Christian friend had a believing disposition, and a desire to be admitted into the Church, received baptism in his stead." It is doubtful whether even the mention of such a ceremony as admissible into our religion would now be listened to for a moment by any Christian community.

MATTHEW, iii, 4-12.

4. And the same John had his raiment of camel's hair, and a leathern girdle about his loins; and his meat was locusts and wild honey. 5. Then went out to him Jerusalem, and all Judæa, and all the region round about Jordan, 6. And were baptized of him in Jordan, confessing their sins.

7. But when he saw many of the Pharisees and Sadducees come to his baptism, he said unto them, "O generation of vipers, who hath warned you to flee from the wrath to come? 8. Bring forth therefore fruits meet for repentance: 9. And think not to say within yourselves, We have Abraham to our father: for I say unto you, that God is able of these stones to raise up children unto Abraham. 10. And now also the axe is laid unto the root of the trees: therefore every tree which bringeth not forth good fruit is hewn down, and cast into the fire.

MARK i, 4-8.

4. John did baptize in the wilderness, and preach the baptism of repentance for the remission of sins. 5. And there went out unto him all the land of Judæa, and they of Jerusalem, and were all baptized of him in the river of Jordan, confessing their sins. 6. And John was clothed with camel's hair, and with a girdle of a skin about his loins; and he did eat locusts and wild honey:

XXII.] DOCTRINES OF JOHN THE BAPTIST. 207

1. *John's preaching and doctrines.*

The peculiar doctrines of John the Baptist may be seen in the following passages from the early part of the four Gospels concerning his first appearance as a teacher. But as regards the place where he preached, a discussion, which reasonable persons will pass over as needless, has arisen about the name Bethany which appears in the Vulgate and certain editions of the original Greek text, whereas in our authorized version Bethabara is the place where the Baptist carried on his ministry. All the earliest MSS read Bethany, and it was Origen who restored what he conceived to be the true name. A copyist may have inadvertently written the well-known Bethany for the less known Bethabara, but the additional words *beyond Jordan* sufficiently indicate the locality of the village.

LUKE iii, 7-18.

7. Then said he to the multitude that came forth to be baptized of him, "O generation of vipers, who hath warned you to flee from the wrath to come? 8. Bring forth therefore fruits worthy of repentance, and begin not to say within yourselves, We have Abraham to our father: for I say unto you, That God is able of these stones to raise up children unto Abraham. 9. And now also the axe is laid unto the root of the trees: every tree therefore which bringeth not forth good fruit is hewn down, and cast into the fire." 10. And the people asked him, saying, "What shall we do then?" 11. He answered and saith unto them, "He that hath two coats, let him impart to him that hath none; and he that hath meat, let him do likewise." 12. Then came also publicans to be baptized, and said unto him, "Master, what shall we do?" 13. And he said unto them, "Exact no more than that which is appointed you." 14. And the soldiers likewise demanded of him, saying, "And what shall we do?" And he said unto them, "Do violence to no man, neither accuse any falsely; and be content with your wages." 15. And as the people were in expectation,

JOHN i, 15-28.

15. John bare witness of him, and cried, saying, "This was he of whom I spake, He that cometh after me is preferred before me: for he was before me. 16. And of his fulness have all we received and grace for grace. 17. For the law was given by Moses, but grace and truth came by Jesus Christ. 18. No man hath seen God at any time; the only begotten Son, which is in the bosom of the Father, he hath declared him." 19. And this is the record of John, when the Jews sent priests and Levites from Jerusalem to ask him, "Who art thou?" 20. And he confessed, and denied not; but confessed, "I am not the Christ." 21. And they asked him, "What then? Art thou Elias?" And he saith, "I am not." "Art thou that prophet?" And he answered, "No." 22. Then said they unto him, "Who art thou? that we may give an answer to them that sent us. What sayest thou of thyself?" 23. He said, "I am the voice of one crying in the wilderness, Make straight the way of the Lord, as said the prophet Esaias." 24. And they which were sent were of the Pharisees. 25. And they asked him, and said unto him, "Why baptizest thou then, if thou

MATTHEW iii, 4-12.　　　　　　MARK i, 4-8.

11. "I indeed baptize you with water unto repentance: but he that cometh after me is mightier than I, whose shoes I am not worthy to bear: he shall baptize you with the Holy Ghost, and with fire: 12. Whose fan is in his hand, and he will throughly purge his floor, and gather his wheat into the garner; but he will burn up the chaff with unquenchable fire."

7. And preached, saying, "There cometh one mightier than I after me, the latchet of whose shoes I am not worthy to stoop down and unloose. 8. I indeed have baptized you with water: but he shall baptize you with the Holy Ghost."

There are some unimportant differences between the four evangelists in these extracts:

St Matthew says that the words, " O generation of vipers &c." were addressed to the Scribes and Pharisees—St Luke, to the multitude. The first three Gospels represent the Baptist as saying, vaguely and in general terms, that a greater than himself was coming, without specifying him more minutely; but St John is more definite—"There standeth one among you, whom ye know not." The record of John concerning himself, " I am the voice of one crying in the wilderness, Make straight the way of the Lord, &c." [John i, 23] is represented by the three other evangelists

---

MATTHEW iii, 13-17.　　　　　　MARK i, 9-11.

13. Then cometh Jesus from Galilee to Jordan unto John, to be baptized of him. 14. But John forbad him, saying, "I have need to be baptized of thee, and comest thou to me?" 15. And Jesus answering said unto him, "Suffer it to be so now: for thus it becometh us to fulfil all righteousness." Then he suffered him. 16. And Jesus, when he was baptized, went up straightway out of the water: and lo, the heavens were opened unto him, and he saw the Spirit of God descending like a dove, and lighting upon him: 17. And lo a voice from heaven, saying, "This is my beloved Son, in whom I am well pleased."

9. And it came to pass in those days, that Jesus came from Nazareth of Galilee, and was baptized of John in Jordan. 10. And straightway coming up out of the water, he saw the heavens opened, and the Spirit like a dove descending upon him: 11. And there came a voice from heaven, saying " Thou art my beloved Son, in whom I am well pleased."

XXII.] JESUS MEETS THE BAPTIST.

Luke iii, 15-18.	John i, 25-28.
and all men mused in their hearts of John, whether he were the Christ, or not; 16. John answered, saying unto them all, "I indeed baptize you with water; but one mightier than I cometh, the latchet of whose shoes I am not worthy to unloose: he shall baptize you with the Holy Ghost and with fire: 17. Whose fan is in his hand, and he will throughly purge his floor, and will gather the wheat into his garner; but the chaff he will burn with fire unquenchable." 18. And many other things in his exhortation preached he unto the people.	be not that Christ, nor Elias, neither that prophet?" 26. John answered them, saying, "I baptize with water: but there standeth one among you, whom ye know not; 27. He it is, who coming after me is preferred before me, whose shoe's latchet I am not worthy to unloose." 28. These things were done in Bethabara beyond Jordan, where John was baptizing.

as coming not from John himself, but from the writer [comp. Matt. iii, 3: Mark i, 3: and Luke iii, 4]. This peculiarity, of running the thoughts of the writer into the mouth of the person speaking, is not uncommon with all the four evangelists, especially with the last, as we shall have frequent occasion to remark.

2. *First meeting of Jesus and the Baptist.*

The second class of extracts from the four Gospels, concerning the Baptist, informs us of the mode in which Jesus first met him and was baptized by him in Jordan.

Luke iii, 19-22.	John i, 29-36.
19. But Herod the tetrarch, being reproved by him for Herodias his brother Philip's wife, and for all the evils which Herod had done, 20. Added yet this above all, that he shut up John in prison. 21. Now when all the people were baptized, it came to pass, that Jesus also being baptized, and praying, the heaven was opened, 22. And the Holy Ghost descended in a bodily shape like a dove upon him, and a voice came from heaven, which said, "Thou art my beloved Son; in thee I am well pleased."	29. The next day John seeth Jesus coming unto him, and saith, "Behold the Lamb of God, which taketh away the sin of the world. 30. This is he of whom I said, After me cometh a man which is preferred before me: for he was before me. 31. And I knew him not; but that he should be made manifest to Israel, therefore am I come baptizing with water." 32. And John bare record, saying, "I saw the Spirit descending from heaven like a dove, and it abode upon him. 33. And I know him not: but he that sent me to baptize with water, the same said unto me, Upon whom thou shalt see the Spirit descending, and remaining on him, the same is he which baptizeth with the Holy

There is here, also, a variation in the four different accounts—of some importance. Three of the Gospels relate a miraculous appearance, which, though seen by a multitude of persons, yet seems to have produced no result, and to have attracted no notice. But the fourth evangelist, it will be observed, limits the miraculous appearance to the physical or mental vision of the Baptist alone. "John bare record, saying, I saw the spirit descending from heaven, &c." In other words we have, in St John's Gospel, the miracle related, not as a well-known occurrence, but resting on the word only of the Baptist. And it would appear from what follows, "And I knew him not, &c." that the miracle was intentionally revealed to John the Baptist, to enable him to

MATTHEW iv, 12-17.	MARK i, 14-15.
12. Now when Jesus had heard that John was cast into prison, he departed into Galilee; 13. And leaving Nazareth, he came and dwelt in Capernaum, which is upon the sea coast, in the borders of Zabulon and Nephthalim: 14. That it might be fulfilled which was spoken by Esaias the prophet, saying, 15. The land of Zabulon, and the land of Nephthalim, by the way of the sea, beyond Jordan, Galilee of the Gentiles; 16. The people which sat in darkness saw great light; and to them which sat in the region and shadow of death light is sprung up. 17. From that time Jesus began to preach, and to say, Repent: for the kingdom of heaven is at hand.	14. Now after that John was put in prison, Jesus came into Galilee, preaching the gospel of the kingdom of God, 15. And saying, "The time is fulfilled, and the kingdom of God is at hand: repent ye, and believe the gospel."

There is no doubt that John the Baptist was imprisoned by Herod's orders, for we have the independent testimony of Josephus and of all the four evangelists; but there is an uncertainty as to the time, in relation to Christ's ministry, at which the imprisonment took place. It is difficult to bring the observation of St John above quoted, "For John was

JOHN i, 34-36.

Ghost. 34. And I saw, and bare record that this is the Son of God." 35. Again the next day after John stood, and two of his disciples: 36. And looking upon Jesus as he walked, he saith, "Behold the Lamb of God!"

distinguish the remarkable person of whom he was the forerunner. The reasonable inference is, that John told the people how he had been enabled to discriminate the Messiah, and that, in process of time, it was popularly believed that the whole multitude had seen the miracle. This opinion is strengthened by the traditions to which we have already alluded in the fourteenth chapter of this volume, of other miraculous appearances seen at the baptism of our Lord, but not recorded in our four Gospels.

3. *Imprisonment of the Baptist.*

The imprisonment of John the Baptist must next be examined.

LUKE iv, 14-15.

14. And Jesus returned in the power of the Spirit into Galilee: and there went out a fame of him through all the region round about. 15. And he taught in their synagogues, being glorified of all.

JOHN iii, 22-24.

22. After these things came Jesus and his disciples into the land of Judæa; and there he tarried with them, and baptized. 23. And John also was baptizing in Ænon near to Salim, because there was much water there: and they came, and were baptized. 24. For John was not yet cast into prison.

not yet cast into prison," into harmony with what the other three evangelists have written. They all relate that immediately or soon after the baptism, John the Baptist was cast into prison, and that Jesus, hearing of it, departed into Galilee. But the author of the fourth Gospel interposes several important events, and among others the marriage at

Cana in Galilee, and a visit of Jesus to Jerusalem at the feast of the Passover.

The didactic nature of St John's Gospel, apparently the least chronological of the four, would deter us from taking his narrative in preference to that of Matthew and Mark. But, if, as we might infer from the latter, Jesus retired into Galilee from fear of sharing the fate of the Baptist, it would create surprise that he should choose the very dominions of Herod as his place of refuge, to escape falling into his hands.

4. *John's doubts about the Messiahship of Jesus.*

It appears from the general tenour of the first three Gospels that the wonderful works of Christ speedily attracted the notice of John whilst in prison, and of his disciples, who seem still to have had free access to their master. Two interviews between Jesus and the disciples of John are mentioned, but in both of them there is something to arrest attention. The first occasion arose from the disciples of John contrasting their own master's ascetic doctrine with the milder practices of Jesus.

The parallel notices of this matter from the Gospels of Matthew, Mark, and Luke here follow.

MATTHEW ix, 14, 15.	MARK ii, 18-20.	LUKE v, 33-35.
14. Then came to him the disciples of John, saying, "Why do we and the Pharisees fast oft, but thy disciples fast not?" 15. And Jesus said unto them, "Can the children of the bridechamber mourn, as long as the bridegroom is with them? but the days will come, when the bridegroom shall be taken from them, and then shall they fast."	18. And the disciples of John and of the Pharisees used to fast: and they come and say unto him, "Why do the disciples of John and of the Pharisees fast, but thy disciples fast not?" 19. And Jesus said unto them, "Can the children of the bridechamber fast while the bridegroom is with them? as long as they have the bridegroom with them, they cannot fast. 20. But the days will come, when the bridegroom shall be taken away from them, and then shall they fast in those days."	33. And they said unto him, "Why do the disciples of John fast often, and make prayers, and likewise the disciples of the Pharisees; but thine eat and drink?" 34. And he said unto them, "Can ye make the children of the bridechamber fast, while the bridegroom is with them? 35. But the days will come, when the bridegroom shall be taken away from them, and then shall they fast in those days."

But the three evangelists do not wholly coincide in their accounts. St Matthew alone says that the disciples of John came and asked Jesus why his followers did not fast: St

Mark and St Luke place the question in the mouths of the people who are represented as always following Jesus about.

On the second meeting between Jesus and the disciples of John, the only two evangelists who relate it, St Matthew and St Luke, are agreed:

MATTHEW xi, 2-6.	LUKE vii, 18-23.
2. Now when John had heard in the prison the works of Christ, he sent two of his disciples, 3. And said unto him, "Art thou he that should come, or do we look for another?"	18. And the disciples of John showed him of all these things. 19. And John calling unto him two of his disciples sent them to Jesus, saying, "Art thou he that should come? or look we for another?" 20. When the men were come unto him, they said, "John Baptist hath sent us unto thee, saying, Art thou he that should come? or look we for another?" 21. And in the same hour he cured many of their infirmities and plagues, and of evil spirits; and unto many that were blind he gave sight.
4. Jesus answered and said unto them, "Go and show John again those things which ye do hear and see: 5. The blind receive their sight, and the lame walk, the lepers are cleansed, and the deaf hear, the dead are raised up, and the poor have the gospel preached to them. 6. And blessed is he, whosoever shall not be offended in me."	22. Then Jesus answering said unto them, "Go your way, and tell John what things ye have seen and heard; how that the blind see, the lame walk, the lepers are cleansed, the deaf hear, the dead are raised, to the poor the gospel is preached. 23. And blessed is he, whosoever shall not be offended in me."

But it has been thought surprising that John the Baptist, who had before borne such noble testimony to the Messiahship of Jesus, should at last waver in his faith, and send two of his disciples to inquire whether Jesus really was he that should come, or were they to look for some other besides him. It has been justly remarked that John would really have been a reed shaken by the wind, if he could have wavered about so vital a point in so remarkable a manner.

CHAPTER XXIII.

THE TEMPTATION IN THE WILDERNESS.

THE reputed authors of the four Gospels, Matthew, Mark, Luke and John, are said to have been, two of them, of the number of the twelve apostles who were chosen at the first to be Christ's immediate followers; and the other two, Mark and Luke, to have been in the next rank to the apostleship, having been followers, one of St Peter, the other of St Paul. As the events which preceded the choosing of the twelve apostles could not be known to them by the evidence of their own senses, but must have come to them by the recital of others, we might make allowance for any discrepancies between the four evangelists on all those particulars, which they had received from others, and had not themselves witnessed. But it has unfortunately been the custom to ascribe to the four Gospels, *a priori*, a peculiar character, which is to exempt them from examination, on the plea that they wrote, word for word, by divine inspiration. Even viewed in this light they must be tried, and there is no other way of trying them than that which is usual with all other books, and with every kind of evidence admitted among mankind. If two of our Lord's apostles, and two who were followers of other apostles, wrote the Gospels, as we now have them, by direct verbal inspiration, we shall undoubtedly find the most perfect agreement between them in every particular, even on those points which they had not themselves witnessed, but which they learnt from others, whilst the divine inspiration prevented them from making any error about the facts which they were writing. In describing the effects of the divine inspiration, it is not enough to say that it would guard them from material errors—all errors are material, on such a subject. It would guard them from every error whatsoever, or it would be of no value. Indeed, to admit that the writers of the Gospels were inspired, and then to speak of their contemporary character, and the means they had of knowing the truth, is the most futile work of supererogation that can be imagined. For the divine inspiration would alone suffice. Error—mistake—anachronism—are words that could have no place in the vocabulary, and the Gospels would only defy criticism, because they would make good their supernatural pretensions against any test that criticism could apply.

Yet, notwithstanding the supposed aid of such inspiration, and the nearness of the time, the four evangelists have not been able to tell us even the first event of Christ's ministry—his TEMPTATION—without differing one from another. And moreover, if we interpret correctly the account given in John i, 40-44, three disciples, Simon, Andrew, and Philip, had been chosen only the day before the temptation in the wilderness began. The first three Gospels furnish the

XXIII.] THE TEMPTATION. 215

following accounts of the Temptation in the wilderness—
placed in parallel columns:

MATT. iv, 1-2.	MARK i, 12-13.	LUKE iv, 1-2.
Then was Jesus led up of the spirit into the wilderness to be tempted of the devil. 2. And when he had fasted forty days and forty nights, he was afterwards an hungred.	12. And immediately the spirit driveth him into the wilderness. 13. And he was there in the wilderness forty days, tempted of Satan; and was with the wild beasts; and the angels ministered unto him.	And Jesus being full of the Holy Ghost returned from Jordan, and was led by the Spirit into the wilderness, 2. Being forty days tempted of the devil. And in those days he did eat nothing: and when they were ended, he afterward hungered.

So far all the three name the Temptation, but only St
Matthew and St Luke give us the details as they here follow; but even here the order of the temptations is not the
same in both.

MATTHEW iv, 3-11.	LUKE iv, 3-13.
3. And when the tempter came to him, he said, "If thou be the Son of God, command that these stones be made bread." 4. But he answered and said, "It is written, Man shall not live by bread alone, but by every word that proceedeth out of the mouth of God." 5. Then the devil taketh him up into the holy city, and setteth him on a pinnacle of the temple, 6. And saith unto him, "If thou be the Son of God, cast thyself down: for it is written, He shall give his angels charge concerning thee: and in their hands they shall bear thee up, lest at any time thou dash thy foot against a stone." 7. Jesus said unto him, "It is written again, Thou shalt not tempt the Lord thy God." 8. Again, the devil taketh him up into an exceeding high mountain, and showeth him all the kingdoms of the world, and the glory of them; 9. And saith unto him, "All these things will I give thee, if thou wilt fall down and worship me." 10. Then saith Jesus unto him, "Get thee hence, Satan: for it is written, Thou shalt worship the Lord thy God, and him only shalt thou serve."	3. And the devil said unto him, "If thou be the Son of God, command this stone that it be made bread." 4. And Jesus answered him, saying, "It is written, That man shall not live by bread alone, but by every word of God." 5. And the devil, taking him up into an high mountain, showed unto him all the kingdoms of the world in a moment of time. 6. And the devil said unto him, "All this power will I give thee, and the glory of them: for that is delivered unto me; and to whomsoever I will I give it. 7. If thou therefore wilt worship me, all shall be thine." 8. And Jesus answered and said unto him, "Get thee behind me, Satan: for it is written, Thou shalt worship the Lord thy God, and him only shalt thou serve." 9. And he brought him to Jerusalem, and set him on a pinnacle of the temple, and said unto him, "If thou be the Son of God, cast thyself down from hence: 10. For it is written, He shall give his angels charge over thee, to keep thee: 11. And in their hands they shall bear thee up, lest at any time thou dash thy foot against a stone." 12. And Jesus answering said unto him, "It is said, Thou shalt not tempt the Lord thy God."

MATTHEW iv, 11.	LUKE iv, 13.
11. Then the devil leaveth him, and, behold, angels came and ministered unto him.	13. And when the devil had ended all the temptation, he departed from him for a season.

In all three, the Temptation is placed immediately after the baptism of Jesus. The language of Matthew, *Then was Jesus led &c.*, is the least decisive: but Mark is remarkably pointed *And immediately &c.*: and all doubt is wholly dispelled by St Luke, who having in the previous chapter related the descent of the Holy Ghost, now tells us that "Jesus, being full of the Holy Ghost, returned from Jordan, and was led by the spirit into the wilderness."

Thus there is no doubt that all the three, St Matthew, St Mark, and St Luke, place the temptation of Jesus immediately after his baptism in the river Jordan.

If now we turn to the Gospel of St John, we find, to our surprise, that he not only passes over this remarkable scene altogether, but places the marriage at Cana of Galilee on the third day after Christ's baptism.

JOHN i, 35. Again, the *next day after*, John stood, and two of his disciples . . . .
i. 43. The *day following*, Jesus would go forth into Galilee, and findeth Philip, and saith unto him, Follow me, ...

The second chapter opens with the marriage at Cana:

JOHN ii, 1-11. And the *third day* there was a marriage in Cana of Galilee; and the mother of Jesus was there: 2. And both Jesus was called, and his disciples, to the marriage.
3. And when they wanted wine, the mother of Jesus saith unto him, "They have no wine." 4. Jesus saith unto her, "Woman, what have I to do with thee? mine hour is not yet come." 5. His mother saith unto the servants, "Whatsoever he saith unto you, do it."
6. And there were set there six waterpots of stone, after the manner of the purifying of the Jews, containing two or three firkins apiece. 7. Jesus saith unto them, "Fill the waterpots with water." And they filled them up to the brim. 8. And he saith unto them, "Draw out now, and bear unto the governor of the feast." And they bare it.
9. When the ruler of the feast had tasted the water that was made wine and knew not whence it was: (but the servants which drew the water knew ;) the governor of the feast called the bridegroom, 10. And saith unto him, " Every man at the beginning doth set forth good wine; and when men have well drunk, then that which is worse : but thou hast kept the good wine until now."
11. This beginning of miracles did Jesus in Cana of Galilee, and manifested forth his glory; and his disciples believed on him.

By this order of events, the scene of the forty days in the wilderness is altogether excluded, for the very days between the baptism in Jordan and the marriage are numbered. To reconcile such conflicting accounts is impossible, without correcting one of them. It is better to correct the narrative of St John, for three reasons:

1. Because his silence about the temptation does not invalidate the testimony of the other three witnesses who relate it—and the only way to admit their testimony is to break the sequence of events observed by John.

2. Because the distance between the Jordan and Cana of Galilee renders it improbable that Christ could have reached the latter place, seventy miles, in the short space of two days.

3. Because the writer of the fourth Gospel relates incidental matters, which shows that he pays no regard to chronology, but only to Christ's teaching and miracles. He tells us that "his disciples believed on him;" but, seeing that only Philip, Andrew, and Simon Peter had been first brought into the company of Jesus the day before, it is rather premature to speak of his disciples, and it is very surprising that they should have followed him to the distance of seventy miles. But unless they followed him, Jesus had no other disciples who *could* believe on him.

Thus we can only explain these divergences by admitting that there are inaccuracies in the Gospel-histories, as in every other book that ever yet was written; and the way to deal with these is to meet them openly and candidly, not to explain them away in a manner which brings both the Gospels and their annotators into manifest and merited contempt.

Admitting then that the temptation of Jesus followed closely after his baptism, we are startled and offended at the incidents of which it is made up. That the devil should appear personally to the Son of God is certainly not more wonderful than that he should, in a more remote age, have appeared among the sons of God, in the presence of God himself, to tempt and torment the righteous Job. But that Satan should carry Jesus bodily and literally through the air, first to the top of a high mountain, and then to the topmost pinnacle of the Temple, is thought by many to be inadmissible, to be an insult to our understanding, and an affront to our Great Creator and our Redeemer.

If however we listen to this denial of what has by the greater number of Christians been looked upon as an undoubted fact, must we reject the moral as well as the literal acceptation of Christ's Temptation? By no means: the spirit of the Gospel runs through all Christ's history, teeming with life and light, where the letter of those ancient histories would slay. The moral lesson might be taken thus: Jesus, endowed with a master-mind by the gift of his Almighty Father, and yet amenable to the suggestions of his human nature, retires to meditate in that eastern wilderness on the subject of his mission, and to prepare himself by prayer and fasting for encountering the lusts of the world, the stings of ambition, and the pride of life. Who will doubt that Jesus, if he could be supposed to give way to worldly ambition, might have gained that kingdom which he was there tempted to covet, and was afterwards charged with coveting? The thought of all these things, and the sight of the fair land of Judæa, for one moment cast their shadow over his spotless mind, but he spurns the tempter, described in the story as bodily present before him—" Get thee behind me, Satan ; for it is written, Thou shalt not tempt the Lord thy God." Is such a scene less real, less weighty in teaching a moral lesson, because it passes in the mind? Is evil less rife, less pernicious to us, because for eighteen hundred years we have never seen Satan bodily amongst us ? Let us not be deceived by such an imagination ; we are tempted to stray quite far enough from the road to righteousness by the evil passions which we bear in our own bosoms—farther than we should stray even if vice met mankind, as our forefathers believed, in the shape of a being that had horns and hoofs.

CHAPTER XXIV.

THE TWELVE APOSTLES—VARIATION, 1. IN THEIR NAMES; 2. IN THE TIME, PLACE AND MANNER OF THEIR BEING CALLED TO THE APOSTLESHIP—THE SEVENTY.

IT is related by two of the evangelists, Mark, and Luke, that Jesus chose twelve out of those who followed him, to be his immediate attendants. Matthew, without stating that Jesus chose the twelve, seems to imply that such a choice had been made, by naming them " the twelve," the " twelve disciples," &c. All the three furnish a list of their names, the occasion when Christ ordained them as a separate body, and the instructions which he gave to them when he sent them forth to preach.

NAMES OF THE APOSTLES.

MATTHEW x, 1-4.

And when he had called unto him his twelve disciples, he gave them power against unclean spirits, to cast them out, and to heal all manner of sickness and all manner of disease.

2. Now the names of the twelve apostles are these; The first, Simon, who is called Peter, and Andrew his brother; James the son of Zebedee, and John his brother; 3. Philip, and Bartholomew; Thomas, and Matthew the publican; James the son of Alphæus, and Lebbæus, whose surname was Thaddæus; 4. Simon the Canaanite, and Judas Iscariot, who also betrayed him.

MARK iii, 13-21.

13. And he goeth up into a mountain, and calleth unto him whom he would: and they came unto him. 14. And he ordained twelve, that they should be with him, and that he might send them forth to preach, 15. And to have power to heal sicknesses, and to cast out devils: 16. And Simon he surnamed Peter; 17. And James the son of Zebedee, and John the brother of James; and he surnamed them Boanerges, which is, The sons of thunder; 18. And Andrew, and Philip, and Bartholomew, and Matthew, and Thomas, and James the son of Alphæus, and Thaddæus, and Simon the Canaanite, 19. And Judas Iscariot, which also betrayed him: and they went into an house.

20. And the multitude cometh together again, so that they could not so much as eat bread. 21. And when his friends heard of it, they went out to lay hold on him: for they said, He is beside himself.

LUKE vi, 13-19.

13. And when it was day he called unto him his disciples; and of them he chose twelve, whom also he named apostles;
14. Simon (whom he also named Peter), and Andrew his brother, James and John, Philip and Bartholomew, 15. Matthew and Thomas, James the son of Alphæus, and Simon called Zelotes, 16. And Judas the brother of James, and Judas Iscariot, which also was the traitor.

17. And he came down with them and stood in the plain, and the company of his disciples, and a great multitude of people out of all Judæa and Jerusalem, and from the sea coast of Tyre and Sidon, which came to hear him, and to be healed of their diseases: 18. And they that were vexed with unclean spirits: and they were healed. 19. And the whole multitude sought to touch him: for there went virtue out of him, and healed them all.

MATTHEW x, 5-16.

5. These twelve Jesus sent forth, and commanded them, saying, "Go not into the way of the Gentiles, and into any city of the Samaritans enter ye not: 6. But go rather to the lost sheep of the house of Israel. 7. And as ye go, preach, saying, The kingdom of heaven is at hand.

8. Heal the sick, cleanse the lepers, raise the dead, cast out devils:

MARK vi, 7-13.

7. And he called unto him the twelve, and began to send them forth by two and two; and gave them power over unclean spirits;

8. And commanded them that they should take nothing for their

LUKE ix, 1-6.

Then he called his twelve disciples together, and gave them power and authority over all devils, and to cure diseases. 2. And he sent them to preach the kingdom of God and to heal the sick.

3. And he said unto them, "Take nothing for your journey, neither

MATTHEW x, 8-16.	MARK vi, 8-13.	LUKE ix, 3-6.
freely ye have received, freely give. 9. Provide neither gold, nor silver, nor brass in your purses, 10. Nor scrip for your journey, neither two coats, neither shoes, nor yet staves: for the workman is worthy of his meat. 11. And into whatsoever city or town ye shall enter, inquire who in it is worthy; and there abide till ye go thence. 12. And when ye come into an house, salute it. 13. And if the house be worthy, let your peace come upon it: but if it be not worthy, let your peace return to you. 14. And whosoever shall not receive you, nor hear your words, when ye depart out of that house or city, shake off the dust of your feet. 15. Verily I say unto you, It shall be more tolerable for the land of Sodom and Gomorrha in the day of judgement, than for that city. 16. Behold I send you forth as sheep in the midst of wolves: be ye therefore wise as serpents, and harmless as doves," &c.	journey, save a staff only; no scrip, no bread, no money in their purse; 9. But be shod with sandals; and not put on two coats. 10. And he said unto them, "In what place soever ye enter into an house, there abide till ye depart from that place. 11. And whosoever shall not receive you, nor hear you, when ye depart thence, shake off the dust under your feet for a testimony against them. Verily I say unto you, it shall be more tolerable for Sodom and Gomorrha in the day of judgement, than for that city."	staves, nor scrip, neither bread, neither money; neither have two coats apiece. 4. And whatsoever house ye enter into, there abide, and thence depart. 5. And whosoever will not receive you, when ye go out of that city, shake off the very dust from your feet for a testimony against them."
Chapter xi. And it came to pass, when Jesus had made an end of commanding his twelve disciples, he departed thence to teach and to preach in their cities.	12. And they went out, and preached that men should repent. 13. And they cast out many devils, and anointed with oil many that were sick and healed them.	6. And they departed, and went through the towns, preaching the gospel, and healing everywhere.

Here we observe only eleven names occurring the same in all the three : Simon Peter and Andrew his brother, James and John, sons of Zebedee, Philip and Bartholomew, Matthew and Thomas, Simon the Canaanite or the Zealot, Judas Iscariot, and James the son of Alphæus. About the twelfth disciple, the evangelists are not agreed. Mark calls him Thaddæus ; Matthew, Lebbæus, " whose surname was Thaddæus ;" Luke calls him Judas, and says that he was " of

James." Our authorized version supplies this blank by inserting the word " brother " on the strength of the first verse in the General Epistle of St Jude ; who, in his salutation "to them that are sanctified" calls himself the "servant of Jesus Christ, and brother of James."

But this reason is insufficient—there is nothing to show that the Jude of the epistle is the same person as the Judas of St Luke : the Greek indeed is Judas in every case where this name occurs, and the variation which appears in the Epistle of " St Jude," would seem to imply that our translators had the wish or the intention to make a distinction between the two. But further, a blank between two proper names, in Greek, is always to be supplied, as in the cases before us, *James of Zebedee, James of Alphæus, Judas of James,* by *son* or *daughter,* according to the sex, not by *brother* or *sister.* We are therefore thrown back to the only explanation of which the case admits, that either St Luke has made a mistake in naming the twelfth disciple Judas, or Matthew and Mark in calling him Thaddæus. Some of the commentaries try to clear up the difficulty by supposing Thaddæus or Theudas and Judas to be the same name. But this, besides being a mere conjecture, would prove too much ; it would admit Judas Iscariot among the possible claimants for the name of Thaddæus, and render the whole subject of these names infinitely more doubtful than before.

There is however a solution of the difficulty regarding the passage in St Matthew's Gospel. It appears by our short summary of various readings given in page 16 of this volume, that the Vatican and the Sinaitic, which are the earliest manuscripts in existence, omit the words " Lebbæus, whose surname was Thaddæus," altogether, and we are led to infer that some writer noticing that only eleven names are found in his copy of St Matthew's Gospel, inserted Lebbæus on the authority of some other copy, and then added the words " whose surname was Thaddæus," in order to reconcile the text with that of the Gospel according to St Mark.

The Gospel of St John, being less minute in historical particulars than the other three, has no list of the names of the twelve apostles.

Now it is remarkable that in a matter apparently so important as this, the three evangelists, who have undertaken to hand down to posterity the names of Christ's apostles, should not agree together in those names. According to the view which this work is written to maintain, there is no difficulty arising from this or any other similar discrepancy, either to the general truth of Christianity or to the cause of general religion. But those who believe that the Gospels are four separate and independent works written by four contemporaries of Christ, under the guidance of verbal inspiration, are bound to explain how it is possible for them to have made a mistake even in the names of those men, to whose labours we owe the establishment of Christ's religion, after their master was removed from the earth.

But we have not yet noticed all the inaccuracies to be found in one or other of the four Gospels respecting the names of Christ's disciples. Matthew, who is termed "the publican" in the Gospel which he is erroneously supposed to have written himself, is elsewhere called Levi by St Luke and Levi the son of Alphæus by St Mark. The parallel accounts of his "call" here follow.

MATTHEW ix, 9-13.	MARK ii, 13-17.	LUKE v, 27-32.
9. And as Jesus passed forth from thence, he saw a man, named Matthew, sitting at the receipt of custom: and he saith unto him, "Follow me." And he arose, and followed him. 10. And it came to pass, as Jesus sat at meat in the house, behold, many publicans and sinners came and sat down with him and his disciples. 11. And when the Pharisees saw it, they said unto his disciples, Why eateth your Master with publicans and sinners?

12. But when Jesus heard that, he said unto them, "They that be whole need not a physician, but they that are sick. 13. But go ye and learn what that meaneth, I will have mercy, and not sacrifice: for I am not come to call the righteous, but sinners to repentance." | 13. And he went forth again by the sea side; and all the multitude resorted unto him, and he taught them. 14. And as he passed by, he saw Levi the son of Alphæus sitting at the receipt of custom and said unto him, "Follow me." And he arose and followed him. 15. And it came to pass, that, as Jesus sat at meat in his house, many publicans and sinners sat also together with Jesus and his disciples; for there were many, and they followed him. 16. And when the scribes and Pharisees saw him eat with publicans and sinners, they said unto his disciples, How is it that he eateth and drinketh with publicans and sinners? 17. When Jesus heard it, he saith unto them, "They that are whole have no need of the physician, but they that are sick: I came not to call the righteous, but sinners to repentance." | 27. And after these things he went forth, and saw a publican, named Levi, sitting at the receipt of custom: and he said unto him, "Follow me." And he left all, rose up, and followed him. 29. And Levi made him a great feast in his house: and there was a great company of publicans and of others that sat down with them. 30. But their scribes and Pharisees murmured against his disciples, saying, Why do ye eat and drink with publicans and sinners?

31. And Jesus answering said unto them, "They that are whole need not a physician; but they that are sick. 32. I came not to call the righteous, but sinners to repentance." |

We cannot doubt that Matthew the publican,—supposing

him to have written the Gospel—knew his own name; but it is very surprising that St Mark and St Luke, his contemporaries, did not know it also. For both of them name Matthew and not Levi, as among the twelve disciples in the later chapters which have been quoted, forgetful, as it would seem, that they had previously related the call of Levi, and the great feast which this disciple had made for Jesus in his house.

There is, in the next place, an historical inaccuracy in either St Luke, or in St Matthew and St Mark, respecting the call of the brothers Peter and Andrew, and likewise in the call of James and John.

MATTHEW iv, 18-22.	MARK i, 16-20.	LUKE v, 1-11.
18. And Jesus, walking by the sea of Galilee, saw two brethren, Simon called Peter, and Andrew his brother, casting a net into the sea: for they were fishers. 19. And he saith unto them, "Follow me, and I will make you fishers of men." 20. And they straightway left their nets and followed him.	16. Now as he walked by the sea of Galilee, he saw Simon and Andrew his brother casting a net into the sea: for they were fishers. 17. And Jesus said unto them, "Come ye after me, and I will make you to become fishers of men." 18. And straightway they forsook their nets, and followed him.	And it came to pass, that, as the people pressed upon him to hear the word of God, he stood by the lake of Gennesaret, 2. And saw two ships standing by the lake: but the fishermen were gone out of them, and were washing their nets. 3. And he entered into one of the ships, which was Simon's, and prayed him that he would thrust out a little from the land. And he sat down, and taught the people out of the ship. 4. Now when he had left speaking, he said unto Simon, "Launch out into the deep and let down your nets for a draught." 5. And Simon answering said unto him, "Master, we have toiled all the night, and have taken nothing: nevertheless at thy word I will let down the net. 6. And when they had this done, they inclosed a great multitude of fishes: and their net brake. 7. And they beckoned unto their partners, which were in the other ship, that they should come and help them. And they came, and filled both the ships,

MATTHEW iv, 21-22.	MARK i, 19-20.	LUKE v, 7-11.
21. And going on from thence, he saw other two brethren, James the son of Zebedee, and John his brother, in a ship with Zebedee their father, mending their nets; and he called them. 22. And they immediately left the ship and their father, and followed him.	19. And when he had gone a little farther thence, he saw James the son of Zebedee, and John his brother, who also were in the ship mending their nets. 20. And straightway he called them: and they left their father Zebedee in the ship with the hired servants, and went after him.	so that they began to sink. 8. When Simon Peter saw it, he fell down at Jesus's knees, saying, "Depart from me: for I am a sinful man, O Lord." 9. For he was astonished, and all that were with him, at the draught of fishes which they had taken: 10. And so was also James, and John, the sons of Zebedee, which were partners with Simon. And Jesus said unto Simon, "Fear not: from henceforth thou shalt catch men." 11. And when they brought their ships to land, they forsook all, and followed him.

The third evangelist represents the four disciples as following Jesus in consequence of the miraculous draught of fishes, but Matthew and Mark, with less likelihood, omit the miracle. All the three lay the scene of their call in Galilee, near the lake of Gennesaret.

It may here be observed that, although the Gospels of St Matthew, St Mark, and St Luke are on the whole tolerably in accordance with one another in the general chronological arrangement of Christ's life, yet St Matthew and St Mark place the call of Simon Peter before the miracle of raising his wife's mother, whereas St Luke places the miracle first, and describes St Peter's election to the apostleship as taking place afterwards.

MATTHEW viii, 14, 15.	MARK i, 29-31.	LUKE iv, 38, 39.
14. And when Jesus was come into Peter's house, he saw his wife's mother laid, and sick of a fever. 15. And he touched her hand, and the fever left her: and she arose, and ministered unto them.	29. And forthwith, when they were come out of the synagogue, they entered into the house of Simon and Andrew, with James and John. 30. But Simon's wife's mother lay sick of a fever, and anon they tell him of her. 31. And he came and took her by the hand, and lifted her up; and immediately the fever left her, and she ministered unto them.	38. And he arose out of the synagogue, and entered into Simon's house. And Simon's wife's mother was taken with a great fever; and they besought him for her. 39. And he stood over her, and rebuked the fever; and it left her: and immediately she arose and ministered unto them.

XXIV.] CALL OF THE TWELVE. 225

In this comparison of the different accounts of the call of these four disciples, we have taken no notice of St John. We must now observe that his account is so entirely at variance with the three already narrated, that all the four cannot at the same time be looked upon as equally chronological, and as such cannot therefore be placed in juxtaposition.

JOHN i, 35-51.

35. Again the next day after John stood, and two of his disciples; 36. And looking upon Jesus as he walked, he saith, "Behold the Lamb of God!" 37. And the two disciples heard him speak, and they followed Jesus.
38. Then Jesus turned, and saw them following, and saith unto them, "What seek ye?" They said unto him, "Rabbi (which is to say, being interpreted, Master), where dwellest thou?" 39. He saith unto them, "Come and see." They came and saw where he dwelt, and abode with him that day: for it was about the tenth hour.
40. One of the two which heard John speak, and followed him, was Andrew, Simon Peter's brother. 41. He first findeth his own brother Simon, and saith unto him, "We have found the Messias," which is, being interpreted, the Christ. 42. And he brought him to Jesus. And when Jesus beheld him, he said, "Thou art Simon the son of Jona: thou shalt be called Cephas, which is by interpretation, a stone."
43. The day following Jesus would go forth into Galilee, and findeth Philip, and saith unto him, "Follow me." 44. Now Philip was of Bethsaida, the city of Andrew and Peter. 45. Philip findeth Nathanael, and saith unto him, "We have found him, of whom Moses in the law, and the prophets, did write, Jesus of Nazareth, the son of Joseph." 46. And Nathanael said unto him, "Can there any good thing come out of Nazareth?" Philip saith unto him, "Come and see."
47. Jesus saw Nathanael coming to him, and saith of him, "Behold an Israelite indeed, in whom is no guile!" 48. Nathanael saith unto him, "Whence knowest thou me?" Jesus answered and said unto him, "Before that Philip called thee, when thou wast under the fig tree, I saw thee." 49. Nathanael answered and saith unto him, "Rabbi, thou art the Son of God: thou art the King of Israel." 50. Jesus answered and said unto him, "Because I said unto thee, I saw thee under the fig tree, believest thou? thou shalt see greater things than these." 51. And he saith unto him, "Verily, verily, I say unto you, Hereafter ye shall see heaven open, and the angels of God ascending and descending upon the Son of man."

In this narrative the first remarkable circumstance is, that Judæa near the Jordan where John was baptizing, and not Galilee, is the country in which Jesus first meets with Peter, Andrew, and a third disciple who is supposed to be John. Secondly, these three, certainly two of them, seem to have been already disciples of the Baptist, and now, as it were by a sudden impulse, become followers of Christ. Thirdly, a strange name, Nathanael, next occurs in conjunction with Philip, though it is not found in either of the first three Gospels, and only in one other passage of St John's Gospel, where, however, he is mentioned as if he was one of the twelve apostles or disciples. All this is irreconcilable with

VOL. II. 16

the narratives of Matthew, Mark, and Luke, who know nothing of Nathanael, and who place the call of Simon, Andrew, James, and John, in Galilee, where they usually lived and carried on their trade of fishermen, not in Judæa where John the Baptist was baptizing.

The last particular of disagreement between the evangelists is the silence of three of them on a most significant and important circumstance which is related by the fourth, namely, the appointment of seventy disciples, subordinate to the twelve:

LUKE X, 1-20.

After these things the Lord appointed other seventy also, and sent them two and two before his face into every city and place, whither he himself would come. 2. Therefore said he unto them, "The harvest truly is great, but the labourers are few: pray ye therefore the Lord of the harvest, that he would send forth labourers into his harvest. 3. Go your ways: behold, I send you forth as lambs among wolves. 4. Carry neither purse, nor scrip, nor shoes: and salute no man by the way. 5. And into whatsoever house ye enter, first say, Peace be to this house. 6. And if the son of peace be there, your peace shall rest upon it: if not, it shall turn to you again. 7. And in the same house remain, eating and drinking such things as they give: for the labourer is worthy of his hire. Go not from house to house. 8. And into whatsoever city ye enter, and they receive you, eat such things as are set before you: 9. And heal the sick that are therein, and say unto them, The kingdom of God is come nigh unto you; 10. But into whatsoever city ye enter, and they receive you not, go your ways out into the streets of the same, and say, 11. Even the very dust of your city, which cleaveth on us, we do wipe off against you: notwithstanding be ye sure of this, that the kingdom of God is come nigh unto you. 12. But I say unto you, that it shall be more tolerable in that day for Sodom, than for that city. . . . . . 16. He that heareth you heareth me; and he that despiseth you despiseth me: and he that despiseth me despiseth him that sent me."

17. And the seventy returned again with joy, saying, "Lord, even the devils are subject unto us through thy name." 18. And he said unto them, "I beheld Satan as lightning fall from heaven. 19. Behold, I give unto you power to tread on serpents and scorpions, and over all the power of the enemy: and nothing shall by any means hurt you. 20. Notwithstanding in this rejoice not, that the spirits are subject unto you; but rather rejoice, because your names are written in heaven."

The admonitions and instructions contained in this extract will be seen to be here and there the same as those which Jesus had before delivered to his twelve disciples; but among these we find other sayings not especially adapted for the occasion of these missions, but of a more general tendency, and expressed in that concise language, which caught the attention of Justin Martyr as rendering them so easy to be retained in the memory: this happened, as we contend, before they were embodied among those miraculous deeds which with them have since formed the four Gospel histories. Although this fact would neither invalidate the truth of these missions nor impugn the accuracy of Christ's teaching, yet we might reasonably doubt whether the admonitions and sayings, which now form the most valuable records of his ministry, have been always placed in the exact order and on the real occasions when they were delivered. It might also be contended that the writers of the Gospel history, in imitating, as they appear to have done, the scheme of the Old Testament, have also in this case imitated the form of administration, which we find to have prevailed at the earliest period of Jewish history, where the numbers twelve and seventy are prominent and have been thought to have a mysterious significance. But if there was a fixed intention of our Lord to establish a peculiar form for his church, it is remarkable that St Luke alone has recorded the mission of the Seventy, whilst the other three take no notice of it at all. And it appears equally remarkable that in the Gospel according to St John, we find nothing said of the mission either of the twelve or of the seventy, and yet we read in St Luke's Gospel (vi, 12), not only that the disciples went out and preached repentance, as John the Baptist had done before, but that they "cast out many devils, and anointed with oil many that were sick and healed them." From the privilege of performing these miracles we cannot imagine the beloved disciple John to have been excluded, and it is on this account the more surprising that in the Gospel which has come down to us under his name no mention is made of the mission either of the seventy or of the twelve. This omission, therefore, must be ascribed to the compiler who in the next generation put together the details of which the fourth Gospel is made up, and if in doing so he has introduced, as a sort of framework, the favourite Jewish numbers twelve and seventy, or, as is more likely still, has copied them from the Old Testament in imitation of the twelve tribal princes and the seventy elders whom God chose to assist Moses in his duties, such a mode of writing the history would not be alien either from the customs of the East or from the mythical tendency of Jewish writers during the years which not only preceded but which also followed the Christian era.

Some bold critics might therefore contend that the single mission of the twelve had gradually been expanded by tradition into two, one of which was assigned to the twelve, the other to the seventy, before the history had been set down in writing.

CHAPTER XXV.

SERMON ON THE MOUNT.

THAT the four Gospels do not follow a strictly chronological order in the events which they relate, has long been admitted even by their warmest advocates. With the exception of a certain rough outline, that Christ's ministry lay first and mainly in Galilee, and afterwards in Judæa and Jerusalem, we cannot obtain anything like an approximate scheme of his travels through the countries and cities which he visited. Even where an attempt is made by the evangelists to connect the performance of a great miracle, or the delivery of a beautiful parable, with some event as following or preceding it, we find in many cases that the four Gospels differ in the attendant circumstances.

This is remarkably so in the case of the Sermon on the Mount, a most beautiful discourse, containing the heads of a moral law, that has been the admiration of every nation and of all ages: so excellent indeed is it in every point of view, that charity can find no other reason than its surpassing and impracticable excellence for the apathy with which men seem agreed, whilst admiring it in theory, to reject it wholly in practice!

The Sermon on the Mount consists of a series of maxims, each complete in itself, yet occasionally connected with those which follow or precede it, as the case may be, with parables and occasional apostrophes introduced, which give it a remarkably vivid and energetic character throughout, and render it a perfect specimen of all the peculiar modes in which Christ conveyed to his hearers the new and beautiful morality which he taught.

Yet, in spite of all these qualities, and of the far-famed reputation which this Discourse has met with throughout all Christendom, there is some ground for believing that such a collective body of maxims was never at any one time delivered from the lips of our Lord, but that a number of separate and shorter discourses, spoken at different times, have been put together to form this more lengthened and much admired Sermon. The reasons for entertaining this belief will be readily gathered from the following table, in which the Sermon on the Mount of St Matthew is placed in juxtaposition with the disjointed maxims of it, which are found in the other Gospels, showing certain peculiarities which deny to it the character of being a distinct and independent discourse.

MATTHEW v, 1-12.

And seeing the multitudes, he went up into a mountain: and when he was set, his disciples came unto him: 2. And he opened his mouth, and taught them, saying, 3. "Blessed are the poor in spirit: for theirs is the kingdom of heaven. 4. Blessed are they that mourn: for they shall be comforted. 5. Blessed are the meek: for they shall inherit the earth. 6. Blessed are they which do hunger and thirst after righteousness: for they shall be filled. 7. Blessed are the merciful: for they shall obtain mercy. 8. Blessed are the pure in heart: for they shall see God. 9. Blessed are the peacemakers: for they shall be called the children of God. 10. Blessed are they which are persecuted for righteousness' sake: for theirs is the kingdom of heaven. 11. Blessed are ye, when men shall revile you, and persecute you, and shall say all manner of evil against you falsely, for my sake.

12. Rejoice, and be exceeding glad: for great is your reward in heaven: for so persecuted they the prophets which were before you.

LUKE vi, 20-22.

20. And he lifted up his eyes on his disciples, and said, "Blessed be ye poor: for yours is the kingdom of God. 21. Blessed are ye that hunger now: for ye shall be filled. Blessed are ye that weep now: for ye shall laugh. 22. Blessed are ye, when men shall hate you, and when they shall separate you from their company, and shall reproach you, and cast out your name as evil, for the Son of man's sake.

LUKE vi, 23-25.

23. Rejoice ye in that day, and leap for joy: for, behold, your reward is great in heaven: for in the like manner did their fathers unto the prophets. 24. But woe unto you that are rich! for ye have received your consolation. 25. Woe unto you that are full! for ye

MATTHEW v, 13-24.	MARK ix, 50.	LUKE vi, 25-27.
		shall hunger. 26. Woe unto you that laugh now! for ye shall mourn and weep. 27. Woe unto you, when all men shall speak well of you! for so did their fathers to the false prophets.
		LUKE xiv, 34, 35.
13. Ye are the salt of the earth: but if the salt have lost his savour, wherewith shall it be salted? it is thenceforth good for nothing, but to be cast out, and to be trodden under foot of men. 14. Ye are the light of the world. A city that is set on an hill cannot be hid. 15. Neither do men light a candle, and put it under a bushel, but on a candlestick; and it giveth light unto all that are in the house. 16. Let your light so shine before men, that they may see your good works, and glorify your Father which is in heaven. 17. Think not that I am come to destroy the law, or the prophets: I am not come to destroy, but to fulfil. 18. For verily I say unto you, Till heaven and earth pass, one jot or one tittle shall in no wise pass from the law, till all be fulfilled.	50. Salt is good: but if the salt have lost his saltness, wherewith will ye season it? Have salt in yourselves, and have peace one with another.	34. Salt is good: but if the salt have lost his savour, wherewith shall it be seasoned? 35. It is neither fit for the land, nor yet for the dunghill; but men cast it out. He that hath ears to hear, let him hear.
	MARK iv, 21.	LUKE viii, 16.
	21. And he said unto them, "Is a candle brought to be put under a bushel, or under a bed? and not to be set on a candlestick?"	16. No man, when he hath lighted a candle, covereth it with a vessel, or putteth it under a bed; but setteth it on a candlestick, that they which enter in may see the light.
		Repeated at xi, 33.
		33. No man, when he hath lighted a candle, putteth it in a secret place, neither under a bushel, but on a candlestick, that they which come in may see the light.
		LUKE xvi, 17.
		17. And it is easier for heaven and earth to pass, than one tittle of the law to fail.

19. Whosoever therefore shall break one of these least commandments, and shall teach men so, he shall be called the least in the kingdom of heaven: but whosoever shall do and teach them, the same shall be called great in the kingdom of heaven. 20. For I say unto you, That except your righteousness shall exceed the righteousness of the scribes and Pharisees, ye shall in no case enter into the kingdom of heaven.

21. Ye have heard that it was said by them of old time, Thou shalt not kill; and whosoever shall kill shall be in danger of the judgement: 22. But I say unto you, That whosoever is angry with his brother without a cause shall be in danger of the judgement; and whosoever shall say to his brother, Raca, shall be in danger of the council: but whosoever shall say, Thou fool, shall be in danger of hell fire. 23. Therefore if thou bring thy gift to the altar, and there rememberest that thy brother hath ought against thee; 24. Leave there thy gift before the altar, and go thy way; first be reconciled to thy brother, and then come and offer thy gift.

XXV.] SERMON ON THE MOUNT.

MATTHEW v, 25-31.	MARK ix, 43.	LUKE xii, 58, 59.
25. Agree with thine adversary quickly, whiles thou art in the way with him; lest at any time the adversary deliver thee to the judge, and the judge deliver thee to the officer, and thou be cast into prison. 26. Verily I say unto thee, Thou shalt by no means come out thence, till thou hast paid the uttermost farthing. 27. Ye have heard that it was said by them of old time, Thou shalt not commit adultery: 28. But I say unto you, That whosoever looketh on a woman to lust after her hath committed adultery with her already in his heart. 29. And if thy right eye offend thee, pluck it out, and cast it from thee: for it is profitable for thee that one of thy members should perish, and not that thy whole body should be cast into hell. 30. And if thy right hand offend thee, cut it off, and cast it from thee: for it is profitable for thee that one of thy members should perish, and not that thy whole body should be cast into hell.	43. And if thy hand offend thee, cut it off: it is better for thee to enter into life maimed, than having two hands to go into hell, into the fire that never shall be quenched: where their worm dieth not, and the fire is not quenched. And if thine eye offend thee, pluck it out: it is better for thee to enter into the kingdom of God with one eye, than having two eyes to be cast into hell fire: where their worm dieth not and the fire is not quenched.	58. When thou goest with thine adversary to the magistrate, as thou art in the way, give diligence that thou mayest be delivered from him, lest he hale thee to the judge, and the judge deliver thee to the officer, and the officer cast thee into prison. 59. I tell thee thou shalt not depart thence, till thou hast paid the very last mite.

Repeated at xviii, 8, 9.

[8. Wherefore if thine hand or thy foot offend thee, cut them off and cast them from thee; it is better for thee to enter into life halt or maimed, rather than having two hands or two feet to be cast into everlasting fire. 9. And if thine eye offend thee, pluck it out and cast it from thee: it is better for thee to enter into life with one eye, rather than having two eyes to be cast into hell fire.]

MARK x, 4.

31. It hath been said, Whosoever shall put away his wife, let him give her a writing of divorcement:	4. Moses suffered to write a bill of divorcement, and to put her away.

Repeated at xix, 7.

[7. Why did Moses then command to give a writing of divorcement, and to put her away?]

MATTHEW v, 32-43.	MARK x, 11, 12.	LUKE xvi, 18.
32. But I say unto you, That whosoever shall put away his wife, saving for the cause of fornication, causeth her to commit adultery: and whosoever shall marry her that is divorced committeth adultery.	11. And he saith unto them, "Whosoever shall put away his wife, and marry another, committeth adultery against her. 12. And if a woman shall put away her husband, and be married to another, she committeth adultery."	18. Whosoever putteth away his wife, and marrieth another, committeth adultery: and whosoever marrieth her that is put away from her husband committeth adultery.

Repeated at xix, 9.

[9. And I say unto you, Whosoever shall put away his wife, except it be for fornication, and shall marry another committeth adultery; and whoso marrieth her that is put away, doth commit adultery.]

33. Again, ye have heard that it hath been said by them of old time, Thou shalt not forswear thyself, but shalt perform unto the Lord thine oaths: 34. But I say unto you, Swear not at all; neither by heaven; for it is God's throne: 35. Nor by the earth, for it is his footstool: neither by Jerusalem, for it is the city of the great King. 36. Neither shalt thou swear by thy head, because thou canst not make one hair white or black. 37. But let your communication be, Yea, yea; Nay, nay: for whatsoever is more than these cometh of evil.

38. Ye have heard that it hath been said, An eye for an eye, and a tooth for a tooth: 39. But I say unto you, That ye resist not evil: but whosoever shall smite thee on the right cheek, turn to him the other also. 40. And if any man will sue thee at the law, and take away thy coat, let him have thy cloke also. 41. And whosoever shall compel thee to go a mile, go with him twain.	
	LUKE vi, 29, 30.
	29. And unto him that smiteth thee on the one cheek offer also the other; and him that taketh away thy cloke forbid not to take thy coat also.
42. Give to him that asketh thee, and from him that would borrow of thee turn not thou away.	30. Give to every man that asketh of thee; and of him that taketh away thy goods ask them not again.
	LUKE vi, 27-28.
43. Ye have heard that it hath been said, Thou shalt love thy neighbour, and hate thine enemy. 44. But I say unto you, Love your enemies, bless them that curse you, do	27. But I say unto you which hear, Love your enemies, do good to them which hate you, 28. Bless them that curse you, and pray for them which despitefully use you. . . . .

MATTHEW v, 44-48.	LUKE vi, 32-36.
good to them that hate you, and pray for them which despitefully use you, and persecute you; 45. That ye may be the children of your Father which is in heaven: for he maketh his sun to rise on the evil and on the good, and sendeth rain on the just and on the unjust. 46. For if ye love them which love you, what reward have ye? do not even the publicans the same? 47. And if ye salute your brethren only, what do ye more than others? do not even the publicans so?	32. For if ye love them which love you, what thank have ye? for sinners also love those that love them. 33. And if ye do good to them which do good to you, what thank have ye? for sinners also do even the same. 34. And if ye lend to them of whom ye hope to receive, what thank have ye? for sinners also lend to sinners, to receive as much again. 35. But love ye your enemies, and do good, and lend, hoping for nothing again; and your reward shall be great, and ye shall be the children of the Highest: for he is kind unto the unthankful and to the evil.
48. Be ye therefore perfect, even as your Father which is in heaven is perfect.	36. Be ye therefore merciful, as your Father also is merciful.

MATTHEW vi, 1-10.

Take heed that ye do not your alms before men, to be seen of them: otherwise ye have no reward of your Father which is in heaven. 2. Therefore when thou doest thine alms, do not sound a trumpet before thee, as the hypocrites do in the synagogues and in the streets, that they may have glory of men. Verily I say unto you, They have their reward. 3. But when thou doest alms, let not thy left hand know what thy right hand doeth: 4. That thine alms may be in secret: and thy Father which seeth in secret himself shall reward thee openly.
5. And when thou prayest, thou shalt not be as the hypocrites are: for they love to pray standing in the synagogues and in the corners of the streets, that they may be seen of men. Verily I say unto you, They have their reward. 6. But thou, when thou prayest, enter into thy closet, and when thou hast shut thy door, pray to thy Father which is in secret; and thy Father which seeth in secret shall reward thee openly. 7. But when ye pray, use not vain repetitions, as the heathen do: for they think that they shall be heard for their much speaking. 8. Be not ye therefore like unto them: for your Father knoweth what things ye have need of, before ye ask him. 9. After this manner therefore pray ye:

	LUKE xi, 2.
Our Father which art in heaven, Hallowed be thy name. 10. Thy kingdom come. Thy will be done in earth, as	Our Father which art in heaven, Hallowed be thy name, Thy kingdom come. Thy will be done, as in Heaven, so in

MATTHEW vi, 10-22.
it is in heaven. 11.
Give us this day our
daily bread. 12. And
forgive us our debts, as
we forgive our debtors.
13. And lead us not
into temptation, but
deliver us from evil:
For thine is the kingdom, and the power,
and the glory, for ever.
Amen.
14. For if ye forgive
men their trespasses,
your heavenly Father
will also forgive you:
15. But if ye forgive not
men their trespasses,
neither will your Father
forgive your trespasses.
16. Moreover when
ye fast, be not, as the
hypocrites, of a sad
countenance: for they
disfigure their faces,
that they may appear
unto men to fast. Verily
I say unto you, They
have their reward. 17.
But thou, when thou
fastest, anoint thine
head, and wash thy
face; 18. That thou
appear not unto men to
fast, but unto thy
Father which is in
secret: and thy Father
which seeth in secret,
shall reward thee
openly.
19. Lay not up for
yourselves treasures
upon earth, where
moth and rust doth
corrupt, and where
thieves break through
and steal: 20. But lay
up for yourselves treasures in heaven, where
neither moth nor rust
doth corrupt, and where
thieves do not break
through nor steal: 21.
For where your treasure is, there will your
heart be also.
22. The light of the
body is the eye: if
therefore thine eye be

MARK xi, 25-26.

And when ye stand
praying, forgive if ye
have aught against any:
that your Father also
which is in heaven may
forgive you your trespasses. But if ye do
not forgive, neither will
your Father which is in
heaven forgive your
trespasses.

LUKE xi, 2.
earth. Give us day by
day our daily bread.
And forgive us our sins;
for we also forgive every
one that is indebted to
us. And lead us not
into temptation; but
deliver us from evil.

LUKE xii, 33.
Sell that ye have, and
give alms; provide
yourselves bags which
wax not old, a treasure
in the heavens that
faileth not, where no
thief approacheth, neither moth corrupteth.
For where your treasure
is, there will your heart
be also.

LUKE xi, 34.
The light of the body
is the eye: therefore
when thine eye is single,

MATTHEW vi, 22-30.	LUKE xi, 34.
single, thy whole body shall be full of light. 23. But if thine eye be evil, thy whole body shall be full of darkness. If therefore the light that is in thee be darkness, how great is that darkness!	thy whole body also is full of light; but when thine eye is evil, thy body also is full of darkness. Take heed therefore that the light which is in thee is not darkness. If thy whole body therefore be full of light, having no part dark, the whole shall be full of light, as when the bright shining of a candle doth give thee light.
	LUKE xvi, 13.
24. No man can serve two masters: for either he will hate the one, and love the other, or else he will hold to the one, and despise the other. Ye cannot serve God and mammon.	No servant can serve two masters: for either he will hate the one, and love the other; or else he will hold to the one, and despise the other. Ye cannot serve God and mammon.
	LUKE xii, 22-27.
25. Therefore I say unto you, Take no thought for your life, what ye shall eat, or what ye shall drink; nor yet for your body, what ye shall put on. Is not the life more than meat, and the body than raiment? 26. Behold the fowls of the air: for they sow not, neither do they reap, nor gather into barns; yet your heavenly Father feedeth them. Are ye not much better than they?	22. And he said unto his disciples, "Therefore I say unto you, Take no thought for your life, what ye shall eat; neither for the body, what ye shall put on. 23. The life is more than meat, and the body is more than raiment. 24. Consider the ravens: for they neither sow nor reap; which neither have storehouse nor barn; and God feedeth them: how much more are ye better than the fowls?
27. Which of you by taking thought can add one cubit unto his stature? 28. And why take ye thought for raiment? Consider the lilies of the field, how they grow; they toil not, neither do they spin: 29. And yet I say unto you, That even Solomon in all his glory was not arrayed like one of these. 30. Where-	25. And which of you with taking thought can add to his stature one cubit? 26. If ye then be not able to do that thing which is least, why take ye thought for the rest? 27. Consider the lilies how they grow: they toil not, they spin not; and yet I say unto you, that Solomon in all his glory was not arrayed like one

MATTHEW vi, 30-34.	MARK iv, 24.	LUKE xii, 28-31.
fore, if God so clothe the grass of the field, which to-day is, and to-morrow is cast into the oven, shall he not much more clothe you, O ye of little faith? 31. Therefore take no thought, saying, What shall we eat? or, What shall we drink? or, Wherewithal shall we be clothed? 32. (For after all these things do the Gentiles seek:) for your heavenly Father knoweth that ye have need of all these things. 33. But seek ye first the kingdom of God, and his righteousness; and all these things shall be added unto you. 34. Take therefore no thought for the morrow: for the morrow shall take thought for the things of itself. Sufficient unto the day is the evil thereof.		of these. 28. If then God so clothe the grass, which is to-day in the field, and to-morrow is cast into the oven; how much more will he clothe you, O ye of little faith? 29. And seek not ye what ye shall eat, or what ye shall drink, neither be ye of doubtful mind: 30. For all these things do the nations of the world seek after: and your Father knoweth that ye have need of these things. 31. But rather seek ye the kingdom of God; and all these things shall be added unto you.

MATTHEW vii, 1-4.		LUKE vi, 37-41.
Judge not, that ye be not judged. 2. For with what judgement ye judge, ye shall be judged: and with what measure ye mete, it shall be measured to you again.	24. And he said unto them, "Take heed what ye hear: with what measure ye mete, it shall be measured to you: and unto you that hear shall more be given."	37. Judge not, and ye shall not be judged: condemn not, and ye shall not be condemned: forgive, and ye shall be forgiven: 38. Give, and it shall be given unto you; good measure, pressed down, and shaken together, and running over, shall men give into your bosom. For with the same measure that ye mete withal it shall be measured to you again.
3. And why beholdest thou the mote that is in thy brother's eye, but considerest not the beam that is in thine own eye? 4. Or how wilt thou say to thy brother, Let me pull the mote out of thine eye; and behold a beam is in thine own eye?		39. And he spake a parable unto them, Can the blind lead the blind? shall they not both fall into the ditch? 40. The disciple is not above his master: but every one that is perfect shall be as his master. 41. And why beholdest thou the mote that is in thy

MATTHEW vii, 5-13.	LUKE vi, 41-42.
5. Thou hypocrite, first cast out the beam out of thine own eye; and then shalt thou see clearly to cast out the mote out of thy brother's eye. 6. Give not that which is holy unto the dogs, neither cast ye your pearls before swine, lest they trample them under their feet, and turn again and rend you.	brother's eye, but perceivest not the beam that is in thine own eye? 42. Either how canst thou say to thy brother, Brother, let me pull out the mote that is in thine eye, when thou thyself beholdest not the beam that is in thine own eye? Thou hypocrite, cast out first the beam out of thine own eye, and then shalt thou see clearly to pull out the mote that is in thy brother's eye.
	LUKE xi, 9.
7. Ask, and it shall be given you; seek, and ye shall find; knock, and it shall be opened unto you; 8. For every one that asketh receiveth; and he that seeketh findeth; and to him that knocketh it shall be opened. 9. Or what man is there of you, whom if his son ask bread, will he give him a stone? 10. Or if he ask a fish, will he give him a serpent? 11. If ye then, being evil, know how to give good gifts unto your children, how much more shall your Father which is in heaven give good things to them that ask him?	9. And I say unto you, Ask, and it shall be given you: seek, and ye shall find; knock, and it shall be opened unto you. For every one that asketh receiveth; and he that seeketh findeth; and to him that knocketh it shall be opened. If a son shall ask bread of any of you that is a father, will he give him a stone? or if he ask a fish, will he for a fish give him a serpent? Or if he ask an egg, will he offer him a scorpion? If ye then, being evil, know how to give good gifts unto your children: how much more shall your Heavenly Father give the Holy Spirit to them that ask him?
	LUKE vi, 31.
12. Therefore all things whatsoever ye would that men should do to you, do ye even so to them: for this is the law and the prophets.	31. And as ye would that men should do to you, do ye also to them likewise.
	LUKE xiii, 24.
13. Enter ye in at the strait gate: for wide is the gate, and broad is the way, that leadeth to destruction, and many there be which	24. Strive to enter in at the strait gate: for many, I say unto you, will seek to enter in, and shall not be able.

MATTHEW vii, 14-21.
go in thereat: 14. Because strait is the gate, and narrow is the way, which leadeth unto life, and few there be that find it. 15. Beware of false prophets, which come to you in sheep's clothing, but inwardly they are ravening wolves. 16. Ye shall know them by their fruits. Do men gather grapes of thorns, or figs of thistles? 17. Even so every good tree bringeth forth good fruit; but a corrupt tree bringeth forth evil fruit. 18. A good tree cannot bring forth evil fruit, neither can a corrupt tree bring forth good fruit. 19. Every tree that bringeth not forth good fruit is hewn down, and cast into the fire. 20. Wherefore by their fruits ye shall know them.

Repeated at iii, 10.

[10. And now also the axe is laid unto the root of the trees: therefore every tree which bringeth not forth good fruit is hewn down and cast into the fire.

And at xii, 33.

33. Either make the tree good, and his fruit good; or else make the tree corrupt and his fruit corrupt: for the tree is known by his fruit.]

21. Not every one that saith unto me, Lord, Lord, shall enter into the kingdom of heaven; but he that doeth the will of my Father which

LUKE vi, 43-45.
43. For a good tree bringeth not forth corrupt fruit; neither doth a corrupt tree bring forth good fruit. 44. For every tree is known by his own fruit. For of thorns men do not gather figs, nor of a bramble bush gather they grapes. 45. A good man out of the good treasure of his heart bringeth forth that which is good; and an evil man out of the evil treasure of his heart bringeth forth that which is evil; for of the abundance of the heart his mouth speaketh.

LUKE iii, 9.
9. And now also the axe is laid unto the root of the trees: every tree therefore which bringeth not forth good fruit is hewn down and cast into the fire.

LUKE vi, 46.
46. And why call ye me Lord, Lord, and do not the things which I say?

MATTHEW vii, 22-29.	MARK i. 22.	LUKE vi, 47-49.
is in heaven. 22. Many will say to me in that day, Lord, Lord, have we not prophesied in thy name? and in thy name have cast out devils? and in thy name done many wonderful works? 23. And then will I profess unto them, I never knew you: depart from me, ye that work iniquity.		
24. Therefore whosoever heareth these sayings of mine, and doeth them, I will liken him unto a wise man, which built his house upon a rock: 25. And the rain descended, and the floods came, and the winds blew, and beat upon that house; and it fell not: for it was founded upon a rock. 26. And every one that heareth these sayings of mine, and doeth them not, shall be likened unto a foolish man, which built his house upon the sand: 27. And the rain descended, and the floods came, and the winds blew, and beat upon that house; and it fell: and great was the fall of it."		47. Whosoever cometh to me, and heareth my sayings and doeth them, I will show you to whom he is like: 48. He is like a man which built an house, and digged deep, and laid the foundation on a rock: and when the flood arose, the stream beat vehemently upon that house, and could not shake it: for it was founded upon a rock. 49. But he that heareth and doeth not, is like a man that without a foundation built an house upon the earth; against which the stream did beat vehemently, and immediately it fell; and the ruin of that house was great.
28. And it came to pass, when Jesus had ended these sayings, the people were astonished at his doctrine: 29. For he taught them as one having authority, and not as the scribes.	22. And they were astonished at his doctrine: for he taught them as one that had authority and not as the scribes.	

The Reasons, which this harmony furnishes, for doubting the original separate character of a Sermon on the Mount, are these.

1. Because it is only in Matthew's Gospel that the Discourse so called is found in a perfect state.

2. Because in all the other Gospels no such consecutive discourse is found, but only a variety of maxims, used by Christ on different occasions, in part the same as those which have been gathered by Matthew under one head.

3. Because some of the very maxims which Matthew includes in the Sermon on the Mount, occur elsewhere again even in St Matthew's own Gospel as spoken by Christ at other times.

4. Because some of the said maxims are found elsewhere, as spoken not by Jesus, but by John the Baptist.

5. The appellation "Sermon on the Mount" has been adopted in later times to designate a discourse which does not stand forward with any particular prominence under an especial name, even in the Gospel according to St Matthew.

6. Because the beginning and the end of Matthew's Sermon on the Mount are given by St Luke, but with every circumstance of time, place and manner diametrically opposed to what is found in the Gospel according to St Matthew, as will appear from a few words of explanation.

As regards the time, we read in the Gospel according to St Matthew, that Jesus, having returned from the wilderness of Judæa into Galilee, calls Simon Peter, Andrew, James, and John, and immediately afterwards heals all that are brought unto him, and, seeing the multitudes, goes up into a mountain and delivers the Sermon on the Mount. The time therefore is evidently fixed by Matthew at the very beginning of Christ's ministry. But in the parallel history of St Luke, a much longer space of time is supposed to have passed between the Temptation in the wilderness and the Sermon on the Mount; all the numerous events in the fourth, the fifth, and half of the sixth chapters are interposed between them.

The place where the Sermon was delivered, according to St Matthew, was the mountain, into which Jesus went up: but in St Luke, vi, 12, he is represented as having first gone up "into a mountain to pray," where he "continued all night in prayer to God;" after which he is said to have gone down again from the mountain in the morning before he addressed the multitude; as we read in the seventeenth verse, "And he came down with them and stood in the plain." These two versions of the story are irreconcilable the one with the other.

But the Manner in which Christ delivered this discourse is also differently set forth by the two evangelists. In St Matthew's Gospel (v, 1) he is made to address the people in a sitting posture. "And seeing the multitudes, he went up into a mountain and when he was set, his disciples came unto him." But in St Luke's account he is said to have gone down and *stood* in the *plain*.

Thus we have not conformity, either of *time, place,* or *manner,* in the accounts of the two evangelists who have told us all we know about the Sermon on the Mount; and we are led by this and the other reasons above stated, to doubt whether it ever was delivered at all as a separate discourse, whether its present state is not rather an embodiment of various maxims and sentences grouped together by tradition, or by the arrangement of the compiler, who wished to combine methodical with moral teaching, whilst at the same time delivering historical facts. From this conclusion the only alternative, certainly more attractive and interesting to the devout believer, is however less open to demonstration, namely that such a discourse was actually delivered by Jesus, but that imperfect accounts of it were circulated, and that each of the Evangelic writers recorded what he knew.

CHAPTER XXVI.

The Lord's Prayer.

If we would derive from the books of the New Testament the benefit which they are best qualified to furnish, we shall dwell less upon their historical accuracy, and more upon their practical and moral use. The subjects, which have occupied our attention in the preceding chapters, must have led the reader to perceive that the four Gospels cannot be received as accurate and complete histories, but only as Memoirs or Memorials, combined into one work with the doctrines and teaching of Jesus which give to that work its chief value. In our anxiety to hold fast on those beautiful truths contained in this cherished book, which were taught us in our childhood, we must acknowledge the propriety of casting overboard certain parts in order to escape making shipwreck of the whole. Our true consolation is that the spirit of the Christian book will still remain with us, when we no longer reverence its letter. The Apostle speaks of three great Christian virtues, Faith, Hope, and Charity; but the greatest of these he says is Charity. With the sanction then of the great Apostle who spake these words, we may proceed with our work, without hesitation—certain that the greatest of Christian virtues is as safe from danger by these speculations as the rock of adamant amid the waves which fall and are broken against its base. The Christian religion has always suffered from the rash zeal of its real or pretended adherents. Its merciful doctrines, found in the New Testament, have ever been clouded by the deep shadows cast upon them by the literal interpretation of that book. By freeing the New Testament from the trammels which involve it, we may alone hope to give it a more vital circulation in the hearts rather than in the lips or in the hands of the multitude. There is no way so certain of bringing the gifts of providence into contempt, as to magnify them beyond the place which they justly occupy in the scale of things. In proportion as this evil is great, is its remedy difficult. Hence the vulgar apprehension that long established error is safer than novel truth; and hence the feeling, too common, but culpably erroneous, that on the most serious and momentous of all the subjects which can interest us, it is possible for ignorance to be bliss, and that it may be folly to be wise. If it has been proved by the arguments contained in the last chapter that the Sermon on the Mount may be regarded rather as a compilation of Christ's sayings, possessing no separate original character of its own, though we may cease henceforth to regard it in this latter light, yet our respect for the moral lessons which it conveys will suffer no diminution. In the same way, we find a similar want of verbal accuracy in what is commonly called "The Lord's prayer," a short and beautiful effusion, adopted by Christians in every age and clime, and bearing the character of having been delivered by Christ to his disciples, at their own request, as a mode of addressing their Father which is in Heaven, and of pouring out their petitions to the throne of grace. It must be remembered, that what we are here concerned with, is simply to bring the evidence which the "Lord's Prayer" furnishes to bear upon the question, about what time the Gospels, in which that Prayer is found, were written. Without raising a doubt or a question whether the Lord's Prayer was really given by Christ or not—such a surmise would be only worthy of that senseless scepticism which doubts every thing—we yet are justified in suggesting a doubt as to the time when that beautiful and simple prayer was first reduced to writing, and also as to the historical accuracy of language in which it has been handed down.

Two copies of the Lord's Prayer have come to us: they are found in the Gospels of St Matthew, vi, 9-13, and St Luke, xi, 2-4.

The texts of the Prayer in the words of the respective

THE LORD'S PRAYER.

Gospels, as we read in the authorized version, may be seen at page 233 of this volume arranged in parallel columns.

The first difference to be noticed between the two Gospels on the subject of the Lord's Prayer, regards the occasion when each of the two represents it as having been delivered. St Matthew introduces it into the Sermon on the Mount, and therefore refers it to the very beginning of Christ's ministry. But St Luke says, at xi, 1 ;

And it came to pass, that, as he was praying in a certain place, when he ceased, one of his disciples said unto him, Lord, teach us to pray, as John also taught his disciples.
2. And he said unto them, when ye pray, say, Our Father &c.

This took place at a much more advanced period of Christ's ministry, than that at which the Sermon on the Mount was delivered ; and the account of St Luke is also more probable, by its giving an occasion for the delivery of the Prayer. Christ's disciples, unwilling to be at a disadvantage with the disciples of John the Baptist, ask their master to furnish them also with a form of prayer, as John had already done to his followers, and they receive that short form, which has been used in the Church thenceforward down to the present time. But, secondly, the two copies of the Lord's Prayer do not agree together. Whilst St Matthew records the prayer that God will give us "to-day" our daily bread, St Luke has "day by day ;" and whilst according to the former we pray God to "forgive us debts as we forgive our debtors," according to the latter we pray God to "forgive us our sins, for we also forgive every one who is indebted to us." In our prayer books, it will be observed neither the version of St Matthew nor that of St Luke has been followed ; we pray that God will "forgive us our trespasses as we forgive them that trespass against us."

Again, St Matthew's copy adds a whole sentence, "For thine is the kingdom, the power, and the glory, for ever," which is omitted by St Luke. These verbal variations are trifling in the eyes of those who regard our Gospels as containing all that could be saved from the wreck of time, when tradition was no longer able to carry on the knowledge of the fading past ; nor indeed ought they to cause any difficulty to those who know that Christ's disciples and apostles were Jews and did not speak Greek ; but those who refer these writings to direct verbal inspiration, are bound to explain the principles upon which they can ascribe to such a source two documents so important and in such general use among Christians, yet differing so much the one from the other.

But it may not be out of place to hear what others have said, in confirmation of the views here suggested, and also what emendations have been suggested by which the meaning of our authorized translation may be improved. In the first place on the Greek word *epi-ousion* translated 'daily,' a late eminent bishop of our church, Dr Hinds, suggests that, whereas the etymology of the word is similar to that of *peri-ousion*, which indicates *substance over*, *i.e. superfluous*, the preposition *epi* 'to' or 'for', substituted in the compound word for *peri*, would seem to give it the signification of merely *sufficient for us*. The learned prelate seems to be less successful in taking the words, ὁ ἐν τοῖς οὐρανοῖς "which art in heaven" to have been originally a side-note which has by accident been admitted into the text. He is right in saying that ὁ 'the' is not equivalent to ὅς 'who,' but no Greek scholar ever said that it was: the word to be supplied is ὤν 'being,' which is a participle, and not εἰς 'art' or ἐστὶν 'is,' which is a verb and therefore inadmissible in such a sentence. The same explanation applies to 'Abba, father' in Galatians, iv, 6, and to the two passages in St Matthew's Gospel, v, 16, and 45, where the words "Father which is in heaven" are represented in Greek by the article, just as in the Lord's prayer which we are now considering. And another example occurs in the Acts, xiii, 9, where we have *Saulos ho kai Paulos* which is interpreted in our version by "Saul who is also called Paul."

Whilst then no other satisfactory explanation has or can be given for the existence of two copies of so important a document it is not only lawful to propose but difficult to resist an inference which must constantly recur to the mind of the reader, that in the city of Antioch, where Greek was the language of the people, where also as our own books tell us the early converts were first called Christians, and where Lucian alludes in no obscure terms to the compilation of Christian books—it is difficult, I say, to resist the inference that those which now form our Canon, as well as numerous others perhaps, were put together at that very time, and in consequence of various circumstances which were then concurrently in action.*

---

* In Bunsen's work entitled *Hippolytus and his Age*, vol. iii, p. 265, is a curious development of the six clauses of the Lord's Prayer, in connection with the Christian ritual in the early ages of our religion.

CHAPTER XXVII.

JESUS ALWAYS ACCOMPANIED BY A MULTITUDE OF FOLLOWERS.

THE four Gospels are all marked with a dramatic or scenic character, well fitted for purposes of doctrine, but remarkably improbable if we regard them as relating absolute matters of fact. Thus we find that the Scribes and Pharisees, who seem to have been Christ's open enemies, are always at hand, to find fault with him and to discuss his most trivial actions. An instance of this we have in the walk through the cornfields on the Sabbath day, as related by the first three evangelists.

MATTHEW xii, 1-8.	MARK ii, 23-28.	LUKE vi, 1-5.
At that time Jesus went on the sabbath day through the corn, and his disciples were an hungred, and began to pluck the ears of corn, and to eat. 2. But when the Pharisees saw it, they said unto him, "Behold, thy disciples do that which is not lawful to do upon the sabbath day."	23. And it came to pass, that he went through the corn fields on the sabbath day; and his disciples began, as they went, to pluck the ears of corn. 24. And the Pharisees said unto him, "Behold, why do they on the sabbath day that which is not lawful?"	And it came to pass on the second sabbath after the first, that he went through the corn fields; and his disciples plucked the ears of corn, and did eat, rubbing them their hands. 2. And certain of the Pharisees said unto them, " Why do ye that which is not lawful to do on the sabbath day?"
3. But he said unto them, "Have ye not read what David did, when he was an hungred, and they that were with him; 4. How he entered into the house of God, and did eat the showbread, which was not lawful for him to eat, neither for them which were with him, but only for the priests? 5. Or have ye not read in the law, how that on the sabbath day the priests in the temple profane the sabbath, and are blameless? 6. But I say unto you, That in this place is	25. And he said unto them, "Have ye never read what David did, when he had need, and was an hungred, he, and they that were with him? 26. How he went into the house of God in the days of Abiathar the high priest, and did eat the showbread, which is not lawful to eat but for the priests, and gave also to them which were with him?" 27. And he said unto them, "The sabbath was made for man, and not man for the sabbath:	3. And Jesus answering them said, " Have ye not read so much as this, what David did, when himself was an hungred, and they which were with him; 4. How he went into the house of God, and did take and eat the showbread, and gave also to them that were with him; which is not lawful to eat but for the priests alone?"

MATTHEW xii, 7, 8.	MARK ii, 28.	LUKE vi, 5.
one greater than the temple. 7. But if ye had known what this meaneth, I will have mercy, and not sacrifice, ye would not have condemned the guiltless. 8. For the Son of man is Lord even of the sabbath day."	28. Therefore the Son of man is Lord also of the sabbath."	5. And he said unto them, "That the Son of man is Lord also of the sabbath."

How the Pharisees could have time to follow Jesus about in this way on all occasions, it is hard to conjecture. They surely did not attend on him as friends; nor is it easy to suppose that from hatred of him they would have taken so much trouble. The various transactions of Christ's life, whilst he was on earth, have evidently derived a colouring, suited to place them in the most striking and picturesque light before the eyes of the world. Unless we admit this principle of interpretation, it is impossible to find our way through the mass of extraordinary facts which we meet with. If we take the accounts literally, we must believe that the whole political state of Jerusalem, if not of all Judæa and Galilee, was arrested to watch the career of our Lord: Pharisees, Sadducees, Priests, and Scribes, seem to have had nothing else to do, or to leave every thing else undone. It may be admitted that we know very little of these Scribes, Priests, Pharisees, and Sadducees; hardly any thing, indeed, beyond what we read of them in the New Testament. But we know, at all events, that they were the leading men of the Jews, and, though subordinate to the authority of the Roman procurator, yet engaged in administrating a considerable portion of the public government, and consequently of too high rank to follow so obscure a person as Christ appeared to be.

Neither do we find sufficient testimony in the writers of that period, to the truth of the supposition that a Messiah was generally expected at that time by the Jews. We certainly find allusion to an opinion of this kind being afloat forty or fifty years after Christ's crucifixion, but not earlier. This is an important difference. An expectation of a Messiah should have preceded the appearance of Christ, if it is to be accepted as an explanation of the great attention with which the rulers of the Jews watched all his motions. But an expectation of a Messiah, following so long after Christ's appearance on earth, may have had its origin in Christ's own history, and so be of no weight in settling such questions as the present.

Even this however is admitting too much; for all the passages quoted from the ancient authors in this matter prove that the expectation was rather of a ruler of the world than of a Messiah, strictly so called.

We may briefly dismiss the well-known eclogue of Virgil, written in compliment to his patron Augustus, as having not the most remote bearing upon the events which passed in Judæa some twenty years afterwards:

Magnus ab integro sæclorum nascitur ordo!

A great revolution, it is true, was about to come; but it was the royal family of the Cæsars, not the humble family in the inn at Bethlehem, of which the poet was speaking. How vain, then, the endeavours of weak-minded men to enlist the Roman Virgil among the harbingers of Christ and of his religion!

A second indication of Christ's coming and of a general expectation concerning him, is supposed to be contained in Suetonius's Life of Vespasian, § 4.

In the journey through Greece among the companions of Nero, he [Vespasian] often either went out when Nero sang, or went to sleep if he remained, and by doing so gave serious offence. For this cause he was excluded from his society, and from salutation in public, and withdrew into a small out of the way city, where he lay concealed, until suddenly, when he was looking out for some extreme punishment, he was intrusted with the government of a province and the command of an army. An old and constant opinion had grown up throughout the whole of the East, that it was fated for the empire of the world at that time to devolve on some one who should go forth from Judæa. This prediction referred to a Roman emperor, as was afterwards evident by the result, but the Jews took it to themselves, and rose in rebellion. Having slain their governor, they moreover routed the lieutenant of Syria, a man of consular rank, who was bringing supplies, and took the standard of the eagle.

This was forty years or more after the crucifixion of our Lord. It is dangerous to say that the old and constant opinion was prophetical of Christ; for if so, prophecy, always obscure until fulfilled, in this case also failed in its fulfilment. The expectation, it seems, was not gratified by Christ's coming. It was still to be realized, and was at last destroyed by the swords of the Romans, who claimed for themselves and for their emperor the fulfilment of the expectation which had grown up among the people of the East.

We find in the History of Tacitus, v, 13, a similar account of this expectation by which the Jews were encouraged to revolt against the Romans.

Many prodigies had happened, but that nation sunk in superstition, and opposed to religion, do not deem it right to expiate these either by victims or by prayers. Armies were seen fighting in heaven, arms rattling, and the temple was illuminated by a sudden light from the clouds. The gates of the forum were suddenly thrown open, and a voice more than human was heard, that "the Gods were leaving"; upon which there was a great move as of persons leaving. These things alarmed some; but the greater number were persuaded that it was written in the ancient writings of their priests, that the East would at this very time gain strength, and the empire of the world devolve on some one who should go forth from Judæa. This ambiguous expression was prophetic of Vespasian and Titus. But the common people, after the custom of human cupidity, interpreting such a magnificent decree of the fates in their own favour, could not be induced even by misfortune to view things in their true light. We have heard that the number of the besieged, of every age, men and women, was six hundred thousand. All took arms, who could bear them, and those who dared to do so, were far more than in proportion to the whole number. Men and women were alike obstinate, and they showed less fear of death than of living in exile. Such was the city, such the people, which Titus Cæsar, seeing that the nature of the ground would not allow of a speedy decision by assault, prepared to assail with mounds and military engines.

MATTHEW xxi, 12-17.	MARK xi, 15-19.
12. And Jesus went into the temple of God, and cast out all them that sold and bought in the temple, and overthrew the tables of the moneychangers, and the seats of them that sold doves, 13. And said unto them, "It is written, My house shall be called the house of prayer, but ye have made it a den of thieves." 14. And the blind and the lame came to him in the temple; and he healed them.	15. And they come to Jerusalem: and Jesus went into the temple, and began to cast out them that sold and bought in the temple, and overthrew the tables of the moneychangers, and the seats of them that sold doves; 16. And would not suffer that any man should carry any vessel through the temple. 17. And he taught, saying unto them, "Is it not written, My house shall be called of all nations the house of prayer? but ye have made it a den of thieves."

Thus, we see no good ground for believing that there was a general expectation of a Messiah, in our sense of the word, prevalent among the Jews at the time when Christ appeared. The aspiration of all nations in distress, finds vent for itself in the wish for a regenerator, and the *Exoriare aliquis* of the poet no doubt found its way into the hearts of the Jews, as it has of most other oppressed nations. But this does not account for the extraordinary concourse of people always following Christ: this seems to be the dramatic framework adopted by the writer in which to represent more forcibly the discourses of our Lord ; and although this may have appeared quite lawful and sanctioned by the hyperbolic and imaginative character of the Eastern intellect, yet the cooler judgement of the western world must make allowance for this feature of the Gospel history and interpret it by the natural tendency of the early Christians to magnify every occasion that concerned the founder of their religion.

CHAPTER XXVIII.

PURIFICATION OF THE TEMPLE.

PERHAPS the most remarkable of all Christ's miracles, because in performing it he put himself in open hostility to the Jewish authorities, was driving out the money-changers and others from the temple of Jerusalem. The miracle is thus related by the four evangelists :—

LUKE xix, 45-48.	JOHN ii, 13-17.
45. And he went into the temple, and began to cast out them that sold therein, and them that bought; 46. Saying unto them, " It is written, My house is the house of prayer: but ye have made it a den of thieves."	13. And the Jews' passover was at hand, and Jesus went up to Jerusalem, 14. And found in the temple those that sold oxen and sheep and doves, and the changers of money sitting : 15. And when he had made a scourge of small cords, he drove them all out of the temple, and the sheep, and the oxen ; and poured out the changers' money, and overthrew the tables ; 16. And said unto them that sold doves, " Take these things hence ; make not my Father's house an house of merchandise."

250   CHRISTIAN RECORDS.   [CHAPTER

MATTHEW xxi, 15-17.	MARK xi, 18, 19.
15. And when the chief priests and scribes saw the wonderful things that he did, and the children crying in the temple, and saying, Hosanna to the son of David; they were sore displeased, 16. And said unto him, "Hearest thou what these say?" And Jesus saith unto them, "Yea; have ye never read, Out of the mouth of babes and sucklings thou hast perfected praise?" 17. And he left them, and went out of the city into Bethany; and he lodged there.	18. And the scribes and chief priests heard it, and sought how they might destroy him : for they feared him, because all the people was astonished at his doctrine. 19. And when even was come, he went out of the city.

There are no striking points of difference in these recitals of the same fact. All of them suggest to the mind a similar picture of the purification of the Temple with its attendant circumstances. But, as regards the time, when this remarkable scene took place, there is an important difference between the four evangelists. Whilst the first three Gospels place it at the end of Christ's ministry, during his stay at Jerusalem which ended with his seizure in the garden of Gethsemane, the fourth evangelist places it at the very beginning of his public life, during one of those previous visits to Jerusalem, which are mentioned in the Gospel of St John alone.

This discrepancy is remarkable, and forbids our thinking that the apostles Matthew and John, both of whom must have been witnesses of the deed, could have, one or the other, made so great an error in relating it.

There is, moreover, a minor discrepancy between St Mark and the others in the day, on which the deed is related to have taken place. Matthew and Luke relate it among the events of the same day, on which Jesus rode on the ass into Jerusalem. Not so Mark: he says at xi, 11 :

And Jesus entered into Jerusalem, and into the temple, and when he had looked round about upon all things, and now the eventide was come, he went out unto Bethany with the twelve.

"Looking about upon all things" certainly commends itself much more to our judgement, and is more consistent with the general character of Christ than the "making a scourge of small cords." But it is on the morrow, at a second visit to the Temple, according to St Mark, that the traders are driven out, and the tables of the money-changers overthrown.

XXVIII.]   PURIFICATION OF TEMPLE.   251

LUKE xix, 47, 48.
47. And he taught daily in the temple. But the chief priests and the scribes and the chief of the people sought to destroy him, 48. And could not find what they might do: for all the people were very attentive to hear him.

JOHN ii, 17.
17. And his disciples remembered that it was written, The zeal of thine house hath eaten me up.

What inference, then, is to be drawn from these conflicting accounts of the evangelists? Some biblical critics have concluded, with St John, that the transaction took place in the early part of Christ's ministry; others at its close. A third body of commentators, unwilling to allow that either of the evangelists is in error, have supposed that the same scene in the Temple was twice enacted, once at the beginning, and again at the termination of Christ's career.

But neither are these explanations satisfactory; for, whilst neither of them wholly disembarrasses the subject of its attendant difficulties, there are other considerations, which suggest another view of the matter, more reconcilable with Christ's character, and might demand our assent no less as a religious than as a reasonable deduction. If we are startled at finding that the witnesses of this deed do not agree about the time when it happened, does it not surprise us still more that such a deed should be related *as a fact* at all? Let us picture to ourselves a single man entering a throng of merchants in London or any other of our populous cities, and forcibly ejecting them from their usual haunts;—that some hundreds of tradesmen should have been driven out by the force of a single arm. It is inconceivable that such a scene could be real. The guards and constables of the city would have interposed, even if the traders themselves had not been firm in defending their property from destruction, and the daring assailant been speedily repulsed. It is painful to imagine such a scene as passing in reality before our eyes: we cannot conceive that the Son of God and the Saviour of men should create a tumult in that Temple which he wished to purify. The people, instead of being astonished at his doctrine, would have been terrified at his power, and would certainly have been little disposed, not many days afterwards, to crowd round the judgement hall, and to cry " Crucify him, crucify him !"

Another principle of interpretation might, then, be adopted; that the transaction was not real, but allegorical and didactic. That the people might be astonished at his doctrine, it was not necessary that the traders should actually be all driven bodily out of the Temple. There were probably hundreds of persons, who sold doves and pigeons for offerings, and changed money in the court of the Temple ; and this without being conscious of doing wrong, for such practices had always been common and were regarded as indifferent, in those external parts of the building which were not looked upon as sacred. It was enough to create astonishment among the people that Jesus should *speak* against these things, and endeavour to open their eyes to the universality of the religious sentiment, to spiritualize their hearts, and freeing them from the formalities of the Jewish ritual, to expand their minds so as to comprehend the infinity of the divine attributes. For this purpose, the whip of small cords was as potent a symbol, as a flying cherubim with a sword of flame. The whip of small cords was allegorical merely. The Saviour chastised with his burning words the traders by whom he was surrounded : he drove them in gesture only, but not in literal reality. He suited the action to the word, like an energetic orator, and whilst he pointed out to them the more elevated view which he took of the Temple his Father's house, he used the whip of small cords only as figurative of his meaning, and making as though he would overthrow the tables of the money-changers, and the seats of them that sold doves. Whether this scenic mode of teaching took place at the beginning or end of his ministry, or at both, becomes now a matter of no consequence : that there should be a doubt as to the time when it happened, shows that the books, in which such doubts are not cleared up, could not have been written, whilst the Holy Ghost was still visibly on earth, to elucidate even more important points than that.

CHAPTER XXIX.

HEALING OF THE CENTURION'S SERVANT.

IT has often been remarked that the same fact, related by several eye-witnesses, is sure to be related in as many different manners as there are relators. Not only will inaccuracies of detail be committed by all, and a different colouring be given by each to almost every distinct transaction, but positive contradictions will occur on many matters of fact, about which, it might be supposed, there could be no possibility of a mistake. Yet all this has never invalidated the separate testimony of each witness, because it is well known that to be wholly free from error is more than human, but that by confronting and comparing the testimony of the separate authorities, an approximate conclusion may be arrived at, sufficient for all the practical purposes of life. We must extend this principle to the four Gospels, if we would wish to obtain a true historical view of them; but we must not, at the same time, argue that being inspired writings, they do not exhibit any of those defects for which alone such a principle of interpretation can be required. Let us see how this principle may be applied to the account of Christ's healing the centurion's servant, related by St Matthew and St Luke.

MATTHEW viii, 5-13.	LUKE vii, 1-10.
5. And when Jesus was entered into Capernaum, there came unto him a centurion, beseeching him, 6. And saying, "Lord, my servant lieth at home sick of the palsy, grievously tormented." 7. And Jesus saith unto him, "I will come and heal him." 8. The centurion answered and said, "Lord, I am not worthy that thou shouldest come under my roof: but speak the word only, and my servant shall be healed. 9. For I am a man under authority, having soldiers under me: and I say to this man, Go, and he goeth; and to another, Come, and he cometh; and to my servant, Do this, and he doeth it."	Now when he had ended all his sayings in the audience of the people, he entered into Capernaum. 2. And a certain centurion's servant, who was dear unto him, was sick, and ready to die. 3. And when he heard of Jesus, he sent unto him the elders of the Jews, beseeching him that he would come and heal his servant. 4. And when they came to Jesus, they besought him instantly, saying, That he was worthy for whom he should do this: 5. For he loveth our nation, and he hath built us a synagogue. 6. Then Jesus went with them. And when he was now not far from the house, the centurion sent friends to him, saying unto him, "Lord, trouble not thy-

MATTHEW viii, 10-13.	LUKE vii, 6-10.
	self: for I am not worthy that thou shouldest enter under my roof: 7. Wherefore neither thought I myself worthy to come unto thee: but say in a word, and my servant shall be healed. 8. For I also am a man set under authority, having under me soldiers, and I say unto one, Go, and he goeth; and to another, Come, and he cometh; and to my servant, Do this, and he doeth it."
10. When Jesus heard it, he marvelled, and said to them that followed, "Verily I say unto you, I have not found so great faith, no, not in Israel. 11. And I say unto you, That many shall come from the east and west, and shall sit down with Abraham, and Isaac, and Jacob, in the kingdom of heaven. 12. But the children of the kingdom shall be cast out into outer darkness: there shall be weeping and gnashing of teeth." 13. And Jesus said unto the centurion, "Go thy way; and as thou hast believed, so be it done unto thee." And his servant was healed in the selfsame hour.	9. When Jesus heard these things, he marvelled at him, and turned him about, and said unto the people that followed him, "I say unto you, I have not found so great faith, no, not in Israel." 10. And they that were sent, returning to the house, found the servant whole that had been sick.

The difference between these two accounts is worthy of observation:

1. According to St Matthew's Gospel, the centurion comes himself: but according to St Luke he sends a message by the "elders of the Jews." Matthew, as one of the twelve, was probably present; for the event takes place immediately after the Sermon on the Mount, which he alone of the four evangelists gives in full. St Luke, not having been of the twelve, may not have been present. So far, therefore, the advantage is in favour of St Matthew, admitting for the moment that these two are writers of the Gospels which bear their names. But there is a difficulty about both these accounts if viewed separately: It is not likely that a Roman centurion would have come himself to solicit the aid of Jesus for one of his servants, as related by St Matthew; and still less so that he should have sent "the elders of the Jews," as we read in the Gospel according to St Luke. The former account is improbable, not only on account of the rank of the centurion, but, as would appear from St Luke's observation that he had built a Jewish synagogue, on account of his riches also. That he would send the "elders of the Jews" is still less likely, because

the Jews were nationally repugnant to the Roman government, and the house of a Roman military officer is almost the last place in which one would expect to find their elders. Of the two accounts that of St Luke is the least probable, and is more complex in its details than that of St Matthew, which is on this account also to be preferred.

2. But, according to St Luke, the centurion sends a second deputation consisting of his own friends, counteracting the message which he had before sent, and "saying unto him, Lord, trouble not thyself: for I am not worthy that thou shouldest enter under my roof" &c. This second message seems to have grown out of the previous particulars. Tradition has handed down the centurion's great faith in Christ's power to work the miracle even at a distance, but according to the writer of the third Gospel, the centurion not having gone himself, a second message was necessary in order to communicate to Jesus the expression of faith, which according to the first Gospel was made by word of mouth. This also awards the preference to the Gospel of St Matthew as more probable from its greater simplicity.

But, whilst we exercise this necessary principle of selection, and reject one narrative for the other, we necessarily protest against the obligation to accept both alike; and we may with reason express a doubt whether two accounts, so different, could have proceeded from contemporary writers, one or both of whom perhaps saw with their own eyes the occurrence which they relate.

CHAPTER XXX.

HEALING OF TWO BLIND MEN NEAR JERICHO—OTHER SUCH CASES.

AMONG the various miracles by which Jesus manifested his divine power, some of the most prominent, I believe, are those which relate to blindness, a calamity to which the inhabitants of hot, as well as those of extremely cold countries, would seem to be peculiarly liable. We may infer that numerous cures of this malady were performed by our Lord, but that the greater number have been omitted by all the four evangelists. Thus we find Jesus answering the question put to him by the emissaries of John the Baptist, at the beginning of his ministry, by an appeal to the works which he had done. "The blind receive their sight." And on numerous other occasions allusion is made to this among other cures which are mentioned in attestation of his divine commission. But, if fewer cases have been given of these healings of blind men and others than the repeated allusion to them would justify, it may be suggested that such healings were not unknown to the Jews as wrought by other agency than that of Jesus. For we read in the Gospel according to St John (v, 3) concerning the five porches at the pool of Bethesda, that—

> In these lay a great multitude of impotent folk, of blind, halt, withered, waiting for the moving of the water. 4. For an angel went down at a certain season into the pool and troubled the water; whosoever then first after the troubling of the water stepped in, was made whole of whatsoever disease he had. (See also Luke iv, 18, and vii, 22.)

No other evangelist confirms this account given in our fourth Gospel, and the authority of MSS has been appealed to against our receiving this narrative as of equal authority with others which have come down to us in the books of the New Testament. Omitting therefore these casual allusions to the general power of healing the blind, we may observe that in the four evangelic histories there are seven passages in which our Lord is said to have opened the eyes of the blind. Three of these concern the miracle of healing the blind performed by Jesus at or near the city of Jericho, and their narrative of this miracle is found in the Gospels of Matthew, Mark and Luke.

MATTHEW xx, 29-34.	MARK x, 46-52.	LUKE xviii, 35-43.
29. And as they departed from Jericho, a great multitude followed him. 30. And, behold, two blind men sitting by the way side, when they heard that Jesus passed by, cried out, saying, "Have mercy on us, O Lord, thou son of David."	46. And they came to Jericho: and as he went out of Jericho with his disciples and a great number of people, blind Bartimæus, the son of Timæus, sat by the highway side begging. 47. And when he heard that it was Jesus of Nazareth, he began to cry out, and say, "Jesus, Thou son of David, have mercy on me."	35. And it came to pass, that as he was come nigh unto Jericho, a certain blind man sat by the way side begging: 36. And hearing the multitude pass by, he asked what it meant. 37. And they told him, that Jesus of Nazareth passeth by. 38. And he cried, saying, "Jesus, thou son of David, have mercy on me."
31. And the multitude rebuked them, because they should hold their peace: but they cried	48. And many charged him that he should hold his peace: but he cried the more a great deal,	39. And they which went before rebuked him, that he should hold his peace: but he cried

BLIND BARTIMÆUS.

MATTHEW xx, 31-34.	MARK x, 48-52.	LUKE xviii, 39-43.
the more, saying, "Have mercy on us, O Lord, thou son of David." 32. And Jesus stood still, and called them, and said, "What will ye that I shall do unto you?" 33. They say unto him, "Lord, that our eyes may be opened." 34. So Jesus had compassion on them, and touched their eyes: and immediately their eyes received sight, and they followed him.	"Thou son of David, have mercy on me." 49. And Jesus stood still, and commanded him to be called. And they call the blind man, saying unto him, "Be of good comfort, rise; he calleth thee." 50. And he, casting away his garment, rose, and came to Jesus. 51. And Jesus answered and said unto him, "What wilt thou that I should do unto thee?" The blind man said unto him, "Lord, that I might receive my sight." 52. And Jesus said unto him, "Go thy way; thy faith hath made thee whole." And immediately he received his sight, and followed Jesus in the way.	so much the more, "Thou son of David, have mercy on me." 40. And Jesus stood, and commanded him to be brought unto him: and when he was come near, he asked him, 41. Saying, "What wilt thou that I shall do unto thee?" And he said, "Lord, that I may receive my sight." 42. And Jesus said unto him, "Receive thy sight: thy faith hath saved thee." 43. And immediately he received his sight, and followed him, glorifying God: and all the people, when they saw it, gave praise unto God.

There can be no doubt, from the great similarity in the attendant circumstances, that the incident is the same in all three Gospels, or, in other words, that the three writers speak of the same miracle: and yet they have related it in a manner so remarkably different, the one from the other, that it is impossible to ascertain the exact nature of the occurrence.

1. St Matthew and St Mark lay the scene of the miracle at Christ's departure out of Jericho: Luke places it at Christ's entry into that city.

2. Matthew says that there were two blind men healed: Mark and Luke confine the incident to one, whom Mark alone calls Bar-timæus, and explains this name as meaning "Son of Timæus."

With these exceptions all the other particulars are exactly similar, and we cannot doubt that they belong to the same miracle. For if Christ once cured a blind Bartimæus, as he was departing from Jericho according to Mark, he must a second time have cured two blind men, as he was leaving that town according to Matthew, and must a third time have healed a single blind man according to Luke, when he was *entering* into Jericho. These arguments prove that the three writers of the Gospels copied tradition, or earlier accounts, and were not themselves eye-witnesses of the fact.

It remains to take notice of the other cases of healing the blind, and the first of these is related by St Matthew, as having occurred when Jesus left the house of the ruler, whose daughter he had just raised, as they supposed, from the dead, but Jesus had said, "The maid is not dead, but sleepeth."

> And when Jesus departed thence, two blind men followed him, crying and saying, "Thou son of David, have mercy on us." 28. And when he was come into the house, the blind men came to him: and Jesus saith unto them, "Believe ye that I am able to do this?" They said unto him, "Yea, Lord." 29. Then touched he their eyes, saying, "According to your faith be it unto you." (ix, 27-29.)

It was not long after this that two more similar miracles were performed by Jesus, sufficiently different from those which have just been detailed, but yet similar in certain particulars which indicate a peculiarity of the writer, if not a peculiar mode used commonly by Jesus in performing his miraculous cures. The first of these cures was performed on a man who was possessed by a devil, besides being blind and dumb, and is recorded by St Matthew. The other case was that of a man who was blind only, and is recorded by St Mark.

> Then was brought unto him one possessed with a devil, blind, and dumb: and he healed him insomuch that the blind and dumb both spake and saw. 23. And all the people were amazed, and said, "Is not this the son of David?" (Matt. xii. 22, 23.)
>
> And he cometh to Bethsaida, and they bring a blind man unto him. 23. And he took the blind man by the hand, and led him out of the town; and when he had spit on his eyes, and put his hands upon him, he asked him if he saw aught. 24. And he looked up and said, "I see men, as trees, walking." 25. After that he put his hands again upon his eyes and made him look up, and he was restored and saw every man clearly. 26. And he sent him away to his house, saying, "Neither go into the town, nor tell it to any in the town." (Mark viii, 23-26.)

Not long before this, Jesus had healed a man who had an impediment in his speech, as we read the narrative in St Mark's Gospel (vii, 33): but the only point to be noticed therein is that "he spit and touched his tongue," as he afterwards spit on the eyes of the blind man at Bethsaida. This process indeed seems to have been customary with our Lord; for in the only instance of his healing the blind, recorded by St John, we find he adopted the same mode of action, when he had just escaped out of the Temple to avoid the stones which the Jews had taken up to cast at him. The man whom he then healed had been blind from his birth, and the miraculous cure wrought on him by Jesus led to a long discussion between the Pharisees and the man, which ended in his being excommunicated by those teachers, into whose presence he had been brought. The details of this incident, occupying the whole of the ninth chapter of St John's Gospel, clearly distinguish this from all the other cases before enumerated; with which indeed it partially agrees in one point only, that in this instance Jesus "spat on the ground and made clay of the spittle and anointed the eyes of the blind man with the clay."

Before concluding this subject, attention may be drawn to the singular fact that in the three narratives of the miracle performed at Bethsaida, the man whose eyes were restored to sight invokes the aid of Jesus as "Thou son of David!" In no other instance do these words of appeal to our Lord appear, but in one of the instances here given it is the multitude who exclaim, when they were amazed at the wonderful manifestation of divine power, "Is not this the son of David?" In the Gospel according to St John this formula does not occur—probably because the object of that work was to inculcate the doctrines of Christianity and the sayings of Jesus, with less regard to historical minutiæ; whereas his descent from the ancient line of Israelitish kings was thought to be an important subject in the other more historical Gospels of Matthew, Mark and Luke.

CHAPTER XXXI.

THE MIRACLE OF THE LOAVES AND FISHES.

AMONG the comparatively few incidents of Christ's life, related by all the four evangelists, without much variation or discrepancy, is the miraculous feeding of the multitude by the multiplication of the loaves and fishes.

The circumstance that preceded and led to this event, according to Matthew and Mark, was the death of John the Baptist, which caused Jesus to retire by *ship* into a desert place for greater security. In Luke's Gospel we read that Herod, having beheaded John, wished to see Jesus, who in consequence retires for safety with his disciples into a desert place, but seemingly by *land*. The fourth evangelist does not mention the death of the Baptist in connection with the feeding of the multitude. The narratives of the four are

MATTHEW xiv, 14-22.	MARK vi, 34-45.
14. And Jesus went forth, and saw a great multitude, and was moved with compassion toward them, and he healed their sick.	34. And Jesus, when he came out, saw much people, and was moved with compassion toward them, because they were as sheep not having a shepherd: and he began to teach them many things.
15. And when it was evening, his disciples came to him, saying, "This is a desert place, and the time is now past; send the multitude away, that they may go into the villages, and buy themselves victuals."	35. And when the day was now far spent, his disciples came unto him, and said, "This is a desert place, and now the time is far passed: 36. Send them away, that they may go into the country round about, and into the villages, and buy themselves bread: for they have nothing to eat."
16. But Jesus said unto them, "They need not depart; give ye them to eat." 17. And they say unto him, "We have here but five loaves, and two fishes." 18. He said, "Bring them hither to me."	37. He answered and said unto them, "Give ye them to eat." And they say unto him, "Shall we go and buy two hundred pennyworth of bread, and give them to eat?" 38. He saith unto them, "How many loaves have ye? go and see." And when they knew, they say, "Five, and two fishes."
19. And he commanded the multitude to sit down on the grass, and took the five loaves, and the two fishes, and looking up to heaven, he blessed, and brake, and gave the loaves to his disciples, and the disciples to the multitude.	39. And he commanded them to make all sit down by companies upon the green grass. 40. And they sat down in ranks, by hundreds, and by fifties.
	41. And when he had taken the five loaves and the two fishes, he looked up to heaven, and blessed, and brake the loaves, and gave them to his disciples to set before them; and the two fishes divided he among them all.
20. And they did all eat, and were filled: and they took up of the fragments that remained twelve baskets full. 21. And they that had eaten were about five thousand men, beside women and children.	42. And they did all eat, and were filled. 43. And they took up twelve baskets full of the fragments, and of the fishes. 44. And they that did eat of the loaves were about five thousand men.

FEEDING THE FIVE THOUSAND.

remarkably in harmony with one another and without a doubt refer to the same incident.

LUKE ix, 10-17.	JOHN vi, 5-17.
10. And the apostles, when they were returned, told him all that they had done. And he took them, and went aside privately into a desert place belonging to the city called Bethsaida. 11. And the people, when they knew it, followed him: and he received them, and spake unto them of the kingdom of God, and healed them that had need of healing. 12. And when the day began to wear away, then came the twelve, and said unto him, " Send the multitude away, that they may go into the town and country round about, and lodge, and get victuals: for we are here in a desert place."	5. When Jesus then lifted up his eyes, and saw a great company come unto him, he saith unto Philip, " Whence shall we buy bread, that these may eat?" 6. And this he said to prove him: for he himself knew what he would do. 7. Philip answered him, "Two hundred pennyworth of bread is not sufficient for them, that every one of them may take a little."
13. But he said unto them, "Give ye them to eat." And they said, "We have no more but five loaves and two fishes; except we should go and buy meat for all this people." 14. For they were about five thousand men. And he said to his disciples, "Make them sit down by fifties in a company." 15. And they did so, and made them all sit down.	8. One of his disciples, Andrew, Simon Peter's brother, saith unto him, 9. "There is a lad here, which hath five barley loaves, and two small fishes: but what are they among so many?" 10. And Jesus said, "Make the men sit down." Now there was much grass in the place. So the men sat down, in number about five thousand.
16. Then he took the five loaves and the two fishes, and looking up to heaven, he blessed them, and brake, and gave to the disciples to set before the multitude.	11. And Jesus took the loaves; and when he had given thanks, he distributed to the disciples, and the disciples to them that were set down; and likewise of the fishes as much as they would.
17. And they did eat, and were all filled: and there was taken up of fragments that remained to them twelve baskets.	12. When they were filled, he said unto his disciples, "Gather up the fragments that remain that nothing be lost." 13. Therefore they gathered them together, and filled twelve baskets with the fragments of the five barley loaves, which remained over and above unto them that had eaten.

262   CHRISTIAN RECORDS.   [CHAPTER

MATTHEW xiv, 22.

22. And straightway Jesus constrained his disciples to get into a ship, and to go before him unto the other side, while he sent the multitudes away.

MARK vi, 45.

45. And straightway he constrained his disciples to get into the ship, and to go to the other side unto Bethsaida, while he sent away the people.

As soon as the multitude are fed, the disciples of Jesus take ship, leaving behind them their master, who at night follows them walking on the sea (Matt. xiv, 25: Mark vi, 48: John vi, 19). So far there is agreement between the evangelists, though there may be uncertainty as to the relative position of the place where the multitude were fed, and the place to which they crossed in the boat. The account of their landing at the latter is given thus:

MATTHEW xiv, 34.

And when they were gone over, they came into the land of Gennesaret.

MARK vi, 53.

And when they had passed over, they came into the land of Gennesaret, and drew to the shore.

JOHN vi, 17.

And went over the sea toward Capernaum.

As Capernaum was a town in the land of Gennesaret, the three narratives of Matthew, Mark, and John, are so far in harmony with one another. The disciples land in Gennesaret; but we see in the last verses of the foregoing harmony, Matt. xiv, 22, and Mark vi, 45, that Christ's instructions were to go before him " unto the other side;" from which we might infer that the feeding of the multitude took place on the eastern side of the lake.

St John however tells us, at vi, 23, that

There came other boats from Tiberias nigh unto the place where they did eat bread, after that the Lord had given thanks.

From which it would appear that the feeding took place on the south-western side, and that Christ with his disciples afterwards sailed in the boat along the shore northward towards Capernaum, also on the western bank of the lake. But this interpretation is not more probable than the other, for the eastern side of the lake was also the territory of

XXXI.]   FEEDING THE FOUR THOUSAND.   263

JOHN vi, 14-17.

14. Then those men, when they had seen the miracle that Jesus did, said, "This is of a truth that prophet that should come into the world."
15. When Jesus therefore perceived that they would come and take him by force, to make him a king, he departed again into a mountain himself alone. 16. And when even was now come, his disciples went down into the sea. 17. And entered into a ship &c.

Herod, and it was the intention of Jesus to retire out of his power.

The remarkable incident, thus carefully and accurately described, would, we might suppose, be of a nature to end all the doubts which Christ's disciples could entertain respecting his divine mission and his miraculous power. "Five thousand men," say two of the evangelists, St Mark and St John, "besides women and children," adds St Matthew, obtain a plentiful meal from five barley loaves and two small fishes: and yet, within a very short space of time, the disciples, who had distributed the food to the multitude, seem to have forgotten the circumstance altogether.

The fourteenth chapter of St Matthew concludes with the arrival of Christ and his disciples at Capernaum, whence he makes a journey into the parts near Tyre and Sidon, returning to the neighbourhood of the sea of Galilee. Then, at verse 32 of the following chapter, is an account of another miraculous feeding of a multitude, corresponding in almost every particular with the former, and not only with no allusion made to the former feeding, but preceded by a doubt on the part of the disciples as to how so large a number should be fed, showing that they either did not know of any other previous miracle of the kind, or (which appears incredible) that they had forgotten it.—This latter miracle is related by Matthew and Mark alone: Luke and John do not notice it.

MATTHEW xv, 32-39.

32. Then Jesus called his disciples unto him, and said, "I have compassion on the multitude, because they continue with me now three days, and have nothing to eat: and I will not send them away fasting, lest they faint in the way."

MARK viii, 1-10.

In those days the multitude being very great, and having nothing to eat, Jesus called his disciples unto him, and saith unto them, 2. "I have compassion on the multitude, because they have now been with me three days, and have nothing to

MATTHEW xv, 33-39.	MARK viii, 3-10.
	eat: 3. And if I send them away fasting to their own houses, they will faint by the way:" for divers of them came from far.
33. And his disciples say unto him, "Whence should we have so much bread in the wilderness, as to fill so great a multitude?" 34. And Jesus saith unto them, "How many loaves have ye?" And they said, "Seven, and a few little fishes."	4. And his disciples answered him, "From whence can a man satisfy these men with bread here in the wilderness?" 5. And he asked them, "How many loaves have ye?" And they said, "Seven."
35. And he commanded the multitude to sit down on the ground. 36. And he took the seven loaves and the fishes, and gave thanks, and brake them, and gave to his disciples, and the disciples to the multitude.	6. And he commanded the people to sit down on the ground: and he took the seven loaves, and gave thanks, and brake, and gave to his disciples to set before them; and they did set them before the people. 7. And they had a few small fishes: and he blessed and commanded to set them also before them.
37. And they did all eat, and were filled: and they took up of the broken meat that was left seven baskets full. 38. And they that did eat were four thousand men, beside women and children. 39. And he sent away the multitude, and took ship, and came into the coasts of Magdala.	8. So they did eat, and were filled: and they took up of the broken meat that was left seven baskets. 9. And they that had eaten were about four thousand: and he sent them away. 10. And straightway he entered into a ship with his disciples, and came into the parts of Dalmanutha.

The points of agreement between the accounts of this and the former miracle are more than the points of difference: hence the following observations seem just and reasonable.

1. In the one case, five thousand, in the other four thousand, is the number fed: but this is a slight difference, such as often creeps silently and accidentally into the most credible histories.

2. St Matthew, in the latter, as well as in the former miracle, adds "besides women and children," omitted by St Mark.

3. In both instances, the disciples make the men sit down, and distribute the food which they receive from the hands of Jesus.

4. In both instances, the scene of the miracle is the wilderness, near the sea of Galilee.

5. In both instances, Jesus embarks on board a ship, immediately after the multitude are fed, and passes across the lake.

These circumstances are so remarkably similar that it is extremely difficult to believe in the separate occurrence of two such miracles. History, it has been said by some, never exactly repeats itself; but here we have two events so precisely alike that it is difficult to distinguish the one from the other. And, to add to our astonishment, it appears from St Matthew and St Mark, that both these remarkable miracles were lost upon the disciples, who shortly after the occurrence of the second, expect a rebuke from their master because they had taken no bread with them in the ship:

MATTHEW xvi, 5-12.	MARK viii, 14-22.
5. And when his disciples were come to the other side, they had forgotten to take bread. 6. Then Jesus said unto them, "Take heed and beware of the leaven of the Pharisees and of the Sadducees." 7. And they reasoned among themselves, saying, "It is because we have taken no bread." 8. Which when Jesus perceived, he said unto them, "O ye of little faith, why reason ye among yourselves, because ye have brought no bread? 9. Do ye not yet understand, neither remember the five loaves of the five thousand, and how many baskets ye took up? 10. Neither the seven loaves of the four thousand, and how many baskets ye took up?	14. Now the disciples had forgotten to take bread, neither had they in the ship with them more than one loaf. 15. And he charged them, saying, "Take heed, beware of the leaven of the Pharisees, and of the leaven of Herod." 16. And they reasoned among themselves, saying, "It is because we have no bread." 17. And when Jesus knew it, he saith unto them, "Why reason ye, because ye have no bread? perceive ye not yet, neither understand? have ye your heart yet hardened? 18. Having eyes see ye not? and do ye not remember? 19. When I brake the five loaves among five thousand, how many baskets full of fragments took ye up?" They say unto him, "Twelve." 20. "And when the seven among four thousand, how many baskets full of fragments took ye up?" And they said "Seven."
11. "How is it that ye do not understand that I spake it not to you concerning bread, that ye should beware of the leaven of the Pharisees and of the Sadducees?" 12. Then understood they how that he bade them not beware of the leaven of bread, but of the doctrine of the Pharisees and of the Sadducees.	21. And he said unto them, "How is it that ye do not understand?"
	22. And he cometh to Bethsaida; and they bring a blind man unto him, &c.

How then is the whole narrative to be viewed? The four accounts of the miraculous multiplication of food fail in almost every condition which would entitle them to be regarded as written by contemporary authors; but, viewing them as later records, we may refer to the fading character of tradition those particulars, which otherwise embarrass us and defy every attempt to explain them.

If reason may be admitted in elucidating so extraordinary an occurrence, we might suggest that Christ only once supplied food miraculously and with beneficent purpose to a smaller number of people, who on that occasion only, and not always, were following him, and that the traditional memory of this event gave birth in time to a written record of two separate miracles, wrought in one case on five thousand, in the other on four thousand men, "besides women and children." In this way only does it seem possible to escape from the double difficulties which the literal interpretation of the text presents. That four or five thousand persons if not more should twice have followed Christ into a desert place, where they stopped three days without anything to eat, and were then fed miraculously with bread and fish, can hardly be accepted literally, for two reasons:

1. Such an event would have led to a thorough revolution in any country ancient or modern, and is utterly out of harmony with all the other miracles of Christ, which were mostly of a private and unostentatious nature.

2. Because immediately after both the miraculous feedings, the very disciples themselves seem not to be aware of an inference which would now occur to the most simple child, that it was unnecessary for them any more to carry with them articles of food, which might be readily supplied by the miraculous powers of their master.

CHAPTER XXXII.

The Demoniac among the Tombs and the Swine.

In three of the Gospels we have an account of a multitude of devils or evil spirits cast out by Jesus and suffered to enter into certain swine, which, in consequence of being thus demoniacally possessed, are driven over a precipice and perish in the sea.

Matthew viii, 28-34.	Mark v, 1-20.	Luke viii, 26-40.
28. And when he was come to the other side into the country of the Gergesenes, there met him two possessed with devils, coming out of the tombs, exceeding fierce, so that no man might pass by that way.	And they came over unto the other side of the sea, into the country of the Gadarenes. 2. And when he was come out of the ships, immediately there met him out of the tombs a man with an unclean spirit,	26. And they arrived at the country of the Gadarenes, which is over against Galilee. 27. And when he went forth to land, there met him out of the city a certain man, which had devils long time, and ware

XXXII.] THE DEMONIACS AND THE SWINE.

MATTHEW viii, 29-32.	MARK v, 3-13.	LUKE viii, 27-33.
	3. Who had his dwelling among the tombs; and no man could bind him, no, not with chains: 4. Because that he had been often bound with fetters and chains, and the chains had been plucked asunder by him, and the fetters broken in pieces: neither could any man tame him. 5. And always, night and day, he was in the mountains, and in the tombs, crying, and cutting himself with stones.	no clothes, neither abode in any house, but in the tombs. 28. When he saw Jesus, he cried out and fell down before him, and with a loud voice said, "What have I to do with thee, Jesus, thou Son of God most high? I beseech thee, torment me not." 29. (For he had commanded the unclean spirit to come out of the man. For oftentimes it had caught him: and he was kept bound with chains and in fetters: and he brake the bands, and was driven of the devil into the wilderness.)
29. And behold, they cried out, saying, "What have we to do with thee, Jesus, thou Son of God? art thou come hither to torment us before the time?"	6. But when he saw Jesus afar off, he ran and worshipped him, 7. And cried with a loud voice, and said, "What have I to do with thee, Jesus, thou Son of the most high God? I adjure thee by God, that thou torment me not." 8. For he said unto him, "Come out of the man, thou unclean spirit." 9. And he asked him, "What is thy name?" And he answered, saying, "My name is Legion: for we are many." 10. And he besought him much that he would not send them away out of the country.	
		30. And Jesus asked him, saying, "What is thy name?" And he said, "Legion:" because many devils were entered into him.
		31. And they besought him that he would not command them to go out into the deep.
30. And there was a good way off from them an herd of many swine feeding. 31. So the devils besought him, saying, "If thou cast us out, suffer us to go away into the herd of swine." 32. And he said unto them, "Go." And when they were come out, they went into the herd of swine: and, behold, the whole herd of swine	11. Now there was there nigh unto the mountains a great herd of swine feeding. 12. And all the devils besought him, saying, "Send us into the swine, that we may enter into them." 13. And forthwith Jesus gave them leave. And the unclean spirits went out, and entered into the swine: and the herd ran vio-	32. And there was there an herd of many swine feeding on the mountain: and they besought him that he would suffer them to enter into them. And he suffered them. 33. Then went the devils out of the man, and entered into the swine: and the herd ran violently down a steep place into the lake, and were choked.

268 CHRISTIAN RECORDS. [CHAPTER

MATTHEW viii, 32-34.	MARK v, 13-20.	LUKE viii, 34-40.
ran violently down a steep place into the sea, and perished in the waters. 33. And they that kept them fled, and went their ways into the city, and told every thing, and what was befallen to the possessed of the devils. 34. And, behold, the whole city came out to meet Jesus: and when they saw him, they besought him that he would depart out of their coasts. MATTHEW ix, 1. And he entered into a ship, and passed over, and came into his own city.	lently down a steep place into the sea (they were about two thousand); and were choked in the sea. 14. And they that fed the swine fled, and told it in the city, and in the country. And they went out to see what it was that was done. 15. And they come to Jesus, and see him that was possessed with the devil, and had the legion, sitting, and clothed, and in his right mind: and they were afraid. 16. And they that saw it told them how it befell to him that was possessed with the devil, and also concerning the swine. 17. And they began to pray him to depart out of their coasts. 18. And when he was come into the ship, he that had been possessed with the devil prayed him that he might be with him. 19. Howbeit Jesus suffered him not, but saith unto him, "Go home to thy friends, and tell them how great things the Lord hath done for thee, and hath had compassion on thee." 20. And he departed, and began to publish in Decapolis how great things Jesus had done for him: and all men did marvel.	34. When they that fed them saw what was done, they fled, and went and told it in the city and in the country. 35. Then they went out to see what was done; and came to Jesus, and found the man, out of whom the devils were departed, sitting at the feet of Jesus, clothed, and in his right mind: and they were afraid. 36. They also which saw it told them by what means he that was possessed of the devils was healed. 37. Then the whole multitude of the country of the Gadarenes round about besought him to depart from them; for they were taken with great fear: and he went up into the ship, and returned back again. 38. Now the man out of whom the devils were departed besought him that he might be with him: but Jesus sent him away, saying, 39. "Return to thine own house, and show how great things God hath done unto thee." And he went his way, and published throughout the whole city how great things Jesus had done unto him. 40. And it came to pass, that, when Jesus was returned, the people gladly received him: for they were all waiting for him.

The purpose for which this remarkable occurrence is here adduced, is neither to uphold nor to deny its real historical character; but to point out from two of its principal features, that it has not been handed down to us by three eye-witnesses: for in one principal feature of the story, the three writers differ from one another, and in another important particular there is an anachronism in the words of two of the writers.

In the first place, St Matthew speaks of two demoniacs, St Mark and St Luke of only one; and it is now impossible, for want of further testimony, to determine which is in the right.

The other inconsistency or anachronism has reference to the answer which the unclean spirit makes to the question, "What is thy name?" And he answered, saying, "My name is *Legion;* for we are many." The four Gospels are written in Greek, and the word legion is Latin: but in Galilee and Peræa, the people spoke neither Latin nor Greek, but Hebrew or a dialect of it. The word *legion* would be perfectly unintelligible to the disciples of Christ and to almost every body in the country, as much so as the English word "regiment" or "brigade" would be to the people of a country where the English arms had never been carried. How then can we account for the Latin word *legion* thus occurring in a vernacular dialogue between men of Galilee and Peræa? It is true that this word occurs in a Greek form in our Gospels; and that the inhabitants of those countries did not speak Greek any more than they spoke Latin. But the Gospels, however they may have been derived from Hebrew sources, or from some kindred Asiatic dialect, have nevertheless been put together in their present form by Grecian editors, who lived at a time when the Hebrew nationality had been destroyed, and every part of Judæa having been overrun by the Roman legions, the inhabitants of every part of it would understand the name and nature of the Roman legion. The word may then have been used, as we now use the word *host,* to describe a large indefinite number, and the compilers so used it, not reflecting that in the time of Christ such usage was unknown, because the country was not then reduced into the perfect tranquillity of a subject province.

CHAPTER XXXIII.

INSTRUCTIONS AND CONDUCT OF JESUS TOWARDS THE SAMARITANS.

THE traditional origin of a book is easily detected in the various forms, often out of harmony with one another, which maxims assume after the death of him who first propounded them. The truth of this assertion will be at once evident to the classical student, who cannot fail to remember the dissonance between the original tenets of Epicurus and those which gradually obtained among the later Epicureans. The same transformation seems to have befallen many particulars of Christ's teaching. Our attention is now invited to the intercourse of himself and his disciples with the Samaritans, presenting two opposite views, which have given much trouble to commentators, and led to a vacillating system of interpretation, from which little advantage is to be gained. The inconsistency is this, that on one occasion Christ seems to forbid all intercourse with Samaritans, at other times he not only allows it but sanctions it by his own conduct.

Thus, at chapter x, verse 5, of St Matthew's Gospel, where Jesus is giving instructions to his disciples, whom he is sending out to preach the Gospel, he says, "Into any city of the Samaritans enter ye not," and no reason is given or can be imagined why the Gospel should be forbidden to a whole nation of men, living between the chief city of the Jewish nationality and Galilee in which our Lord and his disciples principally resided. If we had received more detailed accounts of Christ's ministry, this peculiarity, which appears to be a deviation from the universality of his teaching, would no doubt have been satisfactorily cleared up; but with our present information on this subject, the prohibition to evangelize the Samaritans is somewhat at variance with the acts and sayings of our Lord which are elsewhere so remarkably in their favour.

The parable of the good Samaritan in St Luke's Gospel (x, 30-37), is especially intended to counteract the hostility of the Jews, showing that Jesus not only had no animosity towards the Samaritans but rather sought to free the minds of his hearers from the prejudice which all the Jews entertained towards them. When priest and Levite had both failed to render assistance to their wounded countryman, who had fallen among thieves, a certain Samaritan, who chanced to be travelling that way, performed those duties of benevolence, which not only drew forth the praises of our Lord, but presented a model for the imitation of his followers whom he told to "go and do likewise."

That the inhabitants of Judæa and Jerusalem entertained a national hatred against the Samaritans is manifest from the inference which may be drawn from his words and acts, as we find them related in St John's Gospel (viii, 4-8), "Say we not well that thou art a Samaritan and hast a devil?"

But there are three other narratives concerning the Samaritans, which require to be noticed. We read in the Gospel according to St John (iv, 3-4) that Jesus "left Judæa and departed again into Galilee, and he must needs go through Samaria." Now, as this is related by the writer so early in the life of Jesus, and, if we believe those who defend the chronological character of this Gospel, must have been before the captivity of John the Baptist, and also before the number twelve of the apostles was completed, the details of our Lord's interview with the woman at the well of Sychar, followed by the request of the Samaritans that he would tarry with them, and the granting of their request, seem hardly to sanction the exclusion of them afterwards from the benefits of the Gospel dispensation.

[Jesus] abode there two days. 41. And many more believed because of his own word, 42. And said unto the woman, "Now we believe, not because of thy saying, for we have heard him ourselves, and know that this is indeed the Christ the Saviour of the world." (iv, 40-42.)

According to this narrative Jesus was on his way to Galilee; but he passed through Samaria on two other occasions, according to accounts, both of which are found in the Gospel according to St Luke, unless indeed a similar inaccuracy as to the time has happened in this case also. In the ninth chapter of St Luke, verse 51, we read,

And it came to pass, when the time was come that he should be received up, he stedfastly set his face to go to Jerusalem, 52. And sent messengers before his face; and they went, and entered into a village of the Samaritans to make ready for him. 53. And they did not receive him, because his face was as though he would go to Jerusalem.

It was in consequence of this conduct on the part of the Samaritans, that the disciples James and John asked that fire should be sent down upon the inhospitable nation; but Jesus refused their inhuman request, and "they went to

272   CHRISTIAN RECORDS.   [CHAPTER

another village." This event however, although recorded so early in the Gospel history, happened on his last journey to Jerusalem when the end of his life was approaching; and yet in the seventeenth chapter of the same Gospel, a similar journey to Jerusalem is recorded, in connection with the ten lepers. The narrative of these things is as follows, and can only be reconciled with the foregoing on the supposition that one of the two events is out of place in the book, but that both occurred on the occasion of Christ's last visit to Jerusalem immediately before he was put to death.

> 11. And it came to pass, as he went to Jerusalem, that he passed through the midst of Samaria and Galilee. 12. And as he entered into a certain village, there met him ten men that were lepers, which stood afar off: 13. And they lifted up their voices, and said, "Jesus, master, have mercy on us." 14. And when he saw them, he said unto them, "Go, show yourselves to the priests." And it came to pass that, as they went, they were cleansed. 15. And one of them, when he saw that he was healed, turned back and with a loud voice glorified God, 16. And fell down on his face at his feet, giving him thanks: and he was a Samaritan. 17. And Jesus answering said, "Were there not ten cleansed, where are the nine? There are not found that returned to give glory to God, save this stranger." (Luke xvii, 11-18.)

From these passages it must be inferred that our Saviour's intercourse with the Samaritans was conducted after the same plan which he followed with other nations, but that the minor particulars of that intercourse are less accurate

MATTHEW xxvi, 1-13.	MARK xiv, 1-9.
And it came to pass, when Jesus had finished all these sayings, he said unto his disciples, 2. "Ye know that after two days is the feast of the passover, and the Son of man is betrayed to be crucified." 3. Then assembled together the chief priests, and the scribes, and the elders of the people, unto the palace of the high priest, who was called Caiaphas, 4. And consulted that they might take Jesus by subtilty, and kill him.	After two days was the feast of the passover, and of unleavened bread: and the chief priests and the scribes sought how they might take him by craft, and put him to death.
5. But they said, Not on the feast day, lest there be an uproar among the people.	2. But they said, Not on the feast day, lest there be an uproar of the people.
6. Now when Jesus was in Bethany, in the house of Simon the leper, 7. There came unto him a woman having an alabaster box of very precious ointment, and poured it on his head, as he sat at meat.	3. And being in Bethany in the house of Simon the leper, as he sat at meat, there came a woman having an alabaster box of ointment of spikenard very precious; and she brake the box, and poured it on his head.

than if they had been copied down in writing by those who had been eye-witnesses of the facts. But that the Samaritans were admitted to the same privileges as both Jews and Gentiles is equally manifest from the extracts here given, and is confirmed by the words of the two men, who " stood by them in white apparel " on the occasion when Jesus was taken up into heaven.

> Ye shall receive power, after that the Holy Ghost is come upon you: and ye shall be witnesses unto me both in Jerusalem, and in all Judæa, and in Samaria, and unto the uttermost part of the earth. (i, 8.)

And in accordance with these instructions we read in chapter viii, verse 25, that the apostles "preached the Gospel in many villages of the Samaritans."

CHAPTER XXXIV.

Christ anointed by a Woman at a Feast.

ALL the four evangelic histories speak of a woman who poured ointment or oil upon the head or feet of Jesus, whilst he sat at meat. The parallel accounts here follow.

LUKE vii, 36-50.	JOHN xii, 1-9.
36. And one of the Pharisees desired him that he would eat with him. And he went into the Pharisee's house, and sat down to meat.	Then Jesus six days before the passover came to Bethany, where Lazarus was which had been dead, whom he raised from the dead. 2. There they made him a supper; and Martha served: but Lazarus was one of them that sat at the table with him.
37. And, behold, a woman in the city, which was a sinner, when she knew that Jesus sat at meat in the Pharisee's house, brought an alabaster box of ointment, 38. And stood at his feet behind him weeping, and began to wash his feet with tears, and did wipe them with the	3. Then took Mary a pound of ointment of spikenard, very costly, and anointed the feet of Jesus, and wiped his feet with her hair: and the house was filled with the odour of the ointment.

MATTHEW xxvi, 8-13.   MARK xiv, 4-9.

8. But when his disciples saw it, they had indignation, saying, "To what purpose is this waste? 9. For this ointment might have been sold for much, and given to the poor."

4. And there were some that had indignation within themselves, and said, "Why was this waste of the ointment made? 5. For it might have been sold for more than three hundred pence, and have been given to the poor." And they murmured against her.

10. When Jesus understood it, he said unto them, "Why trouble ye the woman? for she hath wrought a good work upon me. 11. For ye have the poor always with you: but me ye have not always. 12. For in that she hath poured this ointment on my body, she did it for my burial.

6. And Jesus said, "Let her alone: why trouble ye her? she hath wrought a good work on me. 7. For ye have the poor with you always, and whensoever ye will ye may do them good: but me ye have not always. 8. She hath done what she could: she is come aforehand to anoint my body to the burying.

13. Verily I say unto you, Wheresoever this gospel shall be preached in the whole world, there shall also this, that this woman hath done, be told for a memorial of her."

9. Verily I say unto you, Wheresoever this gospel shall be preached throughout the whole world, this also that she hath done shall be spoken of for a memorial of her."

There are here so many striking points of agreement and the words of the descriptions are so nearly the same, that it is impossible to believe they refer to other than the same occurrence. And yet there is such a difference as to time, place, persons, and manner, that it is equally difficult to

JESUS ANOINTED.

LUKE vii, 38-50.

hairs of her head, and kissed his feet, and anointed them with the ointment. 39. Now when the Pharisee which had bidden him saw it, he spake within himself, saying, "This man, if he were a prophet, would have known who and what manner of woman this is that toucheth him: for she is a sinner."

40. And Jesus answering said unto him, "Simon, I have somewhat to say unto thee." And he saith, "Master, say on." 41. "There was a certain creditor which had two debtors: the one owed five hundred pence, and the other fifty. 42. And when they had nothing to pay, he frankly forgave them both. Tell me therefore, which of them will love him most?" 43. Simon answered and said, "I suppose that he, to whom he forgave most." And he said unto him, "Thou hast rightly judged." 44. And he turned to the woman, and said unto Simon, "Seest thou this woman? I entered into thine house, thou gavest me no water for my feet: but she hath washed my feet with tears, and wiped them with the hairs of her head. 45. Thou gavest me no kiss: but this woman since the time I came in hath not ceased to kiss my feet. 46. My head with oil thou didst not anoint: but this woman hath anointed my feet with ointment. 47. Wherefore I say unto thee, Her sins, which are many, are forgiven: for she loved much: but to whom little is forgiven, the same loveth little." 48. And he said unto her, "Thy sins are forgiven." 49. And they that sat at meat with him began to say within themselves, "Who is this that forgiveth sins also?" 50. And he said to the woman, "Thy faith hath saved thee; go in peace."

JOHN xii, 4-9.

4. Then saith one of his disciples, Judas Iscariot, Simon's son, which should betray him, 5. "Why was not this ointment sold for three hundred pence and given to the poor?" 6. This he said, not that he cared for the poor; but because he was a thief, and had the bag, and bare what was put therein. 7. Then said Jesus, "Let her alone; against the day of my burying hath she kept this. 8. For the poor always ye have with you; but me ye have not always." 9. Much people of the Jews therefore knew that he was there: and they came not for Jesus' sake only, but that they might see Lazarus also, whom he had raised from the dead.

---

imagine eye-witnesses could have varied so greatly in relating what they had seen.

1. The four evangelists differ as to the *time* when this took place: Luke relates it in the early part of Christ's ministry; the other three place it within a few days of his crucifixion.

Again, Matthew and Mark seem to say that it was two days, John certainly fixes it at six days before the feast of the Passover.

2. Matthew and Mark say that it took place at the village of Bethany in the house of Simon the leper, of whom we know nothing, for he is not elsewhere mentioned; Luke calls him Simon a Pharisee, and lays the scene "in the city." But John gives us to understand that it was at Bethany in the house of Martha and Mary sister of Lazarus, for he tells us that "Martha served," and he adds (v. 9) that a large number of persons had come together that they might see Lazarus, "whom he had raised from the dead."

3. As to the *manner* of the act, there is equal divergency in the four accounts. The first three evangelists speak of an alabaster *box* or jar of ointment; the fourth of a *pound* of ointment; which apparently she had just bought at a shop, and which might indeed be contained in a box or jar. St Matthew and St Mark say that the woman poured the ointment on his head, as he sat at meat; but Luke and John say that she anointed his feet with it; and Luke, entering more into detail, adds that she stood behind Jesus—a position in harmony with the anointing of his head, but very unfavourable for pouring the ointment over his feet, unless he reclined like the Romans, of which we have no information.

4. The *persons* concerned in this scene are either vaguely described, or are actually different. According to St Matthew and St Mark, it is " a woman " who anoints Jesus : St Luke adds the words " which was a sinner," but St John limits the deed to " Mary " the sister of Lazarus and Martha. As there is no proof that this Mary was a sinner more than any other woman, we are at a loss to reconcile these accounts, and the mind is led to stray in the direction of Mary Magdalene, who indeed from the earliest years of the Christian era has been identified with the woman who anointed Jesus as has been related in the passages that have here been quoted. There were indeed legends throughout all Christendom concerning this conspicuous character of the Gospel history, which have rendered her equally famous in more recent times, and the dedication of churches in her honour has been always accompanied with the belief that she had been raised by our Lord out of the depths of sin and restored to a life of purity and happiness. To examine and see what other women have borne the name of Mary, and how they are to be distinguished the one from the other, will be the subject of a future chapter.

5. Lastly there is not perfect agreement about the person who expostulates with Jesus at the waste of ointment. Matthew and Mark say that it was the disciples who "had indignation" among themselves; John names Judas Iscariot son of Simon; from which it would appear that the traitor who soon afterwards sold his master to his enemies, was the son of the leper (or Pharisee, as he is termed by St Luke); but St Luke himself says that it was Simon himself who complained of the waste of ointment.*

All these circumstances point to the conclusion that we know very little about the real particulars of this occurrence; nothing indeed beyond the fact that a pound of ointment was used by some unknown woman in anointing Jesus; but whether his feet or his head was anointed, and in what place, or at what time, and under what circumstances this happened, we have no certain information.

CHAPTER XXXV.

JESUS RAISES JAÏRUS'S DAUGHTER—HEALS THE WOMAN WHO HAD AN ISSUE OF BLOOD.

WE have it related by the first three evangelists, that soon after the healing of the demoniacs in the country of the Gadarenes, Jesus raised to life the daughter of a certain ruler named Jaïrus. St Matthew (ix, 1) gives us the additional information that he had already returned to his own city, and a further proof that the three narratives refer to the same event is furnished by the concurrent testimony of the evangelists that the woman who had the issue of blood was healed at the same time. The accounts of both cures here follow.

MATTHEW ix, 18-26.	MARK v, 22-43.	LUKE viii, 41-56.
18. While he spake these things unto them, behold, there came a certain ruler, and worship-	22. And, behold, there cometh one of the rulers of the synagogue, Jairus by name, and when he	41. And, behold, there came a man named Jairus, and he was a ruler of the synagogue:

---

* The reader is referred, for the most profuse information about Mary Magdalene, to Dr Smith's Dictionary of the Bible, vol. iii, page 255; but is cautioned against hastily adopting the conclusion that there were two unointings, or that Mary Magdalene could not have been a sinner, because seven devils had been cast out of her.

MATTHEW ix, 18-22.	MARK v, 22-33.	LUKE viii, 41-48.
ped him saying, "My daughter is even now dead: but come and lay thy hand upon her, and she shall live." 19. And Jesus arose, and followed him, and so did his disciples.

20. And behold, a woman, which was diseased with an issue of blood twelve years, came behind him, and touched the hem of his garment: 21. For she said within herself, "If I may but touch his garment, I shall be whole." 22. But Jesus turned him about, and when he saw her, he said, "Daughter, be of good comfort; thy faith hath made thee whole." | saw him, he fell at his feet, 23. And besought him greatly, saying, "My little daughter lieth at the point of death: I pray thee, come and lay thy hands on her, that she may be healed; and she shall live." 24. And Jesus went with him; and much people followed him and thronged him.

25. And a certain woman which had an issue of blood twelve years, 26. And had suffered many things of many physicians, and had spent all that she had, and was nothing bettered, but rather grew worse, 27. When she heard of Jesus, came in the press behind, and touched his garment. 28. For she said, "If I may touch but his clothes, I shall be whole." 29. And straightway the fountain of her blood was dried up; and she felt in her body that she was healed of that plague. 30. And Jesus immediately knowing in himself that virtue had gone out of him, turned him about in the press, and said, "Who touched my clothes?" 31. And his disciples said unto him, "Thou seest the multitude thronging thee, and sayest thou, 'Who touched me?'" 32. And he looked round about to see her who had done this thing. 33. But the woman, fearing and trembling, knowing what was done in her, came and fell down before him, and told him all the truth. 34. And he said unto her, "Daughter, thy faith hath made thee whole; | and he fell down at Jesus's feet, and besought him that he would come into his house: 42. For he had one only daughter, about twelve years of age, and she lay a-dying. But as he went the people thronged him.

43. And a woman, having an issue of blood twelve years, which had spent all her living upon physicians, neither could be healed of any. 44. Came behind him, and touched the border of his garment: and immediately her issue of blood stanched. 45. And Jesus said, "Who touched me?" When all denied, Peter and they that were with him said, "Master, the multitude throng thee, and sayest thou, Who touched me? 46. And Jesus said, "Somebody hath touched me: for I perceive that virtue is gone out of me." 47. And when the woman saw that she was not hid, she came trembling, and falling down before him, she declared unto him before all the people for what cause she had touched him, and how she was healed immediately. 48. And he said unto her, "Daughter, be of good comfort: thy faith hath made thee whole; go in peace." |

JAIRUS'S DAUGHTER.

MATTHEW ix, 23-26.	MARK v, 34-43.	LUKE viii, 49-56.
	go in peace, and be whole of thy plague." 35. While ye yet spake, there came from the ruler of the synagogue's house certain which said, Thy daughter is dead: why troublest thou the Master any further? 36. As soon as Jesus heard the word that was spoken, he saith unto the ruler of the synagogue, "Be not afraid, only believe."	49. While he yet spake, there cometh one from the ruler of the synagogue's house, saying to him, Thy daughter is dead: trouble not the Master. 50. But when Jesus heard it, he answered him, saying, Fear not: believe only, and she shall be made whole.
23. And when Jesus came into the ruler's house, and saw the minstrels and the people making a noise, 24. He said unto them, "Give place: for the maid is not dead, but sleepeth." And they laughed him to scorn. 25. But when the people were put forth, he went in, and took her by the hand, and the maid arose.	37. And he suffered no man to follow him, save Peter, and James, and John the brother of James. 38. And he cometh to the house of the synagogue, and seeth the tumult, and them that wept and wailed greatly. 39. And when he was come in, he saith unto them, "Why make ye this ado, and weep? the damsel is not dead, but sleepeth." 40. And they laughed him to scorn. But when he had put them all out, he taketh the father and the mother of the damsel, and them that were with him, and entereth in where the damsel was lying. 41. And he took the damsel by the hand, and said unto her, Talitha cumi; which is, being interpreted, "Damsel, I say unto thee, arise." 42. And straightway the damsel arose, and walked; for she was of the age of twelve years.	51. And when he came into the house, he suffered no man to go in, save Peter, and James, and John, and the father and the mother of the maiden. 52. And all wept, and bewailed her: but he said, "Weep not; she is not dead, but sleepeth." 53. And they laughed him to scorn, knowing that she was dead. 54. And he put them all out, and took her by the hand, and called saying, "Maid, arise." 55. And her spirit came again, and she arose straightway: and he commanded to give meat.
26. And the fame hereof went abroad into all that land.	And they were astonished with a great astonishment. 43. And he charged them straitly that no man should know it; and commanded that something should be given her to eat.	56. And her parents were astonished: but he charged them that they should tell no man what was done.

The three Gospels of Matthew, Mark, and Luke, agree in fixing the *scene* of this miracle at Capernaum, the *time*, as has been already said, close upon the return of Jesus into Galilee, after casting out the devils which were suffered to enter into the bodies of the swine.

There are however certain differences in the three accounts, which indicate a traditional origin.

1. St Matthew says that the ruler's daughter was already dead, and that the ruler came and asked Jesus to restore her to life: St Mark and St Luke however relate, with greater probability, that the child was lying at the point of death, and that her father requested Jesus to go and heal her.

On their way to the house, the people thronged him, and a woman having an issue of blood, under circumstances told briefly by Matthew and more fully by the other two, was cured by touching him. Immediately after this, messengers from the ruler's house, according to Mark and Luke, bring the information that the child is dead.

2. St Mark and St Luke state that Jesus suffered only Peter, James and John to follow him into the ruler's house: but St Matthew does not mention this circumstance.

3. The conclusion of the history is also different, for whilst we learn from St Matthew that the report of the miracle "went abroad into all that land," St Mark and St Luke relate that Jesus charged the father and mother, who with his three disciples were the only persons that entered the room, "that they should tell no man what was done."

It cannot be denied that the main point is the same in all these narratives, and it is not difficult to suggest that the differences are unimportant and may be explained by the imperfect information which each of the writers had received. We see for instance that, whilst one account begins with the intimation that the maid is dead, in the others a message is first received that she is lying at the point of death. Both of these however agree with St Matthew in relating that she had expired before our Saviour arrived at her father's house.

CHAPTER XXXVI.

CHRIST'S LAST JOURNEY AND TRIUMPHAL ENTRY INTO
JERUSALEM.

THE ministry of Christ in Galilee ends with a journey from Capernaum, where he principally resided, to Jerusalem, into which he entered in triumph, riding upon an ass.

In all the four Gospels notice is taken of this final journey out of Galilee into Judæa in the extracts which here follow.

MATTHEW xix, 1.	MARK x, 1.
And it came to pass, that when Jesus had finished these sayings, he departed from Galilee, and came into the coasts of Judæa beyond Jordan.	And he arose from thence, and cometh into the coasts of Judæa by the farther side of Jordan: and the people resort unto him again, and as he was wont, he taught them again.
LUKE ix, 51.	JOHN xi, 54.
And it came to pass when the time was come that he should be received up, he steadfastly set his face to go up to Jerusalem.	Jesus therefore walked no more openly among the Jews; but went thence to a country near to the wilderness, into a city called Ephraim, and there continued with his disciples.

It can scarcely be doubted that all these narratives describe the last journey which Jesus made out of Galilee into Judæa. That he turned aside into the city called Ephraim near the wilderness for a time, to avoid the enmity of the Jews who sought to kill him, is an incident which apparently was unknown to the three synoptical Gospels: Matthew and Mark indeed speak of his having retired beyond the Jordan, but still within the territory of Judæa.

In the three synoptical Gospels events are now interposed, especially by St Luke, before we arrive at the following passages, from all the four evangelists, in which the triumphal entry of Jesus into Jerusalem is described. The facts are less historically put together in the fourth Gospel, owing to its generally didactic and doctrinal character. Yet even there the sequence of events is sufficiently clear and decided, as having taken place after the triumphal entry into the city, and they occupy one half of the whole book.

MATTHEW xx, 17.

17. And Jesus, going up to Jerusalem, took the twelve disciples apart in the way, and said unto them, 18. "Behold, we go up to Jerusalem," &c.

MARK x, 32.

32. And they were in the way going up to Jerusalem; and Jesus went before them and they were amazed; and, as they followed, they were afraid. And he took again the twelve, and began to tell them what things should happen unto him, 23. Saying, "Behold, we go up to Jerusalem" &c. . . . 46. And they came to Jericho, &c. . . . . .

29. And as they departed from Jericho a great multitude followed him.

MATTHEW xxi, 1.

And when they drew nigh unto Jerusalem, and were come to Bethphage, unto the mount of Olives, then sent Jesus two disciples, 2. Saying unto them, "Go into the village over against you, and straightway ye shall find an ass tied and a colt with her: loose them, and bring them unto me. 3. And if any man say ought unto you, ye shall say, The Lord hath need of them; and straightway he will send them."
4. All this was done, that it might be fulfilled which was spoken by the prophet, saying, 5. "Tell ye the daughter of Sion, Behold, thy King cometh unto thee, meek, and sitting upon an ass, and a colt the foal of an ass."
6. And the disciples went and did as Jesus commanded them, 7. And brought the ass, and the colt, and put on them their clothes, and they set him thereon. 8. And a very great multitude spread their garments in the way; others cut down branches from the trees, and strawed them in the way.

MARK xi, 1.

And when they came nigh to Jerusalem, unto Bethphage and Bethany, at the mount of Olives, he sendeth forth two of his disciples, 2. And saith unto them, "Go your way into the village over against you: and as soon as ye be entered into it, ye shall find a colt tied, whereon never man sat; loose him, and bring him. 3. And if any man say unto you, Why do ye this? say ye that the Lord hath need of him; and straightway he shall send him hither."

4. And they went their way, and found the colt tied by the door without in a place where two ways met: and they loose him. 5. And certain of them that stood there said unto them, "What do ye, loosing the colt?" 6. And they said unto them even as Jesus had commanded; and they let them go. 7. And they brought the colt to Jesus, and cast their garments on him: and he sat upon him. 8. And many spread their garments in the way: and others cut down branches off the trees, and strawed them in the way.

9. And the multitudes that went before, and that followed, cried,

9. And they that went before, and they that followed, cried, saying,

LUKE xvii, 11.
11. And it came to pass, as he went to Jerusalem, that he passed through the midst of Samaria and Galilee.
LUKE xviii, 31, 35.
31. Then he took unto him the twelve, and said unto them, "Behold, we go up to Jerusalem," &c.
35. And it came to pass, that as he was come nigh unto Jericho, &c.
LUKE xix, 1.
And Jesus entered and passed through Jericho, &c.
28. And when he had thus spoken, he went before, ascending up to Jerusalem.
29. And it came to pass, when he was come nigh to Bethphage and Bethany, at the mount called the mount of Olives, he sent two of his disciples, 30. Saying, "Go ye into the village over against you; in the which at your entering ye shall find a colt tied, whereon yet never man sat: loose him, and bring him hither. 31. And if any man ask you, Why do ye loose him? thus shall ye say unto him, Because the Lord hath need of him."

JOHN xi, 55.
55. And the Jews' passover was nigh at hand, &c. . . . .

JOHN xii, 1.
Then Jesus six days before the passover came to Bethany, where Lazarus was which had been dead, whom he raised from the dead. 2. There they made him a supper, &c. . . . . . .

32. And they that were sent went their way, and found even as he had said unto them. 33. And as they were loosing the colt, the owners thereof said unto them, "Why loose ye the colt?" 34. And they said, "The Lord hath need of him." 35. And they brought him to Jesus: and they cast their garments upon the colt, and they set Jesus thereon. 36. And as he went, they spread their clothes in the way.

37. And when he was come nigh, even now at the descent of the

12. On the next day much people that were come to the feast, when

MATTHEW xxi, 9-11.	MARK xi, 9-10.
saying, "Hosanna to the son of David: Blessed is he that cometh in the name of the Lord; Hosanna in the highest."	"Hosanna; Blessed is he that cometh in the name of the Lord: 10. Blessed be the kingdom of our father David, that cometh in the name of the Lord : Hosanna in the highest."

10. And when he was come into Jerusalem, all the city was moved, saying, "Who is this?" 11. And the multitude said, "This is Jesus the prophet of Nazareth of Galilee."

There are three points in these accounts which are more or less at variance one with another.

1. Matthew, Mark and Luke represent Jesus as going up to Jerusalem from Galilee, passing through Jericho, and then riding on the ass from Bethphage and Bethany, into Jerusalem, without stopping at Bethany. John, on the other hand, brings Jesus not from Galilee but from the city of Ephraim where he remained some time ; and he makes him partake of a supper and pass the night at Bethany.

2. Matthew, Mark, and Luke, who agree in bringing Jesus directly out of Galilee, differ about the road which he took. The two former say that he crossed the Jordan and passed along to the east of that river, again crossing it to the westward near Jericho: but Luke says, as plainly, at xvii, 11, that he came by the straight road which led through Galilee and Samaria.

3. A third difference between the evangelists is equally real, but of less importance. Whilst Matthew speaks of an ass and a colt the foal of an ass, the other three name the

LUKE xix, 37-40.	JOHN xii, 12-19.
mount of Olives, the whole multitude of the disciples began to rejoice and praise God with a loud voice for all the mighty works that they had seen: 38. Saying, "Blessed be the King that cometh in the name of the Lord: peace in heaven, and glory in the highest."	they heard that Jesus was coming to Jerusalem, 13. Took branches of palm trees, and went forth to meet him, and cried, "Hosanna; Blessed is the King of Israel that cometh in the name of the Lord." 14. And Jesus, when he had found a young ass, sat thereon; as it is written, 15. Fear not, daughter of Sion: behold, thy King cometh, sitting on an ass's colt. 16. These things understood not his disciples at the first; but when Jesus was glorified, then remembered they that these things were written of him, and that they had done these things unto him. 17. The people therefore that was with him when he called Lazarus out of his grave, and raised him from the dead, bare record. 18. For this cause the people also met him, for that they heard that he had done this miracle.
39. And some of the Pharisees from among the multitude said unto him, "Master, rebuke thy disciples." 40. And he answered and said unto them, "I tell you that, if these should hold their peace, the stones would immediately cry out."	19. The Pharisees therefore said among themselves, "Perceive ye how ye prevail nothing? behold, the world is gone after him."

ass's colt only. The variation may be explained—the word *and* possibly should be rendered *even*; and we get a meaning which at once reconciles Matthew with the other three, " an ass, *even* a colt the foal of an ass."

Nor is this conjecture without some support. The Hebrew style of composition is peculiar, and we have a familiar instance of it in the book of Psalms, where every verse consists of two parts, the latter answering to the former even so as sometimes to repeat the meaning. Thus we read in a prayer of David (Psalm lxxxvi) "Give ear unto my prayer!" at the beginning of verse 6, and the concluding part repeats the sense by the words "Attend to the voice of my supplications." This antiphonal character is especially remarkable in Hebrew poetry. But the very solution here proposed is in itself a more powerful argument against the originality of Matthew's Gospel than the error which it remedies; for it shows that Matthew copied from some original documents which he could not understand, and that he is a compiler from others, instead of being an original authority or eye-witness.

4. Lastly, as regards the honours paid to Christ in his entry into Jerusalem, Matthew says that a "very great multitude" "spread their garments in the way," and he speaks of the "multitudes that went before and that followed." Mark, more moderate in his terms, says that "many spread their garments in the way," and Luke, keeping still closer to probability, says "they," i.e. the disciples, "spread their clothes in the way," and "the whole multitude of the disciples began to rejoice &c." John, however, is at variance with all the three, for having made Jesus rest that night at Bethany, he says that, "on the next day" the multitude who escorted him into Jerusalem consisted of the "much people that were come unto the feast," and now went out expressly to meet him. If so, these visitors were probably the only persons who knew him, a fact which tells strongly against his having often before been at Jerusalem, as we might infer from the narrative of St John. It is, however, seldom that histories written by contemporary authors present such discrepancies as these, and very hard to believe that they could possibly proceed from eye-witnesses of the facts which they relate.

CHAPTER XXXVII.

THE BARREN FIG-TREE.

WHEN our Lord, after receiving such triumphal honours, had entered Jerusalem, he went, in the words of Mark (xi, 11), "into the temple; and when he had looked round about upon all things, and now the eventide was come, he went out unto Bethany with the twelve."

From this time until his crucifixion it was his practice to walk into Jerusalem in the morning, and to return in the afternoon to Bethany. The incident of the barren fig-tree is told by St Matthew and St Mark, and is said to have happened on the first morning after his triumphal entry.

MATTHEW xxi, 18-22.	MARK xi, 12-24.
18. Now in the morning as he returned into the city, he hungered. 19. And when he saw a fig tree in the way, he came to it, and found nothing thereon but leaves only, and said unto it, " Let no fruit grow on thee henceforward for ever." And	12. And on the morrow, when they were come from Bethany, he was hungry: 13. And seeing a fig tree afar off having leaves, he came, if haply he might find any thing thereon: and when he came to it, he found nothing but leaves; for

MATTHEW xxi, 19-22.	MARK xi, 13-24.
presently the fig tree withered away.	the time of figs was not yet. 14. And Jesus answered and said unto it, "No man eat fruit of thee hereafter for ever." And his disciples heard it.
20. And when the disciples saw it, they marvelled, saying, "How soon is the fig tree withered away!"	20. And in the morning, as they passed by, they saw the fig tree dried up from the roots. 21. And Peter calling to remembrance saith unto him, "Master, behold, the fig tree which thou cursedst is withered away."
21. Jesus said unto them, "Verily I say unto you, If ye have faith, and doubt not, ye shall not only do this which is done to the fig tree, but also if ye shall say unto this mountain, Be thou removed and be thou cast into the sea; it shall be done.	22. And Jesus answering saith unto them, "Have faith in God. 23. For verily I say unto you, That whosoever shall say unto this mountain, Be thou removed, and be thou cast into the sea; and shall not doubt in his heart, but shall believe that those things which he saith shall come to pass; he shall have whatsoever he saith.
22. And all things, whatsoever ye shall ask in prayer, believing, ye shall receive."	24. Therefore I say unto you, what things soever ye desire, when ye pray, believe that ye receive them and ye shall have them."

We have in these two accounts, whether taken separately or compared one with the other, marks of something more than a traditional origin, and it may be inferred from the nature of the miracle that we have a very imperfect account of it. We do not find in all the Gospels a similar instance of Christ's power being put forth to do harm rather than good. If the fig-tree was the property of a private man, the owner might justly complain of the wrong done him by the destruction of his property: we therefore may infer that the fig-tree was growing on waste land by the road-side: but even in that case it is difficult to conceive that a tree producing fruit—and fig-trees are highly valued in Eastern countries—would be cursed and perish, because our Lord found no fruit on it. We are therefore justified in suggesting that some particulars, which would have shown the real character of this transaction, have been lost, and this view coincides with the general theory and with other facts, showing that our existing Gospels are, as a traditionary origin would make them, not always wholly in accordance one with another. Nor is the silence of St John without significance in this matter. If any of the disciples were in constant attendance on their Lord, he surely would not be absent, and would scarcely have omitted to mention so striking a manifestation of supernatural power.

Proceeding then to examine the two accounts which are here brought into comparison, we may observe certain points in which they do not perfectly agree. Whilst Matthew seems to say that the fig-tree withered in the sight of the disciples, immediately after the words of Jesus, Mark says that the disciples did not remark that it had withered until the next morning, and that a conversation ensued on the subject between Jesus and Simon Peter. If we might judge of the matter by the test of reason, the latter would seem the most probable of the two, and the account given by Matthew would up to a certain point be in agreement; but according to his account the fig-tree is said to have immediately withered away, and the disciples marvelled at it and said "How soon is the fig-tree withered away!"

But we must not omit to mention another peculiarity in the remarkable avowal of St Mark, that "the time of figs was not yet." That fruit is not found on trees so early as Easter at present and was not to be found on trees at the season of the Passover in the time of Jesus, is a well known fact; but it is less clear how it could be expected that figs would be found on the tree when Jesus was passing with his disciples, nor can we form any clear idea why a tree should be cursed and consigned to barrenness for not bearing fruit, when the season for producing it was not yet come. The real character of the story is somewhat obscure; for, even if we suppose it was meant to inculcate the lesson that men must produce fruit by their deeds, yet we should still seek for other details which are here wanting, whilst those which are given are not completely in harmony. Many of the more minute particulars of our Saviour's life and miracles have no doubt passed into oblivion, and left behind only what the compilers of our Gospel-histories were able to recover from tradition. There can be no doubt that these difficulties would be removed, if we had fuller accounts of the very extraordinary occurrences with which the life of Christ abounds; and that to attempt a conjectural explanation of it is attended with hazard, and may lead to erroneous conclusions.

MATTHEW xxvi, 17-30.

17. Now the first day of the feast of unleavened bread the disciples came to Jesus, saying unto him, "Where wilt thou that we prepare for thee to eat the passover?" 18. And he said, "Go into the city to such a man, and say unto him, The

MARK xiv, 12-26.

12. And the first day of unleavened bread, when they killed the passover, his disciples said unto him, "Where wilt thou that we go and prepare that thou mayest eat the passover." 13. And he sendeth forth two of his disciples, and saith

CHAPTER XXXVIII.

The Last Supper.

THE didactic character of St John's Gospel shows itself most conspicuously in the account of the last supper of which Christ partook with his disciples. The narrative beginning with chapter xiii verse 1, ends at chapter xviii verse 1, where is related the departure of Christ and his disciples from the supper-room: and almost the whole interval of five chapters is filled with his discourses and exhortations. In the middle of these, at the end of the fourteenth chapter, Jesus says, "Arise, let us go hence!" His disciples do not however appear to have departed, but remained still listening to other admonitions which fill the whole of the fifteenth, sixteenth, and seventeenth chapters.

There can be no doubt that the supper, of which I am now speaking, is one of the most interesting and important events of the whole Gospel-history. It is related, more or less fully, by all the four evangelists, and demands the most attentive consideration from all who wish to understand the true nature of the events which then happened. The four accounts here follow; but with a slight transposition of two passages, which occur in almost the same words both in St Matthew and St Mark, in order to render easier their comparison with St Luke.

From St John's Gospel also only such extracts are given as describe what Jesus did or said whilst sitting at supper, but the moral discourses are omitted, and indeed appear to have been inserted here in a body solely that they might be preserved for their intrinsic value and not as especially adapted to this particular occasion.

LUKE xxii, 7-39.	JOHN xiii, 1; xviii, 1.
7. Then came the day of unleavened bread, when the passover must be killed. 8. And he sent Peter and John saying, "Go and prepare us the passover, that we may eat." 9. And they said unto him, "Where wilt thou that we	Now before the feast of the passover, when Jesus knew that his hour was come that he should depart out of this world unto the Father, having loved his own which were in the world, he loved them unto the end.

MATTHEW xxvi, 18-29.

Master saith, My time is at hand; I will keep the passover at thy house with my disciples."

MARK xiv, 13-25.

unto them, "Go ye into the city, and there shall meet you a man bearing a pitcher of water: follow him. 14. And wheresoever he shall go in, say ye to the goodman of the house, The master saith, Where is the guestchamber, where I shall eat the passover with my disciples? 15. And he will show you a large upper room furnished and prepared: there make ready for us."

19. And the disciples did as Jesus had appointed them; and they made ready the passover.

20. Now when the even was come, he sat down with the twelve.

26. And as they were eating, Jesus took bread, and blessed it, and brake it, and gave it to the disciples, and said, "Take, eat; this is my body." 27. And he took the cup, and gave thanks, and gave it to them, saying, "Drink ye all of it; 28. For this is my blood of the new testament, which is shed for many for the remission of sins. 29. But I say unto you, I will not drink henceforth of this fruit of the vine, until that day when I drink it new with you in my Father's kingdom."

16. And his disciples went forth, and came into the city, and found as he had said unto them: and they made ready the passover.
17. And in the evening he cometh with the twelve.

22. And as they did eat, Jesus took bread, and blessed, and brake it, and gave to them, and said, "Take, eat: this is my body." 23. And he took the cup, and when he had given thanks, he gave it to them: and they all drank of it. 24. And he said unto them, "This is my blood of the new testament, which is shed for many. 25. Verily I say unto you, I will drink no more of the fruit of the vine, until that day that I drink it new in the kingdom of God."

LUKE xxii, 9-20.	JOHN xiii, 2-12.
prepare?" 10. And he said unto them, "Behold when ye are entered into the city, there shall a man meet you, bearing a pitcher of water; follow him into the house where he entereth in. 11. And ye shall say unto the good-man of the house, The Master saith unto thee, Where is the guestchamber, where I shall eat the passover with my disciples? 12. And he shall show you a large upper room furnished: there make ready." 13. And they went, and found as he had said unto them: and they made ready the passover. 14. And when the hour was come, he sat down, and the twelve apostles with him. 15. And he said unto them, "With desire I have desired to eat this passover with you before I suffer: 16. For I say unto you, I will not any more eat thereof, until it be fulfilled in the kingdom of God." 17. And he took the cup, and gave thanks, and said, "Take this, and divide it among yourselves: 18. For I say unto you, I will not drink of the fruit of the vine, until the kingdom of God shall come." 19. And he took bread, and gave thanks, and brake it and gave unto them, saying, "This is my body which is given for you: this do in remembrance of me." 20. Likewise also the cup after supper, saying, "This cup is the new testament in my blood, which is shed for you.	2. And supper being ended, the devil having now put into the heart of Judas Iscariot, Simon's son, to betray him; 3. Jesus knowing that the Father had given all things into his hands, and that he was come from God and went to God, 4. He riseth from supper, and laid aside his garments, and took a towel, and girded himself. 5. After that he poureth water into a bason, and began to wash the disciples' feet, and to wipe them with the towel wherewith he was girded. 6. Then cometh he to Simon Peter: and Peter saith unto him, "Lord, dost thou wash my feet?" 7. Jesus answered and said unto him, "What I do thou knowest not now; but thou shalt know hereafter." 8. Peter saith unto him, "Thou shalt never wash my feet." Jesus answered him, "If I wash thee not, thou hast no part with me." 9. Simon Peter saith unto him, "Lord, not my feet only, but also my hands and my head." 10. Jesus saith to him, "He that is washed needeth not save to wash his feet, but is clean every whit: and ye are clean, but not all." 11. For he knew who should betray him; therefore said he, Ye are not all clean. 12. So after he had washed their feet, and had taken his garments and was set down again, he said unto them, "Know ye what I have done to you?" &c.

MATTHEW xxvi, 21-25.	MARK xiv, 18-21.
21. And as they did eat, he said, "Verily I say unto you, that one of you shall betray me." 22. And they were exceeding sorrowful, and began every one of them to say unto him, "Lord, is it I?" 23. And he answered and said, "He that dippeth his hand with me in the dish, the same shall betray me. 24. The Son of man goeth as it is written of him: but woe unto that man by whom the Son of man is betrayed! it had been good for that man if he had not been born." 25. Then Judas, which betrayed him, answered and said, "Master, is it I?" He said unto him, "Thou hast said."	18. And as they sat and did eat, Jesus said, "Verily I say unto you, One of you which eateth with me shall betray me." 19. And they began to be sorrowful, and to say unto him one by one, Is it I? and another said, Is it I? 20. And he answered and said unto them, "It is one of the twelve, that dippeth with me in the dish. 21. The Son of man indeed goeth, as it is written of him: but woe to that man by whom the Son of man is betrayed! good were it for that man if he had never been born."

XXXVIII.] THE LAST SUPPER. 293

LUKE xxii, 21-35.

21. But, behold, the hand of him that betrayeth me is with me on the table. 22. And truly the Son of man goeth, as it was determined: but woe unto that man by whom he is betrayed!" 23. And they began to enquire among themselves, which of them it was that should do this thing.

24. And there was also a strife among them, which of them should be accounted the greatest. 25. And he said unto them, " The kings of the Gentiles," &c. &c.
31. And the Lord said, " Simon, Simon, behold, Satan hath desired to have you, that he may sift you as wheat: 32. But I have prayed for thee, that thy faith fail not: and when thou art converted, strengthen thy brethren." 33. And he said unto him, " Lord, I am ready to go with thee, both into prison, and to death." 34. And he said, "I tell thee, Peter, the cock shall not crow this day, before that thou shalt thrice deny that thou knowest me."
35. And he said unto them, " When I sent you &c."

JOHN xiii, 21-38.

21. When Jesus had thus said, he was troubled in spirit, and testified, and said, " Verily, verily, I say unto you, that one of you shall betray me." 22. Then the disciples looked one on another, doubting of whom he spake. 23. Now there was leaning on Jesus's bosom one of his disciples, whom Jesus loved. 24. Simon Peter therefore beckoned to him, that he should ask who it should be of whom he spake. 25. He then lying on Jesus's breast saith unto him, "Lord, who is it?" 26. Jesus answered, " He it is, to whom I shall give a sop, when I have dipped it." And when he had dipped the sop, he gave it to Judas Iscariot, the son of Simon. 27. And after the sop Satan entered into him. Then said Jesus unto him, " That thou doest, do quickly." 28. Now no man at the table knew for what intent he spake this unto him. 29. For some of them thought, because Judas had the bag, that Jesus had said unto him, Buy those things that we have need of against the feast; or, that he should give something to the poor. 30. He then having received the sop went immediately out: and it was night.

36. Simon Peter said unto him, " Lord, whither goest thou?" Jesus answered him, " Whither I go, thou canst not follow me now: but thou shalt follow me afterwards." 37. Peter said unto him, " Lord, why cannot I follow thee now? I will lay down my life for thy sake." 38. Jesus answered him, " Wilt thou lay down thy life for my sake? Verily, verily, I say unto thee, The cock shall not crow, till thou hast denied me thrice."

MATTHEW xxvi, 30.	MARK xiv, 26.
30. And when they had sung an hymn, they went out into the mount of Olives.	26. And when they had sung an hymn, they went out into the mount of Olives.

In examining these parallel narratives, we find there is a difference as to the *place*, the *time*, the *nature*, and the subordinate *circumstances* of the last supper, which warrant the belief that the accounts of it, thus divergent, have been compiled in a later age, when all the particulars that had been handed down respecting it, were already faint with time, so that many of the minor details are contradictory.

1. As to the *place* of the supper ; it appears from the concurrent testimony of the first three evangelists that it took place at Jerusalem, Jesus having sent some of his disciples that very morning from Bethany into the city to make preparation for the feast. But in the Gospel of St John the supper appears to have been at Bethany, whither Christ returned every evening after the occupation of the day at Jerusalem, and nothing is said of the sending the disciples into Jerusalem in the morning to make preparations for the feast, or of his going thither himself in the evening.

2. The *time*, also, of the supper is not the same in the four Gospels: for, whilst Matthew, Mark, and Luke fix it accurately in the evening, the first day of unleavened bread, i. e. the 14th of the month Nisan (which, according to our modern calendar, would be in that year about the 9th day of April), the Gospel of St John says, " Now *before* the feast of the passover &c.," which words being followed in the next verse by "And supper being ended," can hardly denote any thing else than that the supper was at least on the day before the feast of the passover and was not itself that feast.

3. As regards therefore the *nature* of the supper also, the last evangelist is not in harmony with the other three ; for Matthew, Mark, and Luke all describe it as the passover or paschal feast, "they made ready the passover " ; and Luke especially adds, " With desire I have desired to eat this passover with you before I suffer ": but John has no indication that it was the passover or any thing more than a common meal. These remarks apply to the beginning of the meal in St John's Gospel, not of course to its end ; for the narrative, after five chapters of intervening discourses and admonitions addressed to the disciples, does actually come round to the same point as the other three Gospels ; for,

LUKE xxii, 39.	JOHN xviii, 1.
39. And he came out, and went, as he was wont, to the mount of Olives: and his disciples also followed him.	When Jesus had spoken these words, he went forth with his disciples over the brook Cedron, where was a garden into the which he entered and his disciples.

"When Jesus (xviii, 1) had spoken these words, he went forth with his disciples over the brook Cedron"; coming, it will be remembered, from Bethany, and not, as in Matthew, Mark, and Luke, from Jerusalem.

4. And lastly, the subordinate *circumstances* of the supper are equally divergent.

The first three evangelists relate the message carried by some of the disciples to a man in the city that he should make ready a room at his house for the paschal feast. This circumstance is not noticed by St John, but it is also related differently by the other three. Whilst, according to St Matthew, Christ sends his disciples generally, St Mark says that only two went, and St Luke tells us that these two were Peter and John. Again, in Matthew they are instructed to go to the house of a certain man and give notice that they would eat the passover there that evening. But in St Mark and St Luke, they are instructed to follow a servant who should meet them in the street bearing a pitcher of water into a house where they should find a room prepared for them. These details are not contradictory, and yet the one excludes the other. If they went to the house of a certain man— whereby is implied that Jesus specified the man by name, what was the need of their watching the servant in the street to know where they should go? It is evident that the evangelists have written according to the knowledge of each, and that the traditions which they followed had become divergent one from another.

If we proceed to review the incidents that are said to have happened at the feast, we shall find that these also are very differently told by the four writers.

In the first place Matthew and Mark relate Christ's detection of Judas's treachery as preceding the institution of the Communion: but Luke inverts this order and places the Communion first. John, however, omits all notice of the Communion and instead represents Jesus as washing the feet of his disciples. He also makes Judas Iscariot leave the feast, immediately after his treason was detected. If we insert this fact as having been accidentally omitted by the first three Gospels, we still cannot reconcile the accounts of

Matthew, Mark, and Luke; for if in Matthew and Mark the previous detection of Judas saved him from the sin of partaking in the Communion, yet in Luke, his detection followed after the institution of that ceremony, and he consequently must have partaken of it. But the probability is that Matthew, Mark, and Luke were not aware that Judas left the room, for they do not relate his detection in such explicit terms as John; who alone says that Jesus presented a sop to the traitor who immediately left the room: in the other three evangelists, there is no indication of Judas having been designated so pointedly.

Secondly, Luke places the "strife among the disciples which should be greatest" as one of the incidents of the last supper; but Mark says that it took place as they were on their way to Capernaum some time before.

Thirdly, according to Luke, Christ foretells Peter's denial of him whilst they are still sitting at meat, but Matthew and Mark agree in placing it after their arrival at the mount of Olives, and the accounts which *they* give of it are therefore not quoted above in a parallel column with those of Luke and John. Nor, although there is some little difference in the four descriptions given of Peter's denial, does it seem worth while to make this an additional instance of divergency between the four evangelists.

CHAPTER XXXIX.

Christ's Agony in the Garden of Gethsemane.

From the mount of Olives' Jesus and his disciples withdraw into the neighbouring garden of Gethsemane. The fourth Gospel then immediately relates the coming of Judas and his betrayal of his master, but the other three Gospels interpose a scene generally called the "*Agony in the garden.*"

Matthew xxvi, 36-46.	Mark xiv, 32-42.	Luke xxii, 40-46.
36. Then cometh Jesus with them unto a place called Gethsemane, and saith unto the disciples, "Sit ye here, while I go and pray yonder." 37. And he	32. And they came to a place which was named Gethsemane: and he saith to his disciples, "Sit ye here, while I shall pray." 33. And he taketh with	40. And when he was at the place, he said unto them, "Pray that ye enter not into temptation."

CHRIST'S AGONY IN THE GARDEN.

MATTHEW xxvi, 37-44.	MARK xiv, 33-40.	LUKE xxii, 41-44.
took with him Peter and the two sons of Zebedee, and began to be sorrowful and very heavy. 38. Then saith he unto them, "My soul is exceeding sorrowful, even unto death: tarry ye here, and watch with me."	him Peter and James and John, and began to be sore amazed, and to be very heavy; 34. And saith unto them, "My soul is exceeding sorrowful unto death: tarry ye here, and watch."	
39. And he went a little farther, and fell on his face, and prayed, saying, "O my Father, if it be possible, let this cup pass from me: nevertheless not as I will, but as thou wilt."	35. And he went forward a little, and fell on the ground, and prayed that if it were possible, the hour might pass from him. 36. And he said, "Abba, Father, all things are possible unto thee: take away this cup from me: nevertheless not what I will, but what thou wilt."	41. And he was withdrawn from them about a stone's cast, and kneeled down, and prayed, 42. Saying, "Father, if thou be willing, remove this cup from me: nevertheless not my will, but thine, be done."
		43. And there appeared an angel unto him from heaven, strengthening him. 44. And being in an agony he prayed more earnestly: and his sweat was as it were great drops of blood falling down to the ground.
40. And he cometh unto the disciples, and findeth them asleep, and saith unto Peter, "What, could ye not watch with me one hour? 41. Watch and pray, that ye enter not into temptation: the spirit indeed is willing, but the flesh is weak." 42. He went away again the second time, and prayed, saying, "O my Father, if this cup may not pass away from me, except I drink it, thy will be done." 43. And he came and found them asleep again: for their eyes were heavy. 44. And he left them, and went away again, and prayed the third time, saying the same words.	37. And he cometh, and findeth them sleeping, and saith unto Peter, "Simon, sleepest thou? couldst not thou watch one hour? 38. Watch ye and pray, lest ye enter into temptation. The spirit truly is ready, but the flesh is weak." 39. And again he went away, and prayed, and spake the same words. 40. And when he returned, he found them asleep again, (for their eyes were heavy,) neither wist they what to answer him.	

MATTHEW xxvi, 45, 46.	MARK xiv, 41, 42.	LUKE xxii, 45, 46.
45. Then cometh he to his disciples, and saith unto them, "Sleep on now, and take your rest: behold, the hour is at hand, and the Son of man is betrayed into the hands of sinners. 46. Rise, let us be going: behold, he is at hand that doth betray me."	41. And he cometh the third time, and saith unto them, "Sleep on now, and take your rest: it is enough, the hour is come; behold, the Son of man is betrayed into the hands of sinners. 42. Rise up, let us go; lo, he that betrayeth me is at hand."	45. And when he rose up from prayer, and was come to his disciples, he found them sleeping for sorrow. 46. And said unto them, "Why sleep ye? rise and pray, lest ye enter into temptation."

The first observation called forth by a perusal of this narrative relates to the very remarkable circumstance of its being totally omitted by St John, one of the three selected (if we may believe Matthew and Mark) to be more closely witnesses of it. To explain the omission by supposing that John's Gospel was supplementary to the other three is impossible, for that Gospel frequently mentions at length things of little moment that are also found in Matthew, Mark, and Luke, whilst it fails to supply information on points of great interest that are cursorily treated by the others. The present is an event which would certainly have been a remarkable incident in the life of St John, and would probably have been fully described by him, even if his object had been to supply information that had been omitted by the other evangelists; for, although Matthew, Mark, and Luke relate the Agony in the Garden, yet they do it in such a manner as to give rise to more than one embarrassing question on the subject.

2. From Matthew and Luke we learn that Christ says to his disciples, "Sit ye here, while I go and pray yonder," and that taking with him his three favourite disciples Peter and James and John, he then goes away to some little distance from the others. But at Matthew, v, 38, and Mark, v, 34, we read that he tells even them to remain behind, and going himself alone a little further, throws himself upon the ground in prayer. But in Luke's Gospel we find nothing of the selection of Peter and James and John: Christ only goes alone "about a stone's cast," kneels down and prays.

3. Luke adds the miraculous appearance of an angel sent to strengthen Christ; but neither Matthew nor Mark relates this circumstance; which, we might suppose, would in itself have been a sufficient reason for some notice on the part of St John who was so close a witness of it.

4. Matthew and Mark represent Christ as coming to the

three disciples three times and each time finding them asleep. But in St Luke's Gospel Jesus is represented as coming back once only, not to three of his disciples, but to all the eleven, and it is added that he found them all asleep; "for their eyes were heavy."

CHAPTER XL.

Christ's Arrest and Examination before the High-Priest.

THE agreement between the evangelists, at least between three of them, about the main outlines of Christ's life, is as striking as their want of agreement on all the minor details. Thus, in the account of his arrest, all the four agree in fixing it, for the *time*, on the evening of his last supper, and, for the *place*, in the garden of Gethsemane. These things may have descended to the writers of the Gospels by tradition, and no variation may have been made on points so specific. But in the minute details which the Gospels give of the arrest, it is impossible to reconcile the accounts of the four together. The first three give the account which follows.

MATTHEW xxvi, 47-75.	MARK xiv, 43-72.	LUKE xxii, 47-71.
47. And while he yet spake, lo, Judas, one of the twelve, came, and with him a great multitude with swords and staves, from the chief priests and elders of the people. 48. Now he that betrayed him gave them a sign, saying, "Whomsoever I shall kiss, that same is he: hold him fast." 49. And forthwith he came to Jesus, and said, "Hail, master;" and kissed him. 50. And Jesus said unto him, "Friend, wherefore art thou come?" Then came they, and laid hands on Jesus, and took him.	43. And immediately, while he yet spake, cometh Judas, one of the twelve, and with him a great multitude with swords and staves, from the chief priests and the scribes and the elders. 44. And he that betrayed him had given them a token, saying, "Whomsoever I shall kiss, that same is he; take him, and lead him away safely." 45. And as soon as he was come, he goeth straightway to him, and saith, "Master, master;" and kissed him. 46. And they laid their hands on him, and took him.	47. And while he yet spake, behold a multitude, and he that was called Judas, one of the twelve, went before them, and drew near unto Jesus to kiss him. 48. But Jesus said unto him, "Judas, Betrayest thou the Son of man with a kiss?"

That of St John here follows separately.

JOHN xviii, 3-9.

3. Judas then, having received a band of men and officers from the chief priests and Pharisees, cometh thither with lanterns and torches and weapons.
4. Jesus therefore, knowing all things that should come upon him, went forth, and said unto them, "Whom seek ye?" 5. They answered him, "Jesus of Nazareth." Jesus saith unto them, "I am he." And Judas also, which betrayed him, stood with them. 6. As soon then as he had said unto them, I am he, they went backward, and fell to the ground. 7. Then asked he them again, "Whom seek ye?" And they said, "Jesus of Nazareth." 8. Jesus answered, "I have told you that I am he: if therefore ye seek me, let these go their way;" 9. That the saying might be fulfilled, which he spake, "Of them which thou gavest me have I lost none."

Here, though all agree that Jesus was betrayed by Judas Iscariot, yet the mode in which this was done is differently told by the four evangelists. If, according to St John, Jesus stepped forth and declared himself to be the person whom they were seeking, it is evident that Judas did not indicate him by going up and kissing him, or, at least, it would

---

MATTHEW xxvi, 51-56.	MARK xiv, 47-52.
51. And behold, one of them which were with Jesus stretched out his hand, and drew his sword, and struck a servant of the high priest's, and smote off his ear.	47. And one of them that stood by drew a sword, and smote a servant of the high priest, and cut off his ear.
52. Then said Jesus unto him, "Put up again thy sword into his place: for all they that take the sword shall perish with the sword. 53. Thinkest thou that I cannot now pray to my Father, and he shall presently give me more than twelve legions of angels? 54. But how then shall the scriptures be fulfilled, that thus it must be?"	
55. In that same hour said Jesus to the multitudes, "Are ye come out as against a thief with swords and staves for to take me? I sat daily with you teaching in the temple, and ye laid no hold on me." 56. But all this was done, that the scriptures of the prophets might be fulfilled. Then all the disciples forsook him and fled.	48. And Jesus answered and said unto them, "Are ye come out, as against a thief, with swords and staves to take me? 49. I was daily with you in the temple teaching, and ye took me not: but the scriptures must be fulfilled."
	50. And they all forsook him, and fled.
	51. And there followed him a certain young man, having a linen cloth cast about his naked body; and the young men laid hold on him:
	52. And he left the linen cloth, and fled from them naked.

have been superfluous to do so. If on the other hand the kiss which Judas gave Jesus, was the preconcerted sign by which they might know him, it would be unnecessary for Jesus to declare and so deliver up himself. The narrative of St John is on the whole the most divergent, for he introduces, besides the dialogue between Jesus and the soldiers who arrest him, a very extraordinary display of supernatural power, wholly unnoticed by the other three writers. The omission of this fact is fatal to their claim of having been present at this remarkable scene. That all the four copied from such sources as had come down to their times, and neither were themselves eye-witnesses nor drew from the writings of those who were, is perhaps more evident from the little incident of Peter's smiting the high priest's servant than from any other particular. It is related by the three writers of the Synoptical Gospels immediately after the kiss of Judas; and is noticed also by St John.

LUKE xxii, 49-53.

49. When they which were about him saw what would follow, they said unto him, "Lord, shall we smite with the sword?" 50. And one of them smote the servant of the high priest, and cut off his right ear. 51. And Jesus answered and said, "Suffer ye thus far." And he touched his ear, and healed him.

JOHN xviii, 10, 11.

10. Then Simon Peter having a sword drew it, and smote the high priest's servant, and cut off his right ear. The servant's name was Malchus. 11. Then said Jesus unto Peter, "Put up thy sword into the sheath: the cup which my Father hath given me, shall I not drink it?"

52. Then Jesus said unto the chief priests, and captains of the temple, and the elders, which were come to him, "Be ye come out, as against a thief, with swords and staves? 53. When I was daily with you in the temple, ye stretched forth no hands against me: but this is your hour, and the power of darkness."

The growth of this circumstance from Mark's simple statement that "one of them that stood by drew a sword, and smote a servant of the high priest and cut off his ear," is worthy of notice.

First: Luke adds that all the disciples meant to defend themselves, and asked Jesus, " Shall we smite with the sword ?"

Secondly: Matthew adds that Jesus reproved the author of the deed.

Thirdly: From Luke we learn also that Jesus healed the wounded ear with a touch.

Fourthly: John makes the history complete by adding that it was Peter who struck the blow, and that Malchus was the name of the wounded servant.

This accession of particulars looks exceedingly like the slow process of additional successive details which all such accounts receive, when a number of persons are trying to bring to light what has begun to fade away, and each particular has to be sought after with patient zeal and untiring

MATTHEW xxvi, 57-63.	MARK xiv, 53-60.
57. And they that had laid hold on Jesus led him away to Caiaphas the high priest, where the scribes and the elders were assembled.	53. And they led Jesus away to the high priest: and with him were assembled all the chief priests and the elders and the scribes.
58. But Peter followed him afar off unto the high priest's palace, and went in, and sat with the servants, to see the end.	54. And Peter followed him afar off, even into the palace of the high priest: and sat with the servants, and warmed himself at the fire.
59. Now the chief priests, and elders, and all the council, sought false witness against Jesus, to put him to death, 60. But found none: yea, though many false witnesses came, yet found they none. At the last came two false witnesses, 61. And said, " This fellow said, I am able to destroy the temple of God, and to build it in three days." 62. And the high priest arose, and said unto him, " Answerest thou nothing? what is it which these witness against thee ?" 63. But Jesus held his peace. And the high priest	55. And the chief priests and all the council sought for witness against Jesus to put him to death; and found none. 56. For many bare false witness against him, but their witness agreed not together. 57. And there arose certain, and bare false witness against him, saying, 58. " We heard him say, I will destroy this temple that is made with hands, and within three days I will build another made without hands." 59. But neither so did their witness agree together. 60. And the high priest stood up in the

XL.] CHRIST'S ARREST AND EXAMINATION. 303

perseverance; every contributor being, as it would seem, ignorant of the effect of his discoveries, and careful only to collect facts, which hereafter may be blended together. We may of course make an exception to this process when an isolated fact is recorded as in the case of the young man, named by Mark, who, alarmed at what was going on at night, threw a sheet from the bed round his body, but, surprised and frightened at the sight of the soldiers, left his covering in their hands, and fled naked away.

The company of soldiers meanwhile carry off Jesus; but, though the disciples had at first all taken to flight, Peter came again and followed his master, in company, says the Gospel of St John, with another disciple, who is generally said to have been St John himself. The four narratives proceed thus.

LUKE xxii, 54-71.	JOHN xviii, 12-16.
54. Then took they him, and led him, and brought him into the high priest's house.	12. Then the band and the captain and officers of the Jews took Jesus, and bound him, 13. And led him away to Annas first; for he was father in law to Caiaphas, which was the high priest that same year.
	14. Now Caiaphas was he, which gave counsel to the Jews, that it was expedient that one man should die for the people.
And Peter followed afar off. 55. And when they had kindled a fire in the midst of the hall, and were set down together, Peter sat down among them.	15. And Simon Peter followed Jesus, and so did another disciple: that disciple was known unto the high priest, and went in with Jesus into the palace of the high priest. 16. But Peter stood at the door without. Then went out that other disciple, which was known unto the high priest, and spake unto her that kept the door, and brought in Peter.

MATTHEW xxvi, 63-75.	MARK xiv, 59-72.
answered and said unto him, "I adjure thee by the living God that thou tell us whether thou be the Christ the Son of God." 64. Jesus saith unto him, "Thou hast said: nevertheless I say unto you, Hereafter shall ye see the Son of man sitting on the right hand of power and coming in the clouds of heaven." 65. Then the high priest rent his clothes, saying, "He hath spoken blasphemy; what further need have we of witnesses? behold, now ye have heard his blasphemy. 66. What think ye?" They answered and said, "He is guilty of death." 67. Then did they spit in his face, and buffeted him; and others smote him with the palms of their hands, 68. Saying, "Prophesy unto us, thou Christ, Who is he that smote thee?" 69. Now Peter sat without in the palace: and a damsel came unto him, saying, "Thou also wast with Jesus of Galilee." 70. But he denied before them all, saying, "I know not what thou sayest." 71. And when he was gone out into the porch another maid saw him, and said unto them that were there, "This fellow was also with Jesus of Nazareth." 72. And again he denied with an oath, "I do not know the man." 73. And after a while came unto him they that stood by, and said to Peter, "Surely thou also art one of them; for thy speech betrayeth thee." 74. Then began he to curse and to swear, saying, "I know not the man." And immediately the cock crew. 75. And Peter remembered the word of Jesus, which said unto him, "Before the cock crow, thou shalt deny me thrice." And he went out and wept bitterly.	midst, and asked Jesus, saying, "Answerest thou nothing? what is it which these witness against thee?" 61. But he held his peace, and answered nothing. Again the high priest asked him, and said unto him, "Art thou the Christ, the Son of the Blessed?" 62. And Jesus said, "I am: and ye shall see the Son of man sitting on the right hand of power, and coming in the clouds of heaven." 63. Then the high priest rent his clothes, and saith, "What need we any further witnesses? 64. Ye have heard the blasphemy: what think ye?" And they all condemned him to be guilty of death. 65. And some began to spit on him, and to cover his face, and to buffet him, and to say unto him, "Prophesy:" and the servants did strike him with the palms of their hands. 66. And as Peter was beneath in the palace, there cometh one of the maids of the high priest: 67. And when she saw Peter warming himself, she looked upon him, and said, "And thou also wast with Jesus of Nazareth." 68. But he denied, saying, "I know not, neither understood I what thou sayest." And he went out into the porch; and the cock crew. 69. And a maid saw him again, and began to say to them that stood by, "This is one of them." 70. And he denied it again. And a little after, they that stood by said again to Peter, "Surely thou art one of them: for thou art a Galilæan, and thy speech agreeth thereto." 71. But he began to curse and to swear, saying, "I know not this man of whom ye speak." 72. And the second time the cock crew. And Peter called to mind the word that Jesus said unto him, Before the cock crow twice, thou shalt deny me thrice. And when he thought thereon, he wept.

In these accounts are many particulars, difficult to be reconciled.

1. Whilst in the other three Gospels Jesus is led straight into the palace of the high priest, we find in St John that

XL.] CHRIST'S ARREST AND EXAMINATION. 305

LUKE xxii, 56-71.

56. But a certain maid beheld him as he sat by the fire, and earnestly looked upon him, and said, "This man was also with him." 57. And he denied him, saying, "Woman, I know him not." 58. And after a little while another saw him, and said, "Thou art also of them." And Peter said, "Man, I am not." 59. And about the space of one hour after another confidently affirmed, saying, "Of a truth this fellow was also with him: for he is a Galilæan." 60. And Peter said, "Man, I know not what thou sayest." And immediately, while he yet spake, the cock crew. 61. And the Lord turned, and looked upon Peter. And Peter remembered the word of the Lord, how he had said unto him, Before the cock crow, thou shalt deny me thrice. 62. And Peter went out and wept bitterly.
63. And the men that held Jesus mocked him, and smote him. 64. And when they had blindfolded him, they struck him on the face, and asked him, saying, "Prophesy, who is it that smote thee?" 65. And many other things blasphemously spake they against him.
66. And as soon as it was day, the elders of the people and the chief priests and the scribes came together, and led him into their council, saying, 67. "Art thou the Christ? tell us." And he said unto them, "If I tell you, ye will not believe: 18. And if I also ask you, ye will not answer me, nor let me go. 69. Hereafter shall the Son of man sit on the right hand of the power of God." 70. Then said they all, "Art thou then the Son of God?" And he said unto them, "Ye say that I am." 71. And they said, "What need we any further witness? for we ourselves have heard of his own mouth."

JOHN xviii, 17-27.

17. Then saith the damsel that kept the door unto Peter, "Art not thou also one of this man's disciples?" He saith, "I am not." 18. And the servants and officers stood there, who had made a fire of coals; for it was cold: and they warmed themselves: and Peter stood with them, and warmed himself.
19. The high priest then asked Jesus of his disciples, and of his doctrine. 20. Jesus answered him, "I spake openly to the world; I ever taught in the synagogue, and in the temple, whither the Jews always resort; and in secret have I said nothing. 21. Why askest thou me? ask them which heard me, what I have said unto them: behold, they know what I said." 22. And when he had thus spoken, one of the officers which stood by struck Jesus with the palm of his hand, saying, "Answerest thou the high priest so?" 23. Jesus answered him, "If I have spoken evil, bear witness of the evil: but if well, why smitest thou me?" 24. Now Annas had* sent him bound unto Caiaphas the high priest.
25. And Simon Peter stood and warmed himself. They said therefore unto him, "Art not thou also one of his disciples?" He denied it, and said, "I am not." 26. One of the servants of the high priest, being his kinsman whose ear Peter cut off, saith, "Did not I see thee in the garden with him?" 27. Peter then denied again: and immediately the cock crew.

---

* "Had" is an interpolation of our translators. The original Greek is ἀπέστειλεν, which must apply to a consecutive series of events.

---

he is first led away to Annas the father-in-law of Caiaphas, who was the high priest that same year; and yet within two verses Peter is said to have followed Jesus into the palace of the high priest, having been detained a short time at the door until his companion had obtained for him admission. The discrepancy appears to arise solely from the unhistorical manner in which the fourth Gospel is compiled: often relating facts of which no trace occurs elsewhere, it as often weakens their credibility by the confused order and imperfect manner in which they are related.

2. If, then, setting aside the previous difficulty, we lay the scene of Christ's examination in the palace of the high priest, we have next to observe that St Luke puts off that examination until the next morning early (ver. 66), leaving Jesus for the night in the hands of the servants and officers, who make sport of him, blindfold him, and treat him with many indignities. In this St Luke is not borne out by the other three, all of whom relate the examination as occurring over night, and place the buffeting and smiting, as the immediate consequence of his having been therein declared to be worthy of death.

3. But a third discrepancy, concerning the denial of Christ by Peter, furnishes a still stronger proof that these records have not come down to us with the exactness of a contemporary character, much less with the authority of verbal inspiration. The four accounts of Peter's denial vary very considerably.

The variations will be more intelligible, exhibited in a tabular form.

1st DENIAL.	2nd DENIAL.	3rd DENIAL.
According to MATTHEW—seated in an outer room, by the fire, to a damsel.	Out in the porch, to another maid.	Out in the porch, to the bystanders.
MARK—Agrees with Matthew in all three.		
LUKE—seated in an outer room by the fire, to a damsel.	Still near the fire, to another damsel.	Still near the fire, to a man.
JOHN—On entering, to the damsel who kept the door.	Seated by the fire, to the bystanders.	Still seated by the fire, to one of the servants, who was a relative of Malchus.

The circumstance of the cock crowing is also differently told. Mark alone says that the first crowing was immediately after the first denial, and the second immediately after the third. The other three place the only crowing with which they were acquainted immediately after the third denial.

Such variations do not impugn the idea of the fact, but only the accuracy of the writers; and the introduction of the cock at all seems to militate against all the four alike, for they all place the scene over night, and cocks do not generally crow until the dawn of day.

Lastly, there is a remarkable feature added to the story by St Luke alone—that Jesus, after the third denial, turned and looked at Peter, who was smitten with remorse and went out to weep bitterly. But all the other three evangelists agree that Jesus and Peter were separated from one another— Matthew and Mark even tell us that, whilst the former was led in before the high priest, the latter sat without by the fire. To harmonize these different authorities, without qualifying one of them, is impossible, though it may not be difficult to extract from them a consistent narrative, if reason and not preconceived opinion, be allowed its due weight in conducting the enquiry.

CHAPTER XLI.

The Trial of Jesus before Pontius Pilate, the Roman Procurator.

THE meeting of priests and elders, before whom Jesus was first brought to be examined, appears to have been the Jewish Sanhedrim; but as they no longer had the power of life and death, it was necessary that he should be tried by due form of law before the governor. Whether the previous examination before the Jewish authorities was according to a regular custom, or whether it was exceptional in the present instance, we are not informed. The Romans were willing to allow every safe privilege to the subject states, but insisted on themselves administering the laws of the empire. They also were very careful to extend the language as well as the laws of Rome, and it can hardly be doubted that the trial of our Lord, like all other trials, was conducted in the Latin tongue. We have the testimony of several ancient authors on this subject. Valerius Maximus (ii, 2) has the following passage:

How energetically the ancient magistrates conducted themselves in support of their own majesty and that of the Roman people, may be learned from the fact that among other marks of dignity they persistently took care that no one should reply, even to Greeks, in other than the Latin language.

Cicero also, in his fourth oration against Verres (ch. 66), complains that he had been charged with acting unworthily for having spoken before Greeks in their own tongue. Plutarch too, in his Life of Cato, alludes to a popular report that the Censor during a lengthened stay at Athens delivered to the inhabitants of that city an oration in Greek and in praise of their illustrious ancestors: but his biographer says that this is not true, for that Cato spoke to them through an interpreter. We will then proceed to cite the passages from the four Gospels in which this trial is described. The three Synoptical writers begin this part of their narrative as follows:

MATTHEW xxvii, 1-14.	MARK xv, 1-5.	LUKE xxiii, 1-5.
When the morning was come, all the chief priests and elders of the people took counsel against Jesus to put him to death: 2. And when they had bound him, they led him away, and delivered him to Pontius Pilate the governor. . . . . 11. And Jesus stood before the governor: and the governor asked him, saying, "Art thou the King of the Jews?" And Jesus said unto him, "Thou sayest." 12. And when he was accused of the chief priests and elders, he answered nothing. 13. Then said Pilate unto him, "Hearest thou not how many things they witness against thee?" 14. And he answered him to never a word; insomuch that the governor marvelled greatly.	And straightway in the morning the chief priests held a consultation with the elders and scribes and the whole council, and bound Jesus, and carried him away, and delivered him to Pilate. 2. And Pilate asked him, "Art thou the King of the Jews?" And he answering said unto him, "Thou sayest it." 3. And the chief priests accused him of many things: but he answered nothing. 4. And Pilate asked him again, saying, "Answerest thou nothing? behold how many things they witness against thee." 5. But Jesus yet answered nothing; so that Pilate marvelled.	And the whole multitude of them arose, and led him unto Pilate. 2. And they began to accuse him, saying, "We found this fellow perverting the nation, and forbidding to give tribute to Cæsar, saying that he himself is Christ a King." 3. And Pilate asked him, saying, "Art thou the King of the Jews?" And he answered him and said, "Thou sayest it." 4. Then said Pilate to the chief priests and to the people, "I find no fault in this man." 5. And they were the more fierce, saying, "He stirreth up the people, teaching throughout all Jewry, beginning from Galilee to this place."

The divergences of description given in the Gospel according to St John will be evident from the following extract:

JOHN xviii, 28-38.

28. Then led they Jesus from Caiaphas unto the hall of judgement: and it was early; and they themselves went not into the judgement hall, lest they should be defiled; but that they might eat the passover. 29. Pilate

then went out unto them, and said, "What accusation bring ye against this man?" 30. They answered and said unto him, "If he were not a malefactor, we would not have delivered him up unto thee." 31. Then said Pilate unto them, "Take ye him, and judge him according to your law." The Jews therefore said unto him, "It is not lawful for us to put any man to death:" 32. That the saying of Jesus might be fulfilled, which he spake, signifying what death he should die. 33. Then Pilate entered into the judgement hall again, and called Jesus, and said unto him, "Art thou the King of the Jews?"
34. Jesus answered him, "Sayest thou this thing of thyself, or did others tell it thee of me?"
35. Pilate answered, "Am I a Jew? Thine own nation and the chief priests have delivered thee unto me: what hast thou done?"
36. Jesus answered, "My kingdom is not of this world: if my kingdom were of this world, then would my servants fight, that I should not be delivered to the Jews: but now is my kingdom not from hence."
37. Pilate therefore said unto him, "Art thou a king then?" Jesus answered, "Thou sayest that I am a king. To this end was I born and for this cause came I into the world, that I should bear witness unto the truth. Every one that is of the truth heareth my voice."
38. Pilate saith unto him, "What is truth?" and, when he had said this, he went out again unto the Jews, and saith unto them, " I find in him no fault at all."

At this point of the proceedings St Luke records an incident of which nothing is said by the other three evangelists.

LUKE xxiii, 6-16.

6. When Pilate heard of Galilee, he asked whether the man were a Galilæan. 7. And as soon as he knew that he belonged unto Herod's jurisdiction, he sent him to Herod, who himself also was at Jerusalem at that time. 8. And when Herod saw Jesus, he was exceeding glad: for he was desirous to see him of a long season, because he had heard many things of him; and he hoped to have seen some miracle done by him. 9. Then he questioned with him in many words; but he answered him nothing. 10. And the chief priests and scribes stood and vehemently accused him.
11. And Herod with his men of war set him at nought and mocked him, and arrayed him in a gorgeous robe, and sent him again to Pilate. 12. And the same day Pilate and Herod were made friends together: for before they were at enmity between themselves.
13. And Pilate, when he had called together the chief priests and the rulers, and the people, 14. Said unto them, "Ye have brought this man unto me, as one that perverteth the people: and, behold, I, having examined him before you, have found no fault in this man touching those things whereof ye accuse him: 15. No, nor yet Herod: for I sent you to him; and, lo, nothing worthy of death is done unto him. 16. I will therefore chastise him, and release him."

At this point of the narrative we meet with the notice of Barabbas the robber, mentioned by all the four evangelists, but very briefly by St John.

MATTHEW xxvii, 15-26.	MARK xv, 6-15.	LUKE xxiii, 17-25.
15. Now at that feast the governor was wont to release unto the people a prisoner, whom	6. Now at that feast he released unto them one prisoner, whomsoever they desired. 7.	17. (For of necessity he must release one unto them at the feast.) 18. And they cried out

MATTHEW xxvii, 15-26.	MARK xv, 7-15.	LUKE xxiii, 18-25.
they would. 16. And they had then a notable prisoner, called Barabbas. 17. Therefore when they were gathered together, Pilate said unto them, "Whom will ye that I release unto you? Barabbas, or Jesus which is called Christ?" 18. For he knew that for envy they had delivered him. 19. When he was set down on the judgement seat, his wife sent unto him, saying, "Have thou nothing to do with that just man: for I have suffered many things this day in a dream because of him." 20. But the chief priests and elders persuaded the multitude that they should ask Barabbas, and destroy Jesus. 21. The governor answered and said unto them, "Whether of the twain will ye that I release unto you?" They said, "Barabbas." 22. Pilate saith unto them, "What shall I do then with Jesus which is called Christ?" They all say unto him, "Let him be crucified." 23. And the governor said, "Why, what evil hath he done?" But they cried out the more, saying, "Let him be crucified." 26. Then released he Barabbas unto them: and when he had scourged Jesus, he delivered him to be crucified.	And there was one named Barabbas, which lay bound with them that had made insurrection with him, who had committed murder in the insurrection. 8. And the multitude crying aloud began to desire him to do as he had ever done unto them. 9. But Pilate answered them, saying, "Will ye that I release unto you the King of the Jews?" 10. For he knew that the chief priests had delivered him for envy. 11. But the chief priests moved the people, that he should rather release Barabbas unto them. 12. And Pilate answered and said again unto them, "What will ye then that I shall do unto him whom ye call the King of the Jews?" 13. And they cried out again, "Crucify him." 14. Then Pilate said unto them, "Why, what evil hath he done?" And they cried out the more exceedingly, "Crucify him." 15. And so Pilate, willing to content the people, released Barabbas unto them, and delivered Jesus, when he had scourged him, to be crucified.	all at once, saying, "Away with this man, and release unto us Barabbas:" 19. (Who for a certain sedition made in the city, and for murder, was cast into prison.) 20. Pilate therefore, willing to release Jesus, spake again to them. 21. But they cried, saying, "Crucify him, crucify him." 22. And he said unto them the third time, "Why, what evil hath he done? I have found no cause of death in him: I will therefore chastise him, and let him go." 23. And they were instant with loud voices, requiring that he might be crucified. And the voices of them and of the chief priests prevailed. 24. And Pilate gave sentence that it should be as they required. 25. And he released unto them him that for sedition and murder was cast into prison, whom they had desired; but he delivered Jesus to their will.

JOHN xviii, 39, 40.

39. "But ye have a custom, that I should release unto you one at the passover: will ye therefore that I release unto you the King of the Jews?"
40. Then cried they all again, saying, "Not this man, but Barabbas." Now Barabbas was a robber.

The incident of Pilate's washing his hands before the multitude, is related by St Matthew alone in these terms:

MATTHEW xxvii, 24, 25.

24. When Pilate saw that he could prevail nothing, but that rather a tumult was made, he took water, and washed his hands before the multitude, saying, "I am innocent of the blood of this just person: see ye to it."
25. Then answered all the people, and said, "His blood be on us, and on our children."

St Luke's narrative here ceases and the sequel of history according to the other three here follows.

MATTHEW xxvii, 27-31.	MARK xv, 16-20.	JOHN xix, 1-16.
27. Then the soldiers of the governor took Jesus into the common hall, and gathered unto him the whole band of soldiers. 28. And they stripped him, and put on him a scarlet robe. 29. And when they had platted a crown of thorns, they put it upon his head, and a reed in his right hand: and they bowed the knee before him, and mocked him, saying, "Hail, King of the Jews!" 30. And they spit upon him, and took the reed, and smote him on the head. 31. And after that they had mocked him, they took the robe off from him, and put his own raiment on him, and led him away to crucify him.	16. And the soldiers led him away into the hall, called Prætorium; and they call together the whole band. 17. And they clothed him with purple, and platted a crown of thorns, and put it about his head, 18. And began to salute him, "Hail, King of the Jews!" 19. And they smote him on the head with a reed, and did spit upon him, and bowing their knees worshipped him. 20. And when they had mocked him, they took off the purple from him, and put his own clothes on him, and led him out to crucify him.	Then Pilate therefore took Jesus, and scourged him. 2. And the soldiers platted a crown of thorns, and put it on his head, and they put on him a purple robe, 3. And said, "Hail, King of the Jews!" and they smote him with their hands. 4. Pilate therefore went forth again, and saith unto them, "Behold, I bring him forth to you, that ye may know that I find no fault in him." 5. Then came Jesus forth, wearing the crown of thorns, and the purple robe. And Pilate saith unto them, "Behold the man." 6. When the chief priests therefore and officers saw him, they cried out, saying, "Crucify him, crucify him." Pilate saith unto them, "Take ye him, and crucify him: for I find no fault in him."

7. The Jews answered him, "We have a law, and by our law he ought to die, because he made himself the Son of God." 8. When Pilate therefore heard that saying, he was the more afraid; 9. And went again into

the judgement hall, and saith unto Jesus, "Whence art thou?" But Jesus gave him no answer. 10. Then saith Pilate unto him, " Speakest thou not unto me ? knowest thou not that I have power to crucify thee and have power to release thee?" 11. Jesus answered, " Thou couldest have no power at all against me, except it were given thee from above: therefore he that delivered me unto thee hath the greater sin."

12. And from thenceforth Pilate sought to release him : but the Jews cried out, saying, "If thou let this man go, thou art not Cæsar's friend : whosoever maketh himself a king speaketh against Cæsar." 13. When Pilate therefore heard that saying, he brought Jesus forth, and sat down in the judgement seat in a place that is called the Pavement, but in the Hebrew, Gabbatha.

14. And it was the preparation of passover and about the sixth hour: and he saith unto the Jews, " Behold your King!" 15. But they cried out, " Away with him, away with him, crucify him." Pilate saith unto them, " Shall I crucify your King!" The chief priests answered, "We have no king but Cæsar."

16. Then delivered he him therefore unto them to be crucified.

That the particulars of this trial are of a legendary character, and will not bear a close examination, must be evident to all who are acquainted with Roman history. It is well known that some years before the crucifixion of our Lord, Judæa had been taken possession of by the Romans, reduced to the form of a province, and was governed by a procurator. We learn from John, xviii, 31, as noticed in the foregoing harmony, that the Jews had no longer the power of life and death ; which supplies the reason why it was necessary to bring Jesus before the tribunal of Pilate. That he was so brought before the Roman procurator, is testified by all the evangelists ; but there lies at the outset a discrepancy between John and the other three, as to the place in which this trial was held. For St Matthew, St Mark, and St Luke, all assert that Jesus stood before the governor, and was there accused of many things by the chief priests and elders. But this could hardly be done if the priests and elders remained without and " went not into the judgement hall, lest they should be defiled, but that they might eat the passover." St John, who tells us this, adapts the circumstances of the trial to this beginning of it, and makes Pilate go backward and forward, out from the judgement hall to the people and again in from the people to examine Jesus further. This is said to have happened three times, according to St John, but nothing of the kind is told by the other evangelists ; which causes great perplexity to the mind in forming a true estimate of this remarkable trial. Perhaps there is probably no nation in the world in which the public administration of justice would be rendered so undignified, as that the chief magistrate should quit the judgement seat in the trial of a public criminal, and, in a question of life and death, go backwards and forwards between the accuser and the prisoner, that he might hear what they had to plead. It may be said without hesitation that no Roman governor ever condescended to an act which he would deem so derogatory to his rank and dignity. The writer of the fourth Gospel was no doubt embarrassed by the connection between Christ's death and the Jewish passover; and being aware that in his own previous narrative he had not identified the Last Supper with the paschal feast, he naturally supposed that it was still to come, in which case the Jewish rulers must not disqualify themselves from partaking of it by immediate contact even with the court of the governor. Whether any traditions had already been embodied into this form, out of which the fourth Gospel was compiled, is now uncertain, but this is not unlikely. We may therefore set aside this peculiar feature of St John's Gospel and suppose, with the other three, that accusers and accused stood before the governor.

2. We must next qualify another incident mentioned by St Luke alone, Pilate's sending Jesus to Herod, not because it would be incompatible with Roman customs; on the contrary, it was always agreeable to them that the allied kings should administer justice to their own subjects; but because it is related under many improbable circumstances by Luke, and related by him alone, and also because by admitting it as so related, we should have too many events to occupy the brief space of time which elapsed between the dawn of day and the crucifixion. That so singular an incident as the reference of a state prisoner to another tribunal should have escaped the notice of three out of four contemporary writers, is most significant, and this significancy is increased by the fact that none of their narratives present any break into which the omitted circumstance might be introduced. It is certain that they omitted it because they knew nothing about it. But if it had happened, they could not fail to know it, or, writing by inspiration, they could not but have been inspired with the knowledge of such an important incident. St Mark, at all events, ought to have known it by natural means; for we are told that he wrote what he had heard from St Peter, who was present in the high priest's palace, and no doubt followed his master into the Roman prætorium.

The most improbable circumstance about it is that Herod, a king, " with his men of war set him at nought, and mocked him, and arrayed him in a gorgeous robe, and sent him again to Pilate. It is inconceivable that a man of rank should condescend to such conduct, and would be hard to believe, even if it were recorded by all the evangelists. But as it is related by only one, we are driven to look round for a solution of the difficulty; and a solution at once presents itself in the equally remarkable fact, that this mockery of Jesus is related to have happened at four different times; first, by the servants of the high priest the night before (Luke xxii, 63): secondly, by Herod (Luke xxiii, 11): thirdly, by the Roman soldiers before the order for crucifixion was given (John xix, 2): and fourthly by the same after the order was issued (Matt. xxvii, 27; Mark xv, 17). We cannot resist the feeling that one such incident has here been multiplied into four. The probability is that Jesus was only once mocked—not by Herod who really wished to see Jesus, nor by the Roman soldiers, for that would have been unworthy of their general character, but by the servants of the chief priests, who were perhaps pleased with the opportunity of taunting him who had so often with his truthful irony taunted and baffled their masters.

That Jesus should have been sent to Herod at so early an hour in the morning, is inconceivable; and the multitude of events crowded into so small a space of time throws great improbability[1] on this particular incident; for we learn from Mark xv, 25, that Christ was crucified immediately after the trial, at the third hour or nine o'clock in the morning.

3. Another doubt, with respect to the details of Christ's trial before Pilate, arises from the discordant statements of the evangelists about his scourging Jesus. It is well known that Roman criminals condemned to death were scourged, *virgis cæsi*, before execution. That Jesus was so dealt with, we need not doubt, St Matthew, St Mark, and St John say so; "when he had scourged Jesus, he delivered him to be crucified." But St Luke, who does not actually say that Jesus was scourged, makes Pilate propose to the Jewish people that he should "chastise him and release him." This might be thought to be a flagrant act of injustice in most cases, not only according to the Roman, but to every other code of law or right. But in the inartistic and unprofessional style used by all the evangelists in describing this trial, it is rather difficult to detect the exact crime of which Jesus was accused. Pilate seems to have thought him an enthusiast, and if besides the charge of rebellion and sedition, he was accused of making a disturbance among the people,

---

[1] Herod was probably in Pilate's house at this time, and the difficulty is removed.

Pilate may have been willing to scourge him by way of warning, but not to sentence him to the punishment of death.

In ordinary cases of rebellion and sedition a Roman criminal, like an English criminal, was either found guilty or innocent. If guilty, he was scourged and executed, but if innocent, he was discharged without further suffering. Now all the four evangelists agree that Pilate declared Jesus to be innocent ; he clearly stated his opinion, "I find no fault in him," that is to say, of the more serious charge brought against him. We must therefore look for an explanation of these statements in the simplicity of the early Christians and their want of knowledge of the world. If Pilate had been fully convinced of Christ's innocence, he would probably not have condemned him, though it may be reasonably admitted that he was not unwilling to gratify the Jewish authorities, and therefore perhaps to look at the charges brought against the prisoner in a Jewish and not a Roman point of view.

4. The proceedings related to have taken place at the trial must be much qualified before they can be accepted as historical. The questions asked of Jesus have evidently assumed the irregular character likely to have been given them in later times by the Christians who, like all religious societies, were very little experienced in the ways of the world and possibly altogether ignorant of the formality belonging to a court of justice. In particular, the question "What hast thou done?"—asking the prisoner to state his own offence and convict himself—reminds one rather of a father's expostulation with his son, or of a master's castigation of his pupil than of a trial in a court of justice by the governor of a large and important province, conducted according to the laws of the greatest people that ever yet existed upon the earth.

5. Lastly ; there is a want of uniformity with respect to the custom pleaded by Pilate, of releasing one prisoner, and sacrificing another, on behalf of the people. This custom is nowhere mentioned by any historian, sacred or profane ; and it may be conjectured that the confused manner in which it is alluded to by the evangelists is a proof there was no very clear idea of its meaning or application even in their time. All the four tell us that it was customary for the governor to release unto them a prisoner whom they would ; and Dr Hammond, in a note on St Matthew's Gospel (xxvii, 15), says that "this *seems* not to have been the custom of the Jews, but introduced by the Roman governor as an act of grace, for the purpose of gaining popularity." Yet in John

xviii, 39, Pilate says, " *Ye* have a custom that I should release unto you one at the passover, &c." As if the custom were a Jewish, not a Roman custom—and it *was* Jewish, not Roman, if it prevailed at all ; for the whole of Roman history may be read in vain, without finding any notice of such a custom prevailing at any period of their existence. It may be suspected, indeed, from a passage in John xi, 49, 50, where Caiaphas counsels,

" That it is expedient for us that one man should die for the people," &c.

that some confusion has been made between an act of release and an act of sacrifice,*—that the idea of offering up an innocent victim has been moulded by time into that of releasing a guilty one—a proceeding much more conducive, if not to the glory of God, yet to peace and good-will among men.

CHAPTER XLII.

THE CRUCIFIXION.

THE execution of Jesus followed unusually soon after the sentence had been pronounced. He was brought before Pilate

MATTHEW xxvii, 32-66.	MARK xv, 21-47.
32. And as they came out, they found a man of Cyrene, Simon by name : him they compelled to bear his cross.	21. And they compel one Simon a Cyrenian, who passed by, coming out of the country, the father of Alexander and Rufus, to bear his cross.

---

* See the note about the scapegoat at page 357 of the first volume of this work.

at the dawn of day on the morning of what was perhaps the ninth of April, if, as is probable, the year in which this took place, was the thirtieth of the Christian era. We are also informed by St Mark (xv, 25) that he was crucified at nine o'clock in the morning, which according to the ancient mode of reckoning was the third hour of the day. The haste with which these proceedings were conducted may be explained in various ways. According to the narrative of St John, the Jews, expecting to eat the Passover in the evening of that day, might wish previously to be free from the charge of Jesus who had been given up to Pilate to be disposed of at their will. Or, if we adopt the statement of the other evangelists, that the Passover had been eaten the day before, yet even then, the next day being a Sabbath and being moreover a "high day," seeing that it fell within the Paschal week, they might equally wish to crucify Jesus in time that he might die and be buried, and not remain upon the cross during the ensuing Sabbath. We are indeed assured by Josephus that it was deemed of much importance among his countrymen that the bodies of criminals, who had suffered the extreme penalty of the law, should be buried before the close of day.

The crucifixion of Jesus is described by the four evangelists as follows:

LUKE xxiii, 26-56.	JOHN xix, 16-42.
26. And as they led him away, they laid hold upon one Simon, a Cyrenian, coming out of the country, and on him they laid the cross, that he might bear it after Jesus. 27. And there followed him a great company of people, and of women, which also bewailed and lamented him. 28. But Jesus turning unto them said, "Daughters of Jerusalem, weep not for me, but weep for yourselves, and for your children. 29. For, behold, the days are coming, in the which they shall say, Blessed are the barren, and the wombs that never bare, and the paps which never gave suck. 30. Then shall they begin to say to the mountains, Fall on us; and to the hills, Cover us. 31. For if they do these things in a green tree, what shall be done in the dry?" 32. And there were also two other, malefactors, led with him to be put to death.	16. And they took Jesus and led him away.

MATTHEW xxvii, 33-43.	MARK xv, 22-32.
33. And when they were come unto a place called Golgotha, that is to say, a place of a skull, 34. They gave him vinegar to drink mingled with gall: and when he had tasted thereof, he would not drink. 38. Then were there two thieves crucified with him, one on the right hand, and another on the left.	22. And they bring him unto the place Golgotha, which is, being interpreted, The place of a skull. 23. And they gave him to drink wine mingled with myrrh: but he received it not. 27. And with him they crucify two thieves; the one on his right hand, and the other on his left. 28. And the scripture was fulfilled, which saith, And he was numbered with the transgressors.
35. And they crucified him, and parted his garments, casting lots:	24. And when they had crucified him, they parted his garments, casting lots upon them, what every man should take. 25. And it was the third hour, and they crucified him.
that it might be fulfilled, which was spoken by the prophet, They parted my garments among them, and upon my vesture did they cast lots. 36. And sitting down they watched him there; 37. And set up over his head his accusation written, THIS IS JESUS THE KING OF THE JEWS.	26. And the superscription of his accusation was written over, THE KING OF THE JEWS.
39. And they that passed by reviled him, wagging their heads, 40. And saying, "Thou that destroyest the temple, and buildest it in three days, save thyself. If thou be the Son of God, come down from the cross." 41. Likewise also the chief priests mocking him, with the scribes and elders, said, 42. "He saved others; himself he cannot save. If he be the King of Israel, let him now come down from the cross, and we will believe him. 43. He trusted in God; let him deliver him now, if	29. And they that passed by railed on him, wagging their heads, and saying, "Ah, thou that destroyest the temple, and buildest it in three days, 30. Save thyself, and come down from the cross." 31. Likewise also the chief priests mocking said among themselves with the scribes, "He saved others; himself he cannot save. 32. Let Christ the King of Israel descend now from the cross, that we may see and believe."

THE CRUCIFIXION.

LUKE xxiii, 33-37.	JOHN xix, 17-22.
33. And when they were come to the place, which is called Calvary,	17. And he, bearing his cross, went forth into a place called the place of a skull, which is called in the Hebrew Golgotha:
there they crucified him, and the malefactors, one on the right hand, and the other on the left. 34. Then said Jesus, " Father, forgive them; for they know not what they do." And they parted his raiment, and cast lots.	18. Where they crucified him, and two other with him, on either side one, and Jesus in the midst. 23. Then the soldiers, when they had crucified Jesus, took his garments, and made four parts, to every soldier a part; and also his coat: now the coat was without seam, woven from the top throughout. 24. They said therefore among themselves, "Let us not rend it, but cast lots for it, whose it shall be:" that the scripture might be fulfilled, which saith, They parted my raiment among them, and for my vesture they did cast lots. These things therefore the soldiers did.
38. And a superscription also was written over him in letters of Greek, and Latin, and Hebrew, THIS IS THE KING OF THE JEWS.	19. And Pilate wrote a title, and put it on the cross. And the writing was, JESUS OF NAZARETH THE KING OF THE JEWS. 20. This title then read many of the Jews: for the place where Jesus was crucified was nigh to the city: and it was written in Hebrew, and Greek, and Latin. 21. Then said the chief priests of the Jews to Pilate, " Write not, The King of the Jews; but that he said, I am King of the Jews." 22. Pilate answered, " What I have written I have written."
35. And the people stood beholding.	

And the rulers also with them derided him, saying, "He saved others; let him save himself, if he be Christ, the chosen of God." 36. And the soldiers also mocked him, coming to him, and offering him vinegar, 37. And saying, "If thou be the king of the Jews, save thyself."

MATTHEW xxvii, 43-53.	MARK xv, 32-38.
he will have him: for he said, I am the Son of God." 44. The thieves also, which were crucified with him, cast the same in his teeth.	And they that were crucified with him reviled him.
55. And many women were there beholding afar off, which followed Jesus from Galilee, ministering unto him: 56. Among which was Mary Magdalene, and Mary the mother of James and Joses, and the mother of Zebedee's children.	40. There were also women looking on afar off: among whom was Mary Magdalene, and Mary the mother of James the less and of Joses, and Salome; 41. (Who also, when he was in Galilee, followed him, and ministered unto him;) and many other women which came up with him unto Jerusalem.
45. Now from the sixth hour there was darkness over all the land unto the ninth hour. 46. And about the ninth hour Jesus cried with a loud voice, saying, "Eli, Eli, lama sabachthani?" that is to say, My God, my God, why hast thou forsaken me? 47. Some of them that stood there, when they heard that, said, "This man calleth for Elias." 48. And straightway one of them ran and took a spunge, and filled it with vinegar, and put it on a reed, and gave him to drink. 49. And the rest said, "Let be, let us see whether Elias will come to save him." 50. Jesus, when he had cried again with a loud voice, yielded up the ghost. 51. And, behold, the veil of the temple was rent in twain from the top to the bottom; and the earth did quake, and the rocks rent; 52. And the graves were opened; and many bodies of the saints which slept arose, 53. And came out of the graves after his resurrection,	33. And when the sixth hour was come, there was darkness over the whole land until the ninth hour. 34. And at the ninth hour Jesus cried with a loud voice, saying, "Eloi, Eloi, lama sabachthani?" which is, being interpreted, My God, my God, why hast thou forsaken me? 35. And some of them that stood by, when they heard it, said, "Behold, he calleth Elias." 36. And one ran and filled a spunge full of vinegar, and put it on a reed, and gave him to drink, saying, "Let alone; let us see whether Elias will come to take him down." 37. And Jesus cried with a loud voice, and gave up the ghost. 38. And the veil of the temple was rent in twain from the top to the bottom.

THE CRUCIFIXION.

LUKE xxiii, 39-46.   JOHN xix, 25-30.

39. And one of the malefactors which were hanged railed on him, saying, "If thou be Christ, save thyself and us."
40. But the other answering rebuked him, saying, "Dost not thou fear God, seeing thou art in the same condemnation?
41. And we indeed justly; for we receive the due reward of our deeds: but this man hath done nothing amiss."
42. And he said unto Jesus, "Lord, remember me when thou comest into thy kingdom."
43. And Jesus said unto him, "Verily I say unto thee, To day shalt thou be with me in paradise."
49. And all his acquaintance, and the women that followed him from Galilee, stood afar off, beholding these things.

25. Now there stood by the cross of Jesus his mother, and his mother's sister, Mary the wife of Cleophas, and Mary Magdalene. 26. When Jesus therefore saw his mother, and the disciple standing by, whom he loved, he saith unto his mother, "Woman, behold thy son!" 27. Then saith he to the disciple, "Behold thy mother!" And from that hour that disciple took her unto his own home.

44. And it was about the sixth hour, and there was a darkness over all the earth until the ninth hour. 45. And the sun was darkened, and the veil of the temple was rent in the midst.

28. After this, Jesus knowing that all things were now accomplished, that the scripture might be fulfilled, saith, "I thirst." 29. Now there was set a vessel full of vinegar: and they filled a spunge with vinegar, and put it upon hyssop, and put it to his mouth. 30. When Jesus therefore had received the vinegar,

46. And when Jesus had cried with a loud voice, he said, "Father, into thy hands I commend my spirit:" and having said thus, he gave up the ghost.

he said, "It is finished:" and he bowed his head, and gave up the ghost.

MATTHEW xxvii, 54-60.	MARK xv, 39-46.
and went into the holy city, and appeared unto many. 54. Now when the centurion, and they that were with him, watching Jesus, saw the earthquake, and those things that were done, they feared greatly, saying, "Truly this was the Son of God."	39. And when the centurion, which stood over against him, saw that he so cried out, and gave up the ghost, he said, "Truly this man was the Son of God."
57. When the even was come,	42. And now when the even was come, because it was the preparation, that is, the day before the sabbath,
there came a rich man of Arimathæa, named Joseph, who also himself was Jesus' disciple: 58. He went to Pilate, and begged the body of Jesus. Then Pilate commanded the body to be delivered.	43. Joseph of Arimathæa, an honourable counsellor, which also waited for the kingdom of God, came, and went in boldly unto Pilate, and craved the body of Jesus. 44. And Pilate marvelled if he were already dead: and calling unto him the centurion, he asked him whether he had been any while dead. 45. And when he knew it of the centurion, he gave the body to Joseph.
59. And when Joseph had taken the body, he wrapped it in a clean linen cloth, 60. And laid it in his own new tomb, which he had hewn out in the rock: and he rolled a great stone to the door of the sepulchre, and departed.	46. And he bought fine linen, and took him down, and wrapped him in the linen, and laid him in a sepulchre which was hewn out of a rock, and rolled a stone unto the door of the sepulchre.

LUKE xxiii, 47-54.   JOHN xix, 31-42.

47. Now when the centurion saw what was done, he glorified God, saying, "Certainly this was a righteous man." 48. And all the people that came together to that sight, beholding the things which were done, smote their breasts, and returned.

31. The Jews, therefore, because it was the preparation, that the bodies should not remain upon the cross on the sabbath day, (for that sabbath day was an high day,) besought Pilate that their legs might be broken, and that they might be taken away. 32. Then came the soldiers, and brake the legs of the first, and of the other which was crucified with him. 33. But when they came to Jesus, and saw that he was dead already, they brake not his legs: 34. But one of the soldiers with a spear pierced his side, and forthwith came thereout blood and water. 35. And he that saw it bare record, and his record is true: and he knoweth that he saith true, that ye might believe. 36. For these things were done, that the scripture should be fulfilled, A bone of him shall not be broken. 37. And again another scripture saith, They shall look on him whom they pierced.

50. And behold, there was a man named Joseph, a counsellor; and he was a good man, and a just: 51. (The same had not consented to the counsel and deed of them :) he was of Arimathæa, a city of the Jews: who also himself waited for the kingdom of God. 52. This man went unto Pilate, and begged the body of Jesus. 53. And he took it down, and wrapped it in linen, and laid it in a sepulchre that was hewn in stone, wherein never man before was laid. 54. And that day was the preparation, and the sabbath drew on.

38. And after this Joseph of Arimathæa, being a disciple of Jesus, but secretly for fear of the Jews, besought Pilate that he might take away the body of Jesus: and Pilate gave him leave. He came therefore, and took the body of Jesus. 39. And there came also Nicodemus, which at the first came to Jesus by night, and brought a mixture of myrrh and aloes, about an hundred pound weight. 40. Then took they the body of Jesus, and wound it in linen clothes with the spices, as the manner of the Jews is to bury. 41. Now in the place where he was crucified there was a garden; and in the garden a new sepulchre, wherein was never man yet laid. 42. There laid they Jesus therefore because of the Jews' preparation day, for the sepulchre was nigh at hand.

MATTHEW xxvii, 61-66.

61. And there was Mary Magdalene, and the other Mary, sitting over against the sepulchre.
62. Now the next day, that followed the day of the preparation, the chief priests and Pharisees came together unto Pilate, 63. Saying, "Sir, we remember that that deceiver said, while he was yet alive, After three days I will arise again. 64. Command therefore that the sepulchre be made sure until the third day, lest his disciples come by night, and steal him away, and say unto the people, He is risen from the dead: so the last error shall be worse than the first." 65. Pilate said unto them, "Ye have a watch: go your way, make it as sure as ye can." 66. So they went, and made the sepulchre sure, sealing the stone, and setting a watch.

MARK xv, 47.

47. And Mary Magdalene and Mary the mother of Joses beheld where he was laid.

In comparing these four narratives, we observe that St John, as usual, follows a different line of description from the other three, occasionally making us acquainted with facts which they have omitted, as often omitting circumstances which they have related, and frequently relating the same facts in a manner so contradictory to theirs, that no further argument is needful to prove his Gospel to be a distinct work, and not, as is commonly supposed, supplementary to the others.

There are seven points of divergency in the foregoing harmony; some of which are irreconcilable even by the widest conjecture, whilst all militate against the contemporary character of the writings.

1. In the first place St John says that Jesus bore his own cross to the place of execution, called in Hebrew Golgotha: but St Matthew, St Mark, and St Luke relate that the soldiers laid hold on one Simon a Cyrenian, who was accidentally passing by, and compelled him to carry the cross. The account of John is the most likely to be true; for it was part of the Roman punishment of crucifixion that the criminal should bear his own cross. The opposite statement, though told by three writers, is also less likely, because of the injustice done to Simon an innocent passer-by—for it was not a period of revolution among the Jews, when such an outrage might happen, but of regular lawful government. Some of the German commentators have supposed that the

LUKE xxiii, 55, 56.

55. And the women also, which came with him from Galilee, followed after, and beheld the sepulchre, and how his body was laid. 56. And they returned, and prepared spices and ointments; and rested the sabbath day according to the commandment.

---

designation of Simon, "father of Alexander and Rufus," added by Mark, was intended to refer to two persons known in after times as "Alexander the coppersmith" and "Rufus chosen in the Lord," both of whom are named in various passages of the New Testament, though not in connection with Alexander here mentioned.* Others have imagined that the services of Simon were needful, in consequence of our Lord having fainted beneath the weight of the cross. Both of these ideas are conjectural. The absurd legend, of much later growth, and propagated by the followers of Basileides, that the Cyrenian was thrown in the way by Providence, and was crucified instead of Jesus, need not arrest our attention one moment.

2. A serious discrepancy between John and the other three evangelists concerns the time of the day at which Christ was first tried before Pilate and then crucified. St John (xix, 14) says that it was "about the sixth hour," that is 12 o'clock at noon, when Pilate, in the course of the trial, said "Behold your king." But St Mark (xv, 25) says, "it was the third hour," that is, 9 o'clock in the morning "when they crucified him." It has been suggested, and the suggestion is reasonable, that the Greek numeral *hekté* sixth has been written erroneously for *trité* third in one of the Gos-

---

* See Acts xix, 33; Romans xvi, 13; 1 Timothy i, 20; and 2 Timothy iv, 14: but these evidently were different men of the same name.

pels, or that *trité* has been written erroneously for *hekté* in the other. And it has been said that this emendation is supported by a few MSS that once existed. This is of course a mere conjecture, and we cannot doubt that such a discrepancy between the evangelists would long since have been removed, if it had not been due, not to a clerical error but to a real difference of statement. Another explanation has been given, which will commend itself still less to the judgement of the reader. It has been attempted to show that St John followed a different notation of time from the other three writers: but no conjectural arrangement of the day or mode of calculating time will explain away the difference of three hours which must have elapsed between the third hour named by St Mark and the sixth named by St John. There is not the slightest proof that St John used a different calculation of time, and if he did so, whether by divine inspiration, or by the ordinary mode of procuring information, his leaving us in ignorance of the fact would weaken the authority of any writing in which such an omission had been made. If one of the two accounts is to be rejected, that of St John would seem preferable, because it allows a more reasonable interval for the various incidents which preceded the condemnation of Jesus, than that which results from accepting the early hour in the morning according to the Gospel of St Mark.

3. The third point which requires to be noticed is the fact that some liquor was given to Jesus by those who were present at the crucifixion; but the account of this fact is not the same in the four narratives, nor would it be easy, even if it were important, to discover the real nature of the incident. In the first place, St Matthew tells us that, before the crucifixion, the soldiers gave him vinegar to drink mingled with gall; and that afterwards about the ninth hour, which would be about 3 o'clock in the afternoon, when he would have been six hours on the cross, he cried out "Eli, Eli, lama sabacthani!" upon which one of them that stood by, "ran and took a sponge, and filled it with vinegar, and put it on a reed and gave him to drink."

The account given by St Mark does not differ greatly from the foregoing; but it departs in two particulars from this agreement: instead of vinegar and gall, it is now wine and myrrh that are offered to Jesus the first time, and the second time, when he who ran and got the sponge, gave him it filled with vinegar, whilst we read in Matthew that the rest of the bystanders said in ridicule, "Let alone, let us see whether Elias will come to take him down!" in Mark it is the man himself who offered the vinegar, that used those words.

In the next place, we find in St Luke's Gospel no mention of gall or myrrh; but only that the soldiers "mocked him, coming to him and offering him vinegar," but whether this was done at the beginning, or at the end, just before Jesus breathed his last, does not appear from the narrative of St Luke, where nothing is said of a second offering of vinegar, but only of one such offering made in mockery, whereas neither of the two draughts in Matthew and in Mark was made in mockery, but rather with a benevolent purpose, as perhaps it was customary to do in such cases.

Lastly, in St John's Gospel nothing is said of gall or myrrh, but that "there was set a vessel full of vinegar, and they filled a sponge with vinegar, and put it upon hyssop [*i.e.* a stalk or reed of hyssop] and put it to his mouth:" and it is added that this was done at the request of Jesus himself, who exclaimed "I thirst!"

The divergences in these four narratives are of remarkably little importance, if we explain them reasonably, but if we regard all the four as distinct inspirations, it may justly be asked why one of the evangelists should be directed to speak of a sponge filled with vinegar and placed on a reed of hyssop, whilst the others speak, one of gall, another of myrrh, and the fourth mention none of these details, seeing also that they all vary as to the cause or occasion, for which the draught was offered at all to Jesus on the cross. That the writers of these narratives were not eye-witnesses of what they relate may be inferred from the fact that according to St Luke the soldiers offer Jesus drink in mockery, whilst in the other Gospels it is offered seriously, and it would seem that neither of the writers seems to have had an exact idea of the occurrence, but each wrote faithfully what had come down to him from the memoranda of others or by tradition. Neither of them seems to have been aware that the vinegar named in the Gospels was probably the small sour wine used still in many foreign countries as the ordinary drink of the people, and that, when mingled with myrrh or gall, it was offered to Jesus in kindness, or possibly by custom, for the purpose of deadening the pain of crucifixion: and this perhaps afterwards presented an appearance of mockery to those, who, a hundred and twenty years later, received what was told them by their elders, without having the means of testing the details of the history more accurately for themselves.

4. The words of Christ, as he was hanging on the cross,

are variously reported by the four evangelists, and in particular his last exclamation immediately before his death. The dying words of eminent men are always of interest and have often been recorded in history ; but in hardly one case out of a hundred is there any variation in the accounts about the exact words spoken. In the case of our Lord, however, it is impossible to reconcile the divergent reports of his last words upon the cross. With the exception that Matthew and Mark agree in making him speak twice only, first, " Eli, Eli, lama sabachthani," and then, his last cry, before he died, the other two evangelists differ from both of these, and, multiplying the number of Christ's speeches, differ wholly from one another. For instance, St Luke takes no notice of the exclamation " Eli, eli, lama sabachthani," but tells us of a dialogue between Christ and the thieves ; after which he says that Jesus cried with a loud voice, and, having exclaimed " Father, into thy hands I commend my spirit," gave up the ghost. St John, however, knows nothing of all this, but in its place has a dialogue with Christ's mother, and with the beloved disciple,—" Woman, behold thy son !" " Behold thy mother !" after which he exclaims, " I thirst," and then with the words " It is finished !" bows his head and gives up the ghost. Now in these passages St John and St Luke contradict one another : the one says the last words were " Father, into thy hands I commend my spirit ;" the other says the words were "It is finished." The difference is unimportant—perhaps both these cries were uttered, and we might not wonder at two writers having described the matter differently, if it were not generally believed that both of those writers drew their history as well as their doctrines, not from human sources but from inspiration.

5. A fifth variation between the evangelists is found in their account of the two thieves crucified with Jesus. In Matthew they " cast the same in his teeth ;" in Mark they " revile him :" but in Luke, it is only one of the malefactors that reviles Christ, the other repents, and confessing his sins, is promised immediate happiness with Christ in paradise. The only reasonable explanation of this difference is, that the first two evangelists did not know of the exact particulars, which have been recorded more at length by Luke.

6. The inscription, placed by Pilate upon the cross, occurs in four different forms, according to the Gospel in which it is found ;

MATTHEW has—This is Jesus the King of the Jews.
MARK has—The King of the Jews.

LUKE has—This is the King of the Jews.
JOHN has—Jesus of Nazareth the King of the Jews.

As the value of inscriptions depends wholly upon their being faithfully and exactly copied, it is evident that the inscription now under consideration cannot be relied on for accuracy, but has been handed down in a popular form by divers traditions, each of which has been adopted by one or other of the four evangelists.

7. Neither can we form a very accurate idea of the mode in which the soldiers cast lots for Christ's clothing, seeing that all the accounts of it are vague and discordant.

St Matthew describes the process as if he thought they cast lots on all Christ's garments alike—" they parted his garments, casting lots."

St Mark, following the same idea, explains it more fully, " parted his garments, casting lots upon them, what every man should take."

St Luke uses the very general expression—" parted his garments, and cast lots."

The notion which these terms convey is clearly to the effect that the whole of Christ's clothing was divided into portions, and lots were then drawn, to determine what portion each soldier should take. This interpretation is not weakened by St Matthew's application of a prophecy from the Old Testament to this subject, " They parted my garments among them, and upon my vesture did they cast lots " (*Ps.* xxii, 18): for there is a distinction made in our translation between *garments* and *vesture*, where there is virtually no distinction in the original Greek, ἱμάτια and ἱματισμός. Indeed, even in English, it would be difficult to point out a real difference between *garments* and *vesture*. The truth is that in the connective *and* lies the cause of the confusion. We should read "*even* upon my vesture did they cast lots," and we come to the same conclusion that all the articles of Christ's clothing were distributed by lot among the soldiers.

Turning then to the Fourth Gospel, we find a much more detailed account of the matter. It appears from St John that there were four soldiers, and that the clothes were divided into four parts, one of which in consequence was given without lot to each. But the tunic, χιτών—" coat " in our version of the New Testament—being of a peculiar make, woven in one piece without seam throughout, was not cut into four parts, but reserved entire as having a peculiar value and significance, for which the four soldiers cast lots separately. It is also to be remarked that the same text from the Old Testament is quoted by St John in illustrating this story, which has been already named as quoted by St Matthew. A thought here comes into the mind, which possibly may be accepted as an explanation. Did not St John's narrative grow out of the Greek version of the supposed prophecy, in which there is a fanciful distinction between ἱμάτια garments and ἱματισμός vesture? It is known that popular prophecies tend to bring about their own fulfilment. If it was so here, which looks in every way probable, the idea of the lot having been applied to the *tunic* or seamless coat, has gradually grown out of the necessity of harmonizing the incident with the prophecy of it found in the Book of Psalms.

7. We come to the seventh and last point of difference between the four Gospels concerning those persons who were present at the consummation of Christ's miraculous career.

We learn from St Matthew that there were present, 1. The centurion and Roman soldiers. 2. The chief priests, scribes, and elders, who mocked him saying, " He saved others &c." 3. Many " women, which followed Jesus from Galilee, ministering unto him: among which was Mary Magdalene, and Mary the mother of James and Joses, and the mother of Zebedee's children." Two of these women, Mary Magdalene and the other Mary, followed Christ's body to the sepulchre, and sat down over against it. In St Mark's Gospel also we have Mary Magdalene, and Mary the mother of James the less and Joses, but instead of " the mother of Zebedee's children" is the more particular definition of " Salome," which is supposed to be the name of the same person.

In St Luke's Gospel the names of the women are not given, but some additional circumstances are added. We read that " a great company of people followed him," and " of women, which also bewailed and lamented him." It was to these that Jesus turned and uttered that beautiful address, "Daughters of Jerusalem, weep not for me, but weep for yourselves and for your children"—and if he had ended there, the picture would have been complete, but Luke makes him add, if not without meaning, yet certainly so as to weaken the force of the preceding apostrophe, parts of an address which he had delivered some time before (see Luke xxi, 23), and some words which occur almost verbatim in the Septuagint version of the prophet Hosea (x, 8).

It appears also from verse 49, that all his acquaintance, and the women that followed him from Galilee, stood afar off, beholding his crucifixion.

Between these particulars, recorded on the one hand by Matthew, Mark and Luke, and on the other hand by John, there is not a perfect agreement, for the latter says that the women who followed Christ were his mother's sister the *wife* of Cleophas, and Mary Magdalene, and that they stood " by the cross," and not "afar off," as in Luke's Gospel. Besides these women, the beloved disciple generally thought to be St John was present, and received his master's parting admonition to take charge of his bereaved mother.

The list of the women does not coincide with that given by the other evangelists: they say nothing of Mary the mother of Christ, which is a remarkable omission, and alone is enough to prove the traditional character of the writings. St John moreover does not mention Salome, the mother of Zebedee's children, and instead of Mary the mother of James and Joses, he has Mary the wife of Cleophas. It is not certain that these designations point to the same person: for, at Matthew x, 3, we find that James, commonly called the less, was the son, not of Cleophas, but of Alpheus; and there is no proof that Alpheus and Cleophas were the same person, as some of our commentators have gratuitously assumed. An additional difficulty is occasioned by the mention of the sister of Christ's mother being present. The words are so closely connected with " Mary the wife of Cleophas," that they are generally thought to describe the same person. If so, two sisters bore the same name, Mary: a most remarkable and improbable circumstance in those days, when persons bore only one proper name, and likely to result in great family confusion.

CHAPTER XLIII.

The Resurrection of Christ and the Witnesses thereof.

WE have seen in the preceding chapters that the exact order of time and other particulars regarding the last supper of our Lord with his disciples and the events incidental to his seizure, trial, and crucifixion, cannot now be clearly ascertained. The interval, however, of a Jewish sabbath, or day of rest, when no one stirred abroad, and consequently no fresh events happened requiring to be noticed, gives us a fresh point for starting, and we find that all the four evangelists present a tolerable agreement as to the momentous occurrences which next follow. It is not to be denied that some critics, in a spirit of captiousness as it would seem, object to the terms employed by the several gospel-writers to describe the point of time when the scene re-opens with a visit made by certain women to the tomb of Jesus. Matthew relates that "it was at the end of the sabbath, as it began to dawn toward the first day of the week," and St John tells us that it was early, " when it was yet dark ": but these terms, though apparently contradictory, are yet not so, for who does not know that the dawn begins to show itself faintly in the heavens, whilst the face of the heaven is still dark, though not perhaps densely dark? Strictly speaking, also, the end of the Sabbath means Saturday evening, after six o'clock ; but the qualifying words, "as it began to dawn towards the first day of the week," show plainly that St Matthew was speaking not of

MATTHEW xxviii, 1-15.	MARK xvi, 1-11.
In the end of the sabbath, as it began to dawn toward the first day of the week, came Mary Magdalene and the other Mary to see the sepulchre.	And when the sabbath was past, Mary Magdalene, and Mary the mother of James, and Salome, had bought sweet spices, that they might come and anoint him.
	2. And very early in the morning the first day of the week, they came unto the sepulchre at the rising of the sun.
	3. And they said among themselves, "Who shall roll us away the stone from the door of the sepulchre?"
2. And, behold, there was a great earthquake: for the angel of the Lord descended from heaven, and came and rolled back the stone from the door, and sat upon it.	4. And when they looked, they saw that the stone was rolled away, for it was very great :
3. His countenance was like lightning, and his raiment white as snow: 4. And for fear of him the keepers did shake, and became as dead men. 5. And the angel answered and said unto the women, " Fear not ye : for I know that ye seek Jesus, which was crucified. 6. He is not here : for he is risen, as he said. Come, see the place where the Lord lay. 7. And go quickly, and tell his disciples that he is risen from the dead ; and, behold, he goeth before you into Gali-	5. And entering into the sepulchre, they saw a young man sitting on the right side, clothed in a long white garment; and they were affrighted. 6. And he saith unto them, " Be not affrighted: Ye seek Jesus of Nazareth, which was crucified ; he is risen; he is not here: behold the place where they laid him. 7. But go your way, tell his disciples and Peter that he goeth before you into Galilee : there shall ye see him, as he said unto you."

the evening, but of the morning after the sabbath. The chief difficulty which attends the comparison of the four narratives is the observation of St Mark, "They came unto the sepulchre at the rising of the sun." If the sun were just rising, it could not be yet dark, though probably the interval between the time of the women's setting out from home and their arrival at the sepulchre, in countries near the equator where there is not much twilight, may have been long enough to account for the different descriptions used by the evangelists. After all, it appears unnecessary to harmonize statements which do not differ much from one another; they point out, within an hour or two probably, the time at which the women named by the evangelists set out on a visit to Christ's tomb very early on the morning after his crucifixion. Here however their agreement ends, and we find a series of facts related by all of them, but in so different a manner, that it is impossible to harmonize them exactly.

LUKE xxiv, 1-12.	JOHN xx, 1-18.
Now upon the first day of the week, very early in the morning, they came unto the sepulchre, bringing the spices which they had prepared, and certain others with them,	The first day of the week cometh Mary Magdalene early, when it was yet dark, unto the sepulchre,
2. And they found the stone rolled away from the sepulchre.	and seeth the stone taken away from the sepulchre.
3. And they entered in, and found not the body of the Lord Jesus. 4. And it came to pass, as they were much perplexed thereabout, behold, two men stood by them in shining garments: 5. And as they were afraid, and bowed down their faces to the earth, they said unto them, "Why seek ye the living among the dead? 6. He is not here, but is risen: remember how he spake unto you when he was yet in Galilee, 7. Saying, The Son of man must be delivered into the	

MATTHEW xxviii, 7-15.
lee; there shall ye see him: lo, I have told you."

8. And they departed quickly from the sepulchre with fear and great joy; and did run to bring his disciples word. 9. And as they went to tell his disciples, behold, Jesus met them, saying, "All hail." And they came and held him by the feet, and worshipped him. 10. Then said Jesus unto them, "Be not afraid: go tell my brethren that they go into Galilee, and there shall they see me."

11. Now when they were going, behold, some of the watch came into the city, and showed unto the chief priests all the things that were done.
12. And when they were assembled with the elders, and had taken counsel, they gave large money unto the soldiers,
13. Saying, "Say ye, His disciples came by night, and stole him away while we slept.
14. And if this come to the governor's ears, we will persuade him, and secure you."
15. So they took the money, and did as they were taught: and this saying is commonly reported among the Jews until this day.

MARK xvi, 8-11.

8. And they went out quickly, and fled from the sepulchre: for they trembled and were amazed: neither said they any thing to any man; for they were afraid.

9. Now when Jesus was risen early the first day of the week, he appeared first to Mary Magdalene, out of whom he had cast seven devils. 10. And she went and told them that had been with him, as they mourned and wept. 11. And they, when they had heard that he was alive, and had been seen of her, believed not.

LUKE xxiv, 8-12.	JOHN xx, 2-16.
hands of sinful men, and be crucified, and the third day rise again." 8. And they remembered his words, 9. And returned from the sepulchre, and told all these things unto the eleven, and to all the rest.	2. Then she runneth, and cometh to Simon Peter, and to the other disciple, whom Jesus loved, and saith unto them, "They have taken the Lord out of the sepulchre, and we know not where they have laid him."
10. It was Mary Magdalene, and Joanna, and Mary the mother of James, and other women that were with them, which told these things unto the apostles.	
11. And their words seemed to them as idle tales, and they believed them not. 12. Then arose Peter, and ran unto the sepulchre; and stooping down, he beheld the linen clothes laid by themselves, and departed, wondering in himself at that which was come to pass.	3. Peter therefore went forth, and that other disciple, and came to the sepulchre. 4. So they ran both together: and the other disciple did outrun Peter, and came first to the sepulchre. 5. And he stooping down, and looking in, saw the linen clothes lying; yet went he not in. 6. Then cometh Simon Peter following him, and went into the sepulchre, and seeth the linen clothes lie. 7. And the napkin, that was about his head, not lying with the linen clothes, but wrapped together in a place by itself. 8. Then went in also that other disciple, which came first to the sepulchre, and he saw, and believed. 9. For as yet they knew not the scripture, that he must rise again from the dead.

10. Then the disciples went away again unto their own home.
11. But Mary stood without at the sepulchre weeping: and as she wept, she stooped down, and looked into the sepulchre, 12. And seeth two angels in white sitting, the one at the head, and the other at the feet, where the body of Jesus had lain. 13. And they say unto her, "Woman, why weepest thou?" She saith unto them, "Because they have taken away my Lord, and I know not where they have laid him."
14. And when she had thus said, she turned herself back, and saw Jesus standing, and knew not that it was Jesus. 15. Jesus saith unto her, "Woman, why weepest thou? whom seekest thou?" She, supposing him to be the gardener, saith unto him, "Sir, if thou have borne him hence, tell me where thou hast laid him, and I will take him away." 16. Jesus saith unto her, "Mary!" She turned herself, and saith unto him, "Rab-

boni;" which is to say, Master. 17. Jesus saith unto her, "Touch me not; for I am not yet ascended to my Father: but go to my brethren, and say unto them, I ascend unto my Father, and your Father; and to my God, and your God."

18. Mary Magdalene came and told the disciples that she had seen the Lord, and that he had spoken these things unto her.

When we examine the four narratives here placed in juxtaposition, it is impossible not to notice several remarkable divergences and other peculiarities which we might fancy very unlikely to occur if the writers had been so closely connected with the events which they describe.

1. We may first observe that according to St Matthew, Mary Magdalene and a woman, whom he calls "the other Mary," go to see the sepulchre early on the morning after the Sabbath, which is thus fixed to have been on Sunday morning of the third day from the Crucifixion, according to the Jewish mode of reckoning. St Mark tells us that the women were Mary Magdalene, Mary of James, and Salome: and the translators insert the word mother into our version, as do also the Arabic, Syriac, and Persian translations of the Gospel, although no similar word of parentage is inserted in either the Latin Vulgate, the Ethiopic, or the Greek text. Thus St Mark describes three women, and St Matthew only two. But St Luke's account represents a larger number of women visiting the sepulchre on that morning. Not only Mary Magdalene and Mary the [mother] of James, but instead of Salome, we meet with Joanna, who is elsewhere called the wife of Chusa Herod's steward, and others also, but Salome is not named. Lastly St John names Mary Magdalene only as coming to the sepulchre at that early hour. The explanation given by harmonists and commentators is that each writer has named such women as suited his particular object. But what object could the writers have for making such diverse statements on so simple a subject? There is no ground for believing that the four evangelists wrote each for a special purpose: this is the conjecture of those who find it convenient to have such a basis on which to rest other conclusions equally conjectural. It is more reasonable to suppose that each writer recorded what he had been told or had been able to find out, and that, as tradition varied, so also is there a variation in their accounts. It is true that John was the only disciple who could claim to have been an eye-witness, and he, at least, leaves no room for doubting that Mary Magdalene went alone to the tomb. No sooner did she see that it was

empty than she ran off, which was a most natural thing to do if she was alone, but equally unnatural if any other woman was in her company. This feature of St John's Gospel shows that his account at least cannot be harmonized with the others, though they may perhaps, even as far as this point is concerned, be brought into something like a conventional agreement.

2. But the object which the men had in view by making so early a visit to the tomb, involves a second discrepancy, between St Matthew and St John, who take one view of the matter, and St Mark and St Luke, who take the other. The first and fourth evangelists allege no other motive on the part of the women than the wish, which was exceedingly natural, of seeing again the tomb of their beloved master. But St Mark and St Luke attribute to them the wish to embalm the body of Jesus. We have no means of determining which of these motives was the real one, but, if it should be thought that Mark and Luke have stated the case correctly, it is remarkable that Matthew and John, both of whom were of the number of the twelve apostles, and the latter an eye-witness, should have omitted such a fact, whilst the other two evangelists, who were neither eye-witnesses nor apostles, should have added it. A certain degree of preference may perhaps be claimed for Matthew and John, on the ground, that Joseph of Arimathæa is said to have already embalmed the body before it was consigned to the tomb, but even this fact seems to be involved in as much difficulty as that which it is adduced to illustrate.*

3. A third, and still more serious discrepancy is found in the different ways in which the appearance of the angels is recorded. Matthew mentions only *one angel;* who " descended from heaven, and came and rolled back the stone from the door and sat upon it." This took place of course outside the tomb, and the angel was probably sitting on the stone, when the women came up. The guard of soldiers had fled, frightened at the earthquake and the appearance of the angel, and were therefore no longer there at the arrival of the women. This at least seems more probable, than that the angel came and rolled away the stone, when the women and the soldiers were still present. Mark however relates,

---

* Some writers have doubted whether the practice of embalming existed among the Jews. See II *Chronicles,* xvi, 14, where something is named that seems to be similar to what was done to Jesus : but we know nothing certain on the subject.

that they found the stone rolled away, and entering in, saw a young man sitting on the right side, clothed in a long white garment. St Luke relates, with Mark, that they found the stone rolled away, and entered in; where, as they were perplexed at not finding Christ's body, *two men* stood by them in shining garments. Lastly St John says that Mary Magdalene, finding the tomb empty, ran to call Peter, and having returned in his company, remained behind when he left the tomb, and then, on looking into the tomb, saw two angels in white, sitting, the one at the head, and the other at the feet, where the body of Jesus had lain. It is plain that where the four narratives differ so totally, it is impossible to harmonize them in any other way than by multiplying the vision of the angels and the visits of the women in a surprising manner, and by supposing that the writers closed their eyes to every thing except the very fact which they were relating, no matter how it might be surrounded by other incidents which in the eyes of another writer would give it a totally different character, and lead to a wholly different description. If we were called upon to determine the real nature of the appearances of the angels, as recorded in any other work, it might not be difficult to set aside all the divergencies that lie between the four narratives, and so to extract what remains as common to them all. From such a process we should infer that Mary Magdalene, for certain, and perhaps also some other women in her company, went at an early hour to see the sepulchre of Jesus, and that, when they arrived there, an angel, or perhaps two, appeared and told them that Jesus was already risen. This original and simple story, handed down by tradition, had grown, after a hundred years or more, into the varied narratives which we find in our present gospels.

4. A fourth difference between the evangelists in their description of the same eventful morning, concerns the visit of Peter to the sepulchre. Here again, each writer has a different mode of viewing the matter.

According to St Matthew, the women, as instructed by the angel, go and tell the disciples that their master was risen from the dead, but nothing is said of Peter's visit to the tomb.

In St Mark's gospel, the same turn is given to the account; but the words of the angel are "Go your way, tell his disciples *and Peter* &c." Still the writer does not add that Peter went to the sepulchre to see what had happened.

It is in the third gospel that we first find a hint of this

fact. It is there stated that the women reported what they had seen to the apostles who received the announcement as an idle tale. " Then arose Peter and ran unto the sepulchre; and stooping down, he beheld the linen clothes laid by themselves, and departed, wondering in himself at that which was come to pass." This visit, it will be observed, is still unconnected with that of Mary Magdalene, and is later in point of time.

But in St John's Gospel, the story receives several new features. Mary Magdalene alone runs and calls Peter, to whom John is added, and all three return to the tomb. Peter and John then depart, leaving Mary Magdalene alone; and all this precedes both the appearance of the angels to her and her announcement of Christ's resurrection to the whole body of the apostles. In deciding between the two, whilst, on the one hand, we recognize the supposed authority which John might claim as an eye-witness, yet, on the other hand, his account is less probable than that of the other evangelists, because it multiplies the visits both of the women and of the disciples; because it is less simple than the other accounts; and because it is not likely that Peter and John would have left Mary Magdalene alone weeping at the tomb.

5. A remarkable incident among those which occur at the sepulchre is the appearance of Christ himself to the women, as they leave the spot to fulfil the commands of the angel. In the relation of this occurrence, Mark is more concise than Matthew, but without any other points of difference. St John tells the story in a very different way from St Matthew, partly because he represents Mary Magdalene as being alone. In the first gospel Jesus salutes them, and they at once know him. In St John, Mary does not know him, until he has emphatically called her by name. She even takes him for the gardener and asks him if he knows where the body of Jesus has been carried. This account has not an air of probability about it; for it gives a low idea of Christ's personal appearance to mistake him for the gardener, and the interval of one day could not have produced forgetfulness in Mary's mind. The paleness produced by the death which his body had suffered would even have guided her mind to the recognition,—not to forgetfulness of him. We must therefore choose the account which Matthew gives of this highly interesting interview.

But another objection, drawn from the appearance of Christ so speedily afterwards, lies against the accuracy of the words which were spoken by the angels. St Matthew and St Mark represent the angel as bidding Mary tell his disciples that they should see Christ again in Galilee : and yet the words are hardly spoken before Mary herself sees him there upon the spot, and all the disciples see him that same day in Jerusalem. We must suppose that the conversation between Mary and the angels was preserved a long time by tradition, and gradually assumed a different character, as it flowed, during a hundred years or more, into different channels.

6. It is not unworthy of inquiry why St Matthew alone should have related that the Jewish authorities sealed the stone and set a guard of Roman soldiers, who must have fled at the appearance of the angel that accosted Mary. That so remarkable a precaution against fraud should have been known to only one of the four writers, furnishes a strong probability that the gospels were not written by the apostles themselves, or by their contemporaries ; for they would certainly not have omitted to record such an occurrence, especially when followed by the miraculous appearance of an angel from heaven, which put the guard to flight, and defeated the plans both of the Jewish Sanhedrim and of the Roman governor.

CHAPTER XLIV.

Christ's Appearances after the Resurrection.

From the passages out of the four gospels placed in juxtaposition in our last chapter, it must be inferred that Jesus, on the morning of his resurrection, appeared to Mary Magdalene as she was returning from her visit to his tomb ; but whether other women were in her company or not, is more doubtful ; for whilst St Matthew speaks of "the other woman" who was with her, St John writes as if she were alone, and the other two evangelists do not mention that Jesus immediately after his resurrection appeared near his tomb to any one at all. Setting aside therefore this narrative as forming part of what constitutes the Resurrection, let us next examine the accounts which have come down to us of his having appeared either to his disciples or others, after it was notified to them by the women that he was risen from the dead.

His first appearance to any of his disciples or followers was when, as related by St Mark and St Luke, he showed himself to two of his followers as they were on their way to Emmaus. St Mark (xvi, 12,) says only that he "appeared in another form unto two of them as they walked and went into the country." St Luke gives us the following more detailed narrative.

LUKE xxiv, 13-33.

13. And, behold, two of them went that same day to a village called Emmaus, which was from Jerusalem about threescore furlongs. 14. And they talked together of all these things which had happened.

15. And it came to pass, that, while they communed together and reasoned, Jesus himself drew near, and went with them. 16. But their eyes were holden that they should not know him. 17. And he said unto them, "What manner of communications are these that ye have one to another, as ye walk, and are sad?" 18. And the one of them, whose name was Cleophas, answering said unto him, "Art thou only a stranger in Jerusalem, and hast not known the things which are come to pass there in these days?" 19. And he said unto them, "What things?" And they said unto him, "Concerning Jesus of Nazareth, which was a prophet mighty in deed and word before God, and all the people: 20. And how the chief priests and our rulers delivered him to be condemned to death, and have crucified him. 21. But we trusted that it had been he which should have redeemed Israel: and beside all this, to day is the third day since these things were done. 22. Yea, and certain women also of our company made us astonished, which were early at the sepulchre; 23. And when they found not his body, they came, saying, that they had also seen a vision of angels, which said that he was alive. 24. And certain of them which were with us went to the sepulchre, and found it even so as the women had said: but him they saw not."

25. Then he said unto them, "O fools, and slow of heart to believe all that the prophets have spoken: 26. Ought not Christ to have suffered these things, and to enter into his glory?" 27. And beginning at Moses and all the prophets, he expounded unto them in all the scriptures the things concerning himself. 28. And they drew nigh unto the village, whither they went: and he made as though he would have gone further. 29. But they constrained him, saying, "Abide with us: for it is toward evening, and the day is far spent." And he went in to tarry with them. 30. And it came to pass as he sat at meat with them, he took bread, and blessed it, and brake, and gave to them. 31. And their eyes were opened, and they knew him, and he vanished out of their sight. 32. And they said one to another, "Did not our heart burn within us, while he talked with us by the way, and while he opened to us the scriptures?" 33. And they went and told it unto the residue: neither believed they them.

In this narrative, furnished by only one evangelist, there are no particulars which can be disputed or confirmed by comparison with other evidence. A new feature, however, appears, which nowhere showed itself in the conduct of our Lord before his crucifixion. St Mark, in his short mention of the occurrence, says that Jesus appeared in another form, that is, disguised in some way or other, so that his two followers did not know him, and yet one of the two was Cleophas, who, if we believe previous passages of the gospel history, must have known him intimately before. When his two followers at last recognize him, he vanishes out of their sight, and the two return late in the afternoon to Jerusalem. From Emmaus therefore our attention must now be turned to that city, and the four narratives now again vary much about the events which follow. The account which St Matthew gives is the shortest: he knows nothing of the walk to Emmaus, or of any appearance of Jesus to his followers in Jerusalem. He says:—

MATTHEW xxviii, 16-20.

16. Then the eleven disciples went away into Galilee, into a mountain where Jesus had appointed them. 17. And when they saw him, they worshipped him: but some doubted. 18. And Jesus came and spake unto them, saying, "All power is given unto me in heaven and in earth. 19. Go ye therefore, and teach all nations, baptizing them in the name of the Father, and of the Son, and of the Holy Ghost: 20. Teaching them to observe all things whatsoever I have commanded you: and, lo, I am with you alway, even unto the end of the world. Amen."

The account which St Mark gives is also short, but much at variance with that of St Matthew: he represents the disciples as stopping at Jerusalem and witnessing the ascension of Jesus from the chamber in which they sat at meat.

MARK xvi, 14-20.

14. Afterward he appeared unto the eleven as they sat at meat, and upbraided them with their unbelief and hardness of heart, because they believed not them which had seen him after he was risen. 15. And he said unto them, " Go ye into all the world," &c.

. . . .

19. So then after the Lord had spoken unto them, he was received up into heaven, and sat on the right hand of God. 20. And they went forth, and preached every where, the Lord working with them, and confirming the word with signs following. Amen.

The meeting of the eleven disciples which St Mark here briefly names, but of which St Matthew seems to have known nothing, took place on the evening of the day on which Jesus rose from the dead, and is more fully described by St Luke and St John.

The former of these two evangelists represents the two disciples from Emmaus as finding the eleven sitting at meat in Jerusalem.

LUKE xxiv, 33-53.	JOHN xx, 19-31.
33. And they rose up the same hour, and returned to Jerusalem, and found the eleven gathered together, and them that were with them, 34. Saying, "The Lord is risen indeed, and hath appeared to	19. Then the same day at evening, being the first day of the week, when the doors were shut where the disciples were assembled for fear of the Jews,

AFTER THE RESURRECTION.

LUKE xxiv, 35-49.	JOHN xx, 19-25.
Simon." 35. And they told what things were done in the way, and how he was known of them in breaking of bread.	
36. And as they thus spake, Jesus himself stood in the midst of them, and saith unto them, "Peace be unto you." 37. But they were terrified and affrighted, and supposed that they had seen a spirit. 38. And he said unto them, "Why are ye troubled? and why do thoughts arise in your hearts? 39. Behold my hands and my feet, that it is I myself: handle me, and see; for a spirit hath not flesh and bones, as ye see me have."	came Jesus and stood in the midst, and saith unto them, "Peace be unto you."
40. And when he had thus spoken, he shewed them his hands and his feet. 41. And while they yet believed not for joy, and wondered, he said unto them, "Have ye here any meat?" 42. And they gave him a piece of a broiled fish, and of an honeycomb. 43. And he took it, and did eat before them.	20. And when he had so said, he shewed unto them his hands and his side. Then were the disciples glad, when they saw the Lord. 21. Then said Jesus to them again, "Peace be unto you: as my Father hath sent me, even so send I you."
44. And he said unto them, "These are the words which I spake unto you, while I was yet with you, that all things must be fulfilled, which were written in the law of Moses, and in the prophets, and in the psalms, concerning me." 45. Then opened he their understanding, that they might understand the scriptures, 46. And said unto them, "Thus it is written, and thus it behoved Christ to suffer, and to rise from the dead the third day: 47. And that repentance and remission of sins should be preached in his name among all nations, beginning at Jerusalem. 48. And ye are witnesses of these things. 49. And, behold, I send the promise of my Father upon you: but tarry ye in the city of Jerusalem, until ye be endued with power from on high."	22. And when he had said this, he breathed on them, and saith unto them, "Receive ye the Holy Ghost: 23. Whose soever sins ye remit, they are remitted unto them; and whose soever sins ye retain, they are retained."
	24. But Thomas, one of the twelve, called Didymus, was not with them when Jesus came. 25. The other disciples therefore said unto him, "We have seen the Lord." But he said unto them, "Except I shall see in his hands the print of the nails, and put my finger into the print of the nails, and thrust my hand into his side, I will not believe."

LUKE xxiv, 50-53.

50. And he led them out as far as to Bethany, and he lifted up his hands, and blessed them. 51. And it came to pass, while he blessed them, he was parted from them, and carried up into heaven. 52. And they worshipped him, and returned to Jerusalem with great joy: 53. And were continually in the temple, praising and blessing God. Amen.

JOHN xx, 26-31.

26. And after eight days again his disciples were within, and Thomas with them: then came Jesus, the doors being shut, and stood in the midst, and said, "Peace be unto you." 27. Then saith he to Thomas, "Reach hither thy finger, and behold my hands; and reach hither thy hand, and thrust it into my side: and be not faithless, but believing." 28. And Thomas answered and said unto him, "My Lord and my God." 29. Jesus saith unto him, "Thomas, because thou hast seen me, thou hast believed: blessed are they that have not seen, and yet have believed."
30. And many other signs truly did Jesus in the presence of his disciples, which are not written in this book: 31. But these are written that ye might believe that Jesus is the Christ, the Son of God; and that believing ye might have life through his name.

Of the four evangelists Luke, as we have seen, is the only one who has given us the details of Christ's first appearance to his followers on the road to Emmaus. Mark seems to have had some faint knowledge of such an occurrence, but without indication of either time or place. But on the evening of that same day, on which Jesus quitted the tomb, he showed himself to the eleven disciples in Jerusalem. This fact is recorded by all the three evangelists who have recorded that he appeared at all after his resurrection in that city. But St Mark says that the disciples were sitting at meat, when Jesus appeared among them, and there is some divergency between St Mark and St Luke arising from this statement. The former, not having accurate knowledge of the walk to Emmaus and of Jesus having already broken bread, that is, having made his evening meal or dinner there with the two disciples, represents his first appearance to the disciples whilst they were taking the principal meal of the day at Jerusalem. Now the two disciples at Emmaus had induced Jesus to stop with them, when he made as though he would go further, on the plea that it was toward evening, and the day was far spent. As these two disciples returned to Jerusalem—no doubt on foot —a distance of six miles, it would certainly be unusual that the eleven should be at their evening meal so late in the day. We may indeed suppose that Jesus had the power of transporting himself instantly from one place to another, seeing that he vanished out of sight at Emmaus, and at this meeting stood in the midst of them, although, as St John tells us the doors were shut for fear of the Jews ; but we have no right to suppose that the two disciples were endowed with a similar power of locomotion, and we must therefore suppose that the eleven were taking their meal on that day at a later hour than usual, or that the meeting at Emmaus had taken place at an earlier hour than that which is indicated by the evangelist. In any case it appears that Jesus sat at table with them ; for according to St. Luke, he says to them " Have ye here any meat?" upon which they gave him a piece of a broiled fish, and of an honeycomb. Thus it appears there were two meals on the evening of this day; and we can only suppose that the accounts are in this case divergent only because they are imperfect, and from the want of sufficient data, it may be impossible to determine which of the two should be preferred.

2. The second difference lies between St Matthew and St Mark. Both record only one appearance of Christ to his disciples, but Matthew represents them as having first gone into Galilee, where they meet their master and receive his final instructions. Mark places this scene at Jerusalem, apparently on the evening of the day of the resurrection, and adds that immediately afterwards Jesus was taken up into heaven.

3. A third view is suggested by the words of Luke—that after the exhortations given on the evening of the resurrection, Jesus led his disciples out to Bethany, where he bestowed a blessing upon them, and was immediately afterwards taken up into heaven. The disciples then return to Jerusalem and spend their time continually in the temple, praising and blessing God.

4. In St John's Gospel, we read that on the evening of the resurrection Thomas, not being with the other ten, when Jesus appeared, entertained doubts, which were not dispelled until eight days afterwards when Christ again showed himself to the disciples. The history seems here to end with the observation that there were many other signs done by Jesus in the presence of his disciples, besides those that are " written in this book " : but in chapter XXI, a new series of events begins, the scene of which lies in Galilee, the time, uncertain ; and the disciples, so far from being " continually in the temple praising and blessing God," have gone back to their usual haunts and occupations. Peter with six of

the disciples, "Thomas, Nathanael, the sons of Zebedee, and two others," go out fishing, and the next morning Jesus joins them standing on the shore: they take a meal together, and the scene closes as abruptly as before in the 20th chapter, and almost in the same words respecting the many other things that Jesus did over and above those which the evangelist has related. It seems unnecessary to dwell upon this additional appearance of Jesus in Galilee near the sea of Tiberias, given in the twenty-first chapter of St John's Gospel. It has no counterpart in the other three histories, with which indeed it is wholly irreconcilable; and indeed the most sensible commentators have decided that it is, what it appears, an unauthorized addition to the work in which it is found.

5. The ascension also of Christ into heaven presents some peculiar points of divergency between the narratives of St Mark and St Luke, who alone have left the record of that event. But, as a third account of it is given in the Book of the Acts of the Apostles, it will be more convenient to defer the mention of it here, and to recur to the subject hereafter in our notice of that book.

CHAPTER XLV.

THE DEATH OF JUDAS, AND PURCHASE OF THE POTTER'S FIELD.

THE repentance and death of Judas Iscariot are related by Matthew alone of the evangelists; but in the first chapter of the Acts of the Apostles is a different account of the same matter introduced into a speech of Peter to the apostles, when they elected Matthias to be their colleague in the place of Judas.

MATTHEW xxvii, 3-10.	ACTS i, 16-19.
3. Then Judas, which had betrayed him, when he saw that he was condemned, repented himself, and brought again the thirty pieces of silver to the chief priests and elders, 4. Saying, "I have sinned in that I have betrayed the innocent blood." And they said, "What is that to us? see thou to that."	16. "Men and brethren, this scripture must needs have been fulfilled, which the Holy Ghost by the mouth of David spake before concerning Judas, which was guide to them that took Jesus. 17. For he was numbered with us, and had obtained part of this ministry."

MATTHEW xxvii, 5-10.	ACTS i, 18, 19.
5. And he cast down the pieces of silver in the temple, and departed, and went and hanged himself. 6. And the chief priests took the silver pieces, and said, "It is not lawful for to put them into the treasury, because it is the price of blood." 7. And they took counsel, and bought with them the potter's field, to bury strangers in. 8. Wherefore that field was called, the field of blood, unto this day. 9. Then was fulfilled that which was spoken by Jeremy the prophet, saying, "And they took the thirty pieces of silver, the price of him that was valued, whom they of the children of Israel did value; 10. And gave them for the potter's field, as the Lord appointed me.	18. Now this man purchased a field with the reward of iniquity: and falling headlong, he burst asunder in the midst, and all his bowels gushed out. 19. And it was known unto all the dwellers at Jerusalem; insomuch as that field is called in their proper tongue, Aceldama, that is to say, The field of blood,

These extracts will not detain us long: there are three points to be noticed.

1. St Matthew says that the chief priests bought the field with the thirty pieces of silver: but Peter says that Judas himself was the purchaser.

2. Matthew relates that Judas hanged himself in remorse immediately after the crucifixion of Jesus: Peter knows nothing of his remorse; on the contrary, he shows that Judas bought a field with the money which he had received, and died afterwards, as if by an accident, or a judgement of Providence, but certainly not by his own hand. The supposition that he hanged himself over a precipice, and fell by reason of the rope breaking, is too childish to merit notice.

A singular version of the mode in which Judas came by his death is told by Œcumenius in his Commentary on the Acts of the Apostles (chap. ii) quoting from Papias, bishop of Hierapolis.

Judas walked in this world a great example of impiety. For being swelled so much in flesh that he could not pass through, where a cart passed through easily, he was crushed by the cart so that his entrails were evacuated.

3. The prophecy which, according to Matthew, was fulfilled by the history of Judas, is very different in the Old Testament from what it appears in the New. Zechariah, speaking of himself and his exhortations to the people, proceeds thus (xi, 10-13):

And I took my staff, even Beauty, and cut it asunder, that I might break my covenant which I had made with all the people. 11. And it was broken in that day: and so the poor of the flock that waited upon me knew that it was the word of the Lord. 12. And I said unto them, "If ye think good, give me my price; and if not, forbear." So they weighed for my price thirty pieces of silver. 13. And the Lord said unto me, "Cast it unto the potter:" a goodly price that I was prized at of them. And I took the thirty pieces of silver, and cast them to the potter in the house of the Lord.

It would be difficult to find any analogy between the facts of the gospel-history and those which the prophet imagined: the only connection between them is evidently the number of silver-pieces, which is thirty in both documents, the house of the Lord, and the mention of the potter, although nothing is said of his field. The writers of the gospel history constantly quote passages from the Septuagint version of the Old Testament, and apply them to the events of their own time: but we are not bound to infer that the ancient author, from whose work these passages are taken, wrote them with any intention, or even with the knowledge that they would be so used by others living and quoting them several hundred years after his own time.

CHAPTER XLVI.

DEVELOPMENT OF LATER IDEAS.

A STRIKING witness to the late composition of the gospels is furnished by expressions, denoting ideas that could not have had any being in the time of Christ and his disciples, but must have been developed afterwards, at a time when the Christian religion was established on a broader and still increasing basis.

1. The first instance of this anticipation of ideas occurs in the words which St John's Gospel places in the mouth of John the Baptist:

JOHN i, 15-18.

15. John bare witness of him, and cried, saying, "This was he of whom I spake, He that cometh after me is preferred before me: for he was before me. 16. And of his fulness have all we received, and grace for grace. 17. For the law was given by Moses, but grace and truth came by Jesus Christ. 18. No man hath seen God at any time, the only begotten Son, which is in the bosom of the Father, he hath declared him.

These words appear to have been spoken by John the Baptist, as the record which he bare to Christ. But the latter part, " And of his fulness, &c." could not be spoken by John; for the things there spoken of as resulting from Christ's coming, had not yet resulted. Neither John the Baptist nor the multitude he was addressing, had yet received either grace or fulness from Christ. " The only-begotten Son, which was in the bosom of the Father," had not then " declared him," nor was he at all known to the world, when these words are thought to have been spoken. The truth is that these words were not spoken by John the Baptist at all, but flow from the thoughts of the writer, who knew not where to stop, but having once taken up the words of the Baptist, is borne along in the same tenour, and gives utterance to sentiments, which apply not to the Baptist but to himself, and to the aspect of things in his own time.

2. A still more remarkable form of words is ascribed by the evangelists repeatedly to Christ himself; and an anachronism is the result. The word *cross* is used metaphorically by Christ in numerous passages:

MATTHEW x, 38. And he that taketh not his cross and followeth after me is not worthy of me. xvi, 24. Then said Jesus unto his disciples, "If any man will come after me, let him deny himself, and take up his cross, and follow me."

MARK viii, 34. And when he had called the people unto him with his disciples also, he said unto them, " Whosoever will come after me, let him deny himself, and take up his cross and follow me." x, 21. Then Jesus beholding him loved him, and said unto him, " One thing thou lackest: go thy way, sell whatsoever thou hast, and give to the poor, and thou shalt have treasure in heaven : and come, take up the cross, and follow me."

LUKE ix, 23. And he said unto them all, " If any man will come after me, let him deny himself, and take up his cross daily, and follow me." xiv, 27. And whosoever doth not bear his cross, and come after me, cannot be my disciple."

When these exhortations to patience, fortitude, and perseverance were delivered, the Jews did not know the meaning of the word *cross*, used metaphorically for Christian patience under affliction and perseverance in Christian well-doing. It was only after Christ had suffered on the cross, that the word acquired such a signification, or the thing itself that reverence which it has since received. There may be no doubt that Christ called on the parties to follow him, and to become his disciples, but he would not use for that purpose a word which his hearers could not understand. Some may think that there is an analogy between this misuse of the word *cross* and the exclamation of the Jewish multitude, demanding the execution of our Lord. " Crucify him !

crucify him!" is said to have been their cry, and we might here substitute another word better suited to the modes of execution practised by the Jews, among whom stoning prevailed, as we find it in the laws of Moses: but this argument is not conclusive, for, though the Roman supremacy over Judæa had not long existed, yet it is possible the people of Jerusalem would be sufficiently aware that crucifixion was a common Roman punishment.

3. Again: we observe a similar incoherence of words and ideas in Christ's address to his disciples, concerning John the Baptist, then in prison.

It is related in Matthew's Gospel, chapter 11, verse 2:

> Now when John had heard in the prison the works of Christ, he sent two of his disciples, 3. And said unto him, "Art thou he that should come, or do we look for another?"

When John's messengers were gone, a conversation takes place on the subject between Jesus and his disciples—it is related both by St Matthew and St Luke.

MATTHEW xi, 7-12.	LUKE vii, 24-28.
7. And as they departed, Jesus began to say unto the multitude concerning John, "What went ye out into the wilderness to see? A reed shaken with the wind? 8. But what went ye out for to see? A prophet? behold, they that wear soft clothing are in kings' houses. 9. But what went ye out for to see? A prophet? yea, I say unto you, and more than a prophet.	24. And when the messengers of John were departed, he began to speak unto the people concerning John, "What went ye out into the wilderness for to see? A reed shaken with the wind? 25. But what went ye out for to see? A man clothed in soft raiment! Behold, they which are gorgeously apparelled, and live delicately, are in kings' courts. 26. But what went ye out for to see? A prophet? Yea, I say unto you, and much more than a prophet.
10. For this is he, of whom it is written, Behold, I send my messenger before thy face, which shall prepare thy way before thee.	27. This is he of whom it is written, Behold, I send my messenger before thy face, which shall prepare thy way before thee.
11. Verily I say unto you, Among them that are born of women there hath not risen a greater than John the Baptist: notwithstanding he that is least in the kingdom of heaven is greater than he.	28. For I say unto you, Among those that are born of women there is not a greater prophet than John the Baptist: but he that is least in the kingdom of God is greater than he."
12. And from the days of John the Baptist until now the kingdom of heaven suffereth violence, and the violent take it by force.	

In this recital of the words of Jesus, St Luke is more cautious than St Matthew; for he omits those suspicious words, which Christ could not have spoken; "From the days of John the Baptist *until now*, the kingdom of heaven suffereth violence, and the violent take it by force." All the three parts of this sentence are liable to observation. In the first place, what length of time had elapsed between the "days of John the Baptist" and "now"? Jesus had just dismissed John's disciples, to go back to their master who was in prison, where he had been placed a short time before by Herod. No time at all had elapsed between John the Baptist and Christ, though there is no doubt that when the Gospel of St Matthew was written, a very long time had passed, enough to fully justify the use of the words which we are considering.

But in the second place, the kingdom of heaven could at that time be hardly said to have begun; for John himself only announced that it was at hand; but to say that it suffered violence before the death of our Lord, which was to usher in that kingdom, is hardly in unison with either Christian history or Christian doctrine.

But the third objection to this passage lies partly in the erroneous translation in which we read it, and partly in the erroneous statement which it conveys. The words ἁρπάζουσιν αὐτήν should be rendered "plunder it," and this meaning, unsuitable to the time when Jesus was preaching the advent of the kingdom of heaven, would be appropriate in the time of a later writer, when we know that much harshness was exercised towards the Christians, and many violent men would be ready to plunder them.

4. The title by which the four histories of Christ's life and death are known among Christians, in English *gospel*, in Greek εὐαγγέλιον, in French *evangile*, has a twofold signification, similar to *church* and many other words, which have both an abstract and a concrete meaning. We have already noticed that the word *gospel*, as a title to the evangelic histories, is of late origin, not being found to bear this sense in Justin Martyr or any of the fathers who wrote before the end of the second century. The literal meaning of the Greek, εὐ *well* and ἀγγελία *message, tidings*, is excellently rendered into English by an old Saxon word *gospel*, or *godspell*, that is *good-spell, good tidings*. The word has long been confined to signify the good tidings of the evangelic kingdom, but in its origin it probably might denote any good news whatsoever. In the same way, the Greek word at first bore a general signification, which was gradually narrowed to its present theological meaning. That the preaching of the kingdom of heaven was soon looked upon as good tidings,

and designated by a word bearing that import, may be conceded without difficulty, but it seems unlikely that Christ himself used the word. The word denoting the preacher and the thing preached are so thoroughly of Greek formation, that we are led to ascribe them to Greek writers who lived at a later period, when the Jewish element in Christianity had been eliminated. In no case do we more regret that the books of the New Testament have not come down to us in the Hebrew language which Christ and his disciples spoke. In the following texts the word *gospel* occurs. The reader may distinguish between those cases where the use of the word may be referred to the writer, and those in which Christ himself is made to use it.

MATTHEW iv, 23. And Jesus went about all Galilee, teaching in their synagogues, and preaching the gospel of the kingdom, and healing all manner of sickness and all manner of disease among the people. ix, 35. And Jesus went about all the cities and villages, teaching in their synagogues, and preaching the gospel of the kingdom, and healing every sickness and every disease among the people.

MARK i, 14, 15. Now after that John was put in prison, Jesus came into Galilee, preaching the gospel of the kingdom of God, 15. And saying, "The time is fulfilled, and the kingdom of God is at hand: repent ye, and believe the gospel. viii, 35. For whosoever shall save his life shall lose it; but whosoever shall lose his life for my sake and the gospel's, the same shall save it." x, 29. And Jesus answered and said, "Verily I say unto you, There is no man that hath left house or brethren, or sisters, or father, or mother, or wife, or children, or lands for my sake, and the gospel's, 30. But he shall receive an hundredfold now in this time, houses, and brethren, &c."

MATTHEW xxiv, 14.
And this gospel of the kingdom shall be preached in all the world for a witness unto all nations, and then shall the end come.

MARK xiii, 10.
And the gospel must first be published among all nations.

MATTHEW xxvi, 13.
Verily I say unto you, Whereso- ever this gospel shall be preached in the whole world, there also shall this, that this woman hath done, be told for a memorial of her.

MARK xiv, 9.
Wheresoever this gospel shall be preached throughout the whole world, this also that she hath done shall be spoken of for a memorial of her.

LUKE x, 1.
And it came to pass, that on one of those days, as he taught the people in the temple, and preached the gospel, the chief priests and the scribes came upon him with the elders.

5. The next instance of a later idea prematurely introduced into the Gospels is to be found in the words of Martha, when Jesus says that her brother Lazarus shall rise again; "Yes," says she, "at the last day." But this was a Christian, not a Jewish idea: the Jews are thought to have known

little or nothing of a last day; Christ first taught this belief, and there had not been sufficient time for Martha to have imbibed the idea so deeply as to be able to reply to Jesus by reference to his own doctrine.

6. In the first volume of this work (p. 141) has been noticed a remarkable expression "until this day" which seemed to render it impossible that the writers of the books of the Old Testament were contemporary, but must have lived many years after the events which they have described. In the New Testament also are several forms of speech, from which it might be thought that the writers referred to things belonging to an age that had long since passed away. Such expressions are the following: "It came to pass in those days," and in other cases simply "In those days," "At that time," &c.

The first place in which we find this form of words is in St Matthew's Gospel (iii, 1), "In those days came John the Baptist preaching in the wilderness of Judæa." Seeing that John the Baptist was still preaching in Judæa at the very time that Matthew was following Jesus as one of his twelve disciples, it is difficult to conceive that, in writing a narrative of what himself had witnessed, he would use words that generally designate a period far more remote.

A similar inference may be drawn from the words which introduce us to the miraculous multiplication of food in the Gospel according to St Mark (viii, 1), "In those days the multitude being very great and having nothing to eat." The miracle introduced to our notice by this preface is wholly unconnected with what went before, and might be placed anywhere else in the history with equal propriety. St Luke has indeed, at the beginning of his Gospel, used the same form of words appropriately to the subject of which he is writing. He says in his first chapter, verse 1, "There was in the days of Herod," and again in chapter ii, verse 1, "And it came to pass in those days." The author was speaking of events that had happened before the birth of Christ, and there can be no doubt, even if St Luke be acknowledged to be the writer of the Gospel which bears his name, that fifty years or more had passed since the time of which he was writing. It results therefore that the writers of the Gospel history use this formula to indicate that the period of time in which the miracles and other deeds of our Lord were done, was sufficiently remote from their own times. The expression is indeed well suited for the composition of a narrative which like the Gospels has been compiled out of fragments that have been preserved by individuals and afterwards collected together into one book.

7. In the nineteenth chapter of St Matthew's Gospel, verse 12, we read as follows:—

"For there are some eunuchs, which were so born from their mother's womb; and there are some eunuchs which were made eunuchs of men; and there be eunuchs which have made themselves eunuchs for the kingdom of heaven's sake. He that is able to receive it let him receive it."

It is not to be denied that in all the kingdoms of the East, both ancient and modern, the class of men designated by the name of eunuch has been found, and the Greek emperors of the later period failed to preserve their court and palace from the blot of having eunuchs in their service and at their courts. The Romans do not appear to have been equally guilty: but we can hardly suppose that the Jewish nation, governed as they were by priests and professing a religion of which our own is an offshoot, would encourage amongst themselves any such beings as those named in the passage which we are now considering, to whichever of the three classes they might have belonged. Two of those classes may be passed over, the first as naturally rare, the second as out of place among native Jews; but the third cannot so easily be dismissed, seeing that among the early Christians were to be found more than one who literally made themselves eunuchs for the kingdom of heaven's sake. Had any of the followers of Jesus then, we may ask, ever as yet made themselves eunuchs for his sake, during the time that he was on earth? The answer to this question cannot be doubtful. It was in the second and third centuries that self-mutilation was deemed to be the strongest safeguard of chastity, and pre-eminent among those who inflicted it upon themselves were Melito and Origen, both well known as early writers in the Christian Church.* The case of Origen is authenticated by the strongest evidence: as regards Melito, the writer of his life in Dr Smith's Dictionary of the Bible has expressed his doubt whether another meaning may not be attached to the word, but the expression of Polycrates Μελίτωνα τόν εὐνοῦχον Melito the eunuch, preserved by Eusebius (v, 24) would seem too decided to allow any hesitation as to what meaning it must convey.

Recurring therefore to the passage in St Matthew's Gospel, the only one in the New Testament in which the

---

* See Athenagoras's "Apology for Christianity," sec. 34, and Dr Cave's "Life of Origen," p. 220.

subject is named, we may not unreasonably conclude that the words of Jesus have been expanded by the writer who in a later age did not see that the precepts of Christ on the subject of marriage could receive no illustration in his mouth from customs that had not begun to exist until long after he had himself withdrawn out of the world.

8. In all the four Gospels we meet with the words kingdom of heaven, kingdom of God, Church of God, &c., used to denote the new religious era, which Jesus came to institute. The precursor of Jesus was John the Baptist; he also preached that men should repent, because the kingdom of heaven was at hand; and Jesus immediately after his baptism, made a similar announcement. "From that time" [says St Matthew (iv, 17)] "Jesus began to say Repent; for the kingdom of heaven is at hand!" In chapter iv, verse 33, Jesus preaches the "Gospel of the Kingdom," and in other cases the institution which he came to establish among mankind is designated as the kingdom of heaven and of God, or simply by the name of kingdom, which if we possessed more detailed documents on the subject, might perhaps more fully explain the condemnation of our Lord as having been guilty of endeavouring to found a Jewish kingdom upon earth, instead of that figurative kingdom which was to extend over the minds and not the bodies of his followers, and into which all nations were qualified to enter. We will not now raise the question how far the mention of this heavenly kingdom might be an anachronism whilst Jesus was on earth; for there is another expression which occurs more frequently in almost every book of the New Testament, but which hardly could have been used by Christ himself. The English word church is derived from the German *kirche*, and that from the Greek *kuriake* a feminine adjective which means "belonging or referring to our Lord." As we have no records of the language used commonly by our Lord and his disciples, we are obliged to be content with the books of the New Testament as they have come down to us in the Greek tongue. In these books the word which represents the Christian community is *ecclesia*, a word which in its literal sense would designate a body of men "called out" from the multitude, without any indication of the purpose for which they were summoned. In the various states of Greece this word is used to denote the popular assembly by which the affairs of the state were managed, but since the introduction of Christianity the words *ecclesia* in Greek or Latin, and church in English, are

used to designate the whole body of believers who have adopted the Christian faith. It is not impossible that some Hebrew word may have been used by Jesus and his disciples to denote the community which they were then establishing; nor would it be objected to the use of the word church that its Hebrew equivalent should have been replaced by this word, when the Hebrew began to die out, and the nation no longer preserved a definite existence. But the word church conveys to the mind many ideas which are intelligible to us, but could have had no existence during the life of our Saviour himself. The following passage from the Gospel according to St Matthew (xviii, 15) may be quoted as an illustration of this subject.

"15. Moreover, if thy brother shall trespass against thee, go and tell him his fault between thee and him alone: if he shall hear thee, thou hast gained thy brother. 16. But if he will not hear thee, then take with thee one or two more, that in the mouth of two or three witnesses every word may be established. 17. And if he shall neglect to hear them, tell it unto the church; but if he neglect to hear the church, let him be unto thee as an heathen man and a publican."

In this passage we have allusion to a body of men not merely known for the universal benevolence, piety, humility and modesty of their life, such as would be in perfect harmony with the teaching of their great master, but as having already a sort of ecclesiastical system established among them, whereby offences were withdrawn from the cognizance of the people at large, and the foundation already laid for the superstructure of ecclesiastical law, which began to be built up towards the end of the second century, and which has held the whole Christian world in a species of thraldom even down to the present time. "Let him be unto thee as an heathen man and as a publican," was a precept which in the hands of a later age was thought to be best obeyed by burning a heretic at the stake.

9. That the four Gospels were written by Greeks might be inferred *a priori* from the fact that they are written in the Greek language; and that they were not written by Jews, a necessary corollary from the former inference, seems to derive further support from the Hebrew words and names which occur and which are all explained by a Greek translation or by an equivalent term better known, as we might suppose, to the readers.

But the passages in which these equivalent names occur will hardly fail to suggest the further inference that the books in which they are found were written at a later period, when the names which those equivalents explain had themselves either ceased to exist, or had become so faint by time that without such explanatory affix they would hardly be intelligible to those who read the Gospel histories.

In the sixth chapter of St John, verse 1, mention is made of the "sea of Galilee which is the sea of Tiberias." It might be thought that no reader of St John's Gospel would require explanation about the sea of Galilee, and it would probably be notorious that the sea of Galilee and the lake of Genesareth were one and the same. But when we read that the sea of Galilee is also the sea of Tiberias, we are led to inquire why this explanation should be given of a name that was sufficiently intelligible of itself. It appears then that Tiberias was a city founded by Herod Antipas, not long before the crucifixion of our Saviour, and it follows that the adjoining sea or lake would often be called by the name of the city built upon its banks. This city being strongly fortified, played a prominent part in the later wars between the Jews and the Romans, but does not appear prominently before that time, and the point to which these facts lead is to suggest that the lake which had formerly passed under the name of the sea of Galilee, had probably lost that name and passed under its new name of Tiberias when the gospel histories were written. As regards the Hebrew terms which are used in the Gospels, and which are explained in Greek, it does not seem unreasonable to suppose that a similar explanation may be given.

In Mark x, 46 the name Bartimæus is explained to mean the son of Timæus.

In John v, 3 the pool in which the diseased were healed, is said to have been called in the Hebrew tongue Bethesda, but no Greek equivalent is here added; possibly because the writer did not know the etymology of the word; and indeed this seems even now not to have been clearly ascertained; for whilst some commentators explain it as the "House of Mercy," others suppose it to mean the "House of flowing water," and indeed the oldest MSS vary in the reading, so that we cannot be certain that Bethesda correctly represents the name by which this pool was called.

As illustrations of the same argument may be cited the various Hebrew words spoken at various times by our Lord himself. Thus in St Mark's Gospel (xiv, 36) Jesus is represented as saying "Abba, father, all things are possible unto thee," but as Abba is the Hebrew term for father, we cannot suppose that he used both these words, and it is obvious to suppose that the writer adds the word father to explain the meaning of the Hebrew word Abba by its Greek equivalent. It is unnecessary to quote the other Hebrew words Talitha cumi &c. all of which are followed by a translation or paraphrase which renders them more intelligible to the reader.

10. An anachronism of another character, connected with the geography of the Holy Land, seems to show itself in the account of a woman whose " young daughter had an unclean spirit" and who came and fell at the feet of Jesus. The woman, says St Mark (vii, 26) was a Greek, a Syrophenician by nation; and she besought him that he would cast forth the devil out of her daughter.

It has been doubted by some of the commentators what the word Syrophenician in this passage can mean; but the etymology of the name is evident and seems to carry with it its proper signification. The country was Phœnicia, which may be taken as part of Syria; and we have the same word occurring in other works besides the New Testament. Thus Juvenal (vii, 160) speaks of the " Syrophenician inhabitant of the Idumæan gate," and Lucian (*De cons. Deorum*) fifty years later used the term with great propriety. But the meaning of the name is less important to our present purpose than the question when the name first appears in history, and the answer to this question is unfavourable to the contemporary character of the Gospel in which the name occurs. The woman spoken of is termed a Canaanitish woman by St Matthew (xv, 21) and might, had she lived 100 years later, have been rightly called a Syrophenician. It appears that the emperor Hadrian, in the beginning of the second century, divided Syria into three parts, Syro-Phœnice, Syria Palestine, and Syria proper, and it would follow that until the time when this was done the word Syro-Phœnician could not properly be used to describe the inhabitants of that province, and the inference is either that the narrative, in which the use of this word is anticipated, was not composed before the reign of Hadrian, or that the later term was substituted in place of some other original one since that time.

The foregoing instances are here produced, out of many that occur, pointing to events, practices, and customs, which had hardly begun to exist in the age of which the four Gospels are a record; and are here brought forward to confirm the opinion that the Gospels, compiled out of traditional information derived from the four Apostles themselves, but handed down through intermediate agents, have been supposed to be written textually by those "according to" whom only they were written.

CHAPTER XLVII.

Summary of the Acts of the Apostles, &c.

THE Book of the Acts of the Apostles, which is placed, in the New Testament, immediately after the four Gospels, begins with a short dedication or preface addressed to Theophilus, who is reasonably supposed to be the same to whom the Gospel according to St Luke is inscribed. The book contains the adventures which happened to some of the apostles, and especially to Saul, afterwards St Paul, a new convert, between Christ's ascension into heaven and the year of our Lord 63. A summary of its contents may be convenient to avoid the necessity of constant reference to the New Testament.

Christ's Ascension, 40 days after his Resurrection : chapter i, vv. 3-9.

—" In those days," i, 15,—when the number of the disciples was 120, Matthias is elected into the place of Judas : 26.

—The Holy Spirit is given on the day of Pentecost, ii, 1 ; according to the modern mode of computation, Whitsunday was on or about May 24 in the year A.D. 33.

Soon afterwards, Peter, " standing up with the eleven," addressed the people. " The same day were added unto them about three thousand souls," ii, 41.

Peter and John cure the lame man in the Temple, iii, 1.

—Gamaliel cautions the people not to molest the apostles, for that their doctrines, if false, would die away of their own accord ; and, in illustration of this, he reminds them that the similar attempts of Theudas and Judas the Galilæan, " in the days of the taxing," had been brought to nought, v, 35-36.

—Seven deacons are chosen. " And the word of God increased ; and the number of the disciples multiplied in Jerusalem greatly ; and a great company of the priests were obedient to the faith." vi, 1-7.

Stephen, the deacon, is stoned to death. vii.

The first notice of Paul here occurs in Acts vii, 58, where the witnesses against Stephen, stripping themselves to cast the first stone against their victim, laid down " their clothes at a young man's feet whose name was Saul."

" Saul was consenting unto his [*Stephen's*] death." viii, 1.

—" At that time there was a great persecution against the church which was at Jerusalem ; and they were all scattered abroad throughout the regions of Judæa and Samaria, except the apostles."

" As for Saul, he made havoc of the church, &c." viii, 3. *Marginal date* 34.

Philip preaches Christ in Samaria, viii, 1.

—Saul's journey to Damascus—His conversion on the way, ix, 3-22. A.D. 35. He then preaches Christ at Damascus.

—" After that many days were fulfilled," Saul escapes from Damascus and goes to Jerusalem, ix, 23-27. The disciples at first are afraid of him.

The disciples, hearing that he was a convert and fearing lest the Gentiles should murder him, " brought him down to Cæsarea, and sent him forth to Tarsus." ix, 30.

—" And it came to pass in those days that she [Tabitha or Dorcas] was sick and died." ix, 37.

—" And it came to pass that he [Peter], having raised Dorcas to life, tarried many days in Joppa with one Simon a tanner." ix, 43.

—Peter is warned to go with the messengers of Cornelius from Joppa to Cæsarea. x.

The date given in the margin of our Bibles to these events is A.D. 41.

—" Then departed Barnabas to Tarsus, for to seek Saul, and when he had found him, he brought him to Antioch. And it came to pass that a whole year they assembled themselves with the church and taught much people. And the disciples were called Christians first in Antioch. And in those days came prophets from Jerusalem unto Antioch ; and there stood up one of them named Agabus, and signified by the spirit that there should be great dearth throughout all the world : which came to pass in the days of Claudius Cæsar. Then the disciples, every man according to his ability, determined to send relief unto the brethren which dwelt in Judæa : which also they did, and sent it to the elders by the hands of Barnabas and Saul." xi, 25-30.

—" About that time Herod the king stretched forth his hand to vex certain of the church." James is put to death, and Peter is imprisoned, but escapes by the interference of an angel. . . . . " And he [Herod] went down from Judæa to Cæsarea, and there abode." xii, 1-19.

An approximate date to these events may be obtained from the death of Herod, which happened A. D. 44, and is related in connection with these events. *Acts* xii, 23.

—" Barnabas and Saul returned from Jerusalem when they had fulfilled their ministry, and took with them John, whose surname was Mark." xii, 25.

In chapter 13, it is related that Barnabas and Saul are deputed to preach the Gospel in distant countries, and that they proceed accordingly to Seleucia, and from thence to Cyprus (v. 4), where they visit the principal cities Salamis and Paphos (vv. 5, 6). Here, in the account of their rencontre with Elymas the sorcerer, before Sergius Paulus, the deputy, *i.e.* proconsul, we first learn that Saul was also called Paul (v. 9); and from this time the name of Saul is dropped.

They sail from Paphos to Perga in Pamphylia. John, alias Mark, returns to Jerusalem. xiii, 13.

They depart from Perga to Antioch, where Paul preaches in the synagogue on the two following sabbaths, xiii, 14. Being persecuted by the Jews, they shake off the dust from their feet and depart to Iconium (v. 51).

They preach at Iconium, but, "when there was an assault made both of the Gentiles, and also of the Jews with their rulers," they flee to Lystra and Derbe. xiv, 1-6.

At Lystra Paul cures a lame man; the people take him and Barnabas for gods, but by the intervention of some Jews from Antioch and Iconium, their minds are turned, and they stone Paul, leaving him for dead. On his recovery, he and Barnabas depart to Derbe, thence back to Lystra, Iconium, Antioch, Perga, Attalia (v. 25), and back to Antioch, where they "abode long time with the disciples." xiv, 8-28.

—Paul and Barnabas go up from Antioch to Jerusalem to consult the church about circumcision, and return to Antioch taking with them Judas, surnamed Barsabas, and Silas. xv, 1-35. A.D. 51.

—Paul sets out on his second tour, but quarrels with Barnabas about John surnamed Mark. Barnabas takes Mark and sails to Cyprus. xv, 36-39.

—Paul proceeds on his journey, in company with Silas: they visit Derbe, Lystra, and passing through Phrygia, Galatia, Mysia, Troas, cross to Samothrace, Neapolis, Philippi (where Paul cast out from a woman, a spirit of divination, xvi, 12: and was imprisoned with Silas, but released after the shock of an earthquake), Amphipolis, Apollonia, Thessalonica, Berœa, xvii, 18: Athens, and Corinth, where they "found a certain Jew named Aquila, born in Pontus, lately come from Italy, with his wife Priscilla, because that Claudius had commanded all Jews to depart from Rome." xviii, 2.

—[The date is 54 in margin] after which they "continued there [*i.e.* at Corinth] a year and six months" (Gallio being deputy of Achaia). Here Paul exercises his craft of tentmaking and then with Aquila and Priscilla visits Cenchreæ [where he fulfils a vow by shearing his head], Ephesus, Cæsarea, Jerusalem, and Antioch. xv, 40—xviii, 22.

—After Paul "had spent some time there [at Antioch] " he " went over all the country of Galatia and Phrygia in order "— to Ephesus (where he "disputed daily in the school of one Tyrannus—by the space of two years"), Macedonia, xx, 1: Greece, where he abode three months, Philippi, Troas, Assos, xx, 13: Mitylene, Chios, Samos, Trogyllium, Miletus, Ephesus, xx, 17: Coos, Rhodes, Patara, Tyre, xxi, 3: Ptolemais, Cæsarea, Jerusalem, where he was led before the chief captain Claudius Lysias, who asked him if he was not that Egyptian who had "led into the wilderness 4000 men that were murderers, &c." xxi, 38.

Paul makes his defence, but owing to the clamours of the Jews, they are on the point of scourging him, until it is known that he was a Roman citizen; upon which he is on the morrow set free from his bonds and again examined, on the morrow, face to face with his accusers. xxii, 1-30.

Ananias the high priest commanding to smite Paul, is rebuked by Paul, who does not know that he is the high priest. The Jews conspire to kill Paul, but through his sister's son information thereof is sent to Claudius Lysias who sends him down to Cæsarea. xxxiii, 1-35.

He appears before Felix, and is left bound two years, until Festus was sent to succeed Felix. xxiv, 1-27.

Paul, having been heard by Festus and King Agrippa, appeals to Cæsar. The hearing occupies the whole of chapters xxv and xxvi.

Paul is sent on board ship for Rome, and on his arrival at that city, he dwelt "two years in his own hired house, and received all that came in unto him, preaching the kingdom of God, and teaching those things which concern the Lord Jesus Christ with all confidence, no man forbidding him." Chapters xxvii and xxviii.

The particulars of the voyage, though highly interesting, are of no importance to our present subject, which is neither to defend nor to assail the truth of the history contained in this book, but to show, as has been done in the case of the gospels, that the work is an anonymous compilation, drawn up in a later age, and does not possess the authority of an original contemporary record of the first twenty or thirty years after the death of Christ. The arguments arise, as in the gospel, partly from errors, anachronisms, and contradictions, found in the book itself, partly from a comparison of its contents with other profane histories of the period which it treats of.

From the inscription to Theophilus, it has been argued that the Book of the Acts was written by St Luke; but this inference is based on the supposition that the gospel, bearing his name, was also written by him; and we have shown that no proof of this can be produced beyond the popular tradition; neither can we state with certainty who this Theophilus was. The epithet prefixed to his name, κράτιστος most excellent, denotes somewhat of a diplomatic style, and was thought by Gibbon to designate a man holding a civil or official dignity. It seems not to be a prefix which those contemporary with the apostles would care to give to the humble inspectors or *overseers* of the Christian community, who have since been denominated by the professional and more dignified title of bishops. The sixth bishop of Antioch (A.D. 171) was Theophilus, who appears as the writer of a book addressed to Autolycus, and it has been said that he is the man to whom the Gospel of St Luke and the Acts of the Apostles are inscribed. It is, however, impossible either to confirm or to refute this opinion, although we know, from the example of Paul, who preached the gospel immediately after his conversion, how easy it would be for Theophilus, having been confirmed in his religion by the writer of the third gospel, to publish a work himself in defence of it, after he had been raised to be bishop of the See of Antioch. Nor can we omit to see the close connection between Antioch and the origin of at least one of our gospels, if the Theophilus to whom it is dedicated was the sixth bishop who presided over that See. But all our premises on these points are traditional or conjectural, and the conclusion drawn from them must clearly be conjectural also. There are, however, certain passages in the Acts which are thought to prove that the author of the Acts was at all events contemporary with St Paul, and actually accompanied him on his travels. Thus, in the last chapter, verse 7, the writer says:

In the same quarters were possessions of the chief man of the island, whose name was Publius, who received *us*, and lodged *us* three days courteously.

A similar form of words is found in several other passages of the work. This conclusion might be of weight, if it were certain that the Acts of the Apostles is a distinct original work, as opposed to a compilation in which different traditions and documents are put together in the very words which they bore in their original fragmentary state. This point, however, cannot be proved of the Acts of the Apostles. There is the strongest internal evidence that the work is compiled out of at least two fragments, and that the compiler has united them together so as to make a continuous history, but has not been able to conceal the sutures which join, and yet separate, the several portions of the work. To the compiler of the work,* then, may be due the dedication to Theophilus, as in the case of the gospel, but not the character of having himself witnessed the events which he relates of the apostles generally in the first few chapters, and afterwards of Paul alone.

We may now consider the facts which seem to prove that this view of the work is a reality and not a supposition.

1. *Paul, otherwise called Saul.*

In the first place, after the thirteenth chapter, verse 9, where we learn that Saul was "also called Paul," we hear little or nothing of the twelve apostles, but the history follows the new apostle Paul almost exclusively, and it is only in the travels of Paul that the writer of the history, whoever he may have been, uses the personal pronouns *we* and *us*. A suspicion arises from this fact, that the book of the Acts is made up out of two originals, one the Acts of the Apostles generally, the other the Acts or Travels of St Paul. It would seem that the compiler did not know why the name of Saul was changed to Paul, for he merely tells us that the two names designate the same person, and this view of the case militates strongly against the opinion that the writer was himself a witness of the events which he relates.

2. *The Ascension.*

There is a serious discrepancy between the writer of the Acts of the Apostles and the evangelists on the subject of the Ascension. It will be seen in the harmony of events following the resurrection, given in the 44th chapter, that St Matthew and St John take no notice of this important particular; that, according to Mark (xvi, 19) the ascension took place from the chamber in which the eleven sat at meat in Jerusalem on the evening of the resurrection, but that in Luke's Gospel (xxiv, 50-51), it took place from Bethany,

---

* An apposite illustration of this process may be adduced in the various lives of Thomas-à-Becket, preserved in MSS in various public libraries.—Besides several independent lives of this saint by known writers, there is a compilation from various sources called the "Quadrilogus." No less than six copies of this work are extant, each professing to be the work of a separate author, who has prepared a new preface of his own—but the body of the work is the same in all!

whither Jesus is described as having led them out immediately after his appearance to them on the evening of the resurrection. Now, however, we learn from the Acts (i, 3) that Christ " showed himself alive after his passion by many infallible proofs, being seen of them forty days, and speaking of the things pertaining to the kingdom of God." It is impossible to insert this interval of forty days into the narrative of St Luke between the resurrection which happened in the morning and the ascension which took place at Bethany in the evening. Again in the Acts (i, 4) Jesus tells his disciples "that they should not depart from Jerusalem," until they should " be endued with power from on high " (Luke xxiv, 59), but, in St Matthew's Gospel, they had already gone into Galilee, immediately after the resurrection, and in St John's narrative they appear to have resumed their old occupations, supposing that they had for ever lost their master.

In the latter statement about not departing from Jerusalem, the author of the Acts is at variance with St Matthew, but in the former, about the forty days, he is at variance with St Luke. How then can it be said that the same person wrote the Gospel and the Acts—which are at variance with one another on so important a point as the question whether Christ was seen only one day or forty by his disciples after his resurrection? The two accounts can only be reconciled by supposing them to have been derived from different traditions, which leads to the inevitable inference that the books could not both have been written by apostles or infallible authors.

3. *Simeon and Simon.*

In the fifteenth chapter of the Acts of the Apostles is the notice of a meeting held by Paul and Barnabas and the other apostles and elders respecting the alleged necessity of keeping the law of Moses. Peter then rises, and addresses them as follows:

7. Men and brethren, ye know how that a good while ago God made choice among us that the Gentiles by my mouth should hear the word of the gospel, and believe. 8. And God, which knoweth the hearts, bare them witness, giving them the Holy Ghost, even as he did unto us; 9. And put no difference between us and them, purifying their hearts by faith. 10. Now therefore why tempt ye God, to put a yoke upon the neck of the disciples, which neither our fathers nor we were able to bear? 11. But we believe that through the grace of the Lord Jesus Christ we shall be saved, even as they.

When Peter had ended, Paul and Barnabas address the

meeting ; after which James, commonly called the first Bishop of Jerusalem, begins to speak thus:

13. Men and brethren, hearken unto me: 14. " Simeon hath declared how God at the first did visit the Gentiles, to take out of them a people for his name," &c.

This is an important passage, and it is worth while to consider who is meant by Simeon, and what " visitation of the Gentiles " is here referred to. A note in some of our commentaries on the Bible interprets Simeon, "the same as Simon, meaning St Peter." But this explanation cannot be accepted; *Simeon* is not the same name as *Simon*, either in Hebrew, in Greek, or in any other language. In Greek especially the difference is strongly marked, Σίμων—Συμεών. The mind involuntarily turns to aged Simeon, who is said in the Gospel of St Luke to have come into the temple, when the infant Jesus was presented by his mother, and to have blessed God, and said:

LUKE ii, 29-32.

29. Lord, now lettest thou thy servant depart in peace, according to thy word. 30. For mine eyes have seen thy salvation, 31. Which thou hast prepared before the face of all people; 32. A light to lighten the Gentiles, and the glory of thy people Israel.

But there are difficulties in both views of the matter. If Simon Peter's address to the meeting is what James refers to, why does James now call him Simeon?* Moreover the words which he addressed to the meeting do not convey the meaning which James ascribes to Simeon. The remark which Peter made, was that they knew how God through him had lately admitted the Gentiles to the privileges of the Gospel: but James tells the assembly that Simeon had declared how God *at the first* had chosen the Jews from among the Gentiles, to the honour of his name. There is here some confusion, as if the writer had obtained a faint knowledge of what had been said by aged Simeon fifty years before in the temple, and was unable to explain it more clearly, because it had already become obscure by time.

4. *Theudas and Judas.*

In the fifth chapter of the Acts, verses 36-37, we read:

36. For before these days rose up Theudas, boasting himself to be somebody; to whom a number of men, about four hundred, joined themselves: who was slain; and all, as many as obeyed him, were scattered,

---

* Simeon Peter is found, and not Simon, in the inscription to the second Epistle of St Peter—in the Greek, but not in the English version.

and brought to nought. 37. After this man rose up Judas of Galilee in the days of the taxing, and drew away much people after him: he also perished; and all, even as many as obeyed him, were dispersed.

These words form part of the speech of Gamaliel to the Jewish Sanhedrim, dissuading them from persecuting Peter, lest they should be found to fight against God. Gamaliel enforces his argument by pointing out that all previous impostors had fallen by the weakness of their cause, and he suggests that the apostles also, left to themselves, will not succeed, unless their doctrine is from above.

The cases which Gamaliel cites in support of his argument are those of Theudas and Judas the Galilean. But there is this remarkable difficulty attendant upon the affair, that, when Gamaliel made this address to the Sanhedrim, the insurrection of Theudas and his misguided followers had not taken place! The account of the affair is found in Josephus.

Whilst Fadus was governor of Judæa, [*i. e.* in the fourth year of Claudius A. D. 44] a certain magician [*impostor*], Theudas by name, persuades the greater part of the multitude to take their possessions and follow him to the river Jordan. For he said that he was a prophet, and told them that he would divide the river by his command, and afford them an easy passage. And by saying this he deceived many. Fadus however did not suffer them to reap the fruits of their folly; but sent against them a troop of cavalry, which falling on them unexpectedly, slew many of them, and took many alive. They captured Theudas alive, and cut off his head and carried it to Jerusalem.

Such were the events which happened to the Jews at the time of Cuspius Fadus's government.

2. The successor of Fadus was Tiberius Alexander, son of Alexander who was Alabarch in Alexandria, the first man there of his time both in birth and in wealth, and who for piety towards God also was far above his son Alexander; for the latter did not abide by the customs of his country. It was during the government of these men that the great famine also happened in Judæa, when also the Queen Helena bought corn in Egypt for much money, and dealt it out, as we have already said, to those who were in need. In addition to these were put to death also the children of Judas the Galilean—who led the people to revolt from the Romans, when Cyrenius was the valuer in Judæa, as we have shown in the previous part of this history. *Antiq.* xx, v, 1-2.

Those who defend the genuineness and the accuracy of the Acts of the Apostles, suggest that there may have been two men bearing the name of Theudas, as well as two insurrections, one of which had already happened before the time of

Gamaliel; but there is not the slightest authority for such a supposition, and in any case it is highly improbable that two such events should have happened, so precisely similar, within so short a period.

But the insurrection of Judas the Galilean, is said to have followed that of Theudas, and to have happened at the time of the taxing, which is erroneously supposed by St Luke to have been the occasion which led Christ's parents to visit Bethlehem ten years before, as has been already stated in page 190 of this volume. But instead of happening immediately after the insurrection of Theudas, it happened forty years before, though it appears from the extract above quoted out of Josephus, that the children of Judas the Galilean were put to death immediately after the tumult, begun by Theudas, had been repressed. The connection between the two names, Theudas and Judas, both in the speech of Gamaliel and in the history of Josephus, is at any rate curious, and is a strong argument that the same incidents are referred to, both by the Jewish historian, and the writer of the Acts. No other proof however is wanting that the writer of the Acts of the Apostles has endeavoured to ornament his narrative, like the historians Thucydides and Livy, by placing in the mouths of his characters speeches, which he supposed likely to have been spoken in the circumstances under which those persons were placed.

No other explanation so reasonable can be given for Gamaliel being made to refer in his speech to an event which did not happen until forty years afterwards.

5. *The Conversion of St. Paul.*

The first eight chapters of the Acts of the Apostles bring down the history, according to the margin of our Bibles, from the date of Christ's crucifixion to A.D. 34; embracing an interval of four years, if we place Christ's death in 30, but of one year only, if we place it in the year 33 of our era. This chronological arrangement is exceedingly arbitrary, for we have no sure indication of the time at which any of the events related in the Acts of the Apostles may be supposed to have happened: a few short and vague allusions to the "days of Claudius Cæsar," and similar expressions, are all the data that remain.

The ninth chapter of the Acts opens with the journey of Saul to Damascus, and of his conversion by the way. Three accounts of this event have come down to us—all of them in the Acts—the first in the words of the author or compiler of the book, writing of St Paul in the third person, the other two in the words of Paul, speaking in the first person, first to the people of Jerusalem, and secondly before king Agrippa.

Acts ix, 1-8.	Acts xxii, 5-11.	Acts xxvi, 12-16.
And Saul, yet breathing out threatenings and slaughter against the disciples of the Lord, went unto the high-priest,	5. I received letters unto the brethren, and went to Damascus, to bring them which were there bound unto Jerusalem, for to be punished.	12. Whereupon as I went to Damascus with authority and commission from the chief priests,
2. And desired of him letters to Damascus to the synagogues, that if he found any of this way, whether they were men or women, he might bring them bound unto Jerusalem. 3. And as he journeyed, he came near Damascus: and suddenly there shined round about him a light from heaven:	6. And it came to pass, that, as I made my journey, and was come nigh unto Damascus about noon, suddenly there shone from heaven a great light round about me.	13. At mid-day, O king, I saw in the way a light from heaven, above the brightness of the sun, shining round about me and them which journeyed with me.
4. And he fell to the earth, and heard a voice saying unto him, "Saul, Saul, why persecutest thou me?" 5. And he said, "Who art thou, Lord?" And the Lord said, "I am Jesus whom thou persecutest: it is hard for thee to kick against the pricks."	7. And I fell unto the ground and heard a voice saying unto me, "Saul, Saul, why persecutest thou me?" 8. And I answered, "Who art thou, Lord?" And he said unto me, "I am Jesus of Nazareth, whom thou persecutest." 9. And they that were with me saw indeed the light, and were afraid: but they heard not the voice of him that spake to me.	14. And when we were all fallen to the earth, I heard a voice speaking unto me, and saying in the Hebrew tongue, "Saul, Saul, why persecutest thou me? It is hard for thee to kick against the pricks." 15. And I said, "Who art thou, Lord?" and he said, "I am Jesus whom thou persecutest.
6. And he trembling and astonished said, "Lord, what wilt thou have me to do?" And the Lord said unto him, "Arise, and go into the city, and it shall be told thee what thou must do." 7. And the men which journeyed with him stood speechless, hearing a voice, but seeing no man. 8. And Saul arose from the earth; and when his	10. And I said, "What shall I do, Lord?" And the Lord said unto me, "Arise, and go into Damascus; and there it shall be told thee of all things which are appointed for thee to do." 11. And when I could not see for the glory of that light, being led by the hand of them that were with me, I came into Damascus.	16. But rise, and stand upon thy feet, for I have appeared unto thee for this purpose, to make thee a minister and a witness both of these things which thou hast seen and of those things in the which I will appear unto thee," &c.

Acts ix, 8.
eyes were opened, he saw no man: but they led him by the hand, and brought him into Damascus.

In these accounts we meet with two serious difficulties, leading to a suspicion, not that the writer of the book was guilty of forgery or of dishonesty, but that in the first part of this story he was ignorant of the political relations of Damascus to Judæa, and that, as regards the miraculous event which happened to Paul, he has given, in the same book, three different accounts of it, so little harmonizing one with the other that it is quite evident we have the event second-hand, and not in the words of a contemporary, an eye-witness, or an inspired historian.

1. Let us first explain in what way the writer was ignorant of the political relations between Judæa and Damascus. The chief priests at Jerusalem had no power whatever over persons living at Damascus; that city did not belong to Judæa, any more than Boulogne to the English; and we all know what would be the consequence, if an English magistrate were sent with full powers to seize and bring to London any of the numerous British who reside in that foreign town. The priests of the Jews had no power at Damascus: the Roman empire comprised that city in her extensive territories; the Roman arms and laws were established there in the time of St Paul, and the ecclesiastical rulers of the Jews at Jerusalem had no authority at all over the people of Damascus, which was to them a foreign city. We learn indeed from Dr Cave's note, given in a popular commentary on the Bible, that

The Jewish Sanhedrim had not only the power of seizing and scourging offenders against their law, within the bounds of their own country, but, by the connivance and favour of the Romans, might send into other countries where there were any synagogues that acknowledged a dependence in religious matters upon the council at Jerusalem, to apprehend them.

But this unsupported assertion is not sufficient; so extraordinary an usurpation by the Jewish priests of authority over a Roman city beyond the frontiers of Judæa, requires the strongest confirmation before it can be accepted as a fact, and writers of the present day have accordingly endeavoured to find in the political circumstances of those times a support for the Scripture narrative. The explanation which has been given of this point by Messrs Conybeare and Howson, the learned authors of the Life and Epistles of St Paul, is as follows:

There was war between Aretas, who reigned at Petra, the desert metropolis of Stony Arabia, and Herod Antipas, his son-in-law, the tetrarch of Galilee. A misunderstanding concerning the boundaries of the two principalities had been aggravated into an inveterate quarrel by Herod's unfaithfulness to the daughter of the Arabian king, and his shameful attachment to "his brother Philip's wife." The Jews generally sympathized with the cause of Aretas, rejoiced when Herod's army was cut off, and declared that this disaster was a judgement for the murder of John the Baptist. Herod wrote to Rome and obtained an order for assistance from Vitellius, the governor of Syria. But when Vitellius was on his march through Judæa, from Antioch towards Petra, he suddenly heard of the death of Tiberius (A.D. 37); and the Roman army was withdrawn before the war was brought to a conclusion. It is evident that the relations of the neighbouring powers must have been for some years in a very unsettled condition along the frontiers of Arabia, Judæa, and Syria; and the falling of a rich border-town like Damascus from the hands of the Romans into those of Aretas would be a natural occurrence of the war. If it could be proved that the city was placed in the power of the Arabian Ethnarch under these particular circumstances, and at the time of Paul's journey, good reason would be assigned for believing it probable that the ends for which he went were assisted by the political relations of Damascus. And it would indeed be a singular coincidence if his zeal in persecuting the Christians were promoted by the sympathy of the Jews for the fate of John the Baptist.

But there are grave objections to this view of the occupation of Damascus by Aretas. Such a liberty taken by a petty chieftain with the Roman power would have been an act of great audacity; and it is difficult to believe that Vitellius would have closed the campaign if such a city was in the hand of an enemy. It is more likely that Caligula,—who in many ways contradicted the policy of his predecessor,—who banished Herod Antipas and patronised Herod Agrippa,—assigned the city of Damascus as a free gift to Aretas. This supposition, as well as the former, will perfectly explain the remarkable passage in St Paul's letter, where he distinctly says that it was garrisoned by the Ethnarch of Aretas, at the time of his escape. Many such changes of territorial occupation took place under the emperors, which would have been lost to history, were it not for the information derived from a coin, an inscription, or the incidental remark of a writer who had different ends in view. Any attempt to make this escape from Damascus a fixed point of absolute chronology will be unsuccessful, but, from what has been said, it may fairly be collected, that Saul's journey from Jerusalem to Damascus took place not far from that year which saw the death of Tiberius, and the accession of Caligula.

It would seem hardly needful to make any addition to this extract,—for the writers of the work put forth with much diffidence the two theories, as equally well calculated to explain the political difficulty about the mission of Saul to Damascus. But it is right to point out that both of those explanations are purely conjectural. There is not the slightest allusion in history to the occupation of Damascus by Aretas of Petra: nor is it likely that in a war with Herod, the king of Petra, which lies wholly to the south of Judæa, would have seized on a city, lying to the north of that country, and belonging, not to Herod, but to the Romans. But moreover, even if Damascus had for the moment fallen into the hands of Aretas, it is still very unlikely that this prince would have allowed the quarrel between the Jewish priests and the Christians to be carried to such a length. There is no proof that any persecution of the Christians was yet made or likely to be made in Judæa, when under the tolerant government of the Romans. We may be sure that the judgement of Gallio, who "drave" the parties "from the judgement seat," is a fair index of what would be thought by other Roman magistrates under similar circumstances—"If it were a matter of wrong or wicked lewdness, O ye Jews, reason would that I should bear with you: but if it be a question of words and names, and of your law, look ye to it; for I will be no judge of such matters."

We must then look for another interpretation of St Paul's mission. The simplicity of the early Christians led them to magnify every incident of their past annals into political importance. We must strip from the mission of Saul its public and more showy features, leaving its private and more intrinsic character. That the enmity of the priests was seconded by the zeal of Saul their agent need not be doubted, that he was furnished with letters, &c. is also admissible, but not that the mission was supported by the authority to imprison and persecute the Christians, who were as much the subjects of Rome and under the protection of universal tolerance as the priests themselves.

2. In the miraculous particulars with which the conversion of Saul is more immediately clothed, there is a variation in the accounts which we should not expect to find in contemporary narratives, but only in writings which had been con-

structed many years afterwards from tradition. In the 9th chapter of the Acts, where the first account of Paul's vision occurs, it is said that

The men who journeyed with him stood speechless, *hearing a voice*, but *seeing no man*.

But, in chapter xxii, Paul himself says that

They that were with me *saw indeed the light*, and were afraid; but they *heard not the voice* of him that spake to me.

In both of these descriptions, the latter as well as the former, we may suppose that the men remained standing although speechless through fear; but in chapter xxvi, in another recital of the events which then happened to him, St Paul says,

And when we were all *fallen* to the earth, I heard a voice, &c.

The commentators make a feeble attempt to harmonize these accounts, but it is only by such means as would be wholly rejected in the interpretation of any other human composition, and therefore cannot be readily admitted in interpreting the New Testament. The threefold description of Paul's conversion leads to the conclusion that each description comes from a different document, the author of which had not seen the other two.

6. *Use of the word Christians.*

We learn from Acts xi, 26, that the disciples of Christ were called* "Christians first in Antioch." But it is not related at what time this name was first given to them; and it is not probable that it began to be used at the very outset: for our Saviour's name, whilst he was alive, was not Christ, but Jesus, which is the Greek form of the Hebrew name Joshua. The latter was a more vague title, only applicable to him whom the Jews in Hebrew would call the Messiah. Some time would elapse before the identification of Jesus as *the Christ* would lead the world at large to give him that name generally, or to call his followers by a name derived from it. The etymology of the word, also, is not in favour of its early use; for the termination *anus* is not Greek but Latin, and cannot be supposed to have been introduced into Palestine before the Roman conquest of that country, which was not completed before the siege of Jerusalem in A.D. 70. It is therefore not probable that the disciples were called Christians before that time. This view

---

* I doubt the propriety of the translation of the Greek word. It rather means "acted as Christians"—perhaps called themselves.

of the matter is supported by the very rare occurrence of the word in the New Testament; it is found three times only in that volume; first, in the passage above quoted, secondly in Acts xxvi, 28, where Agrippa says to Paul, "Almost thou persuadest me to be a Christian," and lastly in the 1st Epistle of Peter, iv, 16:

> Yet if any of you suffer as a Christian, let him not be ashamed; but let him glorify God on this behalf.

In the second place where it occurs, an anachronism is involved. For the use of the word Christian grew up too slowly to allow the possibility that Agrippa should have employed it as a well-known and recognized term. He seems to have known nothing whatever of the Christian doctrines before he saw Paul, and we read that it was Festus, who first told him of the "certain man left in bonds by Felix," so that he seems, if we may judge from chapter xxv, 14-21, to have known almost as little as Agrippa.

Lastly, the use of the word *Christian* in an epistle written by St Peter, is quite as unlikely, for the same reason, as in king Aprippa's speech to Paul,—with a further reason, that the allusion to "suffering as a Christian" was not wholly appropriate in the days of the apostles themselves, though it was highly appropriate many years afterwards, when the Roman magistrates, like Pliny, were compelled to use force to put down the system of socialism, liberty, and equality, which was adopted by the Christians, and would, if unchecked, have infallibly subverted all the existing fabric of society. Let not the inference to which this leads be misunderstood or misconstrued. No doubt is here expressed that Agrippa, in his speech, and St Peter in his epistle, used some word equivalent to the word Christian; the only doubtful point is that they used this very word. If "Christian" be a translation of the word they used, then those writings, in which this word is found, are translations, and not the original works of the apostles to whom they are ascribed.

7. *Seeming anticipation of regular Christian worship.*

The two passages which here follow seem to point to a state of things which did not exist at the time when they were written:

1. In Acts xiii, 42-44, the whole city, Gentiles and Jews, meet together on the *sabbath*, not once, but regularly. Is not this a picture of a later age, when the Christians had become a large and increasing body?

2. In Acts xiv, 1, "a great multitude both of the Jews and the Greeks believed." Gentiles and Greeks are the same in the language of Scripture. How came there to be a great multitude of Gentiles in the Jewish synagogue?

8. *Variation in the name of the disciples and brethren of Christ, James, Judas, &c.*

After the ascension of Christ into heaven, we read in Acts i, 12-14,

12. Then returned they unto Jerusalem from the mount called Olivet, which is from Jerusalem a sabbath day's journey. 13. And when they were come in, they went up into an upper room, where abode both Peter and James and John, and Andrew, Philip and Thomas, Bartholomew, and Matthew, James the son of Alpheus, and Simon Zelotes, and Judas the brother of James. 14. These all continued with one accord in prayer and supplication, with the woman, and Mary the mother of Jesus, and with his brethren.

The twelve disciples of Christ are here enumerated as in the Gospel according to St Luke, and not in harmony with the lists of St Matthew and St Mark, which have been given in page 219 of this volume. This disagreement concerning the names of such important persons as the twelve apostles is not sufficient to impair the general testimony and value of the history, but only to show us that the book which contains the Acts of the Apostles is not exempt from the general law of Providence, which is the law of Nature. The energies of the first teachers of Christianity were directed not to hand down to future times the deeds which they themselves had done, but to preach that Gospel which as they felt it to be beneficial to themselves, they thought it their duty to extend if possible to the whole of the human race.

Our examination of these Acts would not be complete if we now omitted to inquire, as in the case of the Gospels, how far the earliest Christian writers were acquainted with the book called the Acts of the Apostles, or have quoted passages which can be proved to have been taken from that book. Such evidence, indeed, is not necessary in proof of its truthfulness, nor does the absence of such evidence prove that the incidents therein recorded are to be set aside as fabulous or legendary. But if no contemporaneous or early writers have quoted the Acts of the Apostles which now forms part of our canon, it results that St Luke, who was one of the earliest disciples of Christianity, could not have been the author of the work. It is then indisputable that no quotation from the Acts of the Apostles is found in any ancient writer until the time of Irenæus, about the year A.D. 170. A few passages have however been quoted by those who maintain the genuineness of form as well as the authenticity of the matter, to prove that the book which we now have was well known to the early writers, in whose works those passages are found. The first of those who are supposed to have quoted the Acts of the Apostles are the five Apostolical Fathers, who will demand but a short notice.

In the epistle of Barnabas, chapter 7, occur the words applied to Christ, " Being about to judge quick and dead," and in Acts x, 42, we read of Christ that he is " judge of quick and dead." But we find in I Peter iv, 5, " ready to judge quick and dead," and in II Tim. iv, 1, " who is about to judge quick and dead." It is evident that these words in the epistle of Barnabas denote an opinion prevalent among all Christians, and have no necessary connection with any book of our canon, nor indeed need be considered as a quotation from any book at all.

The epistle of the Roman Clement also furnishes nothing which directs the attention to the Acts of the Apostles. When in his second chapter he speaks of " Being subject rather than subjecting [others], giving with greater pleasure than receiving," it is by no means necessary to suppose that he had seen the passage in the Acts (xx, 13), where we read " He [Jesus] said It is blessed rather to give than to receive." If Jesus said this, for it is not recorded in the Gospel histories of his life, others must have known it besides the writer of the Acts, and the sentiment expressed in those words would naturally lead to their being quoted among the Christians.

In the Shepherd of Hermas are two passages which are adduced as similar to others in the Acts, Vision iv, 2, compared with Acts iv, 12 ; and Similitude ix, 28, with Acts v, 41; but it would be a waste of time to show—what is well known to everyone—that similarities of word and of thought are found in all writings, particularly in religious works, where set forms of speech and a few specific doctrines are of constant occurrence.

In the Epistle to the Philadelphians, by Ignatius, a sentence in the second chapter is thought to be imitated from Acts xx, 29, because the enemies of the faith are described as wolves in both. And a similar identification of the same author's epistle to the Smyrnæans (iii) with Acts x, 41, is supposed to be established by the reference in both to those who ate and drank with Jesus after his resurrection. But all this was known to others besides the writer of the Acts, and must have been known to Ignatius, even if, as appears from his silence to have been the case, he had never heard of the work in question.

In the Epistle of Polycarp (i) the same inference is vainly drawn from the expression "loosing the pangs of hell," which is thought to have been derived from the words in Acts ii, 24, "loosing the pangs of death." No connection whatever is established by this similarity of expression.

Next to the five Apostolical Fathers comes Justin Martyr, in whose writings no reference to the Acts of the Apostles or quotation from any part thereof is to be found. Nor need we search for any proof of this fact; for Dr Westcott, in his work on the Canon (p. 168), says that "the references to the Acts are uncertain," and Alford, in his Prolegomena to the Greek Testament (ii, p. 20), says that there are none "which, fairly considered, belong to this book."

We cannot doubt that these writers would have quoted from so important a work as the Acts of the Apostles if they had been acquainted with it, and may therefore conclude that up to the time of Justin Martyr, this book was not known to the Christian Church.

CHAPTER XLVIII.

ST PAUL AND HIS EPISTLES.

IN the canon of the Christian Scriptures the book which describes, as it is also named, the Acts of the Apostles, is followed by fourteen epistles, attributed to the Apostle Paul. This great preacher has by many been called the second founder of Christianity, and it may reasonably be allowed that without his agency our religion would hardly have made such rapid progress, after it had received what must have been a serious check by the crucifixion of Jesus Christ.

The eleven disciples, according to Christ's own prophecy, forsook their master and fled immediately after his apprehension; and whether they withdrew to Galilee and resumed their original occupations, or remained in Jerusalem, as according to one injunction of their master's they were bound to do, their proceedings were on a very limited scale compared with those which were carried on so widely and so successfully by the apostle Paul.

It has caused surprise to many readers of the New Testament that a closer bond was not formed between the original disciples and the new convert, but the points of view from which the two parties regarded their religion, and their modes of preaching the gospel, were by no means the same. The old disciples, having witnessed the good deeds and the remarkably practical teaching of Jesus, and having also what might be then thought a better security in their own senses, than in faith like St Paul's, not founded in experience, for the truths which they were to preach, perhaps did not wholly comprehend the vigour and energy which sprung up in the mind of Paul, when converted by so wonderful an intervention of Providence, nor had they anything to compare with his strong feeling that predestination alone had snatched him from his former unbelief. The original disciples had never heard their master compare them to the clay, which the potter formed at his own pleasure to be vessels, some of honour and others of dishonour, and even of the wrath of God; and indeed there was a strong taint of Judaism adhering to all who adopted Christianity and resided in Jerusalem, even later than the time when that city was partially destroyed by the Romans. It was from this source probably that the complaints of false brethren arose, which occur so frequently in the Epistles of St Paul, as we now have them. That the disciples at Jerusalem never wholly harmonized with St Paul derives much confirmation from certain passages which invite our attention. To whom can he refer when he uses those words in 1 Corinthians ix, 1-6?

> Am I not an apostle? am I not free? have I not seen Jesus Christ our Lord? are not ye my work in the Lord? 2. If I be not an apostle unto others, yet doubtless I am to you: for the seal of mine apostleship are ye in the Lord. 3. Mine answer to them that do examine me is this, 4. Have we not power to eat and to drink? 5. Have we not power to lead about a sister, a wife, as well as other apostles, and as the brethren of the Lord, and Cephas? 6. Or I only and Barnabas, have not we power to forbear working?

Paul here, we see, answers some objections that had been made to his claim of being an apostle, and he even asserts that, like the other apostles, he had seen Jesus Christ our Lord whose gospel he was preaching.

In another epistle, inscribed to the Galatians (i, 1), he urges on those whom he is addressing, that he derived his office not from men but from Christ himself, and in the twelfth verse he states more fully of the gospel which he preaches that he "neither received it of man, neither was taught it, but by the revelation of Jesus Christ." That there were violent contentions among the Christians of this early age is manifest from the following extracts:—

2 TIM. ii, 17, 18.

17. Their word will eat as doth a canker: of whom is Hymenæus and Philetus; 18. Who concerning the truth have erred, saying that the resurrection is past already.

1 COR. i, 12.

12. Now this I say, that every one of you saith, "I am of Paul; and I of Apollos; and I of Cephas; and I of Christ."

PHIL. i, 15-17.

15. Some indeed preach Christ of envy and strife; and some of good will: 16. The one preach Christ of contention, not sincerely, supposing to add affliction to my bonds: 17. But the other of love, knowing that I am set for the defence of the gospel.

GAL. ii, 9.

9. But when James, Cephas, and John, who seemed to be pillars, perceived the grace that was given unto me, they gave to me and Barnabas the right hands of fellowship; that we should go unto the heathen, and they unto the circumcision.

GAL. ii, 11.

11. But when Peter was come to Antioch, I withstood him to the face, because he was to be blamed.

Together with these complaints the personality of Jesus is clearly less conspicuous in those epistles than it is in either the Gospels or the Acts; indeed, no persons or facts are brought much into the foreground, but ideas and feelings occupy the first place. The writer never for a moment seems to lose sight of what befel him on the road to Damascus, and to this all-absorbing reflection so many of his admonitions are chiefly due.

Many other passages might be quoted to show that St Paul encountered much opposition from the older disciples who dwelt at Jerusalem. But we do not learn from any part of the New Testament the full extent to which their opposition went. It is in an obscure writing, which has not hitherto had such attention paid to it as it would seem to deserve, that we meet with some startling observations which, if genuine, bear with great force upon the history and ministry of St Paul.

In the eighth chapter of the Acts of the Apostles (verses 9-25) is the account of Simon Magus, who, having thought to obtain for money the same miraculous powers which he had seen exhibited by St Peter, was reproved by the apostle and having declared his repentance was forgiven. This incident, brief as it is here described, is nowhere else referred to in the New Testament, and yet the name of this man has obtained the greatest notoriety in every age and country of the Christian faith. It only concerns our present purpose to notice an ancient writing, in which the name of this Simon is prominent ; and, strange as it may appear, critics of all parties have agreed that under the fictitious name of Simon is to be understood the apostle Paul.

"There can be no doubt," says Dr Westcott, in his work on the Canon of the New Testament (p. 261), "that St Paul is referred to as 'the enemy' in the Epistle of Peter to James prefixed to the Homilies."

These Homilies, formerly ascribed to Clement of Rome, were probably written at the end of the second century ; but their origin is doubtful, and the various questions and opinions that have arisen concerning them forbid us by their extent from entering fully upon that subject here. The general purpose of the writer seems to have been to defend the Judaizing form of Christianity, which prevailed for nearly two hundred years at Jerusalem and elsewhere, against other doctrines which seemed to be more spiritual in their nature and destructive of church government in their results. The whole body of Homilies, twenty in number, is prefaced by a letter from its supposed author Clement to St James, whom he addresses as "master, bishop of bishops, and ruler of the church of the Hebrews at Jerusalem." But prefixed to this is another letter bearing the name of St Peter, also addressed to St James, and containing certain passages which are here given, as illustrating the history of St Paul.

Peter to James the master and bishop of the Holy Church, by the Father of all things, through Jesus Christ, may there be peace for ever ! Knowing, my brother, that thou art earnestly zealous towards that which is expedient for all of us in common, I ask and beg of thee not to impart the books of my preachings, which I have sent thee, either to any of the Gentiles or to any of the same tribe, before having experience of him. But if any one having been tried has been found worthy, then deliver them to him according to the course by which Moses also delivered to the Seventy who received his seat. . . . . . Unless it is so done, our word of truth will be torn asunder into many opinions. This, however, I know, not as being a prophet, but already seeing the beginning of that evil. For some out of the Gentiles have rejected my lawful preaching, having taken to themselves a certain unlawful and vain teaching of the hostile man. . . . . That it may be perceived of what class is Simon who before me first went to the Gentiles, and of what class I happen to be who came after him and succeeded to him as light to darkness, as knowledge to ignorance, and as health to disease. Thus then, as the True Prophet has said, first must come a false gospel from an impostor and then, after the destruction of the holy place, the true gospel be sent to correct future heresies; and after this again at the end first must come Antichrist, and then he who is truly our Christ Jesus, after whom the eternal sun will rise and all darkness be dispersed. *Hom.* ii, 17.

Wherefore before all things remember to avoid that apostle or teacher or prophet who does not first refer his preaching to James called the brother of our Lord, and trusted with managing the church of the Hebrews in Jerusalem, and come to you with witnesses; lest the malice which conversed with the Lord forty days, having effected nothing, should afterwards, like a star falling from heaven, send against you a preacher, as it has sent against us that Simon, preaching under the pretext of truth in the name of our Lord, and sowing the seeds of error. *Hom.* xi, 35.

After delivering this address, Peter sends certain of his followers to Antioch, and three months afterwards went thither himself: and this journey may perhaps be the same which St Paul refers to in his epistle to the Galatians (ii, 11), upon which occasion his own words indicate that a violent altercation arose between him and Peter.

In the seventeenth Homily we have a long discussion between Simon Magus and St Peter, of which the following specimen will be sufficient:

And Simon said: "If thou sayest that visions do not always declare the truth, yet things seen and dreams which are sent by God do not speak falsely about things which he wishes to say." And Peter said, "Thou hast said well that if sent by God they do not speak falsely: but it is uncertain whether he who sees has seen a dream sent by God." And Simon said, "If he who has seen be just, he has seen truly." *Hom.* xvii, 15.

If then our Jesus was seen and known by thee also, and spoke to thee in a vision, being angry with thee as an adversary to him, he, therefore, spoke to thee by visions and dreams, or also by revelations from without. But if a man can be instructed for doctrine through a vision? and if thou sayest it is possible, why did the Teacher abide and converse a whole year* with those who were awake? *Hom.* xvii, 19.

---

* The writer evidently thought that the ministry of Jesus lasted one year only.

The dialogue proceeds in this style, and clearly its benefit to the reader or to its hearers must have been as remote as was the chance of its ever being brought to a satisfactory conclusion. Inward feelings, and supposed manifestations of the Deity, conveyed to the worshipper, have always been favourite subjects with a certain class of enthusiasts or impostors in every age of the world, and have been encountered by the opposite party, as in the present case, with the same demand of more positive and authoritative evidence.

From this digression however let us return to the more immediate subject of this chapter.

The enmity of the sacerdotal Christians residing at Jerusalem, rendered highly probable by St Paul's constant reference to the opposition which he experienced, is a strong argument that we have in some at least of the epistles ascribed to him a genuine reflex of his mind and feelings. There are three points of view from which we may regard these writings. 1. How far the historical details contained in them harmonize with the corresponding narrative of St Paul's ministry as recorded in the Acts of the Apostles. 2. How far it is probable that St Paul would write such epistles as we now have, forming part of the New Testament Canon and written in the Greek language. And 3. What evidence has been produced in favour of their authenticity, and if such evidence is not applicable to all of them, it is important if possible to ascertain which may be considered genuine and which doubtful.

As regards the last question, it may be necessary to state that the genuineness of a book is distinct from the truth of its contents. A work written by any particular author may be accepted as truthful in its contents, but may come before the world under another name and not that of its real writer. It has been not unusual to ascribe authenticity and not genuineness to such a work. In most cases, however, the distinction between these words is not insisted upon, and the two have consequently been often accepted as synonymous, and used indifferently at the pleasure of the writer. If such a distinction, however, be applied to the Epistles of St Paul, there is a class of critics who would ascribe to them authenticity as regards their contents, but not genuineness of form. In other words it might be argued that the teaching of St Paul, his doctrines, and the interesting sketches which he gives us of his life, are authentic in the highest degree, but that the epistolary form in which these have come down to us labours under certain disadvantages which suggest a doubt whether we have those doctrines, that teaching, and those personal details of his life in their genuine original form. That certain of these epistles have been erroneously ascribed to St Paul is an opinion which has been entertained by the best and most learned critics, and which originated in the very earliest ages of our era, and that there was danger of this happening even during his own life-time may be inferred from his own words in the Second Epistle to the Thessalonians (ii, 1),where he cautions them not to be deceived by letters, falsely purporting to be written by him. But that all of these epistles are supposititious, as some have ventured to declare, is an assertion which does not commend itself to the approbation of candid judges. The short summary of the Acts given in the last chapter enables us to form a tolerable idea of the chronology of St Paul's life and ministry.

We read of him first in the book of the Acts as taking a prominent part at the stoning of the martyr Stephen (vii, 58). His conversion, which is the next event in his life (ix, 3), is placed in the year A.D. 35, about five years after the crucifixion, on his way to Damascus. Recovering from the effects of his miraculous vision, he began to preach in the Jewish synagogue of Damascus, with so much success that the Jews sought to kill him, and being let down from the wall in a basket he escaped to Jerusalem, where he joined the disciples and preached, but being again in danger of his life, he escaped to Cæsarea and thence to Tarsus his native town. If our chronology is correct, he remained there till A.D. 41, when he was brought by Barnabas to Antioch, where they preach the gospel during a whole year (xi, 25). We are told in the same chapter that the disciples were called Christians first in Antioch, but it is not necessarily implied that the name was given to them at this very time. At the end of the year Saul and Barnabas carry relief to the brethren at Jerusalem, and return afterwards to Antioch in company with John surnamed Mark (xii, 25). The date of these events is marked in the margin of our Bibles at A.D. 44, and at this time Barnabas and Saul set out on a mission to Cyprus and several of the chief cities in Asia Minor. His name of Saul is now dropped and from this time he is called Paul, a name assumed by him perhaps in compliment to Sergius Paulus the deputy whom he had converted to the new faith in Cyprus (xiii, 7). The two apostles return from their mission to Antioch, where they abode long time with the disciples (xiv, 28). They afterwards attend a meeting of the Christian Church at Jerusalem where they tarried a space (xv, 33), and returned to Antioch A.D. 53. Paul now sets out on his second missionary tour, in the course of which he continued a year and six months at Corinth, and again returned to Jerusalem and Antioch (xviii, 22). In his third tour, he stayed two years at Ephesus, three months in Greece, and after visiting a large number of the Grecian islands and cities he came to Cæsarea and from thence to Jerusalem (xxi, 15), where he was arrested, detained two years (xxiv, 27), and finally sent to Rome, A.D. 62.

Thus the ministry of St Paul lasted nineteen years, from A.D. 41 when he began to preach at Antioch until A.D. 60, when he was put in bonds at Jerusalem. And for the events which befel the Church during this period our attention is divided, at least equally, between Jerusalem and Antioch. We know from profane history that in the years A.D. 64, 65, the emperor Nero, unjustly accusing the Christians of having set fire to Rome, exercised a cruel persecution against all who bore that name; and when we read at the end of the Acts of the Apostles the significant statement that Paul preached two years in that city, "no man forbidding him," we can hardly forbear from drawing the inference that at the end of the two years he was no longer allowed the same freedom of action; and when we find that in the very year when this impunity was at an end the Christians, having become a numerous body, were marked out for punishment, it is very difficult to believe that other inferior and newly converted Christians would be punished and that he their leader would be spared.

The proceedings of St Paul on his first arrival in Rome are interesting and important, and have a strong bearing on the question of his epistles. He is stated in the last chapter of the Acts (13) to have been met, on his arrival in Italy, by the brethren at Appii Forum, and afterwards when he had been at Rome three days, to have called the chief of the Jews together and explained to them the circumstances under which he had been brought to that city. The Jews in reply profess their ignorance on the subject: they had received no "letters" about him, and only knew that the sect to which he belonged was everywhere "spoken against." Paul then declares to them his mission, "and some believed the things which were spoken, and some believed not" (24). He then intimates to them that he shall turn to the Gentiles, " and when he had said these words, the Jews departed, and had great reasoning among themselves (29)." From that time he preached the gospel for two years to all that " came in unto him," and at the end of those two years was begun that cruel persecution of the Christians, in which there is every probability that St Paul himself perished.

We will now turn to the epistles themselves which profess to have been written by the great apostle. At the end of almost every manuscript copy is found a subscription purporting to inform the reader where it was written, and accordingly, at the end of each in our authorized version is added a notice more or less full containing the information here referred to. In the second chapter of this volume (p. 7) is given a table of dates according to the latest opinions that have been held on this subject. How far these opinions are borne out by authority or evidence may appear more clearly from the subscriptions as they are found in two of the oldest MSS which now exist, the Alexandrian and the Vatican, compared with those found in the more common and less ancient MSS, and copied from them into the English authorized version. Taking the epistles in the chronological order which the latest critics have suggested, we find the following results:

I. II. The two EPISTLES TO THE THESSALONIANS are now thought to have been written from Corinth, A.D. 52, but our authorized version has the subscription "written from Athens," with which the Alexandrian MS agrees. The Sinaitic MS has no name of place to any of the epistles; and the Vatican has "from Athens" in handwriting somewhat later than the rest of the book, as it has in all St Paul's epistles.

It was in his second missionary tour that St Paul visited Thessalonica, where there was a Jewish synagogue (Acts xvii, 1). He there "as his manner was," reasoned with them out of the Scriptures three sabbath days. Some of the Jews and many of the Greeks believed, but some did not; a disturbance arose among the people, and Paul accompanied by Silas was sent out of the city for safety to Berœa. He soon after went to Athens, where he addressed the Areopagites concerning the resurrection from the dead. He then went to Corinth where he abode one year and six months. It is difficult to say from which of these two cities St Paul indited the Epistles to the Thessalonians, but it is still more difficult to say why he addressed an epistle to them at all. He had resided among them three or four weeks only, with less success for his preaching than he afterwards obtained among the Beroeans, who were "more noble than those in Thessalonica, in that they received the word with all readiness of mind, and searched the Scriptures whether those things were so" (xvii, 11). But the Jews of Thessalonica followed him to Beroea, and he was compelled by a disturbance among the people to depart from that town also.

The external evidence in favour of the authenticity of these epistles is very slight; they are not mentioned by the Apostolic Fathers, by Justin Martyr, or by any other writer until the end of the second century, when the whole canon of Scripture comes at once into notice, and is extensively quoted by Irenæus and others. The name of Paul occurs in the Epistles of Clement and Polycarp, as we might naturally expect in the case of one to whose ministry the establishment of Christianity was chiefly due. But there are certain peculiarities in these epistles, which may suggest a doubt respecting the time, and also the place where they were written, and possibly also the form in which they have come down to us. The writer says in the First Epistle (i, 7) that the Thessalonians, by their zeal in receiving "the word" were an "ensample to all that believe in Macedonia and Achaia," but this is not in perfect harmony with his abrupt expulsion, after a residence of a few weeks, from that town which he is not known ever to have revisited.

Neither does his statement in the Second Epistle (iii, 8) commend itself to a literal interpretation. In justification of his conduct amongst them he says that he did not eat any man's bread, "but wrought with labour and travail night and day, that we might not be chargeable to any of you." He would probably find some difficulty in working at his trade of tent-making, whilst he was at the same time preaching the gospel for so short a time in the manner which he describes.

A third point, which has not yet been satisfactorily cleared up is, that whereas in the First Epistle he clearly indicates the near approach of Christ's second coming, he in his second letter as clearly warns them not to be deceived on that subject. The two passages will be best examined when exhibited in parallel columns as follows:

1 Thess. iv, 15-18.	2 Thess. ii, 1-5.
15. For this we say unto you by the word of the Lord, that we which are alive and remain unto the com-	Now we beseech you, brethren, by the coming of our Lord Jesus Christ, and by our gathering to-

1 THESS. iv, 15-18.	2 THESS. ii, 1-5.
ing of the Lord shall not prevent [*go before*] them which are asleep. 16. For the Lord himself shall descend from heaven with a shout, with the voice of the archangel, and with the trump of God: and the dead in Christ shall rise first. 17. Then we which are alive and remain shall be caught up together with them in the clouds, to meet the Lord in the air: and so shall we ever be in the Lord. 18. Wherefore comfort one another with these words.	gether unto him, 2. That ye be not soon shaken in mind, or be troubled, neither by spirit, nor by word, nor by letter as from us, as that the day of Christ is at hand. 3. Let no man deceive you by any means: for that day shall not come, except there come a falling away first, and that man of sin be revealed the son of perdition; 4. Who opposeth and exalteth himself above all that is called God, or that is worshipped; so that he as God sitteth in the temple of God, showing himself that he is God. 5. Remember ye not, that, when I was yet with you, I told you these things?

It may fairly be asked whether these epistles have been altered at a later date by some editor and arranged to suit the needs of the Church, when they were embodied with the other writings in the Christian canon.

III. The EPISTLE TO THE GALATIANS also is thought to have been written from Corinth about the same time as the preceding: but the subscription, in the common Greek MSS, and in the authorized version, is "Written from Rome," which is confirmed by the Alexandrian and Vatican MSS, and seems preferable to that which some modern critics have substituted in its place. The "region of Galatia" is briefly mentioned in the Acts (xvi, 6) as having been traversed by Paul in his second tour before he visited Thessalonica, and again (xviii, 23) on his third tour, just before he visited Ephesus, where he disputed two years in the school of Tyrannus. Whether the epistle was written to the Galatians after his first or after his second visit, it is difficult to determine,* for we know nothing of what was done by him in that country, the inhabitants of which, descended from the ancient Gauls, still retained their ancient language in the centre of Asia Minor, with no large cities which might invite the attention of merchants or missionaries. That an epistle should be written to such a people by St Paul is not without the range of probability, but that it should be written in the Greek language is a point which has never been satisfactorily

---

* I have had equal difficulty in determining why Messrs Conybeare and Howson have substituted the words "at my first visit" for "at the first" in Gal. iv, 13, unless it was done to support their view that the apostle had made two visits to Galatia before he wrote the epistle to that nation. The Greek words, *to proteron*, cannot mean *at my first visit*. See John ix, 8.

explained in any other way than by the necessity or expediency of compiling an uniform canon for the whole Christian Church. The Epistles to the Thessalonians, who spoke Greek, are less subject to criticism on this head; but if Christianity was addressed to the lowest class of the community, as is understood generally to have been the case, it is not unreasonable to suppose that a Christian missionary would address the Galatians in the language which they themselves would understand. But St Paul appears as writing in a language which not only those to whom he wrote, but himself also understood imperfectly. On this point we have the evidence of Chrysostom, who cites the interview between St Paul and King Agrippa, whose words, rendered in our version, " Almost thou persuadest me to be a Christian," should rather be rendered, " Why, thou art almost persuading me to be a Christian!" Chrysostom says that Paul misunderstood Agrippa—" so illiterate (οὕτως ἰδιώτης) was he." In his third Homily on 1 Corinthians, chapter i, the same Father says, " Show me if Peter was a literary man, and Paul too, but you cannot. They were ignorant and illiterate." Jerome also in several passages of his commentaries on the epistles states the same fact.

Like the other books contained in the Canon of the New Testament, we have no distinct quotations from this epistle before the time of Irenæus. Certain sayings cited by the Apostolical Fathers and Justin seem to have been the common property of the Church, and here and there find their counterpart in the Epistle to the Galatians. There is one only point which requires to be noticed as involving a discrepancy between what St Paul here writes and what is recorded of him in the Acts of the Apostles. From the latter source (ix, 26) we are led to infer that when he escaped from Damascus by night he went straight to Jerusalem, but in his epistle the course of events is very different.

Acts ix, 25-28.	Gal. i, 15-19.
25. The disciples took him by night and let him down by the wall in a basket. 26. And when Saul was come to Jerusalem, he assayed to join himself to the disciples, but they were all afraid of him, and believed not that he was a disciple, 27. But Barnabas took him, and brought him to the apostles, and declared unto them how he had seen the Lord in the way, and that he had spoken to him, and how he	15. When it pleased God, who separated me from my mother's womb, and called me by his grace, 16. To reveal his Son in me, that I might preach him among the heathen; immediately I conferred not with flesh and blood: 17. Neither went I up to Jerusalem to them which were apostles before me; but I went into Arabia, and returned again unto Damascus. 18. Then after three years I went up to Jeru-

Acts ix, 27, 28.	Gal. i, 18, 19.
had preached boldly at Damascus in the name of Jesus. 28. And he was with them coming in and going out at Jerusalem.	salem to see Peter, and abode with him fifteen days. 19. But other of the apostles saw I none, save James, the Lord's brother.

It is difficult to imagine a greater divergency of description than that which is here presented to our notice. Elaborate attempts have been made to reconcile them: but all these have failed, because their learned authors have not noticed the important feature of both narratives, and have laboured to ascertain which of the numerous visits paid by St Paul as recorded in the Acts is to be identified with that visit which St Paul himself records in the epistle. But the drift of both these narratives is to show, the one that St Paul immediately after his conversion at Damascus went up to Jerusalem and at once began to preach the Gospel in company with the other apostles; whereas it is plainly stated by himself, that he did not go *immediately* to Jerusalem, but only after the lapse of three years, and then saw none of the apostles except Peter and James the Lord's brother, and that even then he only stayed there fifteen days. In the 22nd verse of the 1st chapter, the writer states most emphatically that at this time he was "unknown by face unto the churches of Judæa which were in Christ."

The general tenour of the epistle does not require to be noticed. There are few sentences which can guide us to discover the time or the place at which it was written. The 11th verse of the last chapter is wrongly translated in our English version; it should be, "See with what great letters I have written to you with my own hand!" and it is asserted by the authors of the Life and Epistles of St Paul that the 12th verse of the 5th chapter conveys a meaning far different from that which our English version expresses—a meaning which would attribute to St Paul a levity and perhaps bitterness of language not wholly becoming the character of a Christian teacher. Their interpretation is indeed supported by powerful modern critics and by a certain despotic tone, more congenial to a later period of the Church than to the time in which St Paul lived, in which the punishment of excommunication appears as one of the weapons of the Church. The two versions of the mistranslated passage are as follows:

Gal. v, 12.	Life, &c., chap. xviii.
I would they were even cut off which trouble you.	I could wish that these agitators who disturb your quiet, would execute upon themselves not only circumcision, but excision also.

IV. V. The two EPISTLES TO THE CORINTHIANS are dated in the English version from Philippi; the Vatican MS dates the first from Ephesus and the second from Philippi, but the Alexandrian and Sinaitic have no name of place for either of these epistles; and some modern critics, retaining Ephesus as the place where the first was written, have dated the second vaguely from some place in Macedonia. They are thought to have been written at no wide interval of time between one and the other, probably about the year A.D. 57; and in the dearth of more accurate data, it seems useless to raise doubts that can never be answered on a subject which is not of primary importance. Certain peculiarities are found in both these writings which may be briefly noticed.

In the first place many additional circumstances belonging, as we should infer, to the account of St Paul's conversion are here named. Especially may be mentioned the vision, which was made the subject of jocular conversation in the dialogue of Lucian, of which an extract has been given in page 80 of this volume. We have in the second of these Epistles (xii, 1) the account which St Paul gives of the man whom he knew, and who was carried up "fourteen years ago" into paradise, where he "heard unspeakable words, which it is not lawful for a man to utter." That St Paul here states a vision which he had himself seen, has never been doubted by any who have written commentaries upon the Scriptures.

Connected with visions may be named the gifts of tongues and of prophesying, and the order of ministers in the Church, which are described rather largely in the twelfth, thirteenth, and fourteenth chapters of the first epistle. Other adventures which St Paul met with, not named elsewhere, occur in the same chapters.

The number also of Christ's appearances after his resurrection must also be increased if those here named (1 Cor. xv, 4) by St Paul are additional to those which have been enumerated in the previous books of the New Testament. Nor is it wholly uninteresting to observe that in the sixteenth chapter of the first and in the ninth of the second epistle, we find mention of the collection of money for the use of the saints at Jerusalem, which is named in the Acts of the Apostles. That the labourer is worthy of his hire, no doubt was already admitted among the axioms of the Church; but St Paul in these epistles, as elsewhere, prides himself upon the fact that he did not burden the Corinthians with his maintenance (II Cor. xii, 13) whilst he was among them. Equally remarkable is the constant recurrence to the belief that the second coming of Christ would take place whilst some then living were still alive. " We shall not all sleep, but we shall all be changed" (I, xv, 51), are words still used in the burial service of the Church, but in some of the MSS we read, " We shall all sleep, but we shall not all be changed ; " nor is it difficult to understand why the negative should be intentionally misplaced here in order to release Paul from asserting a belief in the early coming of Christ,* which in process of time was so palpably negatived by fact.

Among the peculiar things to be noticed in these epistles is the account which St Paul gives of the Last Supper. He prefaces this account by saying, " I have received of the Lord that which also I delivered unto you," and unless this was communicated to him in a vision concurrently with what is related of his conversion on the way to Damascus, we have no mention of any other occasion when such a revelation may have been made. He states in I Cor. xi, 23 :—

23. That the Lord Jesus the same night in which he was betrayed took bread : 24. And when he had given thanks, he brake it, and said, "Take, eat: this is my body, which is broken for you : this do in remembrance of me." 25. After the same manner also he took the cup, when he had supped, saying, " This cup is the new testament in my blood : this do ye, as oft as ye drink it, in remembrance of me."

These words, even in the English translation, are remarkably similar to those in which the first three evangelists, and especially St Luke, describe the institution of the Lord's Supper. But in the Greek text the similarity of words is much more remarkable, nor can we avoid the inference that if neither the gospels could have been copied from the epistle nor the epistle from the gospels, the phraseology of both has been taken from some traditional or written original document, which had already been clothed in a Greek dress, before either of these existing narratives had appeared.

VI. THE EPISTLE TO THE ROMANS, in the Alexandrian and Sinaitic MSS, bears no name of place from which it was addressed. The Vatican names Corinth, and the authorized English version has " Written from Corinth to the Romans by Phœbe the deaconess of the church in Cenchreæ." The time when it was written, as in the case

---

* The belief that the reign of Christ on earth was at hand, shows itself indirectly in the words " Anathema Maran-atha," which occur at the end of the First Epistle to the Corinthians. These words are interpreted, " The Lord is coming."

of all the epistles, can only be given from conjecture, which generally assigns this one to the year 57 after Christ.

The belief in the speedy coming of Christ and in the reign of the saints on earth appears in the words, "Now is our salvation nearer than when we believed" (xiii, 11), but the epistle does not enlarge further on this subject. It seems to be the object of the writer to convey general principles of Christian morality to his readers, and whilst he professes his intention to visit Rome when he takes his "journey into Spain," he acknowledges that he has had "a great desire these many years" (xv, 23) to go to Rome, but had hitherto been prevented. At the same time he is persuaded that those to whom he is writing are "full of goodness, filled with all knowledge, able also to admonish one another" (14). The fifteenth chapter ends with the usual benediction, and the sixteenth contains salutations and greetings to a variety of persons, all in the third person, save that in verse 22 are interposed the words, " I Tertius, who wrote this epistle, salute you in the Lord." The names which occur in this chapter, whether of those who are saluted at Rome or of those who join the writer in sending those salutations, afford no decided test as regards the nationality of the one or of the others ; they are partly Roman and partly Greek, and may all be taken to represent Romans, who were much more used to imitate the Greeks than the Greeks to imitate the Romans. It is however remarkable that the persons to whom the Apostle writes are addressed as "you that are in Rome ;" which seems to denote not the Romans generally, but those in Rome who had already become Christians. In what way this bears upon the language in which St Paul addresses the inhabitants of a Latin city must be deferred until the other epistles are briefly noticed.

VII. THE EPISTLE TO THE EPHESIANS, supposed to have been written about the year A.D. 62, is generally admitted to have been erroneously so addressed. The Vatican MS and the English authorized version date it from Rome: the Sinaitic and Alexandrian MSS give no name of place, and the latter of these in the first verse has a blank for the words "at Ephesus," which are added by a later hand. It is generally thought that the epistle was addressed to the Laodiceans ; but for this there is no authority but that of writers who lived much later, and we learn from Colossians iv, 16, that St Paul wrote an epistle "from Laodicea," and not to the people who inhabited that city.

The only point here to be noticed is the great similarity

and even identity of thought and language between this and the epistle addressed to the Colossians and occasionally others of St Paul's letters, and this circumstance has furnished one of the reasons why some modern critics have denied that it was written by St Paul at all.

VIII. THE EPISTLE TO THE PHILIPPIANS also is dated A.D. 62, and the place Rome, in both the Vatican MS and the authorized version. In this short epistle St Paul gives us some account of himself, his origin and creed (iii, 5): also that he had twice received pecuniary aid from the Philippians (iv, 16), and that, whilst he had some adherents even in the prætorium among the servants of the emperor (i, 12), there were some who preached Christ out of contention and envy towards himself (15). There is also here, as in most of the epistles, a reference to the speedy coming of Christ, "The Lord is at hand" (iv, 5). And the word, rendered *concision* in our English version, had already in ancient times suggested a less vague meaning to commentators in connection with the subject not only of circumcision, but of eunuchs also. The Philippians were a colony from Rome.

IX. THE EPISTLE TO THE COLOSSIANS is thought to have been written, A.D. 62, from Rome, as named in our authorized version and in the Vatican MS.

In this short composition we may notice the warning which St Paul so frequently repeats against false teachers, —" Lest any man should beguile you with enticing words (ii, 4)"—" Beware lest any man spoil you through philosophy (ii, 8)," &c. And St Paul's usual warning about circumcision is here repeated; whilst other indications are not wanting, that there were already two systems of doctrine growing up in the Church not yet thoroughly amalgamated, the Judaical derived from the original Church of Jerusalem, and the Pauline as set forth in these epistles. When we consider that hardly thirty years had elapsed since the crucifixion of our Lord, we may be allowed to express surprise that such schisms should in so short a time have found a place among those who were so near to the wonderful career and simple teaching of Jesus Christ.

X. THE EPISTLE TO PHILEMON is thought to have been written in A.D. 62 from Rome, as subscribed in our authorized version, but neither of the three most ancient MSS give any name of place at all. The inscription is not to Philemon alone, but to Appia, to Archippus, and " to the church at thy house." Appia was probably, as stated by Chrysostom, the wife of Philemon. Archippus is named in the Epistle to the Colossians (iv, 17): the church at Philemon's house would mean all his family. The object of the epistle is to ask forgiveness for Onesimus a slave, who had run away from his master. The writer states that he has written the letter with his own hand (19), and he intimates to his friend to prepare for him a lodging; for, whereas he describes himself at the beginning of the letter as " a prisoner of Jesus Christ," he now says " I trust that through your prayers I shall be given unto you." If, as is conjectured, St Paul was set free at first, and was afterwards beheaded there when again arrested, in 64 or 65, his hope of visiting Philemon was fulfilled; but the fact of his release is unsupported by any external evidence, and the internal evidence which the letters themselves furnish has been laboriously worked up out of data insufficient in quantity, vague in reference to time, and altogether conjectural in results.

XI. XII. THE TWO EPISTLES TO TIMOTHY are thought to have been written about A.D. 64 or 65, on the supposition that St Paul escaped from the persecution at Rome in A.D. 62. The first is dated in our English version from Laodicea, and the second from Rome. The Alexandrian MS dates both from Laodicea, but the Sinaitic and Vatican give no name of place.

The uncertainty which attends all the Epistles of St Paul is exemplified by the fact that Dr Burton attributes the first of these addressed to Timothy to the year 52 from Ephesus, and thinks it might have been written from Troas.

The doctrine of predestination and of free grace, which seems to have been the especial mark of St Paul's preaching, is conspicuous in these Epistles to Timothy, and would doubtless recommend them to eastern nations generally.

1 TIM. i, 9.

God (he says), who hath saved us, and called us with an holy calling, not according to our works, but according to his own purpose and grace, which was given us in Christ Jesus before the world began.

The idea of spiritual power in the hands of the Church manifests itself again in the first of these epistles (i, 20), where the writer says of Hymenæus and Alexander, " whom I have delivered unto Satan, that they may learn not to blaspheme." If this phrase means that those men were only cast out of the Church, even supposing that there was also a reference to the doctrine that Satan is the author of bodily disease, as stated by the authors of the Life and Epistles of St Paul (ii, p. 34), the agency of Satan must have been thought to be much less formidable in those days than the Church in general estimates it at present. Nor can it be said that the human mind was less prone to error and wayward thoughts than at any later period; for the various fancies which led men astray from common sense and from the strait path, as enumerated at the beginning of chapter 4 of the First Epistle, might be thought to mark a later period in ecclesiastical history than the lifetime of St Paul himself. Bishops, presbyters, and deacons are all named in this epistle; the first and second of these orders were not then distinct, as they have since become; and deacons appear to have discharged highly important temporal duties, which required that their character should be without reproach. One regulation, common to them and to the bishops, limited them to one wife, whereas the polygamous tendency of all Asiatic nations has given them a greater latitude in this respect than has since been generally allowed by the Church.

XIII. THE EPISTLE TO TITUS bears the subscription, both in our authorized version and in the Alexandrian MS, "from Nicopolis": the Vatican and Sinaitic give no name of place. It is thought to have been written about the year A.D. 64, two years after the persecution of the Christians at Rome, in which antecedent probability would suggest that St Paul the leader of the Christian community would be the first to perish. The writer styles himself in the inscription "a slave of God," rendered in our version a "servant," similarly to the inscription to the Romans a "slave of Jesus Christ," and to the Philippians, where he and Timothy inscribe themselves "slaves of Jesus Christ."

The writer passes some severe remarks on

Many unruly and vain talkers and deceivers, especially they of the circumcision, whose mouths must be stopped, who subvert whole houses, teaching things which they ought not, for filthy lucre's sake.—i. 10, 11.

Titus would seem to be at this time in Crete; for it is against the people of this island that St Paul tells Titus to use severe rebuke, whilst he directs him to ordain elders (or presbyters) in every city, and he here repeats in the case of these elders the injunction to be blameless and to be content with one wife, which he has elsewhere enjoined on bishops and deacons. It is remarked by the authors of the Life and Epistles of St Paul, that the churches in Crete cannot be supposed to have been founded by that apostle; for that "many indications in the Epistle to Titus show that they had already lasted for a considerable time" (vol. ii, p. 487).

XIV. THE EPISTLE TO THE HEBREWS is dated from Italy in our authorized version and by the Vatican MS: the Alexandrian dates it from Rome, but the Sinaitic gives no name of a place. The commentators, wholly unable to assign any certain year, have referred it to that uncertain period, after A.D. 62, of which we have not the slightest original record of St Paul's life remaining.

It has justly been remarked that the absence of any inscription such as those with which every ancient letter used to commence, makes it doubtful whether this is to be looked upon as an epistle at all. On this point opinions are divided, nor is it important here to determine such a question; although to those who refer to its want of the usual greeting at the beginning, we may reply that there is no such want of the usual salutation at the end, for the writer concludes with the words, " Salute all them that have the rule over you, and all the saints. They of Italy salute you."

Neither is it possible now to decide authoritatively whether St Paul is the author; for there has always been a question on this subject from very early times. The tone of it is certainly less fervent than that of other epistles found in our Canon, and there are a few passages which appear to tell against the authorship of Paul. In chapter xiii, verse 23, we read, that "our brother Timothy is set at liberty," but in other passages he is styled "my own son in the Lord" (I Tim. i, 2), and again "my dearly beloved son" (II Tim. i, 2). The tenour and tendency of the whole composition moreover point otherwise than to the same purpose to which the other less doubtful of St Paul's epistles were directed. In most of his other writings the dispute between what is called the Pauline element, and the Judaizing community still subsisting mostly at Jerusalem, occurs incidentally and with a certain brief energy which like a fire lasts but for a time in proportion to its vehemence: but in the Epistle to the Hebrews it is the deliberate and almost the sole purpose to argue the question seriously, and to bring over the Jews to perceive that Christianity is the fulfilment of the law which was given to Moses. In pursuance of this plan, there are almost as many quotations from the Old Testament in this epistle, as in all the other epistles put together, and, like them also, are taken in most instances from the Greek Septuagint and not from the Hebrew text.

If this epistle was written in the year 64-5, as has been suggested by some commentators, it is certainly remarkable that no written record of the wonderful event which took place thirty-four years previously is referred to by the writer, notwithstanding that he was in the company, more than once, of Peter and John who had witnessed every particular of our Lord's life, preaching, and condemnation. But St Paul does not make the slightest mention of their having written anything on those subjects. On the contrary, he pleads that he had seen Jesus as well as they, and had received from him instructions to preach the gospel and also full information as to the nature of that gospel. That he should not, however, have had any knowledge, or left in his epistles any notice, of other Christian writings, may be ascribed to the early period at which he began to preach the Gospel; and on the other hand it is similarly improbable that any of the original disciples remaining at Jerusalem should have had any knowledge of the writings which St Paul might have disseminated over the Gentile world. But it would not be surprising that his followers in preaching Christianity should take notice in their writings of so well-known a preacher as St Paul. It is from this difference in their positions that the Second Epistle of Peter, in which St Paul is named, seems less likely to be genuine; nor is the possibility of its being genuine increased by the fact that St Peter is made to speak of "all the epistles" of St Paul, for we know nothing of their having met but once in Jerusalem and a second time at Antioch; nor is there any certain information that St Peter ever had knowledge of the epistles of St Paul, or that these were written sufficiently early to have ever come to the knowledge of St Peter. These remarks would of course lose their force if the epistle in which St Paul is named were admitted to be undoubtedly genuine.

We shall now briefly refer to the notices of St Paul found in the writings of the Apostolical Fathers, observing however at the same time, that the short tracts which remain, are by many thought to have been written by later authors, who bore the same names as the five contemporaries of the Apostles.

The first of these, Clement, in the 47th section of his Epistle to the Corinthians, has the following passage, referring evidently to St Paul's First Epistle to the Corinthians (i, 12; iii, 22).

Take the epistle of the blessed Paul the Apostle. What did he write first to you in the beginning of the Gospel? In truth he sent to you spiritually about both himself and Cephas and Apollos, because you had made to yourselves factions.

There are two other passages (35 & 47) in St Clement's work which have a slight similitude to Rom. i, 32 and Ephes. iv, 4, 5, 6, but St Paul's name is not mentioned in those places.

In the short epistle of Polycarp to the Philippians (iii) we find three passages which have reference to our present subject.

1. For neither I nor any other like me can attain to the wisdom of the blessed and glorious Paul, who, when he was among you, thoroughly and strenuously taught the word of truth to men then alive, and who also wrote to you letters, &c.

2. Not only in the blessed Ignatius, and Zosimus, and Rufus, but also in others of you, and in Paul himself and the other apostles (ix).

3. Do we not know that the saints shall judge the world? 'as St Paul teaches (1 *Cor.* vi, 2). But I have seen nor heard any thing like it in you, among whom St Paul laboured, and who are praised in the beginning of his epistle to you (xi).

The last of these extracts is found in the Latin text only, and it must be remembered, as may be seen from the summary of the Acts, that St Paul is not related therein to have spent a very long time at Philippi, and not to have met with so much success as Polycarp here seems to indicate, or as St Paul himself seems to speak of in his epistle to the citizens of Philippi.

In the epistle of Ignatius to the Ephesians, § 12, we read as follows:

Ye are the thoroughfare of those who are taken away to God, jointly initiated with Paul the sanctified, the martyred, the worthy of all blessing, beneath whose footsteps may I be found, when I attain to God. He in all his letter makes mention of you in Christ Jesus.

In the remains of Barnabas and Hermas no notice of St Paul is found, nor is there the slightest semblance of argument by which might be established even the faint idea of genuineness which is sometimes alleged in favour of the three preceding apostolical writers.

The few remains of writers who lived towards the end of the second century furnish one or two passages in which St Paul is mentioned. Dionysius of Corinth briefly names him in conjunction with St Peter. Justin Martyr seems to have been wholly ignorant that such an apostle as St Paul ever existed; and Theophilus of Antioch, whilst he quotes the first chapter of St John's Gospel, does not even name or remotely allude to the great apostle to whom the Christian religion is so much indebted, and who resided so often and long in his own city of Antioch.

CHAPTER XLIX.

THE GENERAL EPISTLES OF ST JAMES, ST PETER, ST JOHN, AND ST JUDE.—THE REVELATION OF ST JOHN THE DIVINE.

NEXT to the Epistles of Paul come seven other epistles, one of which is ascribed to James, two to Peter, three to John, and one to Jude: after which follows the Revelation or Apocalypse of St John the Divine, concluding the volume of what is termed the Canon of the New Testament. These seven books, as Dr Westcott well remarks (p. 319), " have been received into the Canon on evidence less complete than that by which the others are supported."

Notwithstanding this admission, the same author suggests that Clement of Rome, in the tenth chapter of his first epistle, quotes from the Epistle of St James (ii, 23) the words, " he [Abraham] was called the friend of God." As Clement nowhere names St James and has no other passage bearing the slightest likeness to anything found in the General Epistle of St James, it cannot be inferred that this epistle, although now canonical, was in existence before the time of Clement. The Shepherd of Hermas also contains no " definite quotation " from St James or from any other part of the Old or the New Testament, and, although the learned author already cited speaks of frequent allusions to the Epistle of St James as well as to the Apocalypse, I find none so definite as to sanction the inference that Hermas was acquainted with either the one or the other of those canonical books. It is not necessary to name any other of the minor Christian writers or Justin Martyr who comes next to them; for the epistle which we are considering, if in existence, seems to have lain in profound obscurity until it appears about the end of the second century with other works then put forward and forming the Christian Scriptures of the new dispensation.

There are certain peculiarities in the work which may be noticed. In chapter v, verse 14, it is directed that if any of the brethren were sick, the elders should pray over him, "anointing him with oil in the name of the Lord.". On the strength of this passage the Roman Catholic doctrine of extreme unction has mainly been founded; but it may fairly be doubted whether the application of oil may not have produced as much benefit medicinally to the patient as the prayers offered over him by the elders. The good Samaritan seems to have had equal faith in the curative properties of oil, which no doubt he applied externally to the wounded man, whilst the wine which he administered was no doubt taken inwardly to support his failing strength.

St James also, like all the other members of the primitive church, believed in the speedy coming of our Lord. "Stablish your hearts" (he says, v, 8): "for the coming of the Lord draweth nigh." But in the third place we find a remarkable passage, which, if the epistle is genuine, gives support to the belief that, even within so short a time after the crucifixion of our Lord, those divisions were already beginning which have ever since caused so much unhappiness and brought so much discredit on the Christian Church. "What doth it profit," says St James (ii, 14), "though a man say he hath faith and have not works? Can faith save him?" We must remember that the author of this epistle was the brother[*] of Jesus Christ, and it is very remarkable that the strife between faith and good works should have been begun so early, or that the writer of this epistle should have written so deliberately about faith, "the evidence of things not seen," when, in the case of his own divine and crucified brother, he had with his own ears heard and with his own eyes seen the very substance of those things, which future ages have of necessity received on the evidence of faith alone. The story of Simon Magus as a personification of St Paul, however improbable in itself, would seem to derive some support from the variation of doctrine, which St James here attempts to

---

[*] See Matthew's Gospel, xiii, 55, where the names of four brothers of Jesus are given. See also Eusebius ii, 1, where James is "called the brother of our Lord," implying certainly some doubt: but it has been vainly attempted to show that the Greek name of brother means sometimes *cousin*: but no real scholar will allow such an application of the term, except when used figuratively—such as in the phrase "All men are brethren."

explain. Seeing also that he was the first man designated by the title of bishop of Jerusalem, and was much respected by the Jews of that city, we need not doubt that there was a Hebrew element of Christianity from the very first, and that it was ultimately merged in the wider range of Christian doctrine due to the superior energy of St Paul. The death of James is recorded by Eusebius, and by Josephus, from whose work an extract will be found in page 63 of this volume.*

II. III. The two GENERAL EPISTLES OF ST PETER follow next, and it might be thought somewhat remarkable that these, in a canon which has been greatly under the influence of the Church of Rome, should have been placed after the Epistle of James, who has never been held to be of such high rank in the Romish Church as St Peter, who has always been esteemed in that church as the prince of the Apostles. But the Christian Canon was formed before the bishops of Rome put forth their claim of universal sovereignty, and the prerogative of St James as bishop of Jerusalem, recognized as we have already quoted it from the Clementine Homilies in page 380 of this volume, had perhaps so strongly secured the first place to the first bishop of Jerusalem in a multitude of manuscripts, that no alteration could afterwards be made of the order in which these three apostles stood.

In the Apostolical Fathers no notice whatever is found of the two Epistles of St Peter; for whereas Polycarp uses the words "not rendering evil for evil or reviling for railing," involved in a longer sentence where he is teaching Christian duty, it is not to be taken for granted that he quotes these words out of St Peter's Epistle; it is quite as likely that they formed part of admonitions which from the first were used both in preaching and in writing by the early Church. It is indeed useless to inquire into the history of this apostle, about whom more legends have been propagated than about any other of the first teachers of Christianity. In addition to what has been previously cited about him, we may add that among the Epistolæ and Decreta of Pope Anacletus, is a statement of his having lived at Antioch before he went to Rome, and that he sent Mark the evange-

---

* It does not diminish the obscurity which, from the want of documents, hangs over all the events of early ecclesiastical history, to find that two men of the name of James were put to death, the Greater in the time of Herod Agrippa, and the Lesser in the time of Ananias.

list to found the Church of Alexandria. It is more to our purpose that Eusebius (iii, 3) considers the first epistle to be genuine, but the second doubtful, and only "read with the other Scriptures because it was useful to many." The same historian names other writings of St Peter, such as his "Acts," the "Gospel according to him," and that which is called the "Preaching and the Revelations of Peter;" adding, however, that he knew nothing of their being handed down as Catholic writings. There are certain points in both these epistles which require notice, and seem indeed to support the theory that even in this early age the Christian sect retained a strongly marked distinction between Jew and Gentile.

The address is to "sojourners of the dispersal" in Pontus and other Asiatic provinces, "elect according to the foreknowledge of God," and in the second chapter, verse 12, he exhorts them to have their "conversation honest among the Gentiles," from which it would seem that the epistle was directed principally to Jews who had become Christians, seeing that some of the Gentiles also had adopted the Christian faith, and these could not accurately be classed, as in the passage before us, distinct from other Gentiles, among whom they dwelt. The term "sojourners of the dispersal" could hardly be applied to other than Jewish Christians; for none but Jews had been dispersed after the taking of Jerusalem, and these no doubt dwelt as sojourners in the various Asiatic countries to which they fled. If this view be correct, it harmonizes well with the accounts already quoted concerning Peter's opposition to St Paul already mentioned, and also with his own statement in his second epistle (iii, 15) where he cautions his correspondents against certain parts of St Paul's epistles, "in which are some things hard to be understood, which they that are unlearned and unstable wrest, as they do also the other Scriptures, unto their own destruction." It is somewhat singular also that St Peter, who must have been known to all the world as one of the most prominent disciples of our Lord, should think it needful, when admonishing the elders (I. v, 1), to add that he "also was an elder, and a witness of the sufferings of Christ."

The statement which he makes elsewhere (II. i, 14), "That shortly I must put off this my tabernacle, even as our Lord Jesus Christ hath showed me," was perhaps more needful as less publicly known, and his remark that the end of all things is at hand (I. iv, 7) is in harmony with the general belief of the age; but the scoffers whom he names in the third chapter of his second epistle, verse 4, seem to have had some apparent reason for doubting that Christ was about immediately to come. "Where is the promise of His coming? for since the fathers fell asleep, all things continue as they were from the beginning of creation."* His allusion to suffering "as a Christian (iv, 16)" is less appropriate, and the salutation which he sends from the "church that is at Babylon," appropriate in itself, if, as is probable, he like other Jews fled to Babylon after their expulsion from Jerusalem, requires still an explanation of the difficulty that the various accounts place him almost at the same time at Antioch, Alexandria, Babylon, and Rome.

IV. V. VI. Of the three GENERAL EPISTLES OF ST JOHN the first only has been considered to be genuine. Eusebius, quoting from Origen, says of this apostle, "He has also left an epistle consisting of very few lines, suppose also a second and a third; for these are not allowed by all to be genuine; but both together consist of less than one hundred lines." The last two are not mentioned, nor is any passage quoted from them by any writer before Irenæus; and the same remark would be applicable to the first also of these epistles, were it not for a sentence in the seventh section of Polycarp's epistle, to the effect that "whosoever does not believe that Jesus Christ is come in the flesh is antichrist." This, although no author is named, is said to be a quotation from I John, iv, 3 ; but the words vary so much, and the idea is so expanded in the case of St John, that no such inference can be allowed. The word antichrist occurring in both, has probably led to the supposed connection between the two; but the apostle tells us in his first epistle (ii, 18), that there were even then many antichrists, and he remarks, when speaking thereof, that it is "the last time," referring doubtless to the expected coming of our Saviour.

There are not many peculiarities found in these three short epistles. It has been remarked in the early part of this volume, that the passage which is generally quoted under the name of the Three Heavenly Witnesses (I John v, 7), is now universally admitted to be an unauthorized interpola-

---

* This is the only clear expression of the obvious answer to those who prophesied too boldly the coming of Christ. The reader may refer to the following passages of the New Testament, where the subject is referred to: Matt. x, 23; xvi, 28; xxiv, 15, 29, 34; Mark ix, 1; x, 23; Luke xix, 11; xxi, 24; II Thes. ii, 26; Heb. x, 37; Rev. vi, 10, 11.

tion in the text. The second and third epistles are addressed, the former to the " Elect Lady and her children," and the latter to " our well-beloved Gaius," but they both profess to be from "the Elder," and this is a title which we can scarcely imagine any of the original witnesses of Christ's wonderful deeds to have assumed.

VII. The GENERAL EPISTLE OF ST JUDE is not named by any ancient writer, nor is there any sentence in either of these that has more than the faintest likeness to any part of this short canonical book. The Canon of Muratori which may be as early as A.D. 170, and may on the other hand be as late as the eighth century, enumerates this epistle as recognized by the Catholic Church; but no one has explained the fact that the Jude or Judas (for the Greek name is the same for both) who wrote this epistle, is therein called the brother of James, whereas the Judas named in the Gospel of St Luke as one of the twelve Apostles must be considered to have been the son of James, as already pointed out in page 221 of this volume. It may be added that St Jude is the only writer in the New Testament who quotes an uncanonical author by name; but it is not certain (though probable) that the book of Enoch, which still exists and has been published, is the same from which St Jude quoted.

VIII. The "REVELATION OF ST JOHN THE DIVINE" is the last book in the Canon of the Church, and it has been remarked by a recent writer* that the " preponderance of evidence and critical opinion assigns it as a genuine work of the Apostle." On this point, however, consent is not universal; for, although many modern writers have allowed it to be possibly or even probably genuine, yet in the time of Eusebius there was still great doubt upon the subject. This historian, quoting from Dionysius, has left us the following statement :—

That it is a John who wrote these things we must believe as himself says so, but what John that is, is uncertain. For he does not say, as he does in many places in the Gospel, that himself was the disciple beloved by the Lord, nor the one who reclined on his breast, nor the brother of James, nor he who himself saw and himself heard the Lord. For he would have said some one of these things before mentioned, if he wished clearly to make himself known. But there is none of these things. He said that he was our brother and associate, and a witness of Jesus, and blessed at seeing and hearing these revela-

---

* The author of Supernatural Religion, vol iii, page 314.

tions. But I consider that there have been many of the same name as John, who through love towards him, and admiration and imitation of him, and the wish to be loved by the Lord equally with him, adopted also the same name; as also Paul is much named and indeed Peter also among the children of the faithful.

There is then also another John in the Acts of the Apostles, surnamed Mark; whom Barnabas and Paul associated with themselves; concerning whom also he again says, "They had also John as their minister." But whether it is he who wrote [the Revelation] I could not say; for neither is it written that he came with them into Asia.

In accordance with this the same historian more than once (iii, 25), in enumerating the books of the New Testament, adds the "Revelation of John, if persons think fit." It would seem then that there is still great doubt both whether the revelation in our Canon was not written by some other John and not by the disciple of our Lord, and this doubt is rather augmented by the epithet the "Divine," or as we might render it the "Theologist" or "Theologian." It may well be doubted whether such a title could with propriety be assumed by the disciple, as much as that St Peter in two of his epistles should have assumed the title of the Elder.

It is indeed well known and recognized among scholars, that the ancients, who have left the immortal works which are read and studied with admiration among all the civilized nations of the world, were nevertheless no better than children in many of the exact sciences which the moderns have since carried to the greatest perfection. In the science of etymology they never progressed beyond the first elements; of languages few knew any but their own; and on questions of genuineness and authenticity they were wholly unable to form a sound and reasonable judgement. Epiphanius, an eminent Father of the Church, although too early to throw much general light upon our present subject, has however left some remarks which, whilst they confirm the doubt acknowledged by Eusebius as to the genuineness of the Revelation, cannot fail to raise a smile at the simplicity of the writer himself. An early heretical sect called the Alogi disputed the genuineness of the Revelation, which enumerates Thyatira among the seven churches of Asia, because the church of Thyatira was not yet founded. Epiphanius (*De Hæres.* 51) does not dispute the fact, but suggests that St John exercised the prophetic spirit in thus classing Thyatira with the other churches, and so extricates himself from a difficulty, which the present age will hardly deny to have revived with increased force since the days of Epiphanius.

CHAPTER L.

UNCERTAINTY IN IDENTIFYING VARIOUS NAMES, JAMES, JUDAS, SIMON, MARY, AND OTHERS IN OUR CANONICAL BOOKS.

AMONG the discrepancies which are noticed in the Gospel history, I have already pointed out that the variation in three of the Gospels touching the names of the twelve Apostles, forbids us to believe that the writers of those Gospels were some of the very apostles whose names have been

MATTHEW.	MARK.
Simon, called Peter	Simon, surnamed Peter . . .
Andrew, his brother	Andrew . . . .
James, son of Zebedee . . .	James, son of Zebedee } surnamed Sons of
John, his brother	John, his brother } Thunder
Philip.	Philip. . . . .
Bartholomew	Bartholomew . . . . . .
Thomas	Thomas . . . .
Matthew	Matthew . . . .
James, son of Alpheus . . .	James, son of Alpheus . . .
Lebbæus [surnamed Thaddæus]	Thaddæus . . . .
Simon the Canaanite	Simon the Canaanite . . . .
Judas Iscariot	Judas Iscariot . . . . . .

But there are many other names occurring in various parts of the New Testament, about which there is great obscurity and confusion; and perhaps no kind of evidence is more conclusive to prove that a long interval had passed before the history was committed to writing than the fact that the writers have differed so greatly in recording the names of men and women with whom they appear to have associated so intimately. It will therefore be of interest to trace some names of various persons, who take part in the events which are recorded in the various books, and if possible to ascertain the identity of each, or to show how far it is difficult, if not impossible, to distinguish one from another.

handed down so differently. In the book of the Acts also
(i, 13), is given a list of the eleven disciples who remained
after the death of Judas Iscariot, corresponding with the list
in the Gospel according to St Luke, and so far in harmony
with the theory that those two histories may have been
written or compiled by the same author. It may be observed
however that the obscurity which rests over the names Lebbæus, Thaddæus and Judas, brother of James, which seem
to denote the same individual, is not cleared away by the fact
that both in the Gospel and in the Acts the word *brother* has
been inserted without authority in our authorized version,
seeing that the elliptical Greek form "Judas of James," save
in well-known cases, requires the word *son*, not *brother* to be
inserted to express the relation between the two. The subject of these different lists has already been noticed, and the
following table of them may perhaps be sufficient to show the
full bearing of the argument.

Luke.	Acts.
Simon, named Peter	Peter.
Andrew, his brother	Andrew.
James.	James.
John	John.
Philip.	Philip.
Bartholomew	Bartholomew.
Thomas	Thomas.
Matthew	Matthew.
James, son of Alpheus . . .	James, son of Alpheus.
Judas [brother] of James . .	Judas [brother] of James.
Simon Zelotes	Simon Zelotes.
Judas Iscariot.	

Setting aside therefore the name of Joseph, the reputed
father of our Lord, seeing that after his marriage with Mary
he does not appear again in the whole of the New Testament, we may observe that in the Gospels according to St
Matthew and St Mark the family of Joseph and Mary are
enumerated as follows.

MATTHEW xiii, 55-56.	MARK vi, 3.
Is not this the carpenter's son? Is not his mother called Mary? and his brethren, James and Joses, and Simon and Judas? 56. And his sisters, are they not all with us? Whence then hath this man all these things?	Is not this the carpenter, the son of Mary, the brother of James, and Joses, and of Juda, and Simon? and are not his sisters here with us? and they were offended at him.

St Luke and St John do not mention these names: the former speaking of Jesus (iv, 22) says only, "Is not this Joseph's son?" and the latter (vi, 41) "Is not this Jesus the son of Joseph, whose father and mother we know?"

Our attention is then called to the remarkable obscurity which not only now hangs over every mention of the disciples and the family of Jesus, but must have hung over it at the time when our present canonical books were written. The names of the twelve disciples are all, except Philip and perhaps Simon, of Hebrew etymology: so also are those assigned to the brothers of Jesus, and are thus strongly contrasted with the names of nearly all who appear afterwards in early ecclesiastical history. Even four of the so-called Apostolical Fathers bear Greek or Latin names— Polycarp, Hermas, Clement, Ignatius—and have no connection whatever with Jerusalem or its people. Barnabas alone, the "son of consolation," bears a name derived from the nationality of our Lord himself. Among the names of those, to whom is assigned the authorship of the Christian canonical books, John, James and Jude [or Judas] alone are derived from a Hebrew origin. Mark, Peter, Paul, Luke also (if Lucas be a short form of Lucanus), and Matthew (if being a tax-gatherer he was also a Roman official) may be classed (the last two with less certainty it is true) among names not wholly derivable from the Hebrew.

If we come down to the second generation after Christ, Hebrew names almost wholly disappear from the list of Christians, orthodox and heretical alike. Aristides, Valentine, Saturninus, Quadratus, Hegesippus, Papias, Justin Martyr, Athenagoras, Theophilus, Montanus, Ammianus, Basileides, Pantænus, Pinytus, Hermias, Celsus, Porphyrius, and many others, present themselves to the student of early Church history, and suggest to the mind that the Christian books are due to Greek writers or compilers, and that the Hebrew or Judaical element of Christianity has had very little to do ultimately with the authorship of our books. So true is the observation made by the late prime minister of this kingdom:

> When Christianity went forth into the world, no sooner had it moved onward from its cradle in Jerusalem, than it assumed the aspect of a Greek religion.—GLADSTONE in *Contemporary Review*, Dec. 1876, p. 4.

It will be remembered that among the twelve earliest disciples there were two named James, two others named Simon, and two named Judas. The two Jameses are distinguished, the one as brother of John and son of Zebedee, the other as the son of Alpheus. The two Simons are distinguished as Simon Peter, and Simon the Canaanite, who was also (we must infer) called Zelotes " the Zealot." Of the two Judases one is surnamed Iscariot, the other is that doubtful disciple, who is called " of James" in two of the lists, Lebbæus or Thaddæus in the other two. It is no doubt remarkable that in the small number of twelve men there should be three pairs bearing the same names ; but greater difficulty is found from the fact that three of those who are mentioned in the Gospel history as brothers of Jesus, Simon, James and Judas, bear names which occur in the list of the twelve Apostles. So great is the difficulty of distinguishing these and their relation to our Lord, that it is a great hindrance to our regarding the books, which leave such things uncertain, as written by any of the apostles themselves, who would so thoroughly have known the subject, and would not, one would think, leave such an interesting point involved in the obscurity which now lies over it.

We will then examine these names more minutely, and bring forward, one after another, all the passages from the New Testament in which these and other names severally occur.

St James. I.

The most important of the apostles at first was undoubtedly St James, and this name is found in the following passages :—

1. Two brethren, James and John, sons of Zebedee, called to be disciples. Matt. iv, 21 ; Mark i, 19 ; Luke v, 10.

2. James and John, sons of Zebedee, and James, son of Alphæus, named among the twelve. Matt. x, 3 ; Mark iii, 18 ; Luke vi, 15, omits " sons of Zebedee ; " Acts i, 13.

3. James, Joses, Judas, and Simon, brothers of Jesus. Matt. xiii, 55 ; Mark vi, 3.

4. James, John, and Peter, present at the transfiguration. Matt. xvii, 1 ; Mark ix, 2 ; Luke ix, 28.

5. James and John ask to sit on right and left hand of Christ in his kingdom. Matt. xx, 20, says Zebedee's sons, omitting " James and John ; " Mark x, 35, says James and John, omitting " Zebedee's sons."

6. Two sons of Zebedee with Peter, witness Christ's agony in the garden. Matt. xxvi, 37 ; Mark xiv, 33, names James, and John, and Peter.

7. James, John, and Peter, taken to witness the raising to life of Jaïrus's daughter. Matt. ix, 22 ; Mark v, 27, names the ruler Jaïrus ; Luke viii, 51, names ruler only.

8. James, and John, ask Jesus on his way to Jerusalem to call down fire from heaven on the Samaritans. Luke ix, 54.

9. James, John, Peter, and Andrew ask Jesus about his prophecy that the Temple should be destroyed. Mark xiii, 3; Matt. xxiv, 3, says "the disciples" ask; Luke xxi, 7, "they" ask.

10. James. "Mary the mother of James and Joses" stood by the cross. Matt. xxvii, 57; Mark xv, 40, says "Mary the mother of James the Less, and of Joses."

11. James. "Mary the [mother] of James" visits the sepulchre. Mark xvi, 1; Luke xxiv, 10.

From this summary, which contains every passage in which the name of James occurs, we find it difficult to extract any satisfactory result concerning the identity of the persons bearing that name. The sons of Zebedee stand out clearly from the rest; and James the son of Alpheus, named once only by three evangelists, has it would seem a distinct existence. But Matthew, as will be observed in No. 10 of the foregoing summary, makes Mary to be the mother of James and Joses, which seems hardly to admit of explanation, seeing that in six other passages he joins James not with a brother Joses, but with a brother John. And Mark also, as in the same clause of the summary, does not clear up the difficulty by naming Mary the " mother of James the Less, and of Joses." Nor does the mention of four brothers of Jesus, named by Matthew and Mark (No. 3), aid us in clearing up this obscurity, for there is nothing in the four Gospels to indicate that any members of our Lord's family took part in promoting the success of his mission. We have indeed, in the Gospel of St John (vii, 3-5), a remarkable reproof from his brethren, accompanied with advice, of which the only explanation appears to be that our existing histories, intended to teach the Christian religion and not to furnish a complete account of every transaction, must be interpreted with reference principally to the main purpose for which they were written.

3. His brethren therefore said unto him, "Depart hence, and go into Judæa, that thy disciples also may see the works that thou doest. 4. For there is no man that doeth any thing in secret, and he himself seeketh to be known openly. If thou do these things show thyself to the world." 5. For neither did his brethren believe in him.

In the Acts of the Apostles the name of James occurs five times, and in the Epistles five times only. They are here subjoined:—

1. Acts i, 13, in the list of the Apostles.
2. Acts xii, 2. Herod kills James the brother of John.

3. Acts xii, 17. Peter having escaped from prison, knocks at the house of Mary the mother of John, whose surname was Mark, and says to the maid " Go show these things to James, and to the brethren."

4. Acts xv, 13. In reply to Barnabas and Saul " James answered saying, ' Men and brethren, hearken unto me.' "

5. Acts xxi, 18. And the day following Paul went in with us unto James; and all the elders were present.

6. In 1 Cor. xv, 7. St Paul, enumerating the appearances of Jesus after the resurrection, says, " After that he was seen of James."

7. Gal. i, 19. St Paul, speaking of his visit to Jerusalem, says, " But other of the Apostles saw I none, save James the Lord's brother."

8. Gal. ii, 9. St Paul says, " James, Cephas, and John, who seemed to be pillars " of the Church. Gal. ii, 12. " For before that certain came from James, he [Peter] did eat with the Gentiles."

9. James i, 1. " James a servant of God, and of the Lord Jesus Christ."

10. Jude i. " Jude the servant of Jesus Christ, and brother of James."

In seven of these ten passages we find nothing to impugn the testimony furnished by the Acts of the Apostles, that one only apostle bearing the name of James takes part in the various incidents recorded throughout the New Testament, and he cannot have been the brother of John, as he was put to death at an early date by Herod the king. Two passages only furnish additions which render the subject obscure. In one of these (No. 7) the same James is termed the Lord's brother, and in the other (No. 10) it is no longer John or Joses, as elsewhere, but Jude, who is connected with James and described as his brother.

Where there are so few dates, and these not perfectly intelligible, it seems needless and almost presumptuous to examine too minutely or to supplement by conjecture. What is wanting is fact, but some of our critics have attempted to simplify the subject which we have been considering by showing that the four names—James, Joses, Judas and Simon, ascribed to brothers of our Lord—do in reality designate his cousins, and they assert that the Greek word ἀδελφοὶ may be applied to other relatives of the male sex, and consequently to cousins, forgetting that in all languages the word brother is used by a kind of metaphor, and not noticing that the word ἀδελφαὶ (sisters) occurs in the same passages, and therefore must be extended similarly in meaning. The subject has been well explained by the historian of the Roman empire in the following extract:—

This appellation [brothers] was at first understood in the most obvious sense, and it was supposed that the brothers of Jesus were the lawful issue of Joseph and Mary. A devout respect for the virginity of the mother of God suggested to the Gnostics, and afterwards to the orthodox Greeks, the expedient of bestowing a second wife on Joseph. The Latins (from the time of Jerome) improved on that point, asserted the perpetual celibacy of Joseph, and justified by many similar examples the new interpretation that Jude, as well as Simon and James, who are styled the brothers of Jesus Christ, were only his first cousins. GIBBON, chap. xvi, vol. ii, 216.

Judas. II.

The name Judas occurring as often as James in our canonical books presents a similar difficulty from the number of persons who bore it. The passages in which it occurs with the name James have already been cited, and the others, in which it occurs separately, are now to be produced.

1. Judas Iscariot is distinctly named or indicated in the following: Matt. x, 4: xxvi, 14-47: xxvii, 3; Mark iii, 19: xiv, 10-43; Luke vi, 16: xxii, 3-47; John vi, 71: xiii, 2-26: xviii, 3-5; Acts i, 16-25.
2. Acts v, 37. Judas of Galilee, who made a sedition in the days of the taxing.
3. — ix, 11. Judas, a citizen of Damascus, in whose house Ananias is told to inquire for Saul.
4. — xv, 22-27. Judas, surnamed Barsabas, is chosen with Silas to accompany Paul and Barnabas from Jerusalem to Antioch.

Enough has been said, in connection with the name James, and also in a former chapter of this work (p. 221), touching the divergence of the names Lebbæus and Judas, assigned by different evangelists to the twelfth disciple, and also concerning the epistle ascribed to Jude; and of the additional passages now quoted, one only, the last, where a new Judas surnamed Barsabas—as well as Barnabas—is mentioned, requires to be considered.

Barnabas and Barsabas. III.

The name Barsabas occurs twice only in the Acts, and nowhere else.

1. In Acts i, 23, where "Joseph called Barsabas who was surnamed Justus," is put forward as a competitor with Matthias for the vacant place among the twelve apostles.

2. In Acts xv, 22, where he is mentioned as "Judas surnamed Barsabas."

To attempt reconciliation between these two passages seems useless, and in the case of any other historical work such an attempt would not be made. But when we examine the passages where the name of Barnabas occurs, the difficulty is much increased.

1. In Acts xi, 22-25-30 : ii, 25 : xiv, 12 : xv, 2-12-37 ; in 1 Cor. ix, 6 ; Gal. ii, 1-9-13 : Barnabas is simply named as a companion to St Paul, and nothing is there found to interfere with all the details of the narrative.

2. In Acts iv, 36, however, we read "Joses, who by the apostles was surnamed Barnabas . . . a Levite, and of the country of Cyprus."

3. In — xiii, 1. Now there were in the church that was at Antioch certain prophets and teachers ; as Barnabas, and Simeon, that was called Niger, and Lucius of Cyrene, and Manaen, which had been brought up with Herod the tetrarch, and Saul.

4. — xiii, 50. The Jews [at Antioch in Pisidia] raised persecution against Paul and Barnabas, and expelled them out of their coasts.

5. In Colos. iv, 10, is the following sentence : "Marcus, sister's son to Barnabas, . . . and Jesus, which is called Justus, who are of the circumcision."

In No. 2 of these five extracts, where Barnabas is named, he is called Joses, and it appears was by place of birth a Cypriot, although by race a Jew and a Levite.

In No. 5 we find a certain Jesus surnamed Justus associated with Marcus the nephew of Barnabas, both of whom were circumcised Jews.

Combining therefore the notices of Judas, Barnabas and Barsabas, we find the following assemblage of names and surnames :—

Judas is surnamed Barsabas.
Joseph is surnamed Barsabas, also surnamed Justus.
Joses is surnamed Barnabas.
Jesus is surnamed Justus.

Again, if we add to this from St Luke vi, 16, that Judas was brother of James, from Eusebius (ii, 1) that James, also first bishop of Jerusalem, was called the Just, and from another text already quoted that James, Joses, Judas, and

Simon were brothers of our Lord, we find an extraordinary combination of difficulties which will be best represented in the following genealogical table :—

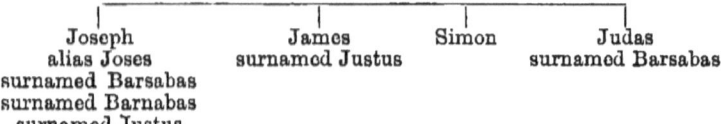

Joseph	James	Simon	Judas
alias Joses	surnamed Justus		surnamed Barsabas
surnamed Barsabas			
surnamed Barnabas			
surnamed Justus			

The only reasonable explanation is that which the first view of the case would suggest—namely, that Jesus, Joseph and Judas were the same person, and that an error has been made by the writer or by a copyist in substituting one name for another. This probability is much increased from the circumstance that one of the names occurs in the former part of the Acts, where Saul's history is given without the explanation that Saul and Paul were the same person; the other is found only in the latter portion of the Acts where Paul's history is the principal subject. It has been remarked above that these two divisions of the Acts seem to have been derived from two different originals; and the beginning of the thirteenth chapter of the Acts, as seen in No. 3 of the extracts last quoted, remarkably supports this suggestion, for it is there stated that among certain prophets and teachers at Antioch were included Saul and Barnabas, as if the writer was not aware that Paul and Barnabas had "assembled themselves together a whole year with the church and taught much people," and that this had already been recorded in the eleventh chapter of the Acts of the Apostles.

Mary. IV.

"Is not his mother called Mary, and his brethren James, and Joses, and Simon, and Judas?" was the question extorted from the neighbours of our Lord by the miraculous deeds which he performed. Whether these four were sons of Joseph alone by a second or by a former wife, or of both Joseph and Mary, we are not told, nor need we stop to inquire; for though it may be important to the speculative theologian to maintain the immaculate character of Mary, and her freedom from all to which the functions of womanhood and motherhood might make her liable, yet those who look only to the facts will leave such questions unanswered, and endeavour only to ascertain who these four were, who are here said to have been brothers of our Lord, and whether they were or were not the same persons, of whom two are named in the lists of the twelve Apostles. But it seems to be a necessary inference from the last two sections, in which the names James and Judas have been passed in review, that we cannot identify any of these four brothers with those who appear under the same names as actors in the history of the early Church. Their mother, however, the Virgin Mary, bears a name which was also borne by others, and we have the same difficulty in distinguishing the several Maries which we had in the case of those who bore the names of James and Judas. The subject will be placed in a clearer light by inspection of the various passages in which the name of Mary occurs, nor is this rendered unnecessary by the fact that the Maries have already been twice produced in a former part of this work, for in those chapters the inquiry had for its object to show that it was uncertain who were the several Maries that anointed our Lord at the feast, or attended at his crucifixion, or at the tomb when he rose from the dead. But we have now to show generally that there is no such distinction between the Maries who occur in the Gospel narrative as must have been made by the more perfect knowledge which the writers would have had, if they had themselves witnessed the events which they relate.

In Matt. i, 16: xiii, 55; Mark vi, 3; Luke i, 27: ii, 5, 16, 19, it is Mary the mother of Jesus who is named; and it is most remarkable that in the Gospel according to St John the name of the Virgin Mary is not found; it is said only in one place (xix, 25) that the mother of Jesus with others stood by the cross. Setting aside those passages, we have to consider the following, where several Maries are named, one of whom, Mary Magdalene, stands out prominently among the rest.

1. *Witnesses of the Crucifixion.*

MATTHEW xxvii, 56.	MARK xv, 40.	JOHN xix, 25.
Mary Magdalene, Mary the mother of James and Joses, and the mother of Zebedee's children.	Mary Magdalene, Mary the mother of James the Less and of Joses, and Salome.	The mother of Jesus, his mother's sister Mary the [wife] of Cleophas, and Mary Magdalene.

2. *The following visit the Tomb.*

MATTHEW xxviii, 1.	MARK xvi, 1.	LUKE xxiv, 10.
Mary Magdalene and the other Mary.	Mary Magdalene, Mary the [mother] of James, and Salome.	Mary Magdalene, Mary the [mother] of Joanna, [mother] of James, and others.

In John (xx, 1-16) Mary Magdalene alone is described as visiting the tomb.

3. *The sisters Martha and Mary.*

In Luke (x, 42) the sisters Martha and Mary are named as entertaining Jesus, not in Bethany, but "in a certain village," which shows that the writer was not aware of the close intimacy which existed between these sisters and our Lord.

In John (xi, 1-20 ; xii, 3) these sisters are named as of Bethany, and Mary appears here as the woman who anointed Jesus.

4. *Other Maries.*

In the Acts (xii, 12) is named Mary the mother of John, whose surname was Mark ; and in Romans (xvi, 6) St Paul greets another Mary " who bestowed much labour on us."

Setting aside all attempt to discriminate and identify these women, it is at all events a remarkable fact that so many, appearing closely in connection with our Lord, should have been known and handed down in history as bearing the same name.

Simon, Peter, Cephas, and Symeon. v.

In the names by which the apostle Peter is designated, both in the Gospels, the Acts, and the Epistles, we find difficulties equal to those already mentioned. Great uncertainty hangs over the distinction to be drawn between the names assigned to St Peter. The original name of this apostle seems to have been Simon, which in one instance only has been most unaccountably exchanged for Symeon. It is remarkable that in the second book of Maccabees the same form, Symeon, has once been substituted for Simon in the narrative which contains the exploits of the famous leader who rescued the Jews from the power of the King of Assyria. But the epithets Cephas and Peter present greater difficulties. The word Cephas signifies a stone or rock, and the name Petros well represents it in Greek. In the majority of texts where the names occur, we may admit without much hesitation that Simon Peter is the apostle described. But in the Epistle to the Galatians (ii, 9), where James, Cephas, and John are named as pillars of the Church, one of the earliest manuscripts omits Cephas, and in the other verses of the same chapter, where the authorized version reads Peter, Cephas is the reading of the three earliest MSS.

It has always been a stumbling-block to the commentators

why Paul should have withstood Peter to the face; and it has also hitherto remained unexplained how Peter could be said to preach the gospel of the *circumcision*, that is, to the Jews only; for it is notorious that a vision was granted to St Peter expressly for the purpose of showing that the wall of partition between Jews and Gentiles was broken down. The words "when Peter was come to Antioch," &c., are quoted by Eusebius, in his Ecclesiastical History (i, 12), but Eusebius, as well as the earliest MSS, reads "*Cephas*," not Peter, "was come to Antioch." His words here follow:—

The story is found in Clement in the fifth of the Hypotyposes, in which he says also that Cephas, of whom St Paul says, "when Cephas was come to Antioch, I withstood him to the face," was one of the seventy disciples, and had the same name as Peter the apostle.

We learn from the History of the Apostles, by Dorotheus, the same fact, that one of the *seventy* disciples—not one of the *twelve*—was Cephas, who was bishop of Cannia, and that it was he whom St Paul withstood to the face at Antioch. A strong suspicion might arise from this that Cephas and Peter were wholly different persons, who were confounded together when the books of the New Testament were compiled. If this be so, and other various discrepancies arise from similar causes, the general character of our books is not impugned, but, on the contrary, is sustained, seeing that all human works are imperfect; and in the case of written works the natural inference is that facts had become faint by time, that the original witnesses had been removed from the world, and many other sources of error had arisen, when the existing histories of Christ and of our religion were put into the shape in which they now appear.

CHAPTER LI.

THE CANON GENERALLY.—THE GREEK LANGUAGE.—ANTIOCH.—
CONCLUSION.

CONCERNING the life and miraculous history of our Lord and the books of the New Testament in which the events of that life and history are recorded, enough has been said in the preceding chapters of this work to suggest to the mind of the reader that our canonical writings are not exempt from the lot of all books that ever were written with the pen. That these books were compiled at a very early period of the Christian religion, and formed into a canon by which Christians still profess to regulate their lives, is consistent with what we know of all human institutions; and, although Christianity is to be regarded rather as a divine than a human institution, yet its affairs were even from the death of its founder committed to the charge of fallible men, and liable to all the chances and vicissitudes to which every thing on this earth is subject. Our task would, however, be incomplete without some remarks on the Canon formed out of the various books which we have passed in review severally in this volume, and on this subject it is obvious to conclude that if none of those books were written before the latter half of the second century, they could not have been gathered into the form in which they now appear, until that same time. That no writer before Irenæus has named these writings or seems to have known either them or their writers, save two or three brief notices of St Paul found in works of suspected antiquity, can hardly lead to any other conclusion than that these books were written immediately preceding the time when they are first mentioned. It was then in the latter half of the second century that the Canon was formed; and, although the collection then made omitted some of the books now found in it, and contained others which since have been excluded, these slight changes are of very little importance, and do not invalidate the fact that our Canon came into existence as early as the date above assigned to it. If however the absence of quotations, and many other peculiarities, which have been already fully developed in the preceding pages, forbid us to attribute an earlier origin to these books and to the canon or collection in which they are contained, there are other peculiarities already slightly alluded to which concern the books collectively, and which equally leading us to the same conclusion, seem sufficiently strong to enable us to fix the place as well as the time when these books were compiled and delivered to the world in the form which they now bear.

Recurring then to the four Gospels which stand first in the volume of the Christian Scriptures, the most hasty reader cannot fail to observe the marked difference between St John's Gospel and the other three, as regards not only the historical order of events, as already pointed out, but the language and style in which the four are written. It is sufficiently remarkable that these four documents, written by those who witnessed the events which they describe, should be written not in the language of the Jewish people, among whom those events took place, but in Greek, a language almost unknown, and rarely studied, as we are informed by the Jewish historian, even by the most educated persons of the Jewish nation. Our surprise becomes greater at finding that the Greek of St John's Gospel is more pure than that of any other part of the New Testament; and such as we should think it impossible for an uneducated Jewish fisherman ever to have produced. But the Gospel of St John presents other peculiarities which have been fully discussed by many modern writers, and which render it difficult to believe that he could have written the book as we now have it. That the facts related in the history have been delivered to us "according to St John," we need not doubt; but we may fairly suggest that if he had written designedly a regular life of Jesus, he would hardly have omitted to insert the Baptism, the Temptation, the Call of himself and his brother James, the Transfiguration, the Sermon on the Mount, the last discourses in the Temple and on the Mount of Olives, the Agony in the Garden, the Institution of the Last Supper, the Ascension, and many other striking things at which he was himself present.

The number of miracles moreover, of parables, and of various incidents which occurred, is remarkably small in the fourth Gospel: with the exception of the last week spent at Jerusalem, the historical part of that Gospel is very limited, and the narrative of events varies considerably from those of the other evangelists. That certain facts are common to St John and to them might with reason be expected, and in all such cases there is great similarity of language, but not that identity of words and phrases which is so remarkable in the other three. Even in the discourses of our Lord, which, as Justin Martyr tells us in a passage which has been quoted in page 131 of this volume, were delivered in short sentences, easy to be remembered, the difference of style may be seen, nor would there be any difficulty in explaining this circumstance, if we could be sure that the Gospel of St John was written, as has been asserted, many years later than the others. Of this however we have no proof, nor are the other three Gospels named or quoted by any ancient author at an earlier date than about the middle of the second century, when the Gospel of St John is quoted also. We are indeed wholly unable, except by conjecture, to ascribe to any book of the New Testament an earlier origin than to the others. They appear forming a canon at the same time, and we are assured on competent authority that, as there are four winds, and four quarters of the world, so the number of the Gospels could be neither more nor less than four. And the Canon also is constructed in imitation of its prototype, the Old Testament, which was the canon of the Jews. If that venerable book consisted of four divisions, so also does the Christian canon. As Moses founded the Hebrew Commonwealth described in the Pentateuch, so also did Christ found the Christian community of which the four Gospels are the record. In the same way the historical books of the Old Testament have their counterpart in the Acts of the Apostles: these writings equally tell us of those by whose labours the two communities were taken up on the death of the first founders, and brought into the perfect form which they afterwards assumed. After these come, in the Old Testament, the moral and didactic writings, Psalms, Proverbs and others, followed by the prophetical books which complete the Jewish canon. Similarly also in the New Testament we have the Epistles, which represent the moral and didactic portions of the older volume, followed by the Revelation, which is the counterpart of the ancient prophetical books.

Thus it would appear so far impossible to disconnect the origin of the Gospel of St John from that of the other three. We cannot conceive any period to have intervened when there were only three Gospels to form the canon, and it consequently results that there is no good external evidence to show that either of the four Gospels was written at a much earlier date than the others. That St John should have written a work in Greek scarcely inferior in style to that of Philo, Josephus and others, who were men of learning, whilst he was a fisherman on the lake of Gennesareth, is sufficiently wonderful, and it is certain that the writer has expanded or contracted or otherwise modified many passages both of the facts and of Christ's sayings, and occasionally introduced many thoughts and expressions of his own.

If we now turn to the other three Gospels, synoptical as they are termed, besides the antecedent improbability that they should have come down to us in the Greek language, we observe such a remarkable similarity as appears in no other works recording, like these, the same events. Their writers agree in relating the same thing not only in the same manner and order, but likewise in the very same words, as must be evident to every reader who has paid the slightest attention to the subject.

A single instance may suffice to show the full bearing of the case; it is taken from the three Gospels where the healing of the sick of the palsy is described, and the comparison, here made through the English version, would be far more striking if the extracts were given in the original Greek.

MATTHEW ix, 2-7.	MARK ii, 5-12.	LUKE v, 20-25.
2. Jesus seeing their faith said unto the sick of the palsy; "Son, be of good cheer; thy sins be forgiven thee."	5. When Jesus saw their faith, he said unto the sick of the palsy, "Son, thy sins be forgiven thee."	20. And when he saw him, "Man, thy sins are forgiven thee."
3. And, behold, certain of the scribes said within themselves, "This man blasphemeth."	6. But there were certain of the scribes sitting there, and reasoning in their hearts, 7. "Why doth this man thus speak blasphemies? who can forgive sins but God only?"	21. And the scribes and the Pharisees began to reason, saying, "Who is this which speaketh blasphemies? Who can forgive sins, but God alone?"
4. And Jesus knowing their thoughts said, "Wherefore think ye evil in your hearts?	8. And immediately when Jesus perceived in his spirit that they so reasoned within themselves, he said unto them, "Why reason ye these things in your hearts?	22. But when Jesus perceived their thoughts, he answering said unto them, "What reason ye in your hearts?
5. For whether is easier, to say, Thy sins be forgiven thee; or to say, Arise, and walk?	9. Whether is it easier to say to the sick of the palsy, Thy sins be forgiven thee; or to say, Arise and take up thy bed and walk?	23. Whether is easier, to say, Thy sins be forgiven thee; or to say, Rise up and walk?
6. But that ye may know that the Son of man hath power on earth to forgive sins, (then saith he to the sick of the palsy,) "Arise, take up thy bed, and go unto thine house."	10. But that ye may know that the Son of man hath power on earth to forgive sins, (he saith to the sick of the palsy,) 11. I say unto thee, Arise, and take up thy bed, and go thy way into thine house."	24. But that ye may know that the Son of man hath power upon earth to forgive sins, (he said unto the sick of the palsy,) I say unto thee, Arise, and take up thy couch, and go into thine house."
7. And he arose, and departed to his house.	12. And immediately he arose, took up the bed and went forth before them all.	25. And immediately he rose up before them, and took up that whereon he lay, and departed to his own house, glorifying God.

This instance is taken without any attempt at selection, because the narrative is found in all the three Gospels: but in the first two Gospels whole chapters, as in Matthew xxiv, 9-35, compared with Mark xiii, 13-32, are found to be expressed throughout almost in the same words.

The agreement between the three evangelists in these passages is remarkable, and leads to the question how such coincidences could arise between works which, from the first years of Christianity until very recent times, were understood to be perfectly independent, and to have had each a separate and independent origin. The answer to this question may be given with tolerable certainty, if we are allowed to judge of this subject according to the rules of reason and common sense, by which all other such difficulties are resolved.

It is remarked by Dr Newman in his Two Essays on Miracles, 1870, p. 232 f. that:—

> Though attention was called to Christianity from the first, yet it is true also that it did not succeed at the spot where it arose, but principally at a distance from it.

The Church at Jerusalem, consisting of Jews and ruled by fifteen circumcised bishops one after another, slumbered for 150 years, and then became extinct; but the more energetic Greeks, who had adopted Christianity, speedily carried it over the whole Roman empire, and have left us the history of it in the books which still form our canon.

Of the Acts of the Apostles, which forms the second division of our canonical Scriptures, little more needs to be said than what has been already noticed in the foregoing pages of this work. It has been remarked by some writers that the first twelve chapters betray by their style the hand of a different writer, and by others that the latter part indicates an author well acquainted with maritime affairs. Some appear to recognize a more classical style in the few verses which form the preface to the work; others attach great weight to the use of the pronouns *we* and *us* in the latter part of the work which traces the history of St Paul.

An eminent German critic Zeller has written an elaborate treatise to show that the book was composed expressly to smoothe down the rivalry between St Peter and St Paul, lest future ages should form an unfavourable view of Christianity, the unity of which was severed by the conflict between the Jewish and the Gentile elements. All these points no doubt have a certain weight, and they justify the inference which the present appearance of the work suggests, that it was not known to the world, before it was included in the Christian canon, immediately before that canon is recognized in the second century by Irenæus.

The third division of our Scriptures consists of the Epistles of Paul, James, Peter, John, and Jude ; and what has been said of these individually is supported by the view which they suggest when considered as part of the Christian canon. In the earliest half of the fourth century, whilst the practical value and use of these epistles was fully recognized by their being read in the churches, the question of genuineness, that is whether they were written by the apostles to whom they were commonly ascribed, had not been satisfactorily answered. Eusebius, whose general credulity and occasional disingenuousness lead us to extend our doubts beyond the limits which he would lay down in matters wherein his own interests and those of the Church were concerned, has told us in the second book of his history (ch. 25) that he deemed it proper to give a summary statement of the books of the New Testament which he had mentioned. It appears from that passage, which has been already given in page 20 of this volume, that five of the seven Catholic Epistles, namely, those of James and Jude, the second and the third of John, and the second of Peter, were of doubtful genuineness even at that late period. Eusebius informs us that the Revelation of St John was not universally received as the work of the apostle, but of a presbyter who bore the same name, and whilst he considers the Epistle to the Hebrews to be not inferior to any of the books acknowledged to be apostolic, he seems to incline to the opinion that it was not written by St Paul, and quoting from Origen (vi, 25) he tells us that it has not that vulgarity of style, which belongs to the apostle and is acknowledged by him, but is written in more pure Greek, as every one will confess who can distinguish difference of style.

To enlarge further on works, which from their first appearance in the world until the year 320, when Eusebius wrote, although admitted into the Canon, were still deemed of doubtful authorship, is superfluous to those who do not deny their value or wish to abrogate their use, but only to establish if possible a reasonable explanation of their authorship, and of the time and place to which their origin is due. It remains then to consider collectively and briefly the Epistles of St Paul, if perchance it may be possible to connect them more closely with their supposed author, from whom according to the most general opinion they are virtually separated by an interval of an hundred years, between the date when he is known to have lived, A.D. 60, and the time when his writings first became known to the world. If it were fully established that the partial account of his own life, given in the Epistle to the Galatians (i and ii) proceeded in its present form from his own hand, we might set aside the other account which differs so widely from it, given in the Acts of the Apostles; but as both these accounts came to the knowledge of the world about the same time, and form part of the same religious code, we must leave them as we find them to the individual judgement of their readers. Whatever internal difficulties may present themselves on this subject are slight in comparison with the fact, which has no parallel in history, that a series of writings, twenty-six in number, having for their subject the original history of the most wonderful revolution ever effected in the world, was composed by the eye-witnesses of the events which they recorded, and among a people who kept aloof from every other people, in a foreign language, which not only was unknown to the people of that nation and those to whom these writings were addressed generally, but, as every probability leads us to believe, unknown even to those who are commonly thought to have been the writers of those histories.

The Epistles of St Paul contain without doubt peculiar sentiments which indicate an individual and peculiar character; but why has he written all his epistles in a language which himself knew very imperfectly and which he might have supposed some of those to whom he wrote would not know at all ? It is beyond our belief that the Romans generally could read the barbarous Greek with which the thoughts of Paul have been clothed in his epistle to the people of that city, which moreover he had then never visited. As it appears from the last chapter of the Acts of the Apostles that his first interview on arriving there was with the Jews, and as it appears he afterwards preached to the whole people, we should infer that he used Hebrew in his conversation with his countrymen and Latin in his preaching to the citizens. Nor is a similar inference unreasonable in the case of his preaching and his Epistles to the Corinthians. For Corinth in the time of St Paul was inhabited by a colony of Romans who spoke Latin. They had been planted by Julius Cæsar, who restored that city many years after it had been wholly destroyed by Memmius. "No one," says Pausanias, "of the ancient Corinthians inhabits Corinth, but colonists sent by the Romans." Modern travellers have confirmed this statement. Dr Clarke, repeating the fact that the Corinthians in the second century consisted entirely of the remains of the Roman colony, speaks of sepulchral caves hewn in the rocks near the sea, and the recesses within them, intended evidently as niches for cinerary urns, denoting a mode of sepulture belonging to the Romans rather than to the Greeks. The names moreover of those whom Paul salutes at the end of his letter betray rather a Roman than a Grecian character; and a passage in the Acts (xviii, 17), which has puzzled some of the commentators, becomes intelligible if we understand the words "all the Greeks" to mean not all the inhabitants, but only all that class of the inhabitants who were of Grecian origin, for no doubt there were many Greeks mixed up for pleasure or business with the far greater Latin population. To these proofs may be added that all the coins, of which there are three hundred and forty distinct types, struck at Corinth from the time of Julius Cæsar to Elagabalus, except three or four, have inscriptions in the Latin language.

The Epistle to the GALATIANS leads to the same conclusion as those which precede. That people was descended from the Gauls, and indeed kept the name, Galatæ both in Greek and Latin, which marked their descent. Their forefathers had invaded Greece, from which they were driven out, and afterwards settled in a central province of Asia Minor, where, as we learn from Jerome (iv, 256 ed. Bened.) they retained their own language even in his time, more than 250 years after the age of St Paul, although the Greek language was also known among them, that is, no doubt, to the officials of the Government and also perhaps to the higher and educated classes.*

The Epistle to the EPHESIANS, which stands next in the Canon, may be passed over in this review, for it has already been remarked that there are doubts whether it was addressed to the inhabitants of Ephesus or of Laodicea, and as regards the language, may have been addressed to either of them, for Greek was the language of both those cities.

Proceeding then to the PHILIPPIANS, I find the following sentence in a popular work which will show the case of Philippi to be the same as that of Corinth, Rome, and Galatia.

---

* The whole of this subject is ably discussed by the author of Palæoromaica, especially at pp. 41, 155, &c. London, 8vo, 1822.

The Philippi, which St Paul visited, the site of which has been described above, was a *Roman colony* founded by Augustus, and the remains which strew the ground are no doubt derived from that city. The establishment of Philip of Macedonia was probably not exactly on the same city; for it is described by Appian as being on a hill.... Nothing would be more natural than that the Roman town should have been built in the immediate neighbourhood of the existing Greek one, on a site more suitable for architectural display.*

Of the remaining epistles little needs to be said. We have difficulty in understanding those addressed to the THESSALONIANS when contrasted with St Paul's short sojourn and adverse treatment in that city; and that which is addressed to the HEBREWS labours under a weight of unfavourable evidence which has always been recognized, whenever the subject has been proposed. But whilst thus abstaining from either admitting or denying the genuineness of form and language in which these writings have come down to us, we fall back upon the general nature of the whole volume of which they form a part. In spite of the slight difference of style which subtle criticism has professed to discover, there is in reality less difference between the language of the four Gospels and the Acts of the Apostles than between any of the classic writers of ancient Greece, and if the other books of our Canon present greater obstacles to the modern student, as indeed every schoolboy who attempts to read them immediately finds out, these are due to the difference of thought and to the need of strange words to express novel ideas rather than to any other cause. The language of Christian as well as of classical philosophy would naturally require the use of words and phrases which could hardly be necessary in works which treated only of history and of fact.

As a conclusion then to this inquiry, which has now reached to more than sufficient length, it is suggested that our volume of the New Testament was put together in the latter half of the second century out of the " Memorials of the Apostles " and the " Sayings of our Lord," both of which are named long before any notice is taken or mention made of the present Gospels or of their writers. That these documents existed separately we cannot doubt, for the latter are named in such a way that they must evidently have been collected in a

---

* By the Rev. J[oseph] W[illiams] B[lakesley] B.D. in Dr Smith's Dictionary of the Bible, Article Philippi.

book, and their existence in those early times in the concise form of which Justin Martyr bears witness, is the strongest evidence in favour of the origin of our religion, being in fact that same evidence which Paley supposes to belong to the existing four Gospels. But those Gospels were compiled out of these sayings, and still embody them, especially the Gospel according to St John, where there are as many of them as in all the three others put together. Nor is it unreasonable to assign the city of Antioch as the place from which our Canon wholly or in great part emanated. Alexandria, which alone is named as a rival claimant, is scarcely mentioned in our books, although it had previously—200 years before— produced the Septuagint version of the Jewish Scriptures. Antioch, on the other hand, is constantly named in the Acts of the Apostles, was moreover a seat of learning, and appears in ecclesiastical history as the frequent residence of St Paul. It is indeed difficult to determine, where authorities differ so much, who was the first that received the office of bishop in either of these two cities. If we find in the chronicle of Eusebius (*apud Hieron.*) that Annianus became the first bishop of Alexandria after St Mark, in the eighth year of Nero, which was the sixty-second or third of the Christian era, it is also recorded in the same chronicle that Evodius was bishop of Antioch in the second year of Claudius, which was the forty-second or third year of the same era, and twenty years before the episcopate of Annianus. But the uncertainty of both chronology and history concerning these early times of our religion precludes the possibility of accurately determining such points as these, which in fact become still more involved and intricate by the statement of the same historian, Eusebius, in his Ecclesiastical History (iii, 36), that " Ignatius, who is celebrated by many even to this day as the successor of Peter at Antioch, was the second that obtained the episcopal office there." It appears moreover from the same source that this city was one of the very first into which the Christian religion* was introduced, if it be true, as the historian informs us, that a great number of Greeks had already "received the faith in Antioch, where the Gospel had been preached by those who were scattered after the persecution at Jerusalem and the death of Stephen." We read also in

---

* At Antioch in the reign of Julian "the majority of the people supported the glory of the Christian name, which had been first invented by their ancestors."—GIBBON, ch. xxiv.

the early part of the Acts of the Apostles (vi, 5) of "Nicolas a proselyte of Antioch," and that Barnabas, closely connected with Antioch, was already a preacher of Christianity before St Paul's conversion, and that by his agency the new convert was introduced to the original disciples at Jerusalem. The travels of St Paul in the book of the Acts are supposed to be delivered to us on the authority of St Luke, who is said to have accompanied him; but we learn from Eusebius (iii, 4) that St Luke was either born at Antioch or of Antiochian parents; that he was by profession a physician, and mostly a companion of St Paul. If to these facts be added the testimony of the heathen Lucian, already given at length (p. 82), that about the middle of the second century the Christians were engaged in collecting their sacred books, and further that all these books have come down to us in the Greek language; that of those to whom these books were addressed several spoke a different language from that in which the books were written, and from that which the writer himself would speak, and, lastly, that the books which present the best and smoothest Greek profess to have been written by those who would be least expected to know Greek at all, we may with reason suggest that the volume concerning which such statements may be made, however worthy of the reverence with which we receive it as being drawn from authentic and truthful sources, cannot reasonably be ascribed to an earlier period than that in which it first became known in the second century, when it was impossible to trust any longer to tradition and to the living voice of the companions and followers of the apostles.

INDEX OF THE PRINCIPAL MATTERS.

ACTS of the Apostles, Summary of, 359; not named by the Apostolical Fathers nor by Justin Martyr, 376.
Ægidius, Sanctus, migrated from Athens to Toulouse, 60.
Agrippa Castor named by Jerome, 139.
Alexander the Great: his kingdom divided among his generals, 40.
Alexander the Alabarch, 367.
Alexandrian MS one of the most ancient, 15; its various readings, 16.
Alphabet of the Jews changed in process of time, 47.
Annunciation, two accounts of the, 174.
Antioch, the rival of Alexandria, 41; closely connected with Apostolic history, 363.
Apocryphal Gospels, mostly of the second century, 18; list of seventy such writings, 21; editions of them, 32 note.
Apostles, names of the twelve, 218.
Apostolical Fathers yield no testimony to the early origin of the New Testament Canon, 88, &c.
Aretas, king of Petra, 371.
Ass's foal tied to a vine, 129.
Athenagoras, author of two works on behalf of the Christians, 140.
Augustus, his remark about Herod, 202.

Baptæ, priests of Cotytto, 205.
Barabbas the robber, 309.
Barnabas, his Catholic epistle, 90; associated with Paul, 365.
Bartimæus, a blind man, healed, 257; son of Timæus, 357.

Bishops and Fathers of second century nearly all Greeks, 59.
Blind men healed, 255.
Brothers of Jesus, their names, 375.
Bunsen, Chevalier, on Hippolytus, 206; 244 note.

Canon of the New Testament, 4.
Cassiodorus, his Chronicle, 196.
Celsus, an early opponent of Christianity, 142.
Census in the time of Cyrenius, 190.
Centuriators of Magdeburg, 111.
Centurion, his servant healed, 253.
Christians, use of the word, 373; worship anticipated, 374.
Church of God, a later idea, 355.
Cicero, his oration against Verres, 308.
Claudius Apollinaris, quoted in the seventh century by the Paschal Chronicle, 143.
Clement of Alexandria acquainted with the Gospels, 138.
Clement of Rome, his epistle, 93, 106, 108; his second epistle one of the Homilies, 111.
Clementine Homilies, 380.
Clinton's Fasti Romani quoted, 183 note, 193 note, 196, 197.
Coined money unknown to the Israelites, 43; first coined by them in the reign of Antiochus, 45.
Commodus, emperor, slain, A.D. 192, 196.
Cureton, his edition of the Ignatian epistles, 101; his discovery of the Ignatian MSS, 112.
Cyrenius holds a census of the Jews, A.D. 10, 190.

430 INDEX.

David buys the threshing-floor of Araunah, 44.
Demoniac among the tombs, 266.
Deutsch, his literary remains, 39, 68.
Development of later ideas, 348.
Dionysius the Areopagite, 109.
Disciples, seventy chosen, 226.
Donaldson, his Christian orthodoxy, 38, 173.

Epictetus names the Galileans, 77.
Epiphanius on Heresies, 196.
Eunuchs, the subject thereof examined, 354.
Eusebius, his Ecclesiastical History quoted, 13, 19, 20, 29, 125; on the writings of Papias, 113; his statement on the order of the Gospels, 153.
Evangelist, original meaning of the term, 125.
Ezekiel quoted, 121 note.

Fabrication of writings in early Christian times, 118.
Fadus, governor of Judæa, 367.
Fire kindled in Jordan, 130.
Flight into Egypt, 198.

Gamaliel, his speech, 367.
Genealogies of Christ examined, 166.
Genesis quoted, 38; 43.
Gough's New Testament Quotations, 52.
Greek language unknown to the Jews, 36.
Greek words in the Old Testament, 38.
Greeks had no intercourse with the Jews before Alexander, 37.
Greek words of unusual form, 55.
Greek words copied from Latin, 54, 56.
Greswell, Rev. Edward, his explanation of the genealogies, 172.

Hadrian, his letter on the degraded state of the Egyptian Christians about the year A.D. 120, 85.
Hebraisms, few or none in the New Testament, 48.
Hebrew words quoted and interpreted in the Gospels, 51.
Hefele, his edition of the Apostolical Fathers, 110.
Hegesippus, his history of Christianity, 144.
Hermas, his Shepherd, 96.
Hermias quotes St Paul, 144.

Herod, his character as given by Josephus; puts to death his sons, 201.
Herodotus quoted, 38.
Hilgenfeld: his Evangeliorum fragmenta, 33.
Homer's Odyssey, quoted, 123.
Hyde, Dr, on the Persian religion, 204.

Ignatius, his epistles mostly forgeries, 97; the Syriac version of them, edited by Cureton, 101, 107.
Innocents, massacre of the, 200.
Irenæus, bishop of Lyons, first writer who recognizes the four Gospels, 137.

Jaddua the High Priest, 39.
James, the brother of Jesus Christ, stoned to death, 63; his general epistle, 399.
Javan supposed to mean Greece,—a late notion, 37.
Jerusalem colonized by Hadrian and called Ælia, 49.
Jesus, his baptism, 199; his place of birth uncertain, 185; time of birth uncertain, 189; tempted in the wilderness, 213; his conduct towards the Samaritans, 270; anointed at a feast, 273; raises to life Jaïrus's daughter, 277; heals the woman having an issue of blood, 277; his last journey and triumphal entry into Jerusalem, 182, 281; curses the barren fig-tree, 286; his last supper, 289; his agony in the garden, 296; his arrest, 299; examination before the high priest, 302; denied by Peter, 306; his trial before Pontius Pilate, 307; mocked four times, 314; crucified, 316; inscription over the cross, 328; his embalmment, 337; his resurrection, 331; his appearances after his resurrection, 340; his ascension, 364.
Jews and Greeks not amalgamated in the time of Herod, 53.
Jews still remain in Jerusalem after the siege by Titus, 49.
John the Baptist, named by Josephus; the mode and reason of his death, 65, 203; his doctrines, 207; first meeting with Jesus, 209; imprisoned, 211; his doubt about the Messiahship of Jesus, 212.

John, St, his Gospel written in purer Greek than the others, 163 ; the last chapter a late addition, 164 ; his general epistles, 399 ; First Epistle quoted, 12 ; Gospel, last chapter doubtful, 12 ; also ch. v, verses 3-4 doubtful, 13.
Joseph of Arimathœa, 337.
Josephus a bad Greek scholar, 42 ; interpreter to the Romans at the siege of Jerusalem, 43 ; spurious passages in his writings, 61, &c.
Judas Iscariot, his death, 346.
Jude, St, his general epistle, 399.
Justin Martyr, list of his works, 119 ; does not name the Gospels, 123 ; names one John ; his quotations compared with those of the Gospels, 132 ; on baptism, 205.

Kingdom of heaven, 355.

Lamech and Ada, Greek names, 37.
Latin words and Latinisms in the Gospels, 53, 54, 56 ; mixed with Greek in the Eastern provinces, 57.
Loaves and fishes, miracle of the, 259.
Lord's Prayer, 241.
Lucian of Samosata : his notice of Christian meetings and allusion to St Paul, 79 ; his account of Peregrinus, 81.
Luke, erroneous translation of the preface, 159 ; later additions made to his Gospel, 161.
Lysanias of Abilene, 193.

Maccabees, book quoted, I, xv, 6 ; p. 45.
Madden's History of the Jewish coinage, 45, 48.
Manichæans, a Christian sect, 204.
Marcus Aurelius names the Christians, 77.
Mark's Gospel quoted, 55-56 ; last twelve verses not authentic, 12 ; the present Gospel not the same which he wrote, 157.
Matthew wrote in Hebrew the *Sayings* of our Lord, not the Gospel, 154.
Melito, his works, 145.
Mishna does not name Christianity, 66, &c.
Money : Persian money used by the Jews ; Jewish money first coined by Simon the Maccabee, 44.

Muratori, Canon discovered by him, 141.

Nicodemus, his interview with Jesus, 178.
Nolan, Dr, his Inquiry into the integrity of the Greek Vulgate, 16.

Orosius quoted, 196.
Otto, his edition of Justin Martyr, 126.

Paley's evidences, 120 ; erroneous statements, 116.
Papias, bishop of Hierapolis, 113.
Paul, St, his conversion, 368 ; his epistles, 377 ; preaches during 19 years, 384 ; his epistles to the Thessalonians, 385 ; Galatians, 387 ; Corinthians, 390 ; Romans, 391 ; Ephesians, 392 ; Philippians, 393 ; Colossians, 393 ; Philemon, 393 ; Timothy, 394 ; Titus, 395 ; Hebrews, 396.
Peter, St, his general epistles, 55, 399.
Philo Judæus, his allegorical works : does not name Christianity, 61.
Pilate washes his hands, 311.
Pliny the younger, his letter about the Christians, 72.
Plutarch, his life of Cato, 308.
Polycarp, his Epistle, doubted by some, defended by others, 104, 107.
Polycrates, bishop of Ephesus, 145.
Porphyry, an early opponent of Christianity, 171.
Potter's Field, purchase of it, 347.

Quadratus, bishop of Athens, 146.

Ramayana quoted, 38.
Rawlinson, Professor, his lecture before the Christian Evidence Society, 192.
Revelation quoted, 8.
Rufinus of Aquileia, 109.

Samaritans, three narratives concerning them, 270.
Samuel, book quoted, 44.
Saul called also Paul, 364.
Sayings of our Lord in general use, 105, &c. ; other sayings not found in the Gospels, 129, &c.
Scene of Christ's ministry, Galilee in the synoptical Gospels, Judæa in John, 180.

INDEX.

Seneca, his notice of the Sabbath, spurious letters between him and St Paul, 76.
Sermon on the Mount, 228.
Sibylline Oracles, 130; quoted by Josephus, 147; the collection of them in fourteen books, 147, &c.
Simeon and Simon, 365, 366 note.
Simon the Cyrenian, 324.
Simon Magus, 381.
Sinaitic MS one of the most ancient, 15; its various readings, 16.
Suetonius, his notice of the Christians, 69, &c.; his life of Vespasian, 247.
Sulpitius Severus, his chronicle, 196.
Syrian coins used by the Jews, 45.
Synoptical, name given to the first three Gospels collectively, 162.
Syrophœnician woman, 358.

Tacitus, his notice of Christ and the Christians, 71; his Annals, 184, 248.
Targums do not name Christianity, 66.
Temple, Purification of the, 249.
Tertullian, his work against the Jews, 197.

Testament, books of the New, names and authors, 5; supposed dates, 7; questions about authorship, &c., not new, 10; only known as a whole, 11; the New framed in harmony with the Old, 35; its language copied from the Septuagint, 51.
Theophilus, his three books addressed to Autolycus, 149; Acts inscribed to him, 362.
Theudas and Judas, their rebellion, 366.
Tischendorf: his apocryphal gospels, acts and revelations, 33.

Vatican MS one of the most ancient, 15; its various readings, 16.

Westcott (Dr) on the Canon, 58; his introduction to the study of the Gospels, 162 note.
Writers, list of twenty-six minor, of second century, 139.

Zacharias, his death related in the Protevangelium Jacobi, 161.
Zonaras quoted, 196.

THE END.

ELZEVIR PRESS:—PRINTED BY JOHN C. WILKINS AND VERNON, 9, CASTLE STREET, CHANCERY LANE.

www.ingramcontent.com/pod-product-compliance
Lightning Source LLC
Chambersburg PA
CBHW020534300426
44111CB00008B/661